Apollon DAVIDSON

CECIL RHODES
and His Time

Progress Publishers
Moscow

BEL[...]

LEALUI

CAPRIVI STRIP
LIVIN[...]

BAMANGWAT[...]

Lake Ngami

ANGOLA

DAMARALAND

Walfisch Bay

KALAHARI
DESERT

GABER[...]

ATLANTIC
OCEAN

PITSANI
MAFEKIN[...]

NAMAQUALAND

R. Molop[...]

BATHOEN

[...]RY

14 STREAMS
LONGLANDS   KLIP[...]
BARKLY WEST   KIM[...]
GRIQUALAND
WEST   BLOEMFONT[...]

Orange

SOUTHERN AFRICA IN 1899

Area of British territory
when Rhodes entered public
life in 1881

Subsequent additions up to
the outbreak of the Boer War
in 1899

CALVINIA

FRASERBURG

CO[...]
MID[...]
N[...]
GRAA[...]
RE[...]

BEAUFORT
WEST

OUDTSHOORN

0   100   200
Miles

Railways   ⊤⊤⊤⊤⊤⊤

Table Bay
CAPE TOWN
SIMONSTOWN

STELLENBOSCH
SOMERSET   SWELLENDAM
WEST

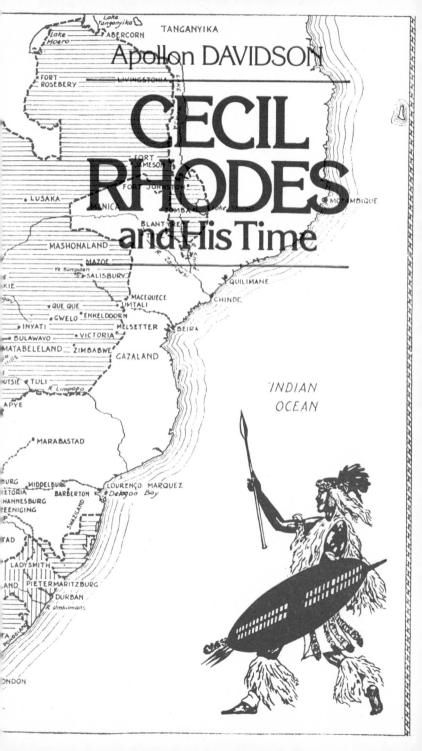

Apollon DAVIDSON

CECIL RHODES

and His Time

Translated from the Russian by CHRISTOPHER ENGLISH

Designed by OLEG GREBENYUK

Jacket: The battle of the Umguza (April 22, 1896), reproduced from Oliver Ransford's book *Bulawayo: Historic Battleground of Rhodesia*, Cape Town, 1968.

Title page: A late nineteenth-century map of Southern Africa showing the countries conquered by Rhodes (from the book *Rhodes* by J. G. Lockhart and Hon. C. M. Woodhouse, London, 1963).

Аполлон Давидсон

СЕСИЛЬ РОДС И ЕГО ВРЕМЯ

На английском языке

© Издательство «Мысль», 1984

English translation of the revised Russian text © Progress Publishers 1988

Printed in the Union of Soviet Socialist Republics

D $\dfrac{0504000000—357}{014(01)—88}$ 21—87

ISBN 5-01-001828-4

CONTENTS

Testament
of a Young Man

A young man, not yet twenty-four years old, sits beneath the scorching African sun contemplating his last will and testament. It preoccupies him constantly, during those oppressively hot nights as he lies sleepless, racked by chest pains; in the evenings, on his return to the inn from the diamond diggings to the raucous merriment of the prospectors, the dice and card games, the air reverberating with the din of men drinking and swearing, and the occasional shattering report of a pistol; in coaches and on wagons, on his thousand mile trek from the African interior to the ocean ports, and it is still in his mind as he paces the deck on interminable journeys to and from Europe, and gazes into the waters of the boundless Atlantic.

The year: 1877. Our young man's time was divided between diamond prospecting in Kimberley and reading for a degree at Oxford. He alternated between the seemingly primeval savannah of Africa and the advanced industrial cities of England. Yet in a way the situation was precisely the reverse... From the seething life of the diamond mines the tranquility of Oxford with its rural landscapes, sheep grazing in its green meadows, its gracious mediaeval buildings, overgrown with moss and ivy. That Oxford where, in the words of the Russian poet Konstantin Balmont,

> *The spires sing out with the chiming of bells*
> *The Colleges dream in their deep-shaded dells.*[1]

In Kimberley the prospectors had long since scared away the wild animals which had once been so plentiful there. Not only the lion disappeared, but even the common antelopes, while in the parks of Oxford deer roamed, freely, nosing right up to the students' windows to be fed.

But this startling diversity is unlikely to have greatly impressed our young man. At that carefree age, when others are giving themselves up to dreams of love and adventure, he was busy composing and refining the clauses of his last will. The problem was not the distribution of his assets and money: these are easy to dispose of. Furthermore, he had already made those arrangements in a will written before his twentieth birthday, but after his first serious heart attack when the official verdict of his doctor was that he had "not six months to live."[2]

No, in this will the young man's design is to shape the destiny of Africa and Europe, no less, even the destiny of the whole world, of all mankind. In his will he plans ". . .the extension of British rule throughout the world . . . the colonization by British subjects of all lands where the means of livelihood are attainable by energy, labour and enterprise, and especially the occupation by British settlers of the entire Continent of Africa, the Holy Land, the Valley of Euphrates, the Islands of Cyprus and Candia, the whole of South America, the islands of the Pacific not heretofore possessed by Great Britain, the whole of the Malay Archipelago, the seaboard of China and Japan, the ultimate recovery of the United States of America as an integral part of the British Empire. . ."

Clearly he had a world-wide empire in mind.

He believed this was a prerequisite for world peace: peace beneath the British aegis. To achieve this, the Imperial Parliament would have to be set up, in which the white settler colonies would be represented. The purpose of this parliament was "the foundation of so great a Power as to hereafter render wars impossible and promote the best interests of humanity."[3]

As his executors he appointed a British colonial official in South Africa, Sidney Shippard and the British Colonial Secretary who was at that time Earl of Carnarvon. There was perhaps some reason for his choice of Shippard: he lived on the South African diamond fields and was a friend. But Carnarvon, on the other hand, could hardly have predicted the role singled out for him by this as yet unknown colonist from the far reaches of the British Empire. . .

There is undeniably something peculiar about this obsession with the composition of wills. It is worthy of note that in his not over-long life he composed no less than six of these! This one, his second, beneath which stood the date 17 September 1877, was to be followed by four more.

If the young man had suddenly died at this stage no one would ever recall these documents today. But he lived on. And unlike many others who have dreamed of shaping the destiny of the world, he did not remain unknown.

His name is Cecil John Rhodes. He entered the annals of history as the "father of the British Empire".

He first expounded his views in a document which he called the *Confession of Faith*.[4] It was finished that same year, 1877, and dated June 2. The *Confession of Faith* begins with the argument that every man has a major goal in life. For some this may be a happy family, for others, wealth. For Rhodes, however, it was "to render myself useful to my country".

Since time immemorial people have sworn undying allegiance to their country and their people—and yet these words are subject to many interpretations. It is interesting to observe how Rhodes interpreted his own goal, which he expressed in such emotional terms.

To him the underlying principle of "useful" service to his country lay in the conviction that Englishmen were the best people on earth. "I contend that we are the finest race in the world and that the more of the world we inhabit the better it is for the human race."

Mankind suffered, he maintained, because the English nation was only increasing in numbers at half its capacity, for the simple reason that they lacked sufficient living space to expand. Perhaps the answer was for the English to emigrate beyond the boundaries of the British Empire? Rhodes did not agree. "It would seem a disgrace to suggest such a thing I think that we all think that poverty is better under our own flag than wealth under a foreign one."

There was only one solution: to extend the British Empire. "Just fancy those parts that are at present inhabited by the most despicable specimens of human beings what an alteration there would be if they were brought under Anglo-Saxon influence... I contend that every acre added to our territory means in the future birth to some more of the English race who otherwise would not be brought into existence."

This, Rhodes believed, would be only one of many benefits to result from the expansion of the British Empire. The unification of the greater part of the world under British control would mean an end to all wars. British domination would therefore lead to the establishment of peace throughout the world. Such was the thrust of Rhodes's argument. As for Africa, "Africa awaits us still, and it is our duty to seize every opportunity of acquiring more territory and we should keep this one idea steadily before our eyes that more territory simply means more of the Anglo-Saxon race, more of the best the most human most honourable race the world possesses".

A "BOYISH DOCUMENT"

Who then was called on to fulfil this duty? Certainly not those who ruled Britain at that time. Rhodes could still only dream of gaining recognition in political circles, but to attain this was no easy task for him, a man with neither name nor connections. It was natural that he should regard Westminster's incumbents as bureaucrats, driven only by self-interest. In a moment of anger Rhodes described the House of Commons as ". . . an assembly of wealth of the men whose lives have been spent in the accumulation of money", and thus who have not had the time to study the past.

He believed strongly in the study of the past, since it furnished many pointers to the realisation of his own ideas. One such example from history was the Catholic Church. "What has been the main cause of the success of the Romish Church? The fact that every enthusiast, call it if you like every madman finds employment in it."

In order to fulfil his duty to mankind—to seize as much territory as possible for the British Empire, it was necessary first to form an organization prepared to shoulder this burden. "Why should we not form a secret society with but one object the furtherance of the British Empire and the bringing of the whole uncivilized world under British rule for the recovery of the United States for the making of the Anglo-Saxon race but one Empire. . . Let us form the same kind of a society a Church for the extension of the British Empire."

Rhodes saw this organisation as appealing to misfits in public life, even men who had grown totally disillusioned. It was only necessary to infect them with the idea of extending the frontiers of the Empire and to convince them of her "greatness".

Rhodes conceived of it as a secret society, with agents in every part of the British Empire. It would derive its material support from its wealthy devotees. This is nowhere stated in its constitution but is clearly implied. Representatives of this society should work in universities and schools, "and should watch the English youth passing through their hands just one perhaps in every thousand would have the mind and feelings for such an object". These recruits would have to be trained, would have to be taught to sacrifice everything else in life to this main purpose, to undergo severe ordeals. And only if the recruit made it through should he be awarded membership of the society and bound to it under oath for the rest of his life. Then he could be granted funds "and sent to that part of the Empire where it was felt he was needed".

Rhodes felt that the right material for this society lay among the younger sons of aristocratic families, and even of families who lacked both titles and large fortunes. He himself had suffered the fate of a younger son. Such sons, wrote Rhodes, have neither the money nor the opportunity to show their worth. The secret society would give them both.

Rhodes was not the only person to focus attention on the "younger sons". Many commentators wrote about the role played in the creation of the British Empire by such peculiarities of the English inheritance system. We find observations on this topic in the most unexpected sources.

"...The younger sons. These were the boys of noble blood who had, however, been cast out of their homes... In this way a new class, a class of 'adventurers' was automatically created..." This is from *The Three Capitals*, written by the well-known Russian monarchist Vassily Shulgin in 1926. In this book he compares the histories of Russia and England, arguing that the absence of a system of primogeniture and the consequent division of principalities amongst the sons of princes at the time of Batu Khan led to the downfall of "Varangian Russia". "Moscow's discovery of primogeniture created the might of Russia", but the absence of an "economic" primogeniture, i.e. "primogeniture in private matters, destroyed this might with the help of the idea of re-distribution of the land."

"In England, on the other hand", Shulgin continues, "they had a sensible system. They had no equal division. There was

Freedom, there was Fraternity, only there was no disastrous Equality..." To such length does Shulgin go in his search for the causes of the collapse of autocracy, that he even envies England.

"So it is that these younger sons are to become the discoverers of new lands. The habit of good living dies hard, and when the pocket is empty and ambition flows in the blood our younger son turns into an adventurer.

"Thus did England grow. The older sons kept a firm grip, preventing it from falling to pieces, and every century its younger sons brought it a new continent."[5]

In the end Shulgin takes his idea too far. But although continents cannot be won solely by the endeavours of a few impoverished aristocrats, it is undeniable that they made a substantial contribution to the creation of the British Empire. It was therefore on them that Cecil Rhodes pinned his hopes.

The full text of the *Confession of Faith* only came to light in 1974, published by the Canadian historian John Flint. Previously only extracts had been published.

This leads one to speculate why no one dared for nearly a hundred years, to publish the document in full.

Flint believes that Rhodes's biographers were afraid to detract from the accepted image of Rhodes, and that a writer "would fear to lose his audience" by publishing this document "of low intellectual content and even less literary merit". In general the story of this secret society's conception is "written almost in the style of the cheap novelettes of the day".

"If Rhodes had composed his *Confession of Faith* at the age of twelve in Bishop's Stortford", argues Flint, "or even at seventeen en route to South Africa, it might be passed off as an immature and childish effusion, such as the attempts at youthful poetry or philosophy that many of us would blush to see if we had not thrown them away long since. But Rhodes was not a child in 1877, he was twenty-four years old, the age at which men marry and rear children, buy homes, settle into careers, or write Ph. D. theses."[6]

Another of Rhodes's biographers, the English historian Basil Williams, describes Rhodes's first political testament as a "boyish document", "that curious mixture of child and prophet so often found in great men."[7]

Naive, perhaps. Boyish, even. But can imperialism be "naive", "boyish"?

"Boyish Imperialism" is in fact the title given by the Russian poet Osip Mandelstam to a chapter of his boyhood memoirs. Even the very architecture of St Petersburg, so formal and splendid, "inspired me with a sort of boyish imperialism. I was besotted with the horse-guards' armour, the Roman helmets of the guardsmen, the silver trumpets of the Preobrazhensky orchestra, and after the May parade my greatest delight was the horse-guards' festival on the feast of the Annunciation."[8]

Did Rhodes perhaps have similar memories, boyish dreams that he cherished into old age?

THE MASONIC AND THE JESUIT SPIRIT

Rhodes paraded these boyish spirits like a banner throughout his life. John Flint again records how in 1891, upon making the acquaintance of the famous English journalist William Stead, Rhodes sent him his *Confession of Faith* with the dedication: "You will see that I have not altered much as to my feelings."[9]

Yet at that stage Rhodes was no lad of twelve, nor even twice that age, but thirty-seven years old. And he was already the gold and diamond king, Prime Minister of the Cape Colony, hero of the day in England. Therefore, if we are to dismiss Rhodes's early ideas as naive, it is only logical to treat his entire philosophy of life in the same way, and to regard his life's work as boyish folly.

What, then, for the most absurd notion, as Flint sees it, of the planned secret society? At first sight it may seem nonsense, yet on closer scrutiny is it so very absurd? We might wonder what suggested the idea of such a society to Rhodes. In the *Confession of Faith* we find the statement: "I look into history and I read the story of the Jesuits." Further on he informs us: "In the present day I become a member of the Masonic order." In other words, on June 2, 1877, on the very day when Rhodes wrote, or at least concluded his *Confession of Faith*, he became a Freemason.

It may happen that new facts come to light for future historians, but for the time being we are left with the impression that Rhodes, like many others before and after him, entered his Masonic lodge as if he were joining a privileged club. It is true, of course, that Masonry had by then lost the aura that had adorned it a century before, but it still carried great prestige. It is interesting to note that the Prince of Wales, the future King Edward VII, was elected Grandmaster of the English Masons in 1875.

Rhodes did not have a particularly reverent attitude to Masonry. After his initiation to a lodge he described the ceremony in great detail to guests at a dinner party, to the horror of his new fellow-masons. In the *Confession of Faith* he expressed the following supercilious opinion of the brotherhood: "I see the wealth and power they possess, the influence they hold and I think over their ceremonies and I wonder that a large body of men can devote themselves to what at times appear the most ridiculous and absurd rites without an object and without an end." At the same time, according to a friend who knew him well, "Rhodes ... retained his interest in Masonry to the close of his life."[10]

Rhodes had an ambivalent attitude to the Jesuits too: "I see what they were able to do in a bad cause and I might say under bad leaders."

But for all his strict censure of the Masons and the Jesuits, features of both orders can be detected in the secret society he proposed to create. His design should not therefore be dismissed as absurd, when such close parallels can be found in reality.

Neither are these parallels confined to history: even today, in the age of space flight, when men have walked on the moon and space probes are studying the surface of Mars, Jupiter and Venus, there exists an organization that calls itself the Broederbond, the Union of Brothers. Its rituals had analogues in the rites and ceremonies of Mediaeval cults. One might think an organization with such obsolete trappings would surely seem a ridiculous parody in the context of modern political life. But the Broederbond is no knock-about farce: it is very real. It was established fully seventy years ago, but its secrets have been so jealously guarded that for the first twenty years or so the world did not even suspect of its existence.

For the first thirty years of its life, the Broederbond concentrated on spreading its influence. But from 1948 until recent times it has managed the affairs of a nation through the agency of an official political party. Neither is this nation some God-forsaken island: its territory is nine times as large as that of Great Britain.

This is the Republic of South Africa. Does this mean that Rhodes's plans have been put into effect, and precisely in the country where they were conceived, in South Africa? They have been put into effect, only not as their author intended, as so often happens. The Broederbond was created not by Englishmen, but by Afrikaners, and it serves not English, but Afrikaner nationalism, and the maintenance of Afrikaner domination over South Africa. Yet in its structure and methods it has much in common with Rhodes's dreams.

We can hardly afford to dismiss the *Confession of Faith*, therefore, as the naive fancy of a man who was never really able to grow up.

We might wonder, though, why it was not published for a a hundred years: was this really because of the ideas it contained? Rhodes reiterated all these in subsequent wills and speeches, which none of his biographers has hesitated to quote.

The full text of the *Confession of Faith* remained unpublished for so long, most probably, for the simple reason that it does not contain much in the way of punctuation, and what there is is used quite haphazardly. Admittedly others before him, like Dumas-père, wasted no time on punctuation marks, leaving it to their clerks to provide these. But Dumas is not to be compared with Rhodes and the latter's biographers could quite justifiably fear that such syntactic sloppiness might detract from the image of the "great Empire-builder".

Young Rhodes's own ideas then, at the end of the eighteen seventies, were neither youthful folly nor a great revelation. In them the spirit of the new age, the age of imperialism, is given perhaps a clearer and more doctrinaire expression than in the writings of his compatriots and contemporaries. Yet if Rhodes's ideas had been mere boyish nonsense would the British really have given his name to entire countries, with an area several times greater than that of Great Britain? Would there ever have been a Southern and a Northern Rhodesia?

"THE ENIGMA OF THE PRESENT AGE"

"It is to such men as Cecil Rhodes that England is indebted for her Imperial greatness".[11]

These are the words of Joseph Chamberlain, the most famous of England's ministers of that time. The sentiment is echoed by Queen Victoria herself, who declared Rhodes to be "a very remarkable ... man" and wished her ministers were more like him.[12]

Even beyond England's frontiers he had countless admirers. Kaiser Wilhelm II, who by rights should have hated everything British, said to Rhodes: "Wenn Sie mein Ministerpräsident waren, so würde ich der grösste Souverän der Welt sein" ("If you had been my Prime Minister I would have been the greatest monarch in the world").[13]

He was admired not only by kings, emperors and ministers: he was also the common man's idol, at least in England, at any rate. "He is the only colonial in the British dominions whose goings and comings are chronicled and discussed under all the globe's meridians, and whose speeches, unclipped, are cabled from the ends of the earth," observed Mark Twain in his book *Following the Equator*.

Rhodes's name was known the world over. Some regarded him with admiration, some with loathing, but none with indifference. Ears would prick up at the mere mention of his name and heated arguments would break out. Everyone had his own opinion of this man. Once again Mark Twain speaks for a great number of people of that time:

"I admire him, I frankly confess it; and when his time comes I shall buy a piece of the rope for a keepsake."

At the same time, like many others, the great American writer regarded Rhodes as an enigma: "...he has done more than enough to pull sixteen common-run great men down; yet there he stands, to this day, upon his dizzy summit under the dome of the sky, an apparent permanency, the marvel of the time, the mystery of the age, an Archangel with wings to half the world, Satan with a tail to the other half... One fact is sure: he keeps his prominence and a vast following, no matter what he does... What is the secret of his formidable supremacy?"[14]

One of the best-known photographs of "the Father of the British Empire"

In our time Rhodes is no longer an idol, not even in his own country. The word Rhodesia has been erased from the maps. In the Republics of Zambia and Zimbabwe, the erstwhile Northern and Southern Rhodesia, monuments to Rhodes have been removed from their pedestals, and streets and squares which once bore his name have been renamed.

But the debates about Rhodes still rage on.

After the collapse of the Rhodesian regime, in the summer of 1980, the journal *Illustrated London News* published a series of letters from readers about Rhodes's historical role. The most extensive of these letters presents Rhodes as a national shrine, a seer gifted with prophetic vision, a man who never deviated from the "three principles ... peace, justice and liberty." The author writes that to him "Rhodes remains one of the great men of history, not least because of his readiness to risk his own life, at the height of his wealth and power, to ensure the survival and future of the embryo of a then obscure nation in Central Africa. . ."[15]

Other opinions were expressed too. The author of another letter, conceding that "without doubt he was a remarkable man", asks whether Rhodes can be regarded as "a carrier of civilization", and poses the question: "Was it necessary to occupy Africa from the Cape to Cairo. . .?"

One letter came from the Republic of Botswana (in colonial times: Bechuanaland). The adulation accorded Rhodes arouses grief and anger in this author. He writes that while such eulogies may still be possible in England, in Africa they are quite unacceptable. They "are frankly insulting to those whose home it was till Cecil Rhodes and his henchmen arrived violently on the scene in the 1890s".[16]

The official British position may be gauged from the remarks of Lord Soames, the last governor of Southern Rhodesia, made in speeches during the independence celebrations of the Republic of Zimbabwe in 1980. Announcing the end of the colonial status of the country, Lord Soames proclaimed his praise of Rhodes. He credited Rhodes with everything the British regarded as achievements of their politics in Rhodesia: the development, "over the past ninety years", of "the forces of economic progress, science and the state, on the one hand, and education and the English language on the other. . ."[17]

Rhodes himself has been the subject of dozens of books and literally thousands of articles.

Nevertheless, in 1969, when there were already a large number of book-length biographies of Rhodes in existence, *The Journal of African History*, the major publication in this field, carried the following statement: "Anything like a definitive biography has yet to be written".[18]

After this, in the seventies and eighties, a number of undoubtedly interesting studies of Rhodes and his activities have been published. These include: John S. Galbraith's *Crown and Charter* and John Flint's *Cecil Rhodes*. In 1983 a lengthy monograph (674 pages) was published by the South African historian Arthur Keppel-Jones, who now lives in Canada, *Rhodes and Rhodesia. The White Conquest of the Land of Zimbabwe, 1884-1902*.

Despite this, in the early 1980s the well-known English Africanist George Shepperson declared: "We are confronted with the fundamental problem, as I see it: there is no adequate biography of Rhodes. In spite of the many millions of words that have been spent on this enigmatic man, he still remains an enigma".[19]

This remark by Shepperson is no off-the-cuff aside, but the main thesis of his lecture "Cecil Rhodes: Some Biographical Problems". In this lecture Shepperson formulates guidelines for a future historian who might one day write the definitive biography of Rhodes. He addresses himself "...to the biographer yet to come, who will tackle the formidable task of giving us, through the great trek through many sources, known and unknown, written and oral, in many countries, that substantial study of Cecil John Rhodes, great Victorian, maker and breaker of empires, conspirator and educator, which we still need, I believe, in spite of nearly a century of writing about him, for the understanding of essential elements in the past, present and future of Europe, America and, of course, his own Africa".

The composition of a truly comprehensive and authentic life of a man like Rhodes is indeed no easy task. The historian finds serious objective difficulties in his path. These are those same difficulties which caused Thomas Carlyle to remark: "A well-written life is almost as rare as a well-spent one".[20]

Even such an accomplished biographer as André Maurois, author of many well-written lives, proved unequal to the task of writing Rhodes' biography and his *Cecil Rhodes* is regarded as one of his least successful books.

Without doubt, it is no easy matter to reconstruct the life of a man—any man—who is no longer amongst the living. It is hard enough to recreate the image of someone very close to you, someone who, it would seem, you know and understand better than all the others. To quote the words of the modern Soviet poet Yevgeny Yevtushenko:

> *Each man has his secret private world.*
> *In this world he has his proudest moment.*
> *In this world he has his hour of shame.*
> *And none of this is known to us.*[21]

There are people about whom it is particularly difficult to write, men who at different times in history have decided the destiny of entire peoples and states.

Can these people be judged by their own words? Only too often these words are used by them as a screen to conceal their real thoughts. Nor can we judge them by their deeds: these are shrouded in mystery. Their private lives are interwoven with state secrets, the intimate affairs of political parties, of gigantic economic and industrial concerns. The more important these secrets and affairs, the closer their link with the cataclysms of history, the harder it is to discover them.

All this is true of Cecil Rhodes.

As for the historical context in which Rhodes lived and worked, this is even harder to reconstruct. It is so easy to put a foot wrong, even if the writer steeps himself in all the available documentary material, explores the streets where Rhodes lived, breathes the same air rising from those pavements. Again and again the words of the great Goethe come to mind:

> *Mein Freund, die Zeiten der Vergangenheit*
> *Sind uns ein Buch mit sieben Siegeln;*
> *Was ihr den Geist der Zeiten heißt,*
> *Das ist im Grund der Herren eigner Geist,*
> *In dem die Zeiten sich bespiegeln.*[22]

Even if Cecil Rhodes does not seem quite the enigma he was to Mark Twain, it is still an arduous undertaking to try to recreate his image today.

It may rightly be wondered why the present author, an inhabitant of Moscow and Leningrad, far removed from the theatre of Cecil Rhodes's activities, has undertaken to write about him. Why should he, when he acknowledges the valuable work done by Rhodes's many other biographers, feel entitled to make his own contribution? What, in fact, is the purpose of this book?

...A South African journalist, now quite forgotten, but well enough known at the time of Rhodes, began his book on the subject with these remarks:

"I am told that the proper thing in a book of this, or indeed of any other narrative nature, is the Preface. Now, I am most exceedingly anxious to do the proper thing. I apprehend, however, that a preface is only of interest and of value when one has anything to say in it; and that is just where my difficulty comes in. Anything I have to say has been said in the book itself. I have no egotistic platitudes to offer here: there is nothing I want to apologise for—I am informed that a great many authors make apology the chief function of a preface—nothing I want to explain; nothing I want to add; nothing I want to retract."[23]

How enviable the author, who can begin his book with such an affirmation (admittedly even he, I might note in parentheses, still proceeded after these rather coquettish remarks to write a preface).

As far as the present book is concerned, a few explanatory remarks are essential.

TO THE READER OF THIS BOOK

By choosing as my title not just *Cecil Rhodes* but *Cecil Rhodes and His Time* I wished to emphasize that its objective is to study Rhodes in his age, as a man who was at one and the same time the product and the personification of the greatest empire in the history of mankind. He symbolized the might of this empire when it was at its very zenith

In addition it seemed vital to me to understand the significance of Rhodes as the embodiment of this entire age, when colonialism was in a state of turbulent growth, and the colonial powers were eagerly carving up the world among themselves.

It is essential to know Cecil Rhodes and the secret of his success in order to make sense of the historical mechanism which united, albeit in a cruel way, by blood and iron, into a single whole the destinies of nations on all continents. Rhodes was one of the chief constructors of that immense machine which bears the name colonialism.

This machine is steadily retreating from us into the past, to confinement in the pages of history. But it is impossible for something which endured for five full centuries and which reached its apogee so recently, at the turn of the twentieth century, to disappear entirely without a trace.

Some countries formed the target of colonial policies, others acted as their initiators—and there are few nations which were not affected by them at all. To this day entire states, even continents, bear the imprint of colonialism in the lives and characters of their inhabitants.

Today, when the political dominion of colonialism has come to an end, it is surely the best time to attempt an overall reassessment of this historical phenomenon, to enquire into its inner springs, to range across the full extent of its influences and consequences, whose true impact is being felt now.

As to Cecil Rhodes, the question inevitably arises: why should it have been Rhodes who became the idol of colonialism in this age of the colonial division of the world? Massive countries were named in his honour, with his own name: an accolade that was accorded to few other men. Yet there were many other empire-builders: in France, Germany, Britain and other countries besides.

Why should it have been Rhodes?

This question has puzzled me ever since my student years. Many years ago, shortly after the Second World War, in supplication for my degree from Leningrad University I submitted a paper on the history of the conquest of Rhodesia. Subsequently I retained my interest in the history of South Africa, Zimbabwe and the neighbouring countries at the end of the 19th century. *Cecil Rhodes and His Time* is a continuation of this same theme.

It is only natural that in the course of so many years' research an historian will acquire a broad range of views on this topic. This diversity is reflected in the pages of this book, too, and I crave in advance the indulgence of those readers who may believe that these associations and considerations disturb the narrative flow or are not strictly consistent with an academic approach.

As I rummaged in the stacks of library and archive hay I

searched for blades of grass which still retained the odour of the past. I endeavoured to catch the flavour of that life, to experience the world of those people, their hopes and fears. I tried to discover what prejudices prevailed at the time, what was taught in and out of school. Alongside historical documents and archive material I also made use of literature, which, so it seemed to me, reflected the spirit of the time, even if it was not directly connected with the events in Rhodes's life. This is how the works of English poets came to be featured in the book, particularly those of Kipling, who has been called the Cecil Rhodes of literature.

Of course, however hard one might try, it is still very difficult to gain a true idea of historical traditions and the national spirit of foreign lands and peoples when observing them from a great distance. It is easy to err when describing the history of England and easier still, with that of South Africa, living so far from both these countries. I tried always to bear this in mind. I was careful too to remain mindful of the great Byron's caveat:

Stop! for thy tread is on an Empire's dust![24]

At the same time I took heart from the conviction that an outsider's view, from a distance, is also legitimate and can be very illuminating. It should also be remembered that the consequences of events directly or indirectly connected with Rhodes's own activities, have been felt far beyond the frontiers of his own country, England, and those countries of Southern Africa where most of his activities took place.

This book was originally written for the Russian reader and it was published in Moscow in Russian. Only very slight alterations have been made for the English edition.

One chapter has been added: "These Events through the Eyes of Contemporary Russian Observers", as I believe that this will be of interest to English-speaking readers.

The translation of books into foreign languages, as is well known, demands a tremendous amount of work and is by far not always successful. Christopher English, in translating the book, did so with great feeling, with a genuine interest for the topic and an overall love for history. The same can be said about his co-workers at Moscow's Progress Publishers who helped to prepare the English edition: Maya Novakova, Larissa Perepechko, Andrei Zur and Yelena Grishilo. In listing their names I certainly do not wish to attribute to them any responsibility for inaccuracies or insufficiencies, almost unavoidable in a book of rather large size and difficult content. I simply want to truly thank them.

Part of the title page of E. P. Mathers's book *Zambesia, England's El Dorado in Africa,* published to attract British settlers to the countries annexed by Rhodes

The Gold
and Diamond
KING

« How Cecil Rhodes Made His Fortune »

On April 20, 1902 the St Petersburg journal *Niva* recounted beneath this heading a remarkable story.

In 1870 a young man sailed into Sydney from the distant Old World. He had no friends in the town and for a long time he was unable to settle down. One night he spent roaming the streets, dreaming of a bite to eat and a roof over his head. By the following dawn he had strayed far from the town, along the ocean-shore. There he encountered a shark-fisher. He took the fisherman's rod and cast out, just for luck. At once he hauled in a twenty-foot shark.

They cut open its belly and inside they found an edition of *The Times* and a notebook: the shark had devoured their owner somewhere off the shores of England. *The Times* was a mere ten days old—a good deal more recent than the newspapers brought by the mailboats.

From the paper the young man learned that the Franco-Prussian war had started in Europe and this had meant a sharp increase in the price of wool. Realising the value of this information in Australia he repaired forthwith to the richest wool-broker in Sydney. Initially the butler refused him entry into his master's house as he was so shabbily dressed. But the young man eventually gained entry and proposed to the dealer that he buy up the entire wool clip. For his part he secured one half of the profits.

When they had concluded the deal the broker turned to his unlikely confederate and said:

"What did you say your name is?"

"Cecil Rhodes."

"It is hard to remember. However, I think you will make it easier by and by, if you live".

The deal went through, and secured to the young stranger the first fortune he ever pocketed.

Appearing as it did in a popular magazine the story undoubtedly attracted the attention of the Russian reading public. After all, Cecil Rhodes was the focus of great interest at that time. The Boer war still raged, and Rhodes was regarded as its primary instigator. Even in the distant reaches of Siberia, in the furthest-flung villages of the Russian Empire, newspapers were adorned with photographs of the bearded Afrikaners and caricatures of Cecil John Rhodes.

The story about the shark must have puzzled its readers. *Niva* gave no commentary, no indication how the story had come to their notice. No signature stood beneath it. It was up to the reader to believe it or not.

But even if one leaves aside the setting of the story (and who knows?—perhaps the much-travelled Rhodes did visit Australia) the story does not stand up to scrutiny. What shark-fishers are these, catching twenty-foot sharks with fishing rods, and hauling them ashore like tench or bream? And then reading a newspaper which has travelled for ten days in the belly of a shark... Even the most outrageous fisherman's tales would not permit such flights of fancy. This story smacks of the writings of Mark Twain.

And indeed, this piece of nonsense did issue from the pen of Mark Twain, although the great American writer may not have invented it himself, merely borrowing and adapting something he heard somewhere. Perhaps he was reminded of the story of how a certain Rothschild, a name as yet unknown to the world, had turned to his advantage the tidings of the battle of Waterloo?

All that *Niva* had done, in fact, was to reprint a chapter from Twain's book, *Following the Equator,*[1] published in 1897 and in Russian translation in 1901, without vouchsafing the reader so much as an explanation.

A great number of rumours and theories circulated about Rhodes's mysterious acquisition of wealth. They were often based on some extraordinary, miraculous stroke of good fortune. In his play *The Simpleton of the Unexpected Isles* Bernard Shaw similarly lampoons Rhodes. The English clerk in the play curses his fate in the following words:

"What am I? An empire builder: that's what I am by nature. Cecil Rhodes: that's me. Why am I a clerk...? Because life never came to me like it came to Rhodes. Found his backyard full of diamonds, he did, and nothing to do but wash the clay off them and be a millionaire."

And he writes his own epitaph: "Here lies a man who might have been Cecil Rhodes if he'd had Rhodes's luck".[2]

What, then, was the secret of Rhodes's sudden acquisition of wealth? Whence did this man, like a magician taking a rabbit from a top hat, pluck his millions?

SON OF A PROVINCIAL VICAR

In June 1870 a young man by the name of Cecil John Rhodes stepped on board the boat *Eudora*, which, on setting sail from Britain, was to take passage round the bulge of Africa, pass Cape Town and put in at the port of Durban, in the territory seized by the British from the Zulus.

But this was not the Cecil Rhodes that we have come to know: time had yet to mould him, and he was still a very young man...

He had pale blue eyes, a fairly sturdy frame, yet the appearance of delicate constitution. The expression on his face was diffident, but he had a fiercely proud manner. He spoke in a thin falsetto, but with confidence. Perhaps this confidence had been lent him by the money his father had advanced him and the two thousand pounds he had received as a gift from Aunt Sophy, his mother's sister.

On board the *Eudora* Rhodes celebrated his seventeenth birthday. As the French poet Arthur Rimbaud, Rhodes's coeval, declared in an early poem: "When you are seventeen you aren't really serious."[3] A few years later Rimbaud too was to set sail for Africa. While Charles Baudelaire, who had rounded the Cape of Good Hope some thirty years before, wrote:

> *The child, in love with globes and maps of foreign parts,*
> *Finds in the universe no dearth and no defect.*
> *How big the world is, seen by lamplight on his charts!*
> *How very small the world is, viewed in retrospect.*[4]

Was Rhodes also drawn to Africa by that beckoning spirit, the Wanderlust that lured successive generations of young Europeans to the dark continent? Africa forms an entire, dazzling chapter in the history of the dreams and aspirations of youth, without which it is impossible to understand the evolution of the human race.

Great numbers of young men set off for Africa in search of adventure, dreaming of exotic landscapes, of hunting fabled beasts in the lush undergrowth of the tropical forest. Rhodes set sail for Africa at the very dawn of this age, even slightly anticipating it. Immediately after him, in 1871, Frederick Selous embarked on his travels. He was to become the most famed of the Great White Hunters in Africa, the prototype of Allan Quatermain, hero of *King Solomon's Mines* and other novels by Henri Rider Haggard. But in those days there were not many like Selous. African safaris had not yet become fashionable among European hunters and adventurers. And the adventure novel with the colonial setting, which in time was to promote the Romanticism of colonial life, was yet to be born.

This was 1870, the eve of the colonial division of the world. The events leading to this great carve-up were already in train. But at the time no one could know to what they would lead.

Yet it was clear that Rhodes was propelled by something more than mere Wanderlust. One of his school-teachers recalls that Rhodes was no dreamer. What in fact was this force that drove him on?

People who think their country shameful, who despise
Its politics, are here; and men who hate their home;
Astrologers, who read the stars in women's eyes
Till nearly drowned, stand by the rail and watch the foam;
Men who must run from Circe, or be changed to swine,
Go tramping round the deck, drunken with light and air,
Thinking that wind and sun and spray that tastes of brine
Can clean the lips of kisses, blow perfume from the hair.[5]

Rhodes was yet to experience profound disillusionment, and, we may be sure, he never experienced loathing of his home country. Could it have been unrequited, youthful love? This we shall never know.

It seems likely that Rhodes cherished the same hopes that spurred Rimbaud to Africa, with dreams of making his millions:

"My day is done; I'm quitting Europe. Sea air will burn my lungs; strange climates will tan my skin. To swim, to trample the grass, to hunt ... to drink liquors strong as boiling metal,— like my dear ancestors around their fires.

"I'll return with limbs of iron, dark skin and furious eye... I will have gold: I will be idle and brutal. Women nurse those fierce invalids, home from hot countries."[6]

Rimbaud did in fact return to his home a cripple, and not in some figurative, Romantic sense, but a real, physical cripple. Nor did he win the veneration of women. Nor did he become a hero with a mysterious past. He returned to die. And when he lay delirious in a Marseilles hospital, ranting about IOU's and accounts, African deserts and trade caravans, the only person by his bedside was his younger sister. Even his own mother refused to come to her prodigal son, to bid him farewell. Fame only came to him posthumously and was in no way connected with his travels.

Rhodes, however, was destined to find in his Africa not only his millions, but power too, and world-wide celebrity.

...Cecil Rhodes's distant travels, his boundless thirst for adventure and his immensely variegated and dizzying career might be a little more understandable if we examine the traditions of his family.

Rhodes's first biographer, Sir Lewis Michell, traced the history of Rhodes's family to the mid-seventeenth century. Cecil's ancestors lived in small villages and towns in the English midlands. Many of them were born and died in the same village. Rhodes's own father, Francis William Rhodes, was neither a sailor, nor an army officer, nor a merchant. He did not embark on distant voyages, he had never been smitten with gold-fever or diamond fever. He led the quiet, patriarchal existence of a parish priest. And his parish was not even on the coast—where the lives of all the inhabitants, irrespective of their professions, are somehow linked with the sea—but inland, in the little town of Bishop's Stortford in Hertfordshire.

It was here that Cecil John Rhodes was born on July 5, 1853, fifth son in a family that was large even by the standards of those times: twelve sons and daughters (although two of them died in infancy).

The Rhodeses were rather influential and quite well-off;

Francis Rhodes's position of the village vicar for nearly three decades made him a prominent figure in the local community.

Cecil was not blessed with good health from the day he was born. As many of his biographers point out, he suffered from consumption right from childhood (and in those days tuberculosis was an incurable disease, scything people down in its relentless path and spreading fear in its wake). From his very earliest years it was also clear that he had a weak heart.

In contrast to his older brothers Cecil did not attend one of Britain's privileged public schools. His father lacked the means to send him either to Eton or Harrow. Rhodes's education was confined to the local grammar school, which had been founded in the reign of Queen Elizabeth I.

How vital those school years are in the development of a person! We are all moulded by our childhood... It is the occupations and enthusiasms of those years, the dreams, even the music we love then, that remains with us to the very end of our days, and explains much in our behaviour, our aspirations, in our very character. But how difficult it is to fathom, to uncover this hidden layer of character! And then when you are writing about a man who lived in another country, in another age, it is all the more difficult to discern his development and spiritual growth. How can we be expected to comprehend his aspirations, his thoughts, as he listened to the admonitions of his teachers?

All this comes so much more easily to the imagination of those who breathed the same English air as Rhodes. Yet there is surprisingly scant information about Rhodes's childhood and boyhood in the biographies by his fellow Englishmen. Admittedly most of these biographies were written at a time when it was not accepted that one should study the influence of childhood impressions on a man's subsequent life. "Concerning his school life not much is known",[7] writes Michell, who was closely acquainted with his hero. Not much, indeed.

André Maurois in his book on Rhodes maintains that even in his childhood years Cecil dreamt of great deeds and power. Maurois quotes an entry from the Rhodes family album. In answer to the question "What is your motto?" thirteen-year-old Cecil wrote: "To do or to die!"[8] But can one really take this childish effusion as the key to the image of Cecil John Rhodes? How many boys at that age have expressed similar sentiments?

It is well-known that Rhodes started school in 1861, that he was fascinated by the ancients, that his favorite subjects were history and geography, that he knew the Bible well, and his favourite writers were Plutarch, Plato, Homer and Aristotle.

The books he read had perhaps more influence on him than books do on boys today. There was, after all, no cinema, nor radio, nor television. Osip Mandelstam once wrote: "The book-case of our early childhood is our companion for all life. The disposition of its shelves, the selection of books, the colour of the bindings are perceived as the colour, height and arrangement of world literature itself. Why, those books which were not in that first bookcase, will never take their place in the ranks of literature, will never enter our universe. Whether we like it or not, every book in that first bookcase is a classic, and we would not throw out so much as the tattered spine of any one of them."[9]

What else could English schoolboys read in the eighteen-sixties? The novels of Walter Scott were already a little old-fashioned. *Tom Sawyer* would only see the light of day in 1876. And youthful readers would have to wait until 1887 to make the acquaintance of another contemporary of Rhodes's—Sherlock Holmes.

The entire reading public were intimately familiar with *Oliver Twist* and *David Copperfield*, and the *Posthumous Papers of the Pickwick Club* were published in editions unparalleled in size—tens of thousands of copies. There were even simplified versions for the common folk. Other popular English writers included Bulwer Lytton, Charles Kingsley, Anthony Trollope, Charles Reade, Wilkie Collins, Lord Alfred Tennyson and George Eliot.

Of the translated writers favourites among young readers were Dumas père, Vicomte Ponson du Terrail—the author of the interminable *Voyages de Rocambole* and the early Jules Verne. Also popular with many were tales of Araby and the recently translated Rubaiyat of Omar Khayyam.

The emergent genre of the detective story was beginning to win devotees at this time, too. Edgar Allan Poe, who had died in 1849, and Émile Gaboriau were both sought after. And there was another, more clandestine vogue in that prim, Victorian England—for the erotic literature which was circulated in manuscript. But pride of place on the bookshelves of England's youth still went to historical and pseudo-historical novels, to naval adventures and the memoirs of hunters and sportsmen.

What of all this might have appealed to the young Cecil Rhodes? Perhaps the historical novels about the conquistadores, about the conquest of the New World, about Admiral Drake and Queen Elizabeth's other "pirates"? We know that later, when he was already in Africa, Rhodes's inseparable companion was a little volume of Marcus Aurelius's *Meditations* which he regarded a veritable font of wisdom. Since his interest in classical studies had been kindled while still at school, it is of course possible that his love of Marcus Aurelius dates from those years.

Rhodes's dream was Oxford. But it proved to be an unattainable dream and when he finished school in 1869 he found himself at a crossroads. The following year it was decided to send him to Southern Africa, where one of his older brothers, the twenty-five-year old Herbert, had already settled.

Why exactly was this decision taken? Some biographers see the reason in Rhodes's poor health, which it was hoped the South African climate would help. Others recall that in English families in those days it was the done thing to dispatch sons to the colonies: there, of course, they would find dangers of many kinds, but it was also possible to make a career more quickly in the colonies and the lucky few would even make their fortunes. It was in the spirit of these convictions that Cecil Rhodes's brothers were dispersed about the world, some in the colonies, others in the army. Not one of them fulfilled his father's wish, and followed in his footsteps. For them the spirit of the time prevailed over family traditions.

Rhodes himself was to comment at a later date, when answering the question about why he had set off for Africa:

"They will tell you that I came out on account of my health, or from a love of adventure, and to some extent that may be true: but the real fact is that I could no longer stand the eternal cold mutton".[10]

Thus did the mature politician, the king of gold and diamonds explain his past. But was it so patently clear to that seventeen-year-old youth?

AT SEVENTEEN

Rhodes took ship on a sailing boat. The wooden vessel *Eudora* was regarded as quite swift for those days: the journey took a mere seventy-two days. Two and a half months!

There was time aplenty for thinking, for remembering the misty shores of England, long since lost to sight below the horizon, and to dream about the hot climes that approached. What else could passengers do during those long days, as they gazed into the endless monotony of the Atlantic waters? Evenings were also a good time for reflection, in the dim light of the swinging oil lamps, and at night, after ten when the lamps were extinguished. To prevent fires there were the severest prohibitions against not only the lighting of candles in the cabins, but even against the striking of matches, a very recent invention. In such manner did Rhodes while away his time, in idle conversation with his fellow-travellers, or musing on the future that lay in store for him.

Many, if not the majority, of the passengers were migrants, people who had decided to begin a new life far from their homes, from a country that was not equally kind to all its inhabitans. Even those who had no intention of permanent migration would be away for a long time. Considering that the journey there and back took well-nigh six months it is unlikely that anyone would have undertaken it purely for pleasure. Most of all, of course, the passengers talked about South Africa. They recalled newspaper reports, they discussed various rumours. Rhodes paid careful attention, making the occasional contribution, too, for he also knew a little about the region, from his brother Herbert's letters.

The passengers would also recall the tales of other travellers. In those days Dr Livingstone was the talk of all Europe. His *Missionary Travels,* published in London in 1857, had been translated into many languages. Then in 1870 people all over the world were alarmed at the news that Livingstone was lost somewhere in tropical Africa. The *New York Herald* responded by sending one of its journalists, H. M. Stanley, at the head of a rescue expedition.

Beyond the stern of the boat raged one of the biggest wars of nineteenth-century Europe: between France and Prussia. It began while the boat was already in mid-Atlantic. But the tele-graph was yet to be invented, and without it news travelled very slowly, so Rhodes and his companions were unable to discuss these events. Instead they recalled other wars. Even in Rhodes's as yet brief life it was a rare year that English soldiers were not dispatched to some corner of the globe to fight and die for the Crown. They went to Russia to fight the Crimean War, to India to supress the Sepoy Mutiny, to China to the Second Opium War, to Japan to storm the ports, to Ethiopia to wage war against the most powerful state in Africa. At one time the air was even charged with the threat of war with the United States.

The distinctive red uniforms were seen everywhere, on board ships and in ports all over the world. Amongst those who sailed with Rhodes on the *Eudora* were many who would later be sent to other distant parts, to extend the frontiers of the British Em-pire, on which "the sun never sets". By no means all of these would return home again. This was naturally the subject of conversa-tion on deck, in the smoking rooms, and in the cabins: by some it was approached with alarm, by others with a haughty and pompous patriotism.

The passengers from more affluent backgrounds discussed socie-ty news, and literary affairs. These would have included the death of Dickens—who died a few days before the *Eudora* em-barked (they did not know of Prosper Merimée's death—he died when they were already lying off the shore of Southern Africa); such new publications as Wilkie Collins' *The Moonstone,* Lewis Carroll's *Alice's Adventures in Wonderland* or the novels of Anthony Trollope, then at the height of fashion. Trollope himself was to take ship a few years later, in order to visit the south of the dark continent and to write his two-volume *South Africa.* Another name on everyone's lips would have been Jules Verne. The heroes of the first of his novels—*Cinq Semaines en Ballon* (Five Weeks in a Ballon)—flew over that same Africa whose scorching winds were even now searing the boards of the ship. The heroes of another—*Adventures de trois Russes et de trois Anglais* (Adven-tures of Three Russians and Three Englishmen)—explored the very same part of the world towards which Rhodes and his com-panions were heading.

Another writer who was greatly in vogue with Rhodes' gener-ation, Émile Gaboriau, had himself served with the cavalry in

Africa. Dumas also belongs in the list. He sent his Vicomte de Bragelonne "to Africa, where men die".[11] He visited Africa himself, and, as he did after all his travels, published several volumes of travel impressions. By this time he was 68 years old, and no longer up to fighting and travelling, with but a few months left to live. Ponson du Terrail, another writer almost as prolific as Dumas, had already joined the fray against the Prussians, in their invasion of French soil.

Such literary reminiscences occupy the attention of only a few of Rhodes's companions. The majority have no interest in such intellectual conversation. Some of the migrants have never read any books before, and are hardly likely to start reading now. After all they are not travelling to foreign shores merely to while away the time, but compelled to do so by their hard lot in life. God knows what awaits them at their destination, and even here, on board ship, misfortune does not abandon them: one falls seriously ill, and there is no suitable medicine; another, in his cups, goes berserk and causes an uproar.

For a seventeen-year-old youth, to have beheld all these sights and heard all this talk must have been quite an education. An education lasting two and a half months, over a six-thousand-mile journey, on board ship and in the ports they visited. Here he was able to see at first hand the wretched life of the poor, and it looked far more terrible and ugly than from the windows of the Bishop's Stortford vicarage. He saw emaciated women, filthy children, helpless old men. Add to these drunkards, card-sharps, prostitutes. . .

Rhodes never recorded his reminiscences of this voyage, nor about any episode in his life. But we may cite instead the memoirs of another man. He also took ship for Africa at the age of seventeen, several years after Rhodes. He wrote: "The six-thou-sand-mile voyage to Durban, Natal, began my education, my teachers were the gamblers, adventurers, and loosely principled women who largely made up the passenger list of the rotten old *Moor*. I suppose I felt my boyhood slipping behind me, and regretted it, for to this day I remember that the fifth night out, after days of severe seasickness, I stood at the stern of the *Moor* and strove to visualize my English home, far across the black waters. In the cabin behind me were hilarious women, noisy gambling, the rough-and-tumble of drunkenness. If I wept a little because of the ache at my heart it was the last time I ever privileged myself. My skin was beginning to thicken".[12]

The impressions of one's youth are engraved into the memory for all one's life. It is possible that these images of ship and port life stood before Rhodes many years later when, as a mature politician, he endeavoured by seizing colonies abroad to diffuse social conflicts at home.

LAND OF THE ZULUS

On September 1, 1870, having rounded the Cape of Good Hope and the southernmost point of Africa, Cecil Rhodes alighted in the port of Durban, in the British colony of Natal. This country, populated by the Zulu people, was a fairly recent acquisition of the realm: it had been seized in the eighteen forties.

Rhodes's older brother was not there to meet him. Unable to wait any longer, Herbert had hurried off to the recently discovered diamond fields. These fields had not yet become the largest in the world, and it was unlikely that anyone at this stage suspected they would: but diamond fever had gripped the land nonetheless.

Cecil Rhodes was not smitten immediately. He began his South African life in Pietermaritzburg, the administrative centre of Natal; here he stayed with friends of his brother. Then Herbert returned, and the brothers tried to grow cotton on Herbert's farm in the Umkomaas valley. It is true that Herbert spent more time in the diamond fields than on the farm, leaving Cecil to run the place largely single-handed, administering a work-force of thirty Zulus.

Rhodes later recalled his life on the farm as an almost idyllic time. He and his brother lived in a little hut, with two beds and a table. Around them stretched green, flowering valleys, above them the clean, azure skies and the brilliant African sun. . . "You feel that every mouthful of this air is a boost to your health, it freshens your chest and senses like bathing in spring water." This rapturous observation from South Africa, "this peaceful and happy corner", comes from the pen of the Russian writer Ivan Goncharov, who visited the continent in the very

year of Rhodes's birth during his travels on the frigate *Pallada.*
And to Rhodes, with his rather frail health, the climate here
must have seemed particularly welcoming after the gloomy skies
of fog-bound England.

An idyllic existence it may have been, but a practical side
to Rhodes's nature also emerged here—in the seventeen-year-old
farm manager's canny treatment of the Africans: "I have lent a
good deal of money to the Kaffirs as it is the hut-tax time, and
they want money, and if you lend it them, they will come and
work it out whenever you want them, besides its getting a very
good name among them, and Kaffirs are really safer than the
Bank of England",[13] he remarked in a letter to his mother.

Rhodes also had a cherished goal: he wanted to save money
to study at Oxford. The reason for this choice Rhodes himself
supplies: ". . .have you ever thought how it is that Oxford men
figure so largely in all departments of public life? The Oxford
system in its most finished form looks very unpractical, yet,
wherever you turn your eye—except in science—an Oxford man
is at the top of the tree".[14]

Business, however, was not going all that well. Two cotton
harvests had brought no great profit. The price of cotton was
falling. And then there was the diamond rush. Rhodes wrote
home: "The people here talk of nothing but diamonds."[15] More
and more white colonists in Natal were abandoning their homes
of many years and hastening to join the diamond rush, hoping
to make a quick fortune.

Cecil Rhodes stayed in Natal for little more than a year. In
October 1871 he too downed tools on the farm and set off for
the diamond fields.

This is about all that is known of his early life in Africa.

To the end of his days Rhodes's favourite author remained
Marcus Aurelius, and he believed in the latter's dictum: "Put
an end once for all to this discussion of what a good man should
be, and be one."

When we examine the sort of man that Rhodes was becoming
it appears that for him the process of growing to manhood was
that of gradual transformation into a colonist. A colonist was
no longer quite a European, not quite an Englishman or a
Frenchman. He was a man whose psychology, morality, whose
entire view of life was shaped by colonialism. Any European

arriving in a colony at once enjoyed privileges which were automatically granted by the colonial system to all those with white skins. In comparison to the native inhabitants he at once became a being of a higher order to whom everything, or almost everything, was permitted. This situation was enshrined in the laws and safeguarded by the authorities, the police and the army.

As a result it often happened that a callow youth, still full of self-doubt and hesitation, on arriving here from Europe would swiftly acquire quite definite and often totally inflexible views. His doubts would recede, and in their place he would display a firm grip on reality. Should he return to his country after a number of years, the difference between him and his co-evals would be very striking.

For many this change in awareness led to a dual moral system: one set of standards applied to their life in the colony, and another, quite different, to their life in Europe.

An interesting reflection of this duality can be seen in a French colonial novel of the time, *L'inutile richesse*, by Georges Ohnet: ". . .Mössler was a man of upright character and a rare goodness. But in Africa ... he would never hesitate to pull the trigger. . . In the Transvaal this was called being a man of action. In France it was called criminal. It was a question of latitude, of the milieu, of circumstances." Elsewhere his wife is implored: "Don't show me your African face. Show me your Paris face. . . It is not the terrible and resolute Madame Mössler, who reigns over the savages amidst the tigers, that I have come to see, it's the charitable and benevolent Madame Mössler who lives on the Avenue des Champs-Elysées. . ."[16]

As the years advanced this moral duality would often disappear. In its place a single system would return, but this, more often than not, would comprise acquired moral categories—acquired in the course of life in the colonies. Thus it happened that in the colonies, amongst "savages", a new breed of people came into existence whose morals were immeasurably worse than those of their compeers at home, in the mother country. Then these same people would return to Europe, where they would be appalled by the unfamiliar "liberalism" they encountered, and would try and inculcate their colonial standards in their fellow countrymen at home.

This fact was neatly observed at the end of the last century by a leading Russian journalist of the day, the London correspondent of the Russian liberal press Isaak Shklovsky. He wrote from England (under the pseudonym Dioneo): "The Member of Parliament for our constituency, since time immemorial, has been an old, retired general. He served somewhere in West Africa; there, with a small detachment and five cannons he planted European culture, i.e. he burnt down so many villages, cut down so many fruit trees and massacred so many Negroes and cattle that the area is still a desert, even though a great many years have passed... He has only attended parliament once or twice, but he made his presence felt. After listening to the opposition's speech the old man declared that, quite frankly, they should be dealt with 'in the African way', that is, send out a few soldiers, haul up a cannon and then: 'Let them have it! Cut and thrust, to left and to right!'"[17]

In this way European colonialism punished the Europeans themselves. No nation which oppresses any other nation can itself be free!

We understand in a general way, from a historical, sociological viewpoint how the colonial face of European democracy came into being. What is not so clear are the specific, tangible features of this development.

It is possible that we are more familiar with the imaginary experiences of Robinson Crusoe, creation of the great Daniel Defoe. We can all recall how Crusoe, working entirely alone, systematically colonizes an uninhabited island and subjugates its solitary aborigine, Man Friday, but little is known about the psychological development of colonists from real life.

Little is known about Rhodes, about the growth of his own personality in this new, colonial life. It is hard to surmise from the biographies and his published letters of those years how he responded to the major events in Europe and Africa. For there were extraordinary happenings. Rhodes alighted on the shores of Africa on the day the French army was routed at Sedan. To his contemporaries the very word "Sedan" had a symbolic sound for many years to come. The Russian poet Fyodor Tyutchev, lying on his death bed in 1873, quipped grimly: "It is my Sedan".[18] Then there was the Paris Commune, which held all Europe at tenterhooks. But we shall never know whether Rhodes was concerned by these events.

Europe had receded from him, and if Rhodes had landed on the shores of another continent, who knows how his personality might have developed. But he arrived in South Africa during a crucial time, a turning-point in history, when the destiny of that country was inextricably linked to that of Europe and the world as a whole.

Not that Europe had neglected the southern extremity of the African continent previously, either. Even Napoléon had a place for this region in his global designs: "If we cannot dislodge England from the Cape, we must take Egypt." After the Battle of Trafalgar, when Admiral Nelson destroyed the French fleet and with it Napoléon's plans to invade overseas countries, the "Emperor of the French" declared: "On the Elbe and on the Oder, we have won our India, our Spanish colonies and our Cape of Good Hope".[19]

But at the end of the eighteen sixties, just before Rhodes's arrival in South Africa, it seemed to his contemporaries that this corner of the Old World was condemned to oblivion. It had lost the role it used to play in the world economy: the role of a major re-fuelling point half-way between Europe and the East, at the most perilous point in this journey, the confluence of the two oceanic currents, the Atlantic and the Indian, where the waters were never still. For entire centuries even the most intrepid captains would cross themselves with undisguised relief when they made it safely into the "tavern of the seas"—the port of Cape Town.

In November 1869 the Suez Canal was opened for shipping. The caravans of ocean-bound vessels no longer had to round the Cape of Good Hope and cast anchor off the shores of South Africa. The South African ports were threatened with losing their cosmopolitan aspect. The polyglot crowds of sailors started to disappear from the streets of Cape Town, depriving the city of one of its most colourful and vibrant features.

Neither was it necessary now to provide supplies for thousands of boats, or to maintain workshops for countless maritime repairs. With the commissioning of the Suez Canal Southern Africa at once found itself out on a limb, cut off from the world trade routes. Neither did it hold any intrinsic interest for capitalist Europe. The colonists here bred cattle and sheep, made wine, exported wool and ostrich feathers to Europe and America. There were barely twenty towns and settlements in all these colonies with populations over a thousand. There was less than sixty miles of railroad.

It seemed that South Africa was doomed to become yet another outpost of Empire, remote and forgotten. The Russian writer Ivan Goncharov pronounced his verdict in the year of Rhodes's birth: "There is no gold here, and no crowds will flock here, as to California or Australia."[20] Nothing, as it happened, could have been further from the truth.

What came next nobody could have foreseen, for it was precisely there, in southern Africa, that the world's greatest deposits of gold and diamonds were found, and these, moreover, were very close to each other, some 250 miles apart. This phenomenon of nature quite stunned the Europe of those days, and it was even called the "second discovery" of South Africa.

Crowds did indeed flock there, in hundreds of thousands. South Africa was born again, to be celebrated thus by Kipling:

> *Lived a woman wonderful*
> > *(May the Lord amend her!)*
> *Neither simple, kind, nor true,*
> *But her Pagan beauty drew*
> *Christian gentlemen a few*
> > *Hotly to attend her.*
> *Christian gentlemen a few*
> > *From Berwick unto Dover;*
> *For she was South Africa,*
> *And she was South Africa,*
> *She was Our South Africa,*
> > *Africa all over!*[21]

California and Australia were nothing to this! No such riches had been found in their soil. The disvcoveries in southern Africa exceeded even the wildest imaginings of any old-time panhandler.

It was in this turbulent stream of events that Cecil Rhodes's personality was formed.

DIAMOND FEVER

For almost two thousand years the world had known only Indian diamonds. The Koh-i-Noor adorned the English crown, the celebrated Orlov diamond sparkled in the sceptre of the Russian czars, the Shah had been presented to Czar Nicholas I by the Shah of Persia in atonement for the murder of the Russian ambassador and playwright Alexander Griboyedov by an angry mob. These were all from India.

But for the last one hundred years or more the word "diamond" has been more closely associated with Southern Africa. It was here that the greatest diamond of all was found: the Cullinan. It is here that the majority of the world's gem-quality diamonds are mined to this day.

Even Brazilian diamonds are thought by scientists to have links with South Africa. According to the hypothesis of the supercontinent, Gondwanaland, South America was once connected to Africa and the Brazilian diamond veins ran into the South African. At any rate, the Brazilian stones closely resemble those from South Africa in form, colouring and other features.

Indian diamonds have inspired countless legends and fables. Such stories as Wilkie Collins' *The Moonstone* or Robert Louis Stevenson's *The Rajah Diamond* at once spring to mind.

But now it is the turn of the South African diamonds to surround themselves in myth and legend. We have probably all heard the theory that the *Titanic* was carrying a cargo of diamonds on its fated journey through the Atlantic in 1912. A new wave of excitement about these diamonds was stirred up at the end of 1985, when a Franco-American expedition located the wreck of the *Titanic* nearly four kilometres below the ocean surface. The diamonds of South Africa now feature in thrillers, ranging from Louis-Henri Boussenard to Wilbur Smith, in Hollywood productions and even in pop songs.

The South African diamonds were discovered near the confluence of the Orange and Vaal rivers. The Afrikaner farmer Schalk van Niekerk once saw a child on his friend Jacobs's farm playing with a sparkling pebble. "Take it away with you, by all means, said Jacobs, if you fancy it." After changing hands a few times the diamond was acquired for five hundred pounds by the governor of the Cape Colony. That was the year 1867.

Two years later van Niekerk had another stroke of luck. He found another such "pebble", only this time a much bigger one, on the farm of a local African witchdoctor. The diamond was measured at eighty-three carats. He knew at once what to do. He sold it to a dealer for eleven thousand pounds, and the dealer then sold it to Lord Dudley for twenty-five thousand. The diamond came to be known as the Star of South Africa.[22]

Rumours about the diamonds travelled throughout the world. The excitement started in mid-1869 and reached its peak by 1870, with Southern Africa now the new Eldorado for all manner of prospectors, adventurers, panhandlers and tricksters. The names of three Boer farms started to appear more and more frequently in European and American newspapers: De Beers, Dutoitspan, Bulfontein. But the name featured most of all was Colesberg Kopje. It was on the slopes of this hill that the prospectors' settlement grew up.

People still had vivid memories of the Californian gold-rush—a mere twenty years before. It was instructive to see how this mania, once described as "the most dangerous illness that could ever grip mankind"—gold-fever, develops. The following account is given in a history of America: "Artisans dropped their tools, farmers left their cattle to die and their crops to rot, lawyers fled from clients, teachers threw aside their books, preachers cast off their cloth, sailors deserted their ships in the harbours, and women left their kitchens—all in one overwhelming rush for the gold-bearing district. Business ceased in the towns; real estate slumped; deserted houses and shops sank into decay. From every direction fortune-hunters swept down like locusts. . ."[23] Diamond fever showed every sign of being just as dangerous.

The first to be smitten with diamond fever were not those who lived closest to the fields. The Africans who lived in these areas could not have imagined how much people in Europe would pay for mere transparent stones. Nor were the Afrikaner farmers interested in the tedious business of prospecting. Having made their new homes deep in the African interior they had long since cut off ties with Europe and forsaken everything European. Van Niekerk with his interest in diamonds was an exception amongst the Afrikaners.

It was the English, the Americans, the German and the French who flocked to the diamond fields. They converged from Cape

Town and the other European settlements in South Africa. They came from much further afield too: from Europe, America and Australia. This was a most colourful assemblage of humanity. They included the "Hale and crippled, young and aged. Paid, deserted, shipped away", to quote Kipling.

There were also men who regarded themselves as gentlemen by birth. Yet they did not think it in the least demeaning to take up a miner's pick and sieve when they graduated from Oxford, as Lord of Salisbury had done, joining the gold rush in Australia. This did not prevent him becoming British Prime Minister in the course of time.

There were Romantics too:

> We were dreamers, dreaming greatly, in the
> man-stifled town,
> We yearned beyond the sky-line where the strange
> roads go down.[24]

Kipling never described what awaited those dreamers in the diamond fields.

The first ordeal was the journey itself. The worst part was not the passage across the ocean, but the trek overland, through South Africa. The diamond deposits were deep in the interior, beyond the Cape Colony and Afrikaner republics of the Orange Free State and the Transvaal. The prospectors had to cover hundreds of miles through the arid veld, hauling heavy baggage: nothing could be purchased once they arrived at their destination. They had to hire or buy large wagons to which they harnessed teams of up to twenty oxen. It was a hard road, with rocky ascents and descents. Along the route and, worse still, at the diamond fields themselves there was practically no woodland, no trees offering shelter from the blazing sun. How could they survive all this? Indeed, there were many who did not survive. Precisely how many is not known: no one kept their tally.

Initially most of the prospectors were not hired hands, but actual claimholders. In these settlements there were no laws and no authority other than the rule of the first or the gun, which everyone kept close at hand. The area of the diamond fields was regarded as no man's land: no European state had managed to seize it by the beginning of the eighteen seventies and Europe then was not inclined to recognize the territorial rights of the African peoples.

The prospectors declared their own republic: the "Diamond Fields Republic" and their own ruling body: the Diggers' Committee. A former English sailor and a man reputed to have great physical strength, Stafford Parker, was elected president. Those opposed to him elected another committee with another president. An attempt to interfere by the British authorities was answered by the Black Flag Rebellion, mounted by a group of anti-British prospectors who raised the Jolly Roger.

The Orange Free State declared that the fields were situated within its territory and were therefore Free State property. The Transvaal also laid claim. But Britain now entered the fray and events proceeded in accordance with the usual development of relations between major and minor states. This is how Mark Twain puts it in his story "The Stolen White Elephant": "...Five years ago, when the troubles concerning the frontier line arose between Great Britain and Siam, it was presently manifest that Siam had been in the wrong."[25]

Thus too in South Africa it soon emerged that the Afrikaner republics had been in the wrong.

In October 1871 the diamond fields area became British (and five years later it was officially annexed to the Cape Colony). This operation was carried out by the British Colonial Secretary Lord Kimberley. It was in his honour that the prospectors' village was named, and on this site there subsequently arose the town of Kimberley. The diamond boom is consequently often called the Kimberley boom, and the ore in which the diamonds were found—kimberlite.

ONE OF THOUSANDS

One day in October 1871 Cecil Rhodes also set off for the diamond fields, taking his final leave of the farm on the shores of the Indian Ocean.

His path lay across the Orange Free State. For the first time Rhodes saw large numbers of Afrikaner farms: in Natal he had lived amongst fellow Englishmen.

Spring had broken, the land was beginning to flower. The animal life in those parts was very rich. Herds of antelope and zebras abounded, giraffes, ostriches, wild cats, hyenas and jackals were plentiful. Lions, elephants and rhinoceroses were also encountered.

The journey was a long one, fully six hundred kilometres even as the crow flies, and it took him through the Drakensberg Mountains, the highest range in South Africa, where he had to cross steep ravines, running streams, and dry river beds. Often there were no paths to follow, and there was never anything like a bridge. Along the entire journey there was only one inn, in Bloemfontein, which at that time was small, nondescript town, capital of an equally nondescript Afrikaner republic, the Orange Free State.

Rhodes hauled food and baggage in a large ox-wagon. His chattels included a spade and bucket for digging up diamonds. He himself rode horseback in front of the wagon, but his pony could not take the hard journey and died. The man proved hardier than the beast: it took him more than a month to reach his goal, but he made it. Rhodes arrived at the diamond fields in November, by which time the diggers' independent republic had been disbanded and the Union Jack flew from the flagpole.

Rhodes made for Colesberg Kopje, the largest settlement of prospectors. It was here that his brother Herbert owned three of the hundreds of claims (each measuring 31 square feet).

In a letter to his mother Rhodes describes this place—it was precisely on this spot that the future town of Kimberley came into existence. "Imagine a small round hill at its very highest part only 30 feet, above the level of the surrounding country, about 180 yards broad and 220 long; all round it a mass of white tents, and then beyond them a flat level country for miles and miles, with here and there a gentle rise... I should like you to have a peep at the kopje from my tent door at the present moment. It is like an immense number of ant-heaps covered with black ants, as thick as can be, the latter represented by human beings; when you understand there are about 600 claims on the kopje and each claim is generally split into 4, and on each bit there are about 6 blacks and whites working, it gives a total of about ten thousand working every day on a piece of ground 180 yards by 220... All through the kopje roads have been left to carry the stuff off in carts... There are constantly mules, carts and all going head over heels into the mines below as there are no rails or anything on either side of the roads, nothing but one great broad chasm below."[26]

Rhodes wished to spare his mother's feelings, and did not add that when the mules and carts plunged into the chasm below they took people with them. Their mangled bodies were brought up afterwards in the same large leather baskets that were used to lift the ore to the surface. Most of these victims were black labourers, who carried out the hardest work: the prospectors hired them for manual labour and tended to remain in the role of supervisors. But some whites perished too.

We do not have such vivid pictures of the South Africa diamond fever as we do of the American gold rush in the Klondike and California. But such accounts of the latter as Bret Harte's "The Luck of Roaring Camp" or Jack London's "The Land of White Silence" do give some idea what life was like in Kimberley.

The sun blazed down. The brown earth was parched dry. There was no fresh produce to be had; even the bare essentials of life were in short supply. What goods were available were terribly dear, because of the distance and difficulty of transporting them. Prices in Kimberley were many times higher than in Cape Town. Drinking water was scarce, epidemics rife.

The problem facing the diggers was how to find a good claim and how to protect it. This meant they lived in a state of permanent anxiety, and tempers flared at the drop of a hat. Murder and suicide were daily occurrences: death was part of everyday life. Illness, even the most serious kind, was nothing. There was only one thing on everyone's mind: diamonds.

The pits grew deeper and deeper and the partitions between them grew narrower by the day, and frequently collapsed. The hill itself grew gradually smaller, eroded by thousands of spades.

Thanks to the combined efforts of the diggers Colesberg Kopje was eventually transformed into the largest man-made hole on the surface of the earth. It was nicknamed the Big Hole. By 1914, when workings were finally terminated, the crater had attained a depth of 1098 metres and more than 3 tons of diamonds had been removed from it. To this day the site is a big tourist attraction.

Rhodes appears to have foreseen this turn of events. "Some day I expect to see the kopje one big basin where once there was a large hill",[27] he wrote.

Diamond fields

One of his biographers, quoting these words, comments: "Little did he realise that when that time came he, Cecil Rhodes, would own it all."[28]

But how did this come about? Was it really enough merely to join the ranks of the diggers, to become just one of those tens of thousands feverishly scratching away at this immense ant heap? We should recall, too, that he was a raw youth of eighteen with no experience of prospecting, and little experience of life in general.

At the most crucial time—right at the very beginning—Cecil Rhodes found himself alone. A mere two weeks after his arrival Herbert left on a long trip, first to Natal, and thence to England. Cecil was left on his own to compete with older and experienced men.

All the more amazing, therefore, that he was able to succeed against such odds. This begs the question: where lies the key to the phenomenon that is Cecil John Rhodes?

THE CAREER OF A KIPLING HERO

It is not easy to divine the secret of such swift and dizzying success stories, to work out the mechanics of their development. This accounts for the proliferation in America of legends about street urchins, shoeshine boys or newspaper sellers, who suddenly, quite out of the blue, become millionaires. Of course, the simplest answer is to put it down to Mother Fortune, "a little bit of luck", as the saying goes.

> *The God of Fair Beginnings*
> *Hath prospered here my hand...*[29]

Yet soon after his arrival at the fields Rhodes wrote to his mother: "I found a $17^5/_8$ carats on Saturday, it was very slightly off, and I hope to get £ 100 for it... Yesterday I found a $3^1/$ perfect stone, but glassy, which I sold for £30... I find on average 30 carats a week".[30] Very soon he was able to start acquiring more claims of his own, no longer content just to work those belonging to his older brother. When Rhodes was eighteen and a half years old his claims were valued at five thousand pounds.

So there was an element of luck. Rhodes certainly cannot be

called unlucky, at least in financial matters. This, however, is not the end of the story.

First and foremost it must be said that, right from the start, Rhodes was never one of the poorer diggers. He never knew real privation. He never had to worry about his next meal or a roof over his head. Even if he had been unsuccessful in South Africa, he could have returned to England and lived there, perhaps not in great luxury, but certainly in sufficient comfort. It was not need that prompted Rhodes to join the rush, like many others, but greed.

We do not know how much money he had when he started: how much his father gave him when he set off, how much he was able to earn in Natal by selling cotton. We only know that he received two thousand pounds from his aunt Sophy, his mother's sister. This sum alone—and it was only part of his capital—was no small amount of money in those days. Many of Rhodes's contemporaries who made their fortunes in the diamond rush started with incomparably less.

The Rhodes brothers were amongst the very few prospectors who possessed their own, individual claims. This was beyond the means of most.

The older brother, despite his restless nature, or perhaps precisely because of it, did Rhodes a great favour. He was among the first diggers to arrive at the diamond fields. But then he kept on going off on long and frequent trips. Either he would be lured by rumours of gold discoveries deep in the African interior, or he would go to sell guns to African chiefs, even including a Portuguese cannon in his merchandise. For this the Portuguese threw him into jail in Lourenço Marques... And just as he had once entrusted the running of his farm to his younger brother now he entrusted the working of his claims to him, and Rhodes found this to be good training. In 1873 Herbert left for good and sold his claims to Cecil. Several years later, having made his way deep into the continent, he died somewhere near Lake Nyasa. The accepted version is that he perished in his hut in a fire caused by a keg of rum exploding. A fitting end to an adventurer's life.

Thus in 1873 Cecil became the sole and undisputed master of several undivided claims. In addition he had money of his own. This, however, still does not explain the mystery of his sudden acquisition of wealth: it took certain qualities of character to increase his capital in this way. Rhodes had these qualities. First and foremost among them was his sense of purpose, which impressed all who knew him, both in his youth and in his mature years. Added to this was his ability to find his bearings swiftly in any difficult situation (a skill which failed him later in life, but which appears to have worked faultlessly in his youth).

Rhodes quickly learnt how to evaluate with total precision the state of the market. He was also constantly searching for new ways of achieving his goals, a search that even extended to technological innovations. To the astonishment of the other prospectors he would engage in schemes like importing a steam engine at great cost, or purchasing a pump to expel water from the mines. One example was the production of ice. Rhodes even started selling it at the diggings. He would quickly abandon any unsuccessful enterprise, but one which showed a profit he would develop and expand.

At an early age Rhodes displayed the talent so essential to the success of any entrepreneur or manager: the ability to find the right people, to get them to work for him and to make good use of them. Rhodes used to say that every man has his price. Once he acquired his wealth he started buying the people he needed. At first his scope was limited, he had to resort to persuasion, pointing out the bright prospects of such cooperation, even using a little flattery. . .

In this way he was able to find his indispensable companion. Charles Rudd was more experienced than Rhodes, nine years older, with an impeccable education—Harrow and Cambridge, a flair for business, and his own money.

In other words, he was to Rhodes what M'Cullough was to Kipling's Anthony Gloster. Rhodes was equally adept at exploiting his new colleague to the full, totally subjugating him to his own ambitions.

In the diamond fields Rhodes came up against all sorts of people. Amongst them was every shade of skin colour, every social class, every character type. In this metier he mastered a complex art: the management of other people. In the first instance these were the blacks, the indigenous population of the great continent in which he was destined to spend his days. Of course, Rhodes was assisted in part by the experience he had

Africans at the diamond fields

gained in Natal, on the cotton farm. But this experience had been limited.

Here, for the first time, Rhodes saw the variety of peoples that populated South Africa. In Natal he had only encountered his own compatriots—other Britons, and of the other tribes only Zulus, as Natal was their country. There were practically no representatives of other African nationalities. But Kimberley was a different story altogether. Here "there are Bushmen, Korannas, Hottentots, Griquas ... Magwata, Mazulu, Maswazi, Matswetswa, Matonga, Matabele, Mabaca, Mampondo, Mampengu, Batembu, Mazosa and more", wrote the African priest Gwayi Tyamzashe from Kimberley at the time. Europeans tended to call them all "kaffirs" from the Arabic word for "infidels". In actual fact that formed a diversity of ethnic and linguistic groups.

The diamond fields presented perhaps the first occasion in African history since the building of the pyramids that so many different peoples had been brought together for the same task. The sources of the industrial revolution in South Africa are to be found in this confluence of toiling masses. This was also the first stage in the formation of an African proletariat. Even then, in Kimberley in 1882, there was a strike of the African labourers, probably the first ever in Africa.

The babel of the diamond fields lived by the law of the jungle. Tribal hostilities were rife, as were fights between the old-timers and newcomers. Here the Africans made their first acquaintance with the life of the white prospectors: with drunkenness, knife-fighting, thieving.

A unique eyewitness report is provided by Gwayi Tyamzashe. In his article "The Native at the Diamond Fields", he writes: "The life then of both colored and whites was so rough that I thought this place was only good for those who were resolved to sell their souls for silver, gold and precious stones, or for those who were determined to barter their lives for the pleasures of time... You would hear nothing but cursing, swearing, scream-ing and shouts of hurrah for newcomers from the interior, for a well-dressed lady, for a diamond being found and so forth."

Forced labour had not yet been introduced in Kimberley. It could hardly be introduced when many of the neighbouring peo-ples were still independent, had not yet been subjugated. We might wonder, then, what it was that drove Africans to work on the diamond fields. Those who came from territories already annexed by Europe came to earn money to pay hut-tax. Those from tribes which still retained their sovereignty came to buy weapons. In the same article Gwayi Tyamzashe later writes: "Those coming from far up in the interior, come with the sole purpose of securing guns. They stay no longer than is necessary to get some £6 or £7 for the guns. Hence you will see hundreds of them leaving the Fields, and as many arriving from the North every day."[31]

Managing this African labour force was no easy matter: if something was not to their liking they would simply down tools and go! But Rhodes succeeded—to the envy of the other prospec-tors.

It was with experiences such as these that he began his career. This was the sort of journey through life which Kipling parodies in his poem "The Mary Gloster". But there was still a long time to pass before Rhodes could be described, like the hero of this poem, "not least of our merchant-princes".[32]

PARADOX?

It may seem paradoxical, but in fact Rhodes's ill health was a spur to his activities, and his bouts of sickness only sharpened his sense of purpose. He was also driven by what today we would call his complexes.

In 1872 he suffered his first severe heart attack. The following year, on his first trip back to England from South Africa, he heard the doctor's verdict: his physician reckoned that he had no more than six months to live. Rhodes was twenty at the time.

He tried to convince himself that there was a good side to his ailment.

"At any rate, Jameson", he remarked to his friend, "death from the heart is clean and quick. There's nothing repulsive about it. It's a clean death, isn't it?"[33]

Even in our day and age, when heart attacks cause more deaths than any other disease, many people try to console themselves with exactly the same words.

Rhodes lived to the age of 48. But when it came his death proved to be agonizing, and anything but clean and quick. It was preceded by weeks of asphyxia.

We might wonder how Rhodes was affected by the heart attacks, which tormented him all through his life.

And most important, how he was influenced by the doctor's verdict, sentencing him to an early death. It is unlikely any man in his position would be able to overcome for long the feeling of being condemned, to suppress the awareness that his days were numbered. It is hard to believe that this would not influence every aspect of his character and conduct. Knowledge of impending death reduces some people to a state of numbness, in which they can only await their final hour with eyes glazed with horror. On others, like Rhodes, it has precisely the opposite effect, spurring them on to a frenzy of activity to fulfill their life's ambitions by any means possible.

Sir Lewis Michell, Rhodes's biographer, mentions in passing that Rhodes was tormented by nightmares. He describes how. "...His friends once found him in his room, blue with fright, his door barricaded with a chest of drawers and other furniture; he insisted that he had seen a ghost".[34] Michell attributes his hero's terror to the fact that his nerves had been shattered by his heart attacks.

Of course, with the passing of years Rhodes accumulated many reasons for nightmares besides his weak heart. But here Michel is probably right: the heart attacks and the constant expectation of his own death were starting to tell on Rhodes's nerves.

Rhodes's behaviour had other quirks too. Everyone who knew him would have agreed with the remark of one acquaintance that even in his youth "Rhodes did not freely yield his interest to women".[35] He never married. None of his contemporaries mentions him having any liaisons. There were women who, like the Polish princess Catherine Radziwill, endeavoured to win his favour, but they were all doomed to failure. Even in prim Victorian England no one could have reproached Rhodes with immoral conduct. Of his nine brothers and sisters only two, his step-sister and one brother, acquired their own families. A biographer, writing almost fifty years ago, cautiously enquires: "Does it mean anything in particular for so many people in a family not to marry, anything that would concern scientists?"[36]

Until quite recently historians have been loath to write about the more intimate aspects of their heroes' lives. This, we presume, was regarded as undignified material for their attention. In this we perhaps see a relic of the prudery of the Victorian age. Even the Soviet historian, Academician Yevgeny Tarle in his well-known study of Napoléon essentially side-steps this aspect of this theme. He confines himself to a few sentences at the very beginning of the book, which he grudgingly puts in: "...to conclude this question once and for all and not to have to return to it". He explains his attitude thus: "Not one of any of the women with whom Napoléon had intimate relations in his life, ever had or even attempted to have the slightest perceptible influence on him..."[37]

"Not one ... ever ... the slightest ..." Such categorical pronouncements are rarely true. In any event it is difficult to believe that this sphere of life, which is of such importance for practically everyone, could be totally divorced from everything else. Besides, are we only influenced by those whose influence we ourselves acknowledge?

Even if we accept this as the truth and that none of Napoléon's women did influence him, surely even the type of women

56

he chose is a reflection of his character? Tarle's "to conclude this question once and for all and not to have to return to it" is hardly the best method of inquiry.

On the other hand, physiological features, their influence on the conscious and the sub-conscious, on the growth and development of the personality, are often adduced nowadays to explain not only character, but even the most diverse peripetia in a person's life. This approach has become so fashionable that pseudo-Freudian conjectures all too frequently take precedence over thorough, objective assessments of historical figures. It is probable that the time will come when a serious and carefully thought out study of the intimate side of life will become an inalienable part of any biographical analysis. But historians and biographers still often rely on mere conjecture.

Cecil Rhodes's biographers agree that Rhodes did not manifest any interest in the opposite sex, or in general in that side of life which occupied so much of the time and energies of the other prospectors.

A French historian depicts life in Kimberley at that time as follows.

...Initially there was not a single white woman in the prospectors' camps. But what a reception they had when they did appear! The first woman was greeted like royalty, like a goddess. An enormous crowd applauded her, people clambered up onto wagons, onto heaps of rubbish, to get a better view. Then more and more women arrived, yet they still remained virtually inaccessible to the prospectors, but infinitely desired. When people started opening up bars and hotels their patrons and residents would spill out onto the street to ogle every smartly dressed woman who passed.

One day a blonde beauty appeared in Kimberley. To everyone who sought to make her acquaintance she said: "You can see me in the evening in Greybittel's Canteen". The news spread like wildfire among the prospectors and that evening the bar was packed. When she saw this even the lady herself was non-plussed. Someone suggested as a solution that they hold an auction. The heroine was lifted up onto some champagne crates, and the bidding began.

"Five pounds and a crate of champagne!"

"Six pounds and a keg of brandy!"

"Ten pounds!"

"Twelve pounds!"

"Twenty pounds and two crates of champagne!"

The bidding was won by a prospector who, waving a wad of banknotes above his head, shouted: "Twenty-five pounds and three crates of champagne!"[38]

In those days that was a large sum of money. His opponents withdrew from the fray. But the victor was not left alone with his spoils: the bidders accompanied him in a large crowd to his tent and set up a terrific din around it...

The healthy young men who flocked to the diamond fields from all corners of the globe naturally made all sorts of resolutions not, under any circumstances, to deviate from their path, from the pursuit of that sacred goal for which they had forsaken their native lands and families, embarked on such a long and arduous journey and now toiled away from morning till night in this hellhole. They swore, with gritted teeth, to dig the hard earth until they dropped on their feet, the sooner to make their fortune and flee from this cursed place.

And yet, for all that it cost them dear, their young flesh proved unequal to these new temptations.

Cecil Rhodes, however, wasted neither his energies, nor his time and money on such pursuits.

"...I do not believe if a flock of the most adorable women passed through the street he would go across the road to see them",[39] wrote one contemporary, who knew him well at that time.

It is hard for us to say what Rhodes's feelings were. But outwardly he always or nearly always remained cold, calculating and sober. It seemed that nothing could distract him from his main purpose. It was as if money, and the power it gave him, took the place of success with women, the warmth of the family heart. Yet was this really the reason?

Direct questions about his relations with women were usually parried by Rhodes with a joke.

"Women! Of course I don't hate women. I like them, but I don't want them always fussing about."

Once Queen Victoria asked him:

"I've been told, Mr Rhodes, that you are a women-hater."

Rhodes answered:

"How could I possibly hate a sex to which Your Majesty belongs?"

Yet Rhodes invariably chose men as his servants. His secretaries were always young bachelors. As soon as they married Rhodes would dismiss them and pass them on to his companions.

The well-known journalist William Stead once expressed the following view: "The history of South Africa would have been different if Rhodes, Dr Jameson, Beit and Milner had been married men".[40]

We would hardly accept this evaluation. Yet we should be careful to avoid the other extreme: we should not underestimate the influence a man's private life and his relations with members of the opposite sex have on his character.

THE TRAGEDY OF THE SMALL PROSPECTOR

The year 1873 brought ruin to many people. This was the year that the "great depression" began, the world economic crisis. In mid-1873 the Austrian stock market collapsed, to be followed by the bankruptcy of some of the apparently most respectable firms and banks in London, Glasgow, Edinburgh, New York and Chicago.

Few investors were interested in diamonds in this crumbling world. The prospectors at once felt the effects of the depression. Most of them were utterly ruined. The lack of any control over production and sale inevitably led to a drop in prices. In addition the upper layers of soil in the fields had already been worked through, and it had become necessary to dig deeper, which entailed large expenditure.

The free-for-all prospecting system with countless tiny claims was doomed, although the majority of prospectors never for a moment suspected this. A new age was inexorably approaching, bringing a new generation with new moral values. The crisis which began in 1873 had the effect of speeding up the process of the concentration of production, bringing nearer and compounding the inevitable tragic fate of the small-time prospector.

Only very shortly before, at the end of 1869 or in 1870, had these people set off for South Africa from England, America or Australia. They were full of radiant hope, they believed in their star, in their own strength. And the world had so much to offer. . .

> *When all the world is young, lad,*
> *And all the trees are green;*
> *And every goose a swan, lad,*
> *And every lass a queen;*
> *Then hey for boot and horse, lad,*
> *And round the world away;*
> *Young blood must have its course, lad,*
> *And every dog his day.*

Now three years had passed. Only three, yet it was as if an entire lifetime was behind them. A few had made their fortune, of course, but the majority, after a dizzying succession of lucky strikes and failures, would eventually lose even the little they had brought with them. Hope gave way to despair, confidence and swagger to weariness and desolation.

Over these three years people exhausted their stores of energy. They never struck lucky. They departed sick, broken men.

> *When all the world is old, lad,*
> *And all the trees are brown,*
> *And all the sport is stable, lad,*
> *And all the wheels run down;*
> *Creep home, and take your place there,*
> *The spent and maimed among:*
> *God grant you find one face there,*
> *You loved when all was young.*[41]

Those who returned home were not the worst off. In order to leave, money was needed, and unluckily for many, the amount required was a large one. Thus many remained behind: defeated, humiliated, unwanted, broke.

The odd one was lucky and managed to change his profession, like the Canadian George McCall Theal, a luckless prospector. Forced to remain in South Africa, he subsequently became its first major historian. But for those who did not have his talents, and nowhere to get the money for their return trip, the only course was to seek employment as a labourer to someone who yesterday was his fellow and equal. Even to a twenty-year-old youth like Cecil John Rhodes.

People sold their claims for pittances, and Rhodes and his associate, Rudd, bought them up.

Over these three years he had altered: his shoulders had sunk, he had started to stoop a little, his long arms hung awkwardly at his side, his face was haggard and his gait stiff and lumbering. His mien already showed slight traces of despotism and cruelty. At a time in history which was to prove fateful for so many prospectors he proved his mettle and rode the crest of the wave.

At the end of 1872 his capital amounted to five thousand pounds, by August or September 1873 he had doubled it and he then doubled it time and time again. Where at the beginning Rhodes had earned, as he wrote to his mother, one hundred pounds a week working in the mines, now he was playing quite a different game and the stakes were immeasurably higher. The pursuit of maximum profits in each claim now gave place to the speculation boom. The frenetic buying up of claims turned into a struggle for survival.

In these new conditions it was essential to understand, with a sort of sixth sense, the laws of capitalist production and the world market, those rules about whose very existence the other prospectors were blissfully unaware. Initially Rhodes did not have much idea about them either.

He did not immediately find his feet in this world of frenzied speculation, among the scheming entrepreneurs, each desperately trying to outsmart and dupe the others. But he was a quick learner. He made a supreme effort to understand the mechanics of playing the stock exchange, to draw experienced people into his orbit and make use of their knowledge. He gained a great deal from his repeated visits to England and his increasing familiarity with the City.

Rhodes was quickly becoming a large-scale entrepreneur, capable of massive speculative deals, prepared to take risks, with a keen sense for anything which might render a profit. He was ruthless in dealings with his weaker rivals and always prepared to reach a compromise with those he was unable to crush.

The main thrust of Rhodes's and Rudd's activities from 1873 was amalgamation: buying up and uniting a mass of small claims under their ownership. Initially they were not concerned with the entire diamond region but concentrated instead on the region of the De Beers farm. Even there they did not immediately gain undivided power. What they did succeed in doing, however was to unite all the prospectors in the region into a single share holders' company.

In pursuit of this policy Rhodes made lengthy overtures to his main rivals in the De Beers mine, Sir Frederick Philipson Stow and Robert English, which eventually led to the registration in March 1881 of their new joint concern. On April 1, 1880, the announcement was made about the establishment of the De Beers Diamond Mining Company, or more simply De Beers with a declared capital of £200,000. Rhodes's portion of this was not in itself sufficiently large to explain the position he held in the company from its very inception. It seems he was helped again by his entrepreneurial talents, thanks to which he gained the important office of Company Secretary. He thus retained considerable power in his own hands.[42]

The year 1882 was in many respects a repeat of 1873. It brought a new world economic crisis. In the diamond fields this first struck those few small-time claim-holders who had beer lucky enough to survive earlier crises. This one proved a much harder ordeal. At the site of Colesberg Kopje there was now an immense hole, three hundred feet deep. In other regions too the workings were so deep that expensive machinery had to be used and it was impossible to operate without pumps to expel the water. Work efficiency dropped. When, in 1970—almost a hundred years later, they washed the old mine-dumps down they found 215 thousand carats of diamonds.

The small-time prospectors had neither money nor machinery. They were powerless to resist the onslaught of the companies One collapse followed another. The companies were able to amalgamate more and more claims. By the end of 1885 in an area which had once contained 3600 separate claims there were only 98 claim-holders left. Yet even this figure does not really indicate how far the process of concentration had advanced. The picture becomes clearer when we realise that of the 98 proprietors in the four diamond mining regions—Colesberg-Kimberley, De Beers, Bultfontein and Dutoitspan—67 had their claims in the last two regions, the least important. Only twelve proprietors were left in Kimberley, and ten in De Beers.

Money begets money. By 1885 the De Beers capital had grown

to £842,000. As the capital grew so did Rhodes's influence. From 1883 he was no longer Company Secretary but President of De Beers. At the age of thirty he was both rich and influential in one of the most promising spheres of world business at that time. In 1885 he said that his yearly income amounted to £50,000.

This was but the beginning. His ambitions were to take him much further yet.

His Road to Politics

At the end of the 1870s Rhodes had formulated his political views in the *Confession of Faith* and in his will. It might be argued that these compositions, albeit not naïve or "boyish effusions", were nonetheless the work of a solitary eccentric, a homespun philosopher from those distant diamond fields, utterly divorced from the active political life of the capital and nourished only by his megalomania.

Let it not be forgotten, however, that of the Englishmen in Southern Africa in those years there were very few who so frequently breathed the air of their native land as did Cecil Rhodes. There were few who had the opportunity to observe and listen to developments in England with such close attention, and at first hand.

Despite the great distance and hardship of travel Rhodes went to England almost every year. He did not merely visit, he took up residence, and for long periods at a time. Nor did he disappear into the provinces, but remained in Oxford and London, where the current spirit of the times was soonest and most keenly felt.

Oxford—not alone, but with the prospects it opened up— was one of Rhodes's persistent obsessions. No sooner had he amassed sufficient funds than he set about realising his cherished dream.

He set off for England in mid-1873, and in October he was admitted as a student of Oxford. He was not accepted into University College: his poor Latin and Greek let him down. He was accepted into another college, also well-known: Oriel, whose rector was related to one of his friends from Natal and diamond-prospecting days. After Christmas Rhodes abandoned his studies and returned to South Africa. The new opportunities for amalgamation opened up by the latest world economic crisis forced him for a while to shelve his hopes of a degree.

The years 1876 and 1877, on the other hand, he spent very largely in Oxford, travelling to the diamond fields only during the summer vacation. He assisted his associate Rudd in his letters with advice and information about the stock market situation. 1878 was spent in almost the same way. But the ordinary degree of Bachelor of Arts was only conferred upon Rhodes in December 1881, after he had been an undergraduate for more than eight years.

Things were not at all easy for him at Oxford. It was hard to return to the school-room after leading so completely different a life. Furthermore, once he had gained admission he felt more of an alien among his fellow students. The writer Felix Gross writes in his book *Rhodes of Africa* that Rhodes, standing as he did on a lower rung of the social ladder and endeavoring to penetrate the category of "Gentlemen", bragged of his African adventures and with extravagant flourishes would cast diamonds onto the table. If this failed to produce the desired effect, he would affect a cynicism, giving vent to supercilious remarks about other people, about mankind and religion.

In order to gain closer access to the *jeunesse dorée* Rhodes also entered the Masonic order while at Oxford, becoming "Brother Rhodes". A document from the Oxford University Lodge is preserved in his archive. It states that Rhodes passed through the ritual of initiation, established by the Supreme Grand Council, and that the treasurer of the lodge "received of Brother C. J. Rhodes the sum of five pounds 10 s" as his life subscription.[1]

Lest too much be made of Rhodes's apparent "inferiority" at Oxford, another biographer hastens to point out that in the official hierarchy he held the same rank as his fellow students, since his father had been to Cambridge and his brothers were army officers.

There was a difference in their social position, however. It made itself felt, and very acutely. Rhodes, at least initially, had neither connections nor position, and his capital did not come all at once. He could hardly be accepted as an equal by the glittering youth of this most privileged university, with their worldly sophistication, their social class and, often, their titles.

All the same, for all the hours of discomfort Rhodes was caused by his humble position in university society, he still gained a great deal from Oxford.

It was not academic learning that benefited him. Even in the pages of *The Times* one of his contemporaries recalls that at Oxford Rhodes was not much given to reading. And when he was reprimanded for missing lectures he would repeat: "I shall pass, which is all I wish to do."[2]

What, then, did he gain from Oxford? Besides, of course, his Bachelor's degree? He gained the very thing which had been so elusive and caused him so much unpleasantness at the beginning: social contact with fashionable young men, those most arrogant and disdainful of beings.

The attraction of Oxford was so great that the scions of aristocracy all over the world were sent there to study. For example, a considerable number of Russian aristocrats received an Oxford education. At the beginning of this century the university admitted through its portals one of the richest members of the Russian gentry: Prince Felix Yusupov, subsequently to marry Nicholas II's niece and to win notoriety for his part in Rasputin's murder.

Rhodes would certainly have met interesting foreigners at Oxford. But far more important to him were his fellow countrymen, the English aristocracy. Those who were preparing to take up the reins of the British Empire, who were being groomed for this by virtue of their birth-right. They felt quite at home in the corridors of power, they had entry to all government departments and, more important, to those houses where the real political decisions were made. They absorbed the mood of the ruling circles like a sponge and brought it back with them to Oxford.

The most famous thinkers of England at that time lectured at Oxford, and new theories and ideas had their first public airing from the lecterns of the university halls. Books that created a sensation were avidly read and debated here (and of course it was often here that they first caused their sensation). Opinions from the most divergent quarters congregated here. Nowhere could those underground tremors, which gave warning of new shifts and fissures in public and political life be felt more clearly.

SIGN OF THE TIMES

It was here, among the chosen ones, that Rhodes detected—and was one of the first to do so—the rumble which announced the coming scramble for the colonial division of the world. This was still a mere rumble, and not the distinct roll of thunder of the eighties and nineties, but it was still audible, both in politics and in society.

It was almost as if the government knew of Rhodes's plans and various wills, so meticulously did they seem to implement his behests. In 1876 the Prime Minister Disraeli declared Queen Victoria Empress of India. A year after Rhodes had sketched out his *Confession of Faith* and will, England seized Cyprus, and a short while later many "inviting" chunks of Africa and Asia.

In 1878, during the Russo-Turkish war, a song rang out from London music halls, driving the public into a frenzy of chauvinism. It was not so much from the words "the Russians shall not have Constantinople" as from the refrain:

> *We don't want to fight, [but]*
> *by Jingo, if we do,*
> *We've got the ships, we've got the man,*
> *we've got the money too.*[3]

The word "Jingo" had been coined long before by Le Motteux in his translation of Rabelais, to avoid mention of ·God and the devil and all possible blasphemy. But this song became such a symbol of British chauvinism that with it the word "jingoism" took its place in the language.

In the 1870s, when John Ruskin took the podium before the students of Oxford, he did not speak of art and aesthetics—the themes of his books then so famous throughout Europe—but on a more topical subject, the greatness of the British nation. He reminded his listeners of their "northern blood", of the Englishman's "firmness to govern and grace to obey", of a fact that a destiny awaited them such as no nation before had been vouchsafed.

What path were they to follow in pursuit of this greatness? England was to found colonies, "as fast and as far as she is able, formed of her most energetic and worthiest men; seizing every piece of fruitful waste ground she can set her foot on, and there teaching these her colonists that their chief virtue is to be fidelity to their country, and that their first aim is to be to advance the power of England by land and sea: and that, though they live on a distant plot of ground, they are no more to consider themselves therefore disfranchised from their native land than the sailors of her fleets do, because they float on distant seas. . . If we can get men, for little pay, to cast themselves against cannon-mouths for love of England, we may find men also who will plough and sow for her, who will behave kindly and righteously for her, and who will bring up their children to love her. . ."[4]

Under the spell of such rhetoric, Rhodes wrote his *Confession of Faith* at Oxford and with it his first political will.

Rhodes was frequently called a Darwinian. The prominent journalist William Stead wrote: "He was a Darwinian, he believed in evolution."[5] It would be closer to the truth to talk of social Darwinism here. Rhodes held that in human society, in the struggle for survival it was the strongest who did and should survive. And he considered the English to be the strongest and the fittest.

A British author of a study of Rhodes takes as his epigraph the following remark, made by Rhodes during his travels through Africa: "I walked between earth and sky, and when I looked down, I said: 'This earth shall be English.' And when I looked up, I said: 'The English shall rule this earth.' "[6]

WE PRACTICAL PEOPLE

"What was attempted by Alexander, Cambyses, and Napoléon we practical people are going to finish,"[7] said Rhodes. In other words, "we practical people" were to unite the entire world under a single dominion. Something the Macedonians, Persians and French had failed to achieve. We the British would do it.

This meant Rhodes considered himself a realist in politics. Here, of course, he was correct. He clearly understood himself better than did his biographers, who regarded him as a dreamer, *par eminence*.

In the early eighties he was still taking his very first steps on the political stage. But even then his actions showed him to have a sober and calculating mind.

At the beginning of 1880 he became a member of the Cape Parliament. The Cape Colony had self-governing status, and its parliament possessed fairly extensive rights in dealing with local matters. Rhodes gained this foothold in Parliament thanks to the fact that the diamond mining region had been allocated six seats. The elections were open and the bribing of voters was also conducted quite openly. At twenty-seven years of age Rhodes was already a wealthy man and influential in the mines. In November 1880 he canvassed in the constituency of Barkly West and was elected. He remained a member for this constituency until he died, i.e. for more than twenty years.

"Rhodes entered Parliament still wearing, as he pointed out, his Oxford tweeds," writes Sarah Gertrude Millin, " 'I think I can legislate in them as well as in sable clothing', he said."[8]

After this Rhodes found it appropriate to appear in Parliament, as everywhere else, in his invariable rumpled cotton trousers. He also violated accepted parliamentary procedure by mentioning the other members in his speeches by name, rather than by constituency.

Rhodes was not renowned for his eloquence in Parliament. But he had one outstanding quality: he always knew exactly what he wanted. He would make this very clear, and was always quick to throw down the gauntlet to his opponents.

Rhodes was a keen yachtsman: the windy reaches of Table Bay gave ample scope to the pursuit of this hobby. Thus, in one of his speeches about his opponents, the "honourable members", he said: "There are honourable members opposite who have racing boats, but I dare to challenge them and to say that they do not know what ports they are sailing for."

Of himself he said: "It is as if I were a little sailing boat in Table Bay and knew exactly what I am starting for."[9]

His membership of the Cape Parliament opened up wide new opportunities to Rhodes. As an MP he gained great influence in administering the colony. His connections were no longer confined to the diamond mines. Gradually, over the course of several years, he was able to acquire influential allies. He cultivated the friendship of people who held key posts, such as Secretary to the British Governor for South Africa, Sir Hercules Robinson. Robinson himself (whose post was officially called Governor of the Cape Colony and High Commissioner to South Africa) at once took an interest in this young man with such ambitious designs. Later he was to support Rhodes in literally every venture.

Besides a Governor, the Cape also had its own government headed by a Prime Minister. Rhodes became closely acquainted with the Cape politicians. In order to gain political influence in the region he bought shares in the *Cape Argus,* one of Cape Town's leading newspapers.

In a word, from the very start, Rhodes proved to be a pragmatist in politics, and, after a few inevitable blunders and miscalculations, quickly got his bearings in the political circles of Cape Town.

At one time, in the years 1882 to 1884, he used to wonder whether he should not perhaps stand as a Conservative candidate for the Westminster Parliament. The imperialist designs of the Conservatives were very close to his own heart. Some years before, while still at Oxford, he and four like-minded friends had written a letter to Disraeli with certain proposals for the expansion of the British Empire.

In 1885, when imperial tendencies were clearly felt in Liberal policies too, Rhodes started to consider seriously whether he should stand for Westminster as a Liberal candidate. But then he decided that he may not have the strength to divide his time between South Africa and England, the way he had in his student years. Instead he concentrated on South African affairs.

Most English politicians at that time regarded the "Boer problem" as the major issue in South Africa. Boers constituted the majority of the white population of the Cape Colony and of South Africa as a whole. It was their independent republics that blocked further British expansion. On the eve of Rhodes's entry into Parliament the whole of "white" South Africa was rocked to its foundations by the First Anglo-Boer War.

In April 1877, after the failure to gain the Boer's agreement to a "union", a "federation" with their colonies, the British authorities sent troops to the capital of the Transvaal, Pretoria, which at that time was a small settlement. There were not very many soldiers, twenty-five to be precise, but even this number proved sufficient to hoist the Union Jack and declare the Transvaal annexed.

The Transvaal Boers, who lived on farms scattered all over the large territory, did not at once discover, still less comprehend, what had happened. The republic had no regular army. The farmers had to decide for themselves what to do next.

They gathered together in groups in the open veld and, gloomily sucking on their long-stemmed pipes, unhurriedly discussed the situation. Most unhurriedly. For more than three and a half years. They recalled their primacy in "white" South Africa, the arrival of the British and their incessant machinations. They sought answers in the Bible—for many, the only book they ever read.

In December 1880 they finally rose up, expelled the British from their country and even invaded British Natal. The war ended with the Battle of Majuba Hill on February 27, 1881. In fact it is hardly worthy of the name "battle". A large British unit under the command of a general, totally unsuspecting, marched along the road. The Boers lay in hiding along the roadside, and each took an officer or a soldier in his sights. It was all over in a matter of minutes. This secured the Boers' reputation through the world as fine marksmen.

It is easy to imagine how this incident must have inflamed passions in the neighbouring Cape Colony, and the upsurge of nationalism it would have excited amongst the Cape Africaners.

Of course the interests of the Afrikaners who had remained in the Cape would not have coincided exactly with those of their fellows, with those who even in the thirties had refused to accept British dominion and, retreating further to the north, had founded there the Transvaal and Orange Free State. Nevertheless they were united by their common historical experience and a shared loathing for the English. It was for this reason that the Battle of Majuba Hill and the restoration of the independence of the Transvaal inspired them too and rendered them more intractable.

Leaders emerged amongst the Cape Boer. The most popular of them was Jan Hofmeyr. The Boers called him "onze Jan"—"our Jan". He was a member of the Cape Parliament, published the largest Boer newspaper, *Die Zuid Afrikaan*, and in 1878 founded the Boeren Beschermings Vereeniging (Farmers' Defence Union). Then in 1879 the first major Boer political party came into existence: the Afrikaner Bond, and three years later Hofmeyr became its leader. In other words, he was a symbol of the awakening nationalism of the Cape Boers, who identified body and soul not with their ancestral home, Holland, but with Africa. To underline this bond they increasingly called themselves Afrikaners—i.e. Africans, although the old names Dutch and Boers (in Dutch: peasants, farmers) were still current.

This was all quite new to Rhodes. In the first ten years of his South African life he had not had frequent encounters with the Afrikaners. There were very few of them in Natal, and even less on the diamond fields. As a result Rhodes was forced when canvassing and in his early Parliamentary days to decide in new and unfamiliar circumstances what line to adopt in dealing with the Afrikaners. This was the first time he had been faced by such a complex political question, and in fact the first time he had entered the arena of politics.

It is interesting to observe how he faced this challenge.

He did not try to foist the ideas of his *Confession of Faith* on Hofmeyr and his confederates. Unlike those who shouted "Remember Majuba!" and called for the Afrikaners' punishment, Rhodes understood that at that stage the battle for a "South African Federation" had been lost and that slow and careful work was now needed to prepare the possibility of any united "white" South Africa in the future.

So he set about demonstrating in every possible way his respect for the national feelings of the Afrikaners. He wooed Afrikaner voters in his constituency with such slogans as "Dutch are the coming race in South Africa." In a conversation with Hofmeyr he maintained that the victory of the Afrikaners at Majuba "has made Englishmen respect Dutchmen and made them respect one another."[10]

Rhodes employed an old and tested method: he would identify the men who might be useful to him and would then seek the right key to each man's heart. He endeavoured to be everyone's friend. Pretending to be on everyone's side he would promise that his policies would primarily serve the interests of South Africa, not England. By this he meant, of course, "white" South Africa.

On the whole the Afrikaners were reluctant to lend too much credence to mere words. They had seen more than their fair share of British politicians over the years. Any number of them, including many MP's, had visited South Africa. They would arrive, talk a lot of claptrap and spread confusion. They would express their opinion on all and sundry and promise the earth. Or they would talk in such a way that they actually said nothing at all:

> *Pagett, M.P., was a liar, and a fluent liar therewith,—*
> *He spoke of the heat of India as 'The Asian Solar Myth'.*
> *. . .I thought of the fools like Pagett who write of their*
> *'Eastern trips',*
> *And the sneers of the travelled idiots who duly misgovern*
> *the land. . .*[11]

The Afrikaners regarded them as useless phrase-mongers and windbags, but altogether lacking any kind of soul, like Kipling's Thomlinson:

> *We have threshed a stock of print and book,*
> *and winnowed a chattering wind,*
> *And many a soul wherefrom he stole,*
> *but his we cannot find.*
> *We have handled him, we have dandled him,*
> *we have seared him to the bone,*
> *And Sire, if tooth and nail show truth he*
> *has no soul of his own.*[12]

Rhodes was a different kettle of fish. He was always able to produce the impression of someone with firm convictions, a strong, practical man with his own, very sober view of life. In other words, the sort of man you could do business with.

He finally got his way. His relations with the Afrikaner Bond and with the leaders of the Cape Afrikaners remained cordial for almost fifteen years. They were sufficiently cordial for the Afrikaners to support him when he ran for office in the Cape government. Rhodes was successful—although his first term of office was brief. From March to May 1884 he was Treasurer of the Cape Colony.

A SUEZ CANAL
INTO THE INTERIOR OF AFRICA

By the early 1880s Rhodes had already earned in "white" South Africa the name of a man capable of putting his ideas into practice. The first demonstration of this, and Rhodes's first achievement, was the annexation of the extensive territory of the

Tswana people. At the time the British called this nation the Bechuana and their country Bechuanaland. In our time this covers the territory of Botswana and, in the south, adjacent areas of the Republic of South Africa.

In itself this territory—mostly stony plateau and the Kalahari desert, did not present any great value. The trade links between Europeans and the Tswana tribes were limited to the purchase of ostrich feathers and ivory. But Rhodes was interested in the land of the Tswana because it offered the most convenient route into the interior of Africa, and above all to the Zambezi basin. The territory to the east of the Tswana had already been taken up by the Transvaal, and that to the west by the Germans. Rhodes called this country "the road to the North, the neck of the bottle", "the Suez Canal into the interior", and the key "of this country's road to the interior".[13]

In the early 1880s, shortly after the Transvaal had recovered its independence, the Transvaal Afrikaners invaded the land of the Tswana. In 1882 and 1883 they founded there two more republics: Stellaland and Goshen. Rhodes's annoyance was unbounded. He was not, however, sufficiently powerful to be able himself to initiate campaigns of territorial expansion, he could only try and persuade the government in London, and that through the intermediary offices of the Cape government. In Rhodes's opinion, London acted with criminal indecision.

The officials in London did indeed hesitate. The defeats suffered in the Zulu and Boer wars had cost the South African adventure a great deal of its former popularity with the British public. The position in the Tswana nation was extremely confused. The Anglo-Boer conflict only compounded the strife among the tribes: the English tried to turn this discord to their own advantage, and the Afrikaners did the same. Some tribal chiefs were considered pro-British, and others pro-Afrikaner.

In addition, London had had many other things to worry about all over the world. Some of the British politicians believed that there was no real hurry here: the "Tswana question" could wait a little while.

Rhodes, however, had many allies. These included men who had no great love for him, but who nonetheless assisted the implementation of his plans. Some spoke of the importance of "imperial interests", others took a philanthropic stance and appealed for the Tswana to be saved from their "plunderers"—the Afrikaners. The missionary John Mackenzie toured twenty-nine towns and villages in England in September and October 1882 and delivered addresses two or three times a day, calling for the annexation of the land of the Tswana. He enjoyed the support of the well-known Aborigines Protection Society.

In March 1883 the British Parliament started to debate the question of the Afrikaner "filibusters" who had violated the rights of the Tswana. In the House of Commons a resolution was at once tabled that the Afrikaner "filibusters" must be expelled so that the Tswana "may be preserved from the destruction with which they are threatened".[14] Joseph Chamberlain said that a military expedition would have to be sent to expel the Afrikaners.

If there were doubts in the British Establishment about the annexation to the British Empire of another, one-hundredth or two-hundredth country, these were altogether dispelled in 1884. In 1884 Germany invaded Africa and immediately seized large chunks of the continent in the west, east and south.

The Germans had started making overtures towards the Afrikaners much earlier. They started calling the Afrikaners their "Low German brothers", reminding them that they were once Germany's neighbours, in the Netherlands. Then at the end of the 1870s there was talk of German patronage over the Transvaal, of "a German African empire",[15] and about the creation there of a "second India" under German control.

In 1884, when the massive territory of the German South West Africa appeared on the maps immediately adjacent to the land of the Tswana, these dreams started to become real.

An interesting first-hand account is provided by sailors from the Russian corvette *Skobelev*. At the end of 1884 it was on its homeward journey from the Pacific, making for Kronstadt, and *en route* it received a secret instruction from the Chief Naval Staff: to inspect Germany's new colony. The corvette sailed along the entire shoreline of the colony, its officers made a careful inspection and compiled their report, entitled: "Some Information on the New German Colony on the Southwestern Shore of Africa, Gathered on a Visit by the Corvette *Skobelev* to this Shore in January 1885".

The main conclusion of the report was formulated thus: "The

question now arises: what possible advantages could Germany derive from such a desolate colony, void of any communication links, of water and of all bare necessities, and what could be its purpose? The truth is that Germany, in all probability, does not mean to confine itself to the territory of Lüderitz and hopes, either by purchasing land or by some other method, to penetrate into Central Africa, which has long been the object of the attention and aspirations of other European states, and there to establish a colony."[16]

In that same year of 1884 Germany concluded a trade agreement with the Transvaal. Moreover, the Germans had started to encroach on the British not only here, on the Atlantic seaboard of South Africa, but, in alliance with the Afrikaners, also on the Indian Ocean side. In August 1884 the Afrikaners established their own "New Republic" in Zululand, and the following month two German agents obtained a "concession" of sixty thousand acres from the Zulu ruler Dinuzulu, and permission to build a railway line from the Transvaal to the Indian Ocean.

One might wonder why the Afrikaners decided to set up these puppet republics. Would it not have been simpler just to extend the frontiers of the Transvaal? The point is that, when England recognized the independence of the Transvaal after Majuba she forbade the Transvaal to extend her frontiers either to the west, i.e. into Tswana territory, or to the east, into Zululand. The Transvaal did not dare disobey the prohibition directly, and instead set up these puppet republics.

This was not the only prohibition. The Transvaal was also forbidden to restore the official name it had held until the British occupation: the South African Republic. The British regarded this as far too presumptuous.

In 1884 Rhodes's idea of seizing the Tswana territory finally prevailed both in the Cape Colony and in Britain. In the process Rhodes, always anxious to maintain good relations with the Afrikaners, was careful not to offend them, not to subject them to any abuse. By contrast, the High Commissioner for South Africa, Sir Hercules Robinson, in his dispatches to London described the Afrikaners who had invaded Botswana territory as "marauders", "plunderers" and "pirates".

This was nothing compared to the reports in the newspapers and other organs of mass propaganda. Both at home and abroad in South Africa the English public was informed daily that the world had yet to see worse villains than those Afrikaners. They took away the Africans' livestock and land. They were bandits and thieves, rotten to the core.

There was one consolation: living alongside these brigands were truly decent people. Such as the Scotsman Smith, nicknamed "Scotty", for example. He was admired by many Englishmen at that time, and even in our day he has been a film hero. It is instructive to see how this most notorious of brigands earned his fame. As the *Southern African Dictionary of National Biography* records, "his name became a byword for cattle robberies and other exploits." Was he no better than the Africaner plunderers?

But this of course could not be. The dictionary goes on to record that he was "temperamentally like the legendary Robin Hood". His robberies were always "mingled with outbursts of good humour".[17] The British could not dream of equating "Scotty" Smith with the Afrikaner brigands. Admittedly, he did sometimes also rob his fellow Britons, something the Afrikaners did not dare. Nevertheless he remains a merry Robin Hood while they are sombre and malicious bandits. This should only seem strange at first glance: after all, history and literature are full of examples of nations glorifying "their own" criminals. In Stevenson's *Treasure Island*—which was published at this very same time, in 1883—Squire Trelawney says of the pirate Flint: ". . .I was sometimes proud he was an Englishman."[18]

It may seem unwarranted to accord such attention to this Scotty, if it were not for the fact that in 1884 he was appointed inspector of the Tswana territory, charged with maintaining law and order. He became one of Rhodes's assistants, for in August the same year Rhodes became deputy to the High Commissioner for South Africa in Bechuanaland. Rhodes's and his assistants' functions were not clearly defined. Indeed it was difficult to define them, since the British government had created the office of administrators for a territory which still had not been occupied. Even then, in the buccaneering age of the division of the world, this must have seemed rather strange. But in his new capacity Rhodes was now able to hold discussions with the chiefs in Stellaland and Goshen. He used to say that he had absolutely no intention of expelling them from the Tswana territory. On the contrary: they could continue exactly as before, but under the British flag. Needless to say, the Afrikaners did not agree.

Then, in December 1884, four thousand British soldiers under the command of General Sir Charles Warren were set ashore in South Africa. The purpose of this excercise was formulated as follows: "The object of this mission and expedition is to remove the filibusters from Bechuanaland, to pacificate the territory, to re-instate the natives on their lands, to take such measures as may be necessary to prevent further depredations, and, finally, to hold the country until its further destination is known."[19]

Having eliminated these Afrikaner republics the British now offered to the Tswana tribes the patronage of Queen Victoria, in other words the status of protectorate. The tribes were less than ecstatic. The Kwena chief stated: "But we wish to see how the Queen's Protectorate will help the other Chiefs which are included in it... Should we find that they are well protected by the Queen, we also shall then be agreeable and without a word of dispute". This was a polite refusal, but Warren reported back to London that the Kwena offered a "cordial reception of the Protectorate."

Kgama I, Chief of the Ngwato, offered to extend the British Protectorate over a massive area—80 thousand square miles. Warren described this as an "unprecedented and friendly offer".[20] But it soon transpired that Kgama I's "friendly offer" was actually to concede to the British land belonging to the Ndebele, with whom he was at war.

All this did not in any way prevent Britain from taking pride in the results of its actions. A military correspondent wrote at the time that "England ... was always to be depended upon (to combine business with philanthropy), and protect the natives against the results of their own ignorant acts, as well as against the intrusion of outside land and cattle grabbers."[21]

In September 1885 London passed a resolution: the southern section of the lands of the Tswana were to be declared a Crown colony—the British Bechuanaland—and the northern section the Bechuanaland Protectorate.

The "road to the north" now lay open. But Rhodes lacked the power to proceed any further.

Battle of the Magnates

To extend the frontiers of an empire money is needed, a great deal of money. And the power that money confers. By the mid-1880s Rhodes was already a very wealthy man, but still not wealthy enough to implement his designs.

So he now bent his efforts towards gaining control over the entire diamond mining operation. By 1887 his company had become the only one in the De Beers region. It had swallowed up the other nine. Rhodes managed to cut the cost of mining between 1882 and 1888 by two and a half times, to increase the dividends eight-fold and the company capital almost twelve-fold from £200,000 to £2,332,000. This he achieved by mechanization and by tightening up anti-theft measures. At the same time he introduced the compound system: housing the African workers in camps, surrounded by iron railings or barbed wire. The workers were forbidden to leave these compounds and their movements were strictly controlled.

Rhodes and his confederates were not the only ones to practice amalgamation. Other massive companies were also coming into existence. The output increased and the price of diamonds on the world market fell. In a mere five years it had fallen by thirty percent, and Rhodes could see that this was only the beginning.

In Rhodes's opinion the market was too limited. He reasoned thus: large-scale purchases were only made infrequently, while the mass consumer was the bridegroom-to-be, buying a diamond ring for his bride. In Europe and America alone there were about four million such marriages a year. In other words, four million diamonds. Rhodes was also aware that the diamond itself would usually be an inexpensive one, of one carat. It cost one pound. This added up to four million pounds—the entire yearly capacity of the world diamond market. If the prices were raised, fewer diamonds would be bought, and if they were lowered, more would be bought, but the limit would remain four million pounds.

There might seem something unconvincing about such deductions based on the psychology of the courting male, made by a man who in all his life never gave any woman any diamond ring whatsoever, but there was still a grain of reason in his arguments. The diamond market was by no means unlimited. This meant that only by monopolizing production could one safeguard against a drop in prices.

CREATION OF THE DIAMOND EMPIRE

In 1887 Rhodes began his last, decisive assault on the diamond industry, aimed at uniting under his power all the diamond fields. By this stage he had only one serious competitor left: Barney Barnato, head of the Kimberley Central Diamond Mining Company. Barnato controlled the richest mines, and his capital exceeded that of De Beers. Rhodes was locked in bitter struggle with Barnato for several years.

In this battle Rhodes displayed certain unflattering traits which are admitted even by such an admiring biographer as Basil Williams: "He always had a purpose, which he pursued with persistence, sometimes even with ruthlessness ... he was not tender with those men who came across his path."[1]

Rhodes would launch attacks, and capitalize on fluctuation in the price of shares; he victimized his opponents and steadily gained control over all those companies which were still independent, even in Kimberley, the citadel of Barnato's empire. By his intricate manipulation of the stock exchange Rhodes placed these companies in a dilemma: they could either face ruin or submit to De Beers.

Rhodes chose the direction in which to strike, but the methods were suggested to him by Alfred Beit, a German national who earned the reputation in South Africa of an outstanding financier and a financial genius. Here too we see evidence of Rhodes' gift for finding and making use of the right people. Beit was an invaluable find. As Flint records: " 'Ask little Alfred', was increasingly Rhodes's response to difficult problems".[2]

Beit is believed to have given Rhodes the most valuable piece of advice he ever received, advice which helped him secure the upport of one of the most influential families of Europe of that ime, and support which was given not merely on one isolated occasion, but constantly from then on. Beit advised Rhodes to apply to the Rothschilds, the leading banking house of England.

The situation was as follows: Rhodes was anxious to buy up he shares of a major Kimberley company, one surpassed only by Barney Barnato's company. If Rhodes had succeeded he would have emerged victorious in his contest with Barnato. But the proprietors of this company, called the French Diamond Mining Company, asked nearly one and a half million pounds for their hares.

It was then that Rhodes turned to Lord Nathaniel Rothschild. Their encounter, which was to play an immense role in Rhodes's ife, has been described in many books. The authors emphasize hat Rhodes was pleasantly surprised by his very cordial reception and that the two new acquaintances made an agreeable mpression on each other. But the man Rothschild saw was no grizzled prospector with uncouth manners and loose morals, such as usually returned from the diamond fields. Rhodes's Oxford education had stood him in good stead.

There was more to it, of course, than manners. As the English historian Colvin subsequently recorded: "Now it was known at that time that the House of Rothschild had its exceedingly keen eyes on the diamond diggings ... it had no doubt been tempted more than once to take a hand in the amalgamation"[3].

Anxious not to miss an opportunity, the House had sent its own observer to the mines. Consequently the Rothschilds were well informed about the situation and knew with whom they were dealing.

Furthermore, Rhodes confided in his interlocutor his ideas about spreading the influence of England throughout the world. This must have impressed Rothschild. It is with good reason that he is called the Banker of the British Empire. In 1875 Nathaniel's father, Lionel, lent the then Prime Minister Disraeli £4,000,000 to buy shares in the Suez Canal Company, and refused to accept any interest. If Rothschild had not done this Disraeli would have had to seek the money from Parliament. The procedure would have been so drawn-out that his plan may well have collapsed.

A few years later another Rothschild, this time Nathaniel,

made a massive loan to Egypt—£8,000,000—vital at that time for Britain's colonial designs. Thus the Rothschilds already had close ties with African politics.

Rhodes asked Rothschild for a million pounds. During their discussions the latter withheld his reply and Rhodes had to leave without knowing how his fate would be decided. But on his return to his hotel he almost at once received a note from Roth schild giving his agreement to Rhodes's request.

At this meeting Rhodes gained a powerful patron, someone who was both financier and politician. It was Rothschild who introduced Rhodes to Joseph Chamberlain, even at that time an influential figure in colonial affairs, and from 1895 Colonial Secretary in Lord Salisbury's government. When Rhodes first went to Lord Salisbury to seek his support in effecting his plan he alluded to Rothschild's patronage.

Rhodes was evidently convinced that Rothschild approved not only of his financial plans but, albeit only partially, of his politi cal designs as well. As evidence of this we can cite the fact that Rothschild is named in Rhodes's third, fourth and fifth political wills as his first executor. In the sixth and last will Rothschild's place is taken by his son-in-law, Lord Rosebery, leader of the Liberal Party and at one time British Prime Minister. The close ness between Rhodes and Rothschild was so carefully concealed from the public that even after Rhodes's death the journalist William Stead, one of his friends and executors, referred to Roth schild in his book on Rhodes's wills as "a financial friend, whom I will call 'X' "[4].

After Rhodes's first meeting with Rothschild, Barnato conti nued to resist. On a purely financial level he was still more than a match for Rhodes. But Rothschild's support meant more than money: his loan showed that he had taken Rhodes's side. After this it was so much easier for Rhodes to win the support of the other financiers too. Added to this was the assistance from the political and business circles of "white" South Africa which Rhodes had managed to secure during his years in Parliament— and this, of course, was something that Barnato did not have.

Rhodes had literally surrounded Barnato on all sides, and his great rival was forced to retreat. We can imagine Barnato's astonishment when he found himself squeezed as in a pair of powerful pincers by a man who was apparently so much weaker than himself in all respects. Even in health and stamina. Barnato was a sportsman, a wrestler and boxer, while his victor was a weakling, with a poor heart and lungs. And, most important: Rhodes had less money than him.

But defeat did not mean ruin for Barnato, Rhodes's propositions did not presuppose that he would be put out of business. Rhodes proposed that they join forces and limit production, initially to four million pounds a year, and thus establish a high level of market prices. Thus the deal was mutually advantageous.

On March 13, 1888, the place of the competing companies was taken by the De Beers Consolidated Mines Company. The Rothschilds' representative acquired great influence in its administration. The company was controlled by a board of directors, but it was effectively run by only three of them: Rhodes, Barnato and Beit. They received the constituent profit. Dividends on normal shares were limited in advance to a fixed revenue and the excess, which was very considerable since profits far exceeded expectations, was divided among these three.

At the very first meeting of the shareholders of De Beers, in May 1888, Rhodes declared that they stood at the head of an enterprise that was almost a state within a state. Nor could Rhodes resist a little showmanship. At a dinner in the Kimberley Club, attended by select guests, he asked his new companion to fill a large basket with diamonds. Before the eyes of all the diners Rhodes scooped up handfuls of these stones and let them trickle through his fingers, like rivulets of magical, sparkling water.

The De Beers Consolidated Mines at once sacked two hundred white miners and lowered production costs. The production of one carat now cost no more than ten shillings. On the world market, however, it cost thirty. The following year, 1889, De Beers took over the mines of Bulfontein and Dutoitspan, and then a few newer mines which had been opened in other regions. Rhodes now controlled the entire diamond mining industry in South Africa and ninety percent of the world production. Even in 1890 De Beers's capital was estimated at 14.5 million pounds —an immense sum in those days. A labour force of twenty thousand Africans worked in its mines.

It was thus that the diamond empire came into existence. It monopolized diamond mining not only in the primary diamond area, South Africa, but subsequently extended its power to other countries and continents too. Rising to the position of one of the world's largest monopolies, De Beers has proved to be very resilient, and even today it controls the world diamond market.

By the time the De Beers consolidation was established such world famous stones as the Star of South Africa, the Victoria (or Imperial), the Du Toit, the Stuart and the Beers had already been discovered in the South African diamond mines. The world's biggest diamond, the Cullinan, however, was only found after Rhodes's death, but in a mine bearing his name.

THE HALF MILE OF HELL

In the meantime gold had been discovered in South Africa. In fact it had already been found in various regions, on different occasions since the sixties. But after the first sensational news reports no significant veins were discovered. Halfway through 1886 a genuinely massive deposit was found—in the Transvaal, on high ground in the watershed between the Orange River and the Limpopo. This area became known as the White Water's Edge—Witwatersrand, or abbreviated, the Rand. The spot to which the gold prospectors swarmed was christened Johannesburg by the Transvaal government. To this day historians argue about which of the many Johanneses in the Transvaal gave his name to this new Babylon.

This deposit proved to be the largest anywhere in the world. To this day, year after year, it yields significantly more than half of the world's entire gold output.

History knows a great many outbursts of gold fever. Frederick Engels wrote that the search for gold was the reason for some of man's earliest migrations and geographical discoveries: "It was *gold* that the Portuguese sought on the shores of Africa, in India and throughout the Far East; *gold* was the magic word which impelled the Spanish across the Atlantic Ocean to America; *gold* was the very first thing the white man demanded as he set foot on a newly discovered shore."[5]

But the discovery of gold in the Transvaal provoked an epidemic of gold fever such as the world had never before seen. It was more frenzied than any gold-rush before or since, in California, Alaska, Australia or Siberia.

The seething mass of humanity in the Transvaal was not only greater in number than the hordes in California and elsewhere, it was also more colorful and varied. The stakes were far higher, and the historical consequences far more significant. If today we do not have such graphic images of the Transvaal gold rush as we do of the Land of White Silence or the gold-mining Urals this is perhaps only because the Transvaal did not engender a Jack London, Bret Harte or Mamin-Sibiryak—the chronicler of the Ural gold mines. The scant memoirs of its participants are therefore all the more valuable to us.

"That gold-rush to Johannesburg in the summer of 1886 was probably the wildest, toughest human stampede the world has ever seen . . . the stampede began. Rich man, poor man, beggar-man, thief—emphasis on the thief—raced across the veld to Witwatersrand. . . On horseback, afoot, in buckboards, and by stage the mob travelled. Plodding oxen were lashed mercilessly; human bodies were driven just as fiercely. . .

". . .Every horse obtainable was purchased or stolen; stages were crowded to the boot, heavy-wheeled transports drawn by oxen were chartered. These, however, proved too slow, and during that dash I saw many men pile from the wagons and hurry on afoot. I saw, too, a human team in action. An old paralytic in Pretoria, unable to buy horses for the trip, hired two native blacks and hitched them to a buck-board. Out across the veld they went, trotting at a heartbreaking speed.

". . .Many who started never gained their goal, for the country was rigorous and demanded its tool. Those who reached the Rand apparently were the rougher, more reckless, ones, for Johannesburg during the next year was probably the toughest place in the world. . ."

This was written by a man called Sam Kemp.[6] Before the discovery of gold he was an overseer of African workers on the diamond mines and was accustomed to use a revolver, a bludgeon or a hippopotamus-hide lash. Later, in the nineties, he served in the mounted police in North America, on the United States' troubled frontiers with Mexico and Canada.

"Yet those two hard American frontiers were picnic-grounds for a Sunday school, kindergarten class, compared to the Rand during the year following 1886. My training, my life, has not been one to lead me into narrow of morality, but Johannesburg seemed a trifle indigestible even to my vitrified stomach", he admitted.

The first action of each new arrival at the Rand was to stake out his own claim. Initially this was easily done. But the claim then had to be defended from all subsequent newcomers. Often the conflicts were resolved by gun-fights.

The settlement on the site of modern Johannesburg was called "Half Mile of Hell". This desolate region had been considered quite barren. There were no forests. For six months a year a searing, dry wind blew, day and night, whipping sand into the miners' faces and eyes and encrusting their lips with yellow dust.

For the prospectors from Europe and North America the scorching African heat was more intolerable even than the biting frosts in the gold-fields of Alaska and Siberia.

Here they were confronted by such basic problems as how to get a roof over their heads. There was no wood: they had to use tin sheets, battered out from large crates and paraffin drums. The resulting dwellings were hardly suitable for habitation but even the meanest of them could not be rented for less than the equivalent of one hundred dollars a month. Even so every available place could have been rented twice over. Those who failed to secure tin shacks erected tents, or lean-tos, or merely slept in the open air.

Foodstuffs and other wares were brought by ox-cart from regions hundreds of miles distant, and the prices were outrageously high. The drought brought the situation to the brink of calamity.

The cattle were struck down with the dreaded rinderpest. The vultures were so glutted with the abundance of food, that people could knock them down with sticks. There was no meat for the miners. And the wagon supply, already a very arduous operation, virtually ceased altogether because the wagons could no longer traverse burnt-out territory where there was no grazing for their oxen.

The prospectors were confronted by such fundamental problems as how to obtain blankets. A seemingly trivial matter, yet blankets were essential if one lived in a tin shack and simply slept out in the open.

"After all, one needed blankets in which to keep one's personal allotment of sand-fleas, cockroaches, snakes, jiggers, and 'seam squirrels', or lice. But try to buy one! It was much easier to steal one, even when it was wrapped around the victim.

"Law and order? None, of course. Or, rather, the law of the gun and fist, the order of might and trickery. Accidents, the first murders were called. After all, an empty blanket or an empty shack was worth securing."

It was a rare man who parted with his gun. Various makes were to be found, but most widely favoured was the 45 calibre, favourite with the bandits of the time, too. Automatic pistols had not yet been invented, but with persistent training some achieved a lethally fast draw. This was done by fanning the hammer with the palm of the left hand, so as to lose no time squeezing the trigger. This innovation was introduced to life on the gold fields by the more enterprising American prospectors.

It must not be imagined that the only way to grow rich on the fields was by toiling from dawn to dusk in the mines. On the contrary, there were far easier paths to follow.

"No gold mine was as good as the leading saloon, no claim as rich as the main gambling-den. And of course, the easiest way of all to get the gold-dust was—hop in and take it from some other fellow. Get him drunk first, or get him in an argument. No one cared what happened to him. The man who kept his hands near his guns during the day became maudlin drunk at night and easy prey."

Most of the fights, robberies and murders took place in gambling houses.

A dance of shadows on the wall,
A knife-thrust unawares. . .

"At midnight thirty or forty of us were gambling in the Queen's Bar. Play had been high at poker, faro, pinto, and the English game of nap. In front of us were our chips and pouches of gold. A stamping of feet sounded, and eight thugs entered. Unmasked, disdaining all preliminaries, they announced their presence with a fusillade of shots aimed over our heads. . . Three of the bandits remained at the door and kept the tables covered. The other five moved forward. One by one they swept the boards clean of gold, all the time vouchsafing insolent and sarcastic remarks. Back to the door they went, and the fun commenced.

The gamblers, as if on a given signal, flashed their guns and began shooting wildly. The bandits leaped into the darkness of the street, but the firing continued. . ."

> *And he may die before the dawn*
> *Who liquored out the day. . .*

By the end of 1886 gold prospectors had decided that the time had come to elect a sheriff, a judge and a bailiff, in other words, "a suicide club should be formed".

Willing candidates were found, although they must have been aware of the high risk of their new positions and that their chances of survival were slim. The sole triumph of the first sheriff was the arrest of the gang of eight who held up the Queen's Bar. When the sheriff and his posse of volunteers caught up with them, to avoid general bloodshed he proposed that he and the leader of the gang fight a duel. In this duel, fought on horseback, the sheriff won, the bandits surrendered, they were put on trial and shot. Admittedly the sheriff, as everyone had predicted, did not surivive his captives by long.

But all this did little to scare many away. The population of Johannesburg increased every day. "The little cemetery on the hill behind the town had many new bunkers in it, but for every funeral there were a hundred newcomers."

The number of gambling dens, pubs, and bars also increased swiftly, with their interminable cursing and brawling. As the South African poet William Plomer puts it in his poem "Conquistadors":

> *Some stole or cheated, some*
> *Made off with their feverish gains,*
> *And many failed, and a foolish few*
> *Blew out their bankrupt brains.*[7]

The majority of the women who travelled to the gold fields to get their own share of the new-found wealth, "were more remarkable for their silk stockings and short, spangled dresses than for any great beauty". In many ways they were a good match for the menfolk. The first "madam" in Johannesburg "could shoot well with either hand, a trick greatly admired in the town, she was afraid of neither man nor the devil, and I have seen her throw out bodily some drunken roisterer who disturbed the so-called dignity of her business house".

Of course, here too, as in all places at all times, people were able to find romance. Here is an excerpt from a private letter of the time: "The only billiard table has never a spare moment. At a saloon where it stands is a Venus-Aphrodite, a barmaid from Kimberley, blessed with great personal charm. She is a good billiardist and can play very well the piano. She is said to have come up from the coast dressed as a man and filled her part very well."[8] It was with such men and women, tents and make-shift tin hovels that the city of Johannesburg, "Golden City", "African New York" and "Little America", had its beginnings.

In the first nine years after its birth in 1886 its population reached one hundred thousand. In 1889, the third year of its existence, Johannesburg had its own horse-tram, and in the following year electricity. And in Europe there were still many big cities that had no electric lighting.

Johannesburg grew up in almost exactly the same way as Kimberley, but their destinies were very different. Diamond mining was not nearly so labour-intensive. Thus it is that to this day Kimberley has remained a comparatively small town. Johannesburg, by contrast, was to become the largest industrial centre on the entire African continent, a position which it still holds today. It was on this very spot, where once there had stood tin shacks made from paraffin drums, that Africa's first skyscrapers were to rise.

Johannesburg has played an incomparably greater role in the history of South Africa than Kimberley, just as the gold industry has come to be a far more significant component of South Africa's economy than diamond mining.

Another distinguishing feature is that diamonds were discovered before big capital appeared in South Africa. South Africa had no millionaires or large companies, capable of taking such a profitable undertaking in hand. It was for that reason that so many free agents remained in play for so long in the Kimberley region and small-time prospectors could stay in contention. Initially they even had a real chance of becoming wealthy men.

The gold industry began in quite different conditions. By now large companies had come into existence. They keenly followed the course of events in Johannesburg and swiftly became involved.

In essence they deprived the small-time prospector of any chance of applying his own forces. This might well have had something to do with the rapid growth of crime.

Cecil Rhodes, who had begun in Kimberley as one of those very same small-time prospectors, entered the stage in Johannesburg in a quite different role.

THE FIGHT FOR THE GOLDEN CROWN

In Johannesburg Rhodes walked without a gun. He had a different weapon: money. And the power which money conferred.

He was not among the very first arrivals at the gold fields, but he did not delay his arrival long. Anyway, his representatives had followed the course of events in Kimberley from the moment the first news broke. The reminiscences of one of them have survived: the doctor Hans Sauer. He took it upon himself to keep Cecil Rhodes informed, and was in all probability the first to bring Rhodes a sample of the gold ore.

This was in June 1886. Having received Sauer and hearing him out one morning, Rhodes asked him to return at one o'clock in the afternoon. When he entered the doctor saw that there were already four men awaiting him: Rhodes, Rudd and two Australians—they had amassed considerable gold-mining skills in their own country. Studying the ore with the aid of special instruments they had brought, the Australians confirmed that it had a high gold content. After this Rhodes called for Sauer again, this time at four o'clock, in the De Beers office, and proposed that he acquire claims on the Rand on Rhodes's behalf. There and then a deal was struck, by which Sauer gained a share and was to receive fifteen per cent of the profit. Rhodes at once wrote Sauer a cheque for two hundred pounds, and the latter was sent off for the Rand urgently, by the following morning at the latest.

At ten in the evening Rhodes himself called on Sauer and warned him that on no account was he to board a carriage there in Kimberley since this might excite suspicion. Furthermore, when Sauer boarded his carriage the following morning a cautious twelve miles from Kimberley, as he mounted the footboard and glanced inside he saw to his astonishment Rhodes and Rudd sitting inside, trying not to be recognized. After this they covered a considerable distance together. To the Afrikaner town of Potchefstroom was a ride of thirty-six hours, and from there the carriage had to travel the entire length of the Rand. "History was being made,"[9] declared Sauer solemnly.

All the same, having displayed such eager interest, Rhodes and Rudd in fact made much less successful use of the possibilities afforded them than, for example, the Kimberley businessman Joseph Robinson. After buying up a considerable number of claims Rhodes and Rudd then started rejecting others which subsequently earned their owners millions. This hesitation seems strange. Decisions had to be made swiftly, on the spot, but the associates at that stage understood nothing about the gold industry. Rudd was sceptical, believing that the samples of ore which he and Rhodes had been shown, were of doubtful value. Nor did the American mining engineer, whom Rhodes consulted, display much enthusiasm.

This was a totally new undertaking. Risks had to be taken. Of course both Rhodes and Rudd were capable of taking risks, but in a way their appetite for risky business had been sated in Kimberley: at this same time Rhodes was preparing for his final showdown with Barnato by amalgamating dozens of claims. In general Rhodes's attention was still largely occupied by his business interests in Kimberley.

There were also reasons of a profoundly personal nature. At the very height of the gold rush, when Rhodes was in the thick of events on the Rand, he was informed from Kimberley that Neville Pickering was seriously ill. He was the first of a series of young men who had served Rhodes as secretaries. Rhodes promptly returned to Kimberley and stood vigil day after day at the bedside of the sick man. At Pickering's funeral he was in such a state of hysteria that he even brought the unemotional Barnato to tears. For a long time after, Rhodes could not bring himself to enter alone into the cottage which he and Pickering had shared. Throughout this period Rhodes, for perhaps the first time in his life, totally lost all interest in business, and despite the promises he had made Sauer he did not even answer his telegrams from the gold-fields. Rhodes's biographers tend to ascribe the relative inefficiency of Rhodes's activities on the Rand to this personal tragedy, occurring at the very time when the future of the richest claims was decided.

The majority of these biographers emphasise how much Rhodes "fell short" in the goldfields. But this only seems like a shortfall when compared with Rhodes's fabulous success in the diamond fields.

It is true that Rhodes never achieved a position of absolute power in the gold-mining world. Yet he did achieve a great deal. Having entered the fray a little late he was still able to catch up with his most zealous rivals. He was forced to pay more for his claims, but he was in a position to do so. Together with Rudd he bought the title deeds to eight or nine excellent claims, mostly in the west of the gold-bearing area, and set up shareholder companies for their development.

In 1887 all these companies were united in the Gold Fields of South Africa, with a capital of £125,000. Rhodes reserved for himself and Rudd the right to one third of the net profits. In 1892 the company was renamed the Consolidated Gold Fields of South Africa with a capital ten times as large. It exists to this day under the same name, and is one of the largest gold-mining companies in the world. In 1894/95 it paid dividends amounting to fifty per cent. In 1896 Rhodes officially announced that he received between three and four hundred thousand pounds net profit a year from his gold mines. In other words, gold earned him twice as much as diamonds.

Lord of the diamond industry and one of the kings of gold, by the end of the eighties Rhodes had become the most influential man in Southern Africa.

In the world of those days that meant a great deal. South Africa's significance in the world economy was growing at a remarkable rate. Gold was discovered in the Transvaal at the very moment when world gold production was at its lowest level since the middle of the nineteenth century. In 1887 the Transvaal produced 40,000 ounces, in 1892 the output passed the million mark, and in 1898 production approached four million ounces and accounted for nearly a third of the world total. While the diamonds exported from the Cape Colony in 1882 alone, according to the calculations of the economist Sally Herbert Frankel, exceeded in value the entire exports of all the other countries of Black Africa.

Gold and diamond mining, the influx of people, required the provision of mining machinery, merchandise, the building of railways... In anticipation of profits capital investments flowed in abundantly. On the London Stock Exchange from the end of the 1880s South African shares (which were then called "Kaffir shares") became the object of frenzied speculation. "At any rate the like of the stock-jobbing that took place in connexion with the Rand mines had never been seen before", writes one historian.[10]

The industrial revolution began in Southern Africa with the rapid growth of the economy, upheavals in every aspect of normal life and fearful burdens for the indigenous people.

The entire capitalist world eagerly lent its ear to any man who could speak on behalf of this new Eldorado. Cecil John Rhodes was destined to be this man and his hour had come.

He was now able to start putting into action his dreams of seizing new countries. Behind him he had a mighty monopoly, an empire of gold and diamonds. When thrashing out the terms of his amalgamation with Barnato he had already secured the right to use the De Beers money for new conquests. Barnato was not much interested in such matters but had little choice but to agree. In the words of the Russian journalist Isaak Shklovsky, "the warriors struck an alliance in which Rhodes's job was to 'pacify' the blacks, win over their princelings with bribes, establish a formal system of slavery and prepare the ground for a future 'African Empire' under the protection of England. Cecil Rhodes was an ambitious man: the possession of millions was not enough for him."[11]

Rhodes was impatient to begin the "amalgamation" of African countries—to deal with them as he had learnt to deal with the claims on the gold and diamond fields. He began preparations for his northwards drive along the Cape-to-Cairo route. Rhodes's favourite expression: "The North is my thought" became the motto of a political campaign.

On July 5, 1888 Rhodes turned thirty-five, attained the peak of a man's life, the high point from which one can survey the years behind and those yet to come. The day's beginning can be seen, the bright dawn, and if one gazes hard, its sunset too. We might wonder whether Rhodes's mind moved along these lines. Or perhaps we can apply to him these words, applicable to so many others, and like all wise words, tinged with sadness: "Only the very young see life ahead, and only the very old see life behind; the rest, those who fall in-between, are so preoccupied with life that they see nothing at all."

It seems most likely that Rhodes did stop to think on such matters. He was not altogether devoid of sentimentality. Perhaps, albeit only subconsciously, he sensed that he was drawing near the *magnum opus* of his life. The moment was approaching when his name would be greeted with praise and adulation by some, but with curses and loathing by thousands of others.

Ahead in Rhodes's path lay entire countries which, by his will, were destined one day to bear his name.

Drawing from *Punch* magazine (1892).

HERO
of the Day

The Land of Ophir Between the Zambezi and the Limpopo

The country between the rivers Zambezi and Limpopo was already known to the Europeans in those days. Travellers and scholars had visited it. Hunters ranged through it. Missionaries endeavoured to convert its heathen peoples to Christianity. It was the site of the ruins of remarkable ancient structures and mines. Africans from those parts came south to work as wage-earners and recounted tales of how their peoples lived, what customs they observed and what paths led into the depths of the country. They told of the hostilities between them, and the grounds for these. The names of their rulers, their characters, how many wives and concubines each had, and which was the favourite. . .

Rhodes, of course, knew this. And he most probably thought that he now knew all there was to know about the inhabitants of the area between the Zambezi and the Limpopo.

As Rhodes saw it, the main obstacle to his designs was Inkosi (chief) Lobengula, together with his warlike people, the Ndebele, or as their neighbours and thereafter the Europeans called them the Matabele, who inhabited the southwest of the territory.

Even in those days many authors had published accounts of the Ndebele and their kindred peoples. One such was Dr Livingstone. It was there, on the borders of the Ndebele territory, in the village of Kuruman, that Livingstone married the daughter of the famous missionary, his fellow-Scot, Robert Moffat.

Lobengula was also a familiar figure to European travellers, missionaries, hunters and traders. A great many tales circulated about the Ndebele king.

THE MAN WHO STOOD IN RHODES'S PATH

We should not, of course, idealize the regimes of patriarchal Africa and its rulers. But even in contemporary accounts by Europeans Lobengula was portrayed as a sensible, thoughtful and, perhaps, genuinely wise man. Seventeen years older than Rhodes, in 1888 Lobengula was already in his fifties, and he had led his people for about twenty years. He was addressed by his subjects as "Baba"—"father". The hunter Frederick Hugh Barber, who was received by Lobengula in 1875, wrote, admittedly with some of the arrogance that characterized many European travellers, "His face was pleasant in conversation, with a humorous twinkle in his eye. He was ready-witted and loved a joke, a grand savage, and every inch a king"[1].

Once an English traveller tried to impress Lobengula and his people by predicting a solar eclipse.

In his novel *A Connecticut Yankee at King Arthur's Court,* Mark Twain gives a most colourful account of the shattering effect this same device had on the "heathens"—King Arthur and his knights of the Round Table.

It did not work so successfully on Lobengula, however. He was of course amazed by the fulfilment of the terrible prediction. But when the eclipse ended the Englishman, who expected, no doubt, to be acclaimed as a god, was bitterly disappointed. In the opinion of the European bystanders, Lobengula did not even admit the possibility that the Englishman might have known in advance about the eclipse. He reckoned that this could only be taken "as a purely accidental verification of the word of the white witch"[2].

Lobengula's response helps explain another similar incident. It has been recorded how the Zulu ruler, Shaka, founder of the "Zulu Empire", reacted to a solar eclipse. Lobengula's father was one of Shaka's army commanders.

The occasion was in 1824. At that time the Zulus had practically no acquaintance with the white people, and there was no-one who could have predicted the eclipse for them. At the very height of the festival of the first fruits, December 20 by the European calendar, while the people rejoiced and sang songs, the light of the sun suddenly faded and a shadow covered seven eighths of its face.

"Shaka stood on the clay mound whence he made national announcements. The people gazed at him with fearful hope. His commanding figure seemed to be magnified to majestic proportions in that weird and unreal light. In his right hand he held the redshafted spear, and in his left the Royal stick. Then he spurted at the sun. He commanded it to return. His spear lunged in the direction of the sun and he kept it pointed there as immobile as a statue. The vast concourse held its breath. The sun was nearly gone.

"An incredulous gasp arose from the multitude. For when the sun was all but gone, it began to wax again. The black shadow of the moon was receding, and the sun's disk rapidly growing.

" 'It is true. It is true', bellowed the multitude. 'The black monster is creeping back, and the sun is chasing it now. Our King has stabbed the beast and it is losing power' "[3].

This description is cited from a book based on Zulu legends. Of course, we can never be entirely certain that in re-working this material for publication the author did not embellish it somewhat. Nevertheless this description seems perfectly authentic. If we accept it as such, then Shaka acted not merely as a courageous and level-headed man, but also as a wise politician: he averted general panic and affirmed his own authority. Yet it was a considerable risk he took: what if the monster had not crept away?

In situations he found confusing Lobengula used to say: "You white men are very artful, but you cannot cure the fever"[4].

This pronounced mistrust—even if it was not always justified —for the power of the white man, whether in the episode with the eclipse or in the curing of fevers, helped Lobengula to preserve the spiritual independence of his people for a number of years.

Like Shaka, Lobengula was not, of course, a naive savage, a Kiplingesque "half-child", but an experienced, tested leader, capable of great self-possession, good sense and resourcefulness in the difficult circumstances.

In his early years Lobengula had regarded the Europeans with benevolence, even though in the thirties the Afrikaners had waged war against his people. He knew a great deal about the Afrikaners, and the British, Germans and Portuguese were also not unknown to him. It was inevitable that he should have been slightly on his guard. Nevertheless, initially his people perhaps did not feel directly threatened by European conquest here, deep inside Africa and far from the major European possessions.

One of the first books to inform Europe about Lobengula and his people was the two-volume work by the German traveller Eduard Mohr. In it he described how "a foreigner, who travels through Zululand or Matabeleland in times of peace, when the ruler reigns supreme in his capital surrounded by his indunas, when he respects the customs of the land, is just as safe and his property just as secure as in the best-governed countries of Europe —even safer, I might say, as the corruption and coarseness which thrives in the dirt of the narrow alleys of our large and overpopulated cities, has still not taken root amongst these barbarians"[5].

Indeed, for many years the famous hunter Frederick Selous travelled through this region, and never did one of the local inhabitants touch so much as a hair on his head. The same could be said of many other hunters, traders and missionaries.

This is how it was, writes Mohr, "in times of peace". How was it in times of war? Mohr did in fact visit the Ndebele at such a time, in 1869, after the death of Mzilikazi, Lobengula's father, but before the question of his succession had been decided. The situation in the country was very charged, major battles were expected between the armies of the two main rivals.

The supreme council of the Ndebele people then summoned the Europeans in the country and ordered them to gather in the village of Mangwe. "Initially I regarded this directive as the ultimate in despotism and injustice", writes Mohr, "but subsequently I realised that it was based on a genuinely benevolent regard for the welfare of the whites. The natives genuinely ... wished to see the foreigners safe. The death of even one of them could result in difficulties with the British colonial administration, and this they wished to avoid."[6]

Mohr fails to recall that, while they protected the Europeans from the fratricidal war which seemed imminent in their land, the Ndebele people had every justification for regarding these same Europeans as the initiators of this bloodshed.

In fact Lobengula was the only real heir to the throne. But rumours arrived from areas of South Africa already under European control that his elder brother Nkulumane, whom the Ndebele thought to be dead, was in hiding there. In the Transvaal

Lobengula

there was even an impostor who claimed to be Nkulumane. It was only natural that all those who, for any reason, were opposed to the coronation of Lobengula should support his mythical rival.

Mzilikazi died in 1868, and Lobengula's rule was firmly established only in 1870, the same year that Rhodes first set foot on South African soil. For eighteen months the country was torn by strife, leading to bloody confrontation between rival armies. The Ndebele had every reason to believe that the rumours about Nkulumane were being fuelled by the Europeans, yet there were no direct hostilities against the latter and Lobengula himself even retained his friendly disposition towards them.

Eduard Mohr had an interview with him on October 6, 1869 and afterwards he described the impression made on him by the "future king of the Matabele". "I was meant to see him from a more likeable side. He expressed his regrets that for the moment he was unable to do anything to comply with my request, but asked me not to be anxious ... and either they (the indunas—*Tr.*) or he himself would soon see to my requests"[7]. In other words, even though Lobengula would not have known the expression "noblesse oblige", he certainly acted in accordance with its principle.

During dinner Lobengula noticed the medallion hanging round Mohr's neck: a portrait of his mother. Lobengula asked to be shown the portrait. Observing the family likeness and learning that Mohr's mother had died, he said: "Yes, you whites are fortunate people, your art is so great that you still see those who are no longer alive, your hearts have no need to be sour"[8].

Quoting these words, Mohr adds, "A child of our own civilization could not have expressed himself with greater tact"[9].

There was much that amazed Mohr. For example, the fact that "...a Matabele never lets himself be taken by surprise". He found it "astounding how many natives know exactly what is going on in their own country"[10].

...In 1870 Lobengula was confirmed in office as inkosi—supreme ruler. Ndebele scouts sought Nkulumane everywhere, even far beyond the boundaries of the territory between the Zambezi and the Limpopo, but they never found him. We can only surmise that he had been killed in childhood, as had been believed earlier, because of certain factional hostilities in the Ndebele hierarchy.

On his accession to power Lobengula—let it be emphasized once again—did not immediately become mistrustful of the Europeans. At first he even permitted certain people to prospect for gold in the interior of his country—or, as they put it, gave them a "concession".

He only endeavoured to regularize relations with the Europeans, to bring them under his control. In "Lonbengula's Proclamation to Hunters and Traders", he stated: "All travellers, hunters or traders wishing to enter Matabeleland are required to come by the main road leading from Ba Mangwato to Manyami's outpost where they are to report themselves as usual and receive permission to come onward to the King's residence and obtain their respective licences.

"The hunter's fee for the districts South and West of the Shashani river will be one gun of the value of £15 British Sterling, one bag of powder and one box of caps. No occupation of the country is allowed nor are any houses to be built except by the King's special permission."[11]

There were other such documents in circulation issued on Lobengula's instructions. They bore his seal with the figure of an elephant. Lobengula himself was not literate. These documents were taken down from his words by Europeans who lived in his main kraal; other Europeans even called them Lobengula's "secretaries".

When translating these words and attempting to express in European terms the ideas they contained, they may involuntarily have distorted their meaning. Of course there were also instances of deliberate distortion, although Lobengula resisted such efforts. Having instructed one European to translate and transcribe his words, he might then summon another and, showing him the paper, ask what was written on it. With the help of this sort of checking system he hoped to control the whites.

Later, however, Lobengula's attitude to the Europeans changed.

The Englishman Captain Robert R. Patterson, who visited Lobengula in 1878, wrote of him: "As a young man, and for some time after he became king, he associated much with white people and adopted their dress. He built for himself a house, welcomed them to the country, and ensured their safety. Of late a change has come over him. With the return to a garb of a few strings of monkey-skin, he appears to have resumed an analogous condition of mind, rejects all improvements, restricts trade, discountenances missionaries, and does not defend white men from attack and insult."[12]

"What do you think of the missionaries and their belief?" Lobengula was once asked by the Englishman Walter Kerr. "I suppose it is right, because they say so," he answered, but added at once: "but then they are paid for saying so".

Kerr remarks: "I imagined that Lobengula had little sympathy with missionary efforts"[13]. And he points out that over twenty-five years of missionary activity Christianity had failed to make a single convert in Lobengula's country.

During the first years of Lobengula's reign his favourite sister Ningi enjoyed great influence. She had her own "court". White hunters and traders had audiences with her, if Lobengula was away. And she welcomed them. It was figures such as this Ningi that gave Rider Haggard the inspiration for the heroine of one of his best novels—*She*—about the mighty queen of an African country. To this day film versions are being made of Haggard's novels.

But Ningi was put to death in 1880. According to one English historian, Lobengula feared her growing influence. But perhaps it was her close contacts with the Europeans that brought her into disfavour?

We may wonder what caused this sudden change in Lobengula. Captain Patterson writes: "Whether this change is one of real feeling, or is a political design, is difficult to say. Surrounded by men still greater haters of civilization than himself, he is a man of whom we can have little hope".[14]

This Englishman was a true son of his age and espoused all the received ideas current in his country about Africans. He simply affixed the label of "hater of civilization" to Lobengula, without troubling to ask why this leader, who at first had been so well-disposed towards the Europeans, suddenly changed his attitude.

Nor can the answer be found in other sources. It is true that many European visitors to Africa were quick to criticize one another. The missionaries deplored the indecent behaviour of the traders, the hunters in their turn criticized the conduct of the missionaries. . . We get the impression, however, that not one of them ever tried once in earnest to consider the situation from the other side: what sort of impression they all made on the Africans and what reaction they were likely to provoke. Or what effect all this might have on the African rulers, like Lobengula.

Let us for a moment consider how the Africans might have reacted to the Europeans who arrived in their territory, especially when the numbers of these new-arrivals continued to grow. The majority of them, after all, were cast in the same mould as the Transvaal gold prospectors, those men who in Johannesburg would never go anywhere without their Colt .45, and would draw it at the very least provocation.

For the stereotype of the hunter we may look once again to the books of Rider Haggard. Allan Quatermain, hero of many of his African adventures, was regarded by the European reading public as a very admirable figure—not only courageous and resolute, but also noble and generous, a big-hearted man. In a word, a gentleman. This image was created to delight and inspire the youth of Europe, and especially of Britain. Haggard's success was considerable. It is testimony to his ability that his novels continue to be re-issued and re-printed in many different languages to the present day.

What concerns us here, though, is Quatermain's attitude to the Africans. In the novel *Maiwa's Revenge: or, the War of the Little Hand* Quatermain recounts how in the course of a hunting expedition he enters the land of a people very similar to the Ndebele, at least to the European stereotype of the Ndebele. Quatermain's conduct amongst these people is quite illuminating.

When the head of the African guides and porters says that he and his people do not wish to proceed further into the land of a foreign people, Quatermain points his rifle at him: "Now if you or any of those men walk one step back from here . . . I shall fire at you; and you know that I don't miss".[15]

Then Quatermain begins, without so much as a by-your-leave, to hunt in the lands of this people. But when the headman of one of the villages comes to him and politely seeks a meeting, Quatermain starts shouting at him for the benefit of everyone around.

"What did he mean by disturbing me in this rude way? How did he dare to cause a person of my quality and evident importance to be awakened in order to interview his entirely contemptible self?" Quatermain explains to his friends why he has thus raised his voice: "I spoke thus because I knew that it would produce an impression on him".[16]

When the chief sends a detachment of soldiers in pursuit of Quatermain, after the latter has invaded a people's territory without permission, Quatermain considers poisoning the warriors with strychnine, but his supplies of strychnine prove to be too limited...

Let us not forget that these are the thoughts and actions not of some social outcast, but of the exalted, romanticized hero of boys' adventure stories. Very few readers would have seen anything shameful in the way a mere "savage" is callously duped.

Among the European settlers there were, of course, some who were anxious to preserve their good name and tried not to let it be sullied in any way. Some of the missionaries, for example, were genuine zealots: it was, after all, no easy matter to leave Europe for the African interior, and not for a month or a year, but for the rest of their lives!

But they too believed that the Africans had no spiritual values of their own. They proceeded from the conviction that it was both possible and necessary to destroy the entire fabric of the Africans' spiritual and moral existence.

Whatever had been the intentions of the Europeans who first set foot on African soil, the fact remains that objectively they blazed a trail for those who followed. Kipling celebrated these men in his poetry, seeing them as the very vanguard of colonialism.

> *There's a Legion that never was 'listed,*
> *That carries no colours or crest,*
> *But split in a thousand detachments,*
> *Is breaking the road for the rest.*
> *Our fathers they left us their blessing—*
> *They taught us, and groomed us, and crammed;*
> *But we've shaken the Clubs and the Messes*
> *To go and find out and be damned*
> *(Dear boys!)*
> *To go get shot and be damned.*[17]

While Kipling and Rhodes understood this, it is also true that Lobengula was beginning to understand it too. News was continually reaching him of the fate of other African peoples whose lands had been invaded by white men, first in the guise of missionaries, hunters, traders, naturalists and travellers. . .

The first years of Lobengula's rule coincided with the beginning of the "division" of Africa: the rumble of the approaching colonial wars grew ever louder in the territory between the Zambezi and the Limpopo, as the European powers encroached further into Africa. Lobengula could hear it too. It is hardly surprising, therefore, that his attitude to the British should have changed so abruptly.

Unmistakable portents of the imminent danger first appeared in the late 1870s. In 1877 Britain annexed the Transvaal, and in 1878 the British administrator of the Transvaal promptly dispatched to the Ndebele an expedition, led by that very same Captain Patterson who was so disparaging of Lobengula. Patterson was charged with persuading Lobengula to lift all restrictions on the movement of Englishmen in his country. For himself and his team Patterson was to secure permission to traverse the entire territory of the Ndebele and to reach Victoria Falls on the Zambezi. The purpose of this excercise was to enable Patterson to carry out a reconnaissance of this extensive territory for future annexation.

One intended member of Patterson's teem was the then quite unknown Rider Haggard, aged twenty-two, a minor colonial official in the Transvaal. But on the eve of departure he was held back by administrative commitments.

En route to Lobengula's territory Patterson carefully studied the country through which he travelled. He assessed its wealth and potential. "The country is rich in natural resources", he wrote. "The soil is good, it is well-watered, has a fine climate, and trees of great variety and size. . . The bread-fruit-tree, palms, cotton, olive and all kinds of wild fruit-trees also flourish. . . The Mashona and Tati districts are reported to contain gold in considerable quantities, iron also is plentiful."[18]

Lobengula knew exactly why this expedition had been sent. Patterson never did get permission to move freely through the country. But he still demanded that he and his companions be allowed to travel to Victoria Falls. Lobengula limited himself o advising them in the most insistent terms not to make the journey, and warned them of its dangers, of the many poisoned wells along the route.

Patterson ignored the warnings and set off for the Zambezi. On the eighteenth day of the journey, all the members of the expedition died. Local rumours had it that they had drunk some water from a poisoned well.

In Britain it was assumed that the expedition had been murdered on the orders of Lobengula and his commanding officers. But there was no proof. The British authorities sent a number of inquiries to Lobengula, but he categorically denied that he had anything to do with the expedition's tragic end.

It is easy to imagine Rider Haggard's feelings when he learnt that only by a miracle had he escaped the same fate. Perhaps this is the reason why the area between the Zambezi and the Limpopo is depicted by him in *King Solomon's Mines*, written a few years later, and in his other novels, as a country of such mystery and so hostile to white men.

Whatever the reasons for its tragic end, Patterson's ill-fated expedition exacerbated relations between Lobengula and his people on the one side, and the British on the other. From documents left behind by Patterson describing his talks with Lobengula his contemporaries concluded that "wildest suspicions were aroused by the extraordinary mission from the British", and that "the 'big talk' ended in nothing but bad feeling"[19].

The Patterson episode demonstrated that conditions for an incursion by the British into the territory between the Zambezi and Limpopo were not propitious. The demands made by the British emissaries were not backed by real force: Queen Victoria's soldiers were nearby, in the Transvaal, but only from 1877 to 1881, until the Afrikaners' victory at Majuba, and they were few in number and had other concerns.

But by 1888 the situation had changed. This was partly because Rhodes and his confederates had extended the British sphere of influence to include the neighbouring lands of the Tswana, and had thereby prepared the path for the invasion.

Also, the number of whites actually living north of the Limpopo had steadily increased. When gold was discovered in the Transvaal rumours at once spread that there were even richer deposits further north. Why, otherwise, had the natives

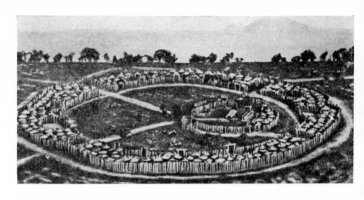

Bulawayo: a contemporary drawing

left so many mine workings?... The tales, seemingly long since forgotten, of the mediaeval Portuguese travellers were passed on by word of mouth. Their ancient maps were reprinted, bearing the alluring legend: "Here is gold".

Prospectors flocked to Lobengula for "concessions" to seek gold. His capital Bulawayo became a place of pilgrimage and the centre of English, German, Portuguese and Afrikaner intrigue.

"The white people ... come in here like wolves without my permission and make roads to my country"[20] wrote Lobengula on March 1, 1887 to the British officials. He tried to take measures, to restrict entry into his country, but the flood of Europeans only continued to grow. "To-day is peace," he warned, "but I don't know what to-morrow may bring."[21]

Lobengula was in a tricky position. Amongst his own people there was growing discontent with the Europeans, and his young warriors were calling for war. Lobengula said to them: "You want to drive me into the lion's mouth."[22]

With his age and experience Lobengula was wise enough to realize that he simply was no match for the Europeans. He needed all the skills of a true diplomat to stand up to the Europeans and prevent matters from coming to war, on the one hand, and, on the other, to restrain his own warriors, but n such a way that they did not rise up against him instead.

Perhaps even then he had already realised that war was inevitable? And if so, he wished to put it off as long as possible,
as his people were doomed to almost certain defeat...

Rhodes, on the other hand, most certainly comprehended that
some sort of military confrontation was inevitable if they were to
achieve total annexation of this new territory. He looked into
the future with a certain measure of wariness: there were good
reasons for him to be wary.

A PEOPLE TO BE ADMIRED

A Zulu "can move faster and cover a longer distance in
twenty-four hours than a horse. As an English painter says,
their smallest muscles stand out, hard and steely, like whipcord",[23]
wrote Frederick Engels one hundred years ago.

By repeating the admiring opinions of eye-witnesses Engels
was giving expression to his praise for the bravery of the Zulus.
The Zulus, he wrote, "did what no European army can
do. Armed only with pikes and spears and without firearms,
they advanced, under a hail of bullets from the breech loaders,
right up to the bayonets of the English infantry—acknowledged
as the best in the world for fighting in close formation—throwing them into disorder and even beating them back more than
once; and this, despite the colossal disparity in arms".[24]

This refers to the events of 1879, when British forces invaded
the land of the Zulus. At the time this war was one of the major
events in the world. In Europe people everywhere were full of
admiration for the feats of Cetshwayo and spoke with amazement of the battle of Isandhlwana, in which the Zulus had
attacked and annihilated a large British detachment that had
invaded their country. And although the Zulu spears were being
pitted against the very latest in European military technology,
casualties on the British side numbered more than eight
hundred men and officers, and almost five hundred "native
troops"—Africans recruited by British authorities.

This was the first time in history that African warriors had
inflicted a defeat on European armed forces.

The Anglo-Zulu War also influenced events in Europe. In
England itself it provoked widespread dissatisfaction with Prime

Minister Disraeli and contributed to his fall from office. Yet prior to this war he had been at the very zenith of his power. Even the Anglican bishop of Natal condemned the aggression of his fellow-Britons.

In a minor skirmish the Zulus killed a young man who went under the nickname Prince Lulu, but whose full name was Eugène Louis Jean Joseph Napoléon, Prince Imperial of France. He was the only son of the last French emperor, Napoléon III. Although France had been a republic for a number of years, since the time of the Franco-Prussian War and the Paris Commune, the Bonapartists swiftly rallied their forces and, convinced they would soon come to power, proclaimed the prince their leader with the title Napoléon IV in 1874, the year of his majority. The Bonapartists believed he only lacked military glory, for the French people to see him as a true Bonaparte. Napoléon III's widow, the Empress Eugénie, and Queen Victoria, who had given her asylum in her exile, despatched their darling to Southern Africa in search of this glory. They reckoned it would not be hard to find there. The French geographer Élisée Reclus quipped: the Prince hoped "that his feats of arms against the Zulus would one day earn him over the French"[25]. European newspapers made ready to describe the young prince's military exploits. "According to rumours, Prince Louis-Napoléon will record all his experiences in South Africa in a diary, which will be published..." reported the St Petersburg newspaper *Golos* in April 1879. But the Zulu assegai destroyed the plans of the Bonapartists and rocked the policies of those European cabinets that had until then reckoned with the possibility of a restoration of the empire in France.

Even Disraeli, one of the prime instigators of the Zulu war, was unable to conceal his amazement: "What an amazing people they are: they can beat our generals, make converts of our priests, and bring to the conclusion the history of a French dynasty"[26].

The fine martial qualities of the Zulus made such a lasting impression on the entire world that many years later, in January 1942, the most critical period of World War II, the *New York Herald Tribune* published an article entitled: "Vast Reservoir of Warriors for Allies in Africa", which said: "The greatest fighting race in Africa has not been used in either the first world

Cetshwayo

war or in this—the famous Zulu Nations of South Africa."[27]

What, it might be asked, is the relevance of all this here, in a consideration of Rhodes's plans to seize the territory between the Zambezi and the Limpopo?

Naturaly enough, the Anglo-Zulu War made an immense impression on Rhodes. After all, its battles were fought in Natal, where he had spent the first year of his South African life. Peitermaritzburg, the town to which he had come as a seventeen-year-old youth, was seized in the grip of panic.

There were other analogies too. The events of the Zulu War graphically demonstrated to Rhodes the true capabilities of the Africans, those same people who toiled daily in his diamond mines. Rhodes of course knew that some Zulu soldiers were armed with rifles, and that the money to buy these guns had originally been earned in Kimberley. The thought may have occurred to him that the same men who worked for him, Rhodes, had participated in the killing of the French prince. . .

Rhodes was an impressionable man in matters concerning his own life, and, as the prince's exact contemporary, he was bound to be deeply affected by news of his untimely death. The incident demonstrated that even a "small" colonial war is still war, in which people are killed without regard for rank or title.

A few years later Rhodes himself very nearly departed for the next world by the same route as the hapless Napoléon. During a colonial "expedition" against the small Korana nation, the man riding alongside Rhodes received a stomach wound and died on the spot. Rhodes would afterwards repeat with horror: "Fancy! That might easily have been my stomach instead of his." In the words of one of his friends, Rhodes "got the shock of his life",[28] and for years after was careful to avoid all possible risks.

At the same time we might wonder how important the lesson of the Anglo-Zulu War was for Rhodes. A number of years had since elapsed, and anyway his objectives lay in different regions, far from the ill-starred Isandhlwana. There would be other peoples living there, with different customs and mores. . .

But the truth of the matter was that Rhodes was to meet the very same customs and mores there, and—most important— the very same Zulu warriors.

Lobengula's father, as we have already seen, had once, in Shaka's reign, been a commander of the Zulus. Lobengula himself, when asked by an English traveller for the current name of his people, replied: "The proper name for my people is Zulu."[29]

Let us see how this came to be. The lands of Lobengula's people lay more than a thousand kilometres from Natal, the Zulu territory. But this, as Engels reminds us, would not bother a people that could cover a longer distance in twenty-four hours than a horse. The journey from Natal to the north of the Limpopo had once been traversed by the Ndebele. Not all at once, but in two migrations, many years apart: in fact, by two different generations.

Lobengula's father Mzilikazi—"Big Trace"—was Shaka's favourite, one of his most gifted confederates and commanders. Accordng to legend, after a particularly successful raid Mzilikazi concealed several herds of cattle from Shaka. Shaka dealt graciously with Mzilikazi: he dispatched couriers to him demanding that he return the missing cattle. Mzilikazi responded with unprecedented audacity. He cut off the plumes which adorned the heads of the couriers and sent them back as they were, with no further message.

"'Wo!' said Shaka sorrowfully when he saw their shorn plumes, 'my child has voided its diarrhoea on me'."[30]

By early 1823 Shaka's patience was finally exhausted. Mzilikazi and his Ndebele clan were forced to flee to the north. Initially they settled north of the Vaal River, but in 1836 the Afrikaners arrived, to set up their new republic of the Transvaal. After two years of clashes Mzilikazi had to retreat further northwards and the Ndebele finally established themselves beyond the Limpopo River.

Thus it was that Zulu customs and traditions, and with them the Zulu language, were transplanted far from Zululand itself to the Zambezi-Limpopo area. Travellers were amazed to discover here the very same military organization that, as with the Zulus, formed the cornerstone of the entire social structure.

The country, like that of the Zulus, was divided into military districts. The young men underwent a severe upbringing, turning them into disciplined warriors, hardened and fearless. With constant training they learnt, like the Zulu warriors, to cover more ground in a day than a horse, and their bodies were as muscular as those of their southern cousins.

The supreme ruler here was called the inkosi, commanders and heads of administrative regions—indunas, a unit of warriors an impi, and so forth. In fact, just as with the Zulus.

In western literature the Ndebele, like the Zulus, are frequently described as "bloodthirsty", ruthless in their dealings with other peoples and in their own society. There is no denying that the Ndebele way of life, like the Zulu, was Spartan and harsh. Shaka believed, for example, that any form of footwear softened the character. The skin of his warriors' feet had to be tougher than the sole of a shoe. They were not allowed to have throwing spears: the enemy was only to be confronted in hand-to-hand combat. Any warrior who lost his weapon in the field of battle was punished by death. During the reigns of Shaka and Mzilikazi this fate could be extended to an entire unit which had suffered defeat against the enemy, but it seems that Lobengula was not as harsh as this.

Lobengula used to say that he had no prisons and he regarded it inhuman to hold people in prison as the Europeans did. Misdemeanours were therefore either pardoned, or punished by death.

All this might provoke us to exclaim: *O tempora! O mores!* Yet are these customs so shockingly cruel? Do we not find something similar in the history of European nations? European history is also written in blood, and sorry reflection though it may be, it is those rulers who treated their subjects with greatest cruelty that people remember most distinctly.

Let us return again to Ritter: "Shaka, no doubt, was cruel at times: what great soldier is not? Titus, most 'humane' of Roman emperors, crucified 1000 Jews a day at the siege of Jerusalem... Shaka burnt sixteen women alive. Crassus, after defeating Spartacus, crucified 6000 of the revolted slaves. When Tilly sacked Magdeburg in 1631, the women of the town were raped. Shaka's troops would have been put to death for this crime."[31]

Thus, however cruel the customs of the Ndebele and Zulus may seem to us now, from a moral and ethical point of view they were far more natural for that society than the terrible carnage and vicious slaughter perpetrated at that same time, and even later in history, by the so-called "civilized" states of Europe.

THE MOST INDUSTRIOUS
AND SKILFUL TRIBE

The Ndebele were not very numerous. Making their base in the southwest of the region they did not take up the entire territory between the Zambezi and the Limpopo. The other areas were occupied as before by the Shona, greater in numbers than the Ndebele, but lacking their coherent military organization. Some groups of Shona lived in a tributary state to the Ndebele, others retained their independence.

When Cecil Rhodes hatched his plans to annexe the watershed area the Shona naturally concerned him far less than the Ndebele. He did not expect any serious military opposition from them. Furthermore, Rhodes even hoped that the Shona would see the white men as their liberators from the domination of the "blood-thirsty" Ndebele. Rhodes's supporters sought to spread the view that the Shona were subjected to constant oppression by the Ndebele.

It is quite true that the Shona did not have the martial repute of the Ndebele, but were better known for their industry in agriculture and animal husbandry and their skill as craftsmen. The missionary John Mackenzie, who knew them well, wrote that the Shona were "...the most industrious and skilful tribe in all South Africa... [They] are also first among all the tribes for their knowledge of agriculture, their skill in smelting metals, and especially for their superior work in iron implements, such as spears, hoes, axes, adzes, etc."[32]

The Shona had lived in the area for immeasurably longer than the Ndebele.

In modern times the name of the Shona has become linked with historical events that have puzzled scholars for centuries.

European travellers exploring the region between the Zambezi and the Limpopo, frequently encountered the remnants of a civilization that struck them as out of place in Africa. These included hundreds of deep mine-shafts, and a number of massive stone structures, with tall towers and thick walls. The local inhabitants called the largest of these "Zimbabwe", and in modern times it has become known as Great Zimbabwe.

These discoveries quite baffled the scholars. In Rhodes's day most Europeans would not have dreamed that Africans could, independently, have developed a comparatively sophisticated culture. Yet, the very first travellers had recorded that the Shona, the main inhabitants of the region, were mining gold, albeit in insignificant quantities, and that they, as Eduard Mohr declares, "are said to have sunk the mines."[33] But no one paid any attention to these accounts. The leading British archaeologist J. Theodore Bent declared authoritatively in 1892 with reference to Great Zimbabwe that "the ruins and the things in them are not in any way connected with any known African race" and that they are "incompatible with the character of the African native".[34]

This was how the conjecture first arose, dressed, as it were, in scholarly guise, that the territory between the Zambezi and the Limpopo was the true site of the fabled land of Ophir, described in the Bible. It was from here that King Solomon was supposed to have brought the gold to adorn his temple in Jerusalem. Rider Haggard's novel, *King Solomon's Mines*, published in 1885, was born out of this very conjecture.

There were many different theories. Scholars argued whether the culture of Zimbabwe had been created by the Phoenicians, Arabs or Indians.

Today the historian's job has been made much easier. With the aid of radio-carbon dating it has been established that the structures of Great Zimbabwe go back not to the Antiquity, but to the middle of our own millennium, that is they were built some four or five hundred years ago. This means that they cannot at any rate have had any connection with King Solomon and the Phoenicians. In modern times it has been definitely proved that the culture of Great Zimbabwe was of local, African origin.

Admittedly, even today not all the puzzles have been solved. Archaeologists have found great numbers of beads, very similar to those of Zanzibar, India and Indonesia. Most scholars regard these finds as evidence of undiscovered and unexplored links and contacts between the continents. But to others, they still suggest that the cultural elements were introduced into the civilization of Zimbabwe from outside.

The debates continue, although not, perhaps, as stormy as they were in Rhodes's day, when the origin of Zimbabwe ruins was not only the object of academic discussion, but even a fashionable topic in aristocratic salons. It also engaged Rhodes's attention. During the years of British expansion into the territory of the Ndebele and Shona he amassed a handsome collection of relics from Great Zimbabwe in his house in Cape Town.

In the mid-1890s he often showed them to his distinguished guests and they would argue heatedly about the origins of the ruins, whether they had been built by Phoenicians or Arabs of the pre-Mohammedan era.

Rhodes's views are recounted by the French scholar and traveller Pierre Leroy-Beaulieu. Rhodes called for the *Book of Kings*, read out the extracts pertaining to Solomon and the voyages of Hiram in search of gold to the land of Ophir; then taking a translation of Diodorus Siculus, he read the passages in which the author described the gold mines lying south of Egypt and the manner in which they were worked. Rhodes believed that the remains of the gold mines in Mashonaland and Matabeleland corresponded to those described by Diodorus Siculus.

Leroy-Beaulieu quotes him as saying: "I do not claim that those same mines were worked by the Egyptians; but they were most certainly worked by people from the same civilization."

Then, continues the French author, taking up a gold medallion also found near these ruins but clearly of much more recent date, Rhodes would talk of the numerous Jesuit missions to this country in the 16th century. " 'And all this has been lost', he would say at last, as it were with a shade of melancholy". According to Leroy-Beaulieu, Rhodes most certainly regarded this as justification for the seizure of these countries by a superior race, whose mission was to reintroduce to them a civilization which the barbarians had destroyed and which the Portuguese, after a first great effort, had been unable to establish.[35]

Thus, even an ancient African culture was viewed by Rhodes through the prism of his political interests.

RHODES'S VIEW OF THE NDEBELE AND SHONA

It is important for us to know what Rhodes thought of the contemporary Africans, the Shona and the Ndebele, the nations he was about to subjugate, and not only to gain a better understanding of Rhodes himself. For his views reflected the typical attitudes to the African peoples held by most of his fellow-countrymen and contemporaries.

Rhodes assimilated the views current among those with whom he mixed, and in his turn he personally had an immense effect on shaping the image of the peoples of Africa both in England and in Europe as a whole. This image and these views, with a few minor changes, survived for decades and frequently served to justify and to explain colonial policies.

Today the scientific and technological revolution has made the whole world so easily visible and, it seems, so small, that even the most distant nations need to grow familiar with one another. To understand this process we must first discover how one nation's view of another is formed, and we must ascertain the origins of every prejudice. It is with good reason that the branch of science concerned with this is gaining increasing numbers of adherents.

The views of Rhodes and his confederates mark one stage in the history of racial prejudice and colonial psychology. There are, however, considerable problems in ascertaining Rhodes's view of the territory between the Zambezi and the Limpopo and its people. Rhodes did not keep a diary, nor did he have any literary aspirations. Even his epistolary legacy consists largely of laconic memoranda and telegrams.

At home in Kimberley and Cape Town he had every possibility to familiarize himself with all the existing literature on the Shona and Ndebele and to hear all the stories circulating about them. It is doubtful, though, how much of this information was authentic or how accurate a picture it gave.

Rhodes would probably have gleaned some information from eye-witnesses, but even this would have been distorted.

The first reason for this distortion was the attitude of the Africans themselves. With some justification, a contemporary British author claimed that the African, when questioned by a white man, would reason more or less as follows: "Who are you that I should answer all your questions? Why should I tell you all about ourselves, our country, our possessions, our government, our homes? How should I know what you are, or what your object is? For aught I know you may be a spy, and may turn out a bitter foe."[36]

Thus the information imparted by the Africans themselves was by no means always true.

A second source of distortion was the prejudice of the European eye-witness.

This was the age in which the French writer Gustave Flaubert wrote his *Le Dictionnaire des Idées Reçues,* completed in 1856. In it he records the standard conceptions held by the Parisian bourgeoisie for every eventuality in life. It took a very exceptional person not to subscribe to these received ideas. Similar prejudices and biassed notions were widely held about Africans.

When they arrived in Africa, most Europeans firmly believed that, whatever their occupation, they were doing good. They were bringing the light of civilization and culture, the only true ideas and way of life. The "greatness" of their mission blinded them to the reality around them. Thus they believed that only hopelessly backward races, "savages" and "haters of civilization", could nourish any sort of hostility or mistrust of them. What could be more convenient than thus to identify with progress, to believe they were its standard-bearers? With such a belief there was no need to enquire any further, to try and understand, the significance of their actions.

It was from the reports of men such as these that Europe was to judge Africa, men who could only see the familiar stereotype of the continent and its inhabitants which they brought with them from home. Even in 1843 John Stuart Mill had written: "The information which an ordinary traveller brings back from a foreign country, as the result of the evidence of his senses, is almost always such as exactly confirms the opinions with which he set out. He has had eyes and ears for such things only as he expected to see."[37]

It is not only social and economic factors which help determine the image we have of people living in other countries. This image is also influenced by the subtlest and sometimes inscrutable features of the age in which we live. It is these subtle features which can—and in history often do—provide the breeding ground for preconceived ideas and prejudices.

There is yet another source of distortion: the mind of the person who receives the information, whether he hears it from an eye-witness or reads it in a book. In the present instance we are concerned with the mind of Cecil Rhodes. In his case, information which, as we have seen, had already been distorted twice, passed through the prism of his perception and was distorted a third time.

Rhodes did not have a particular interest in knowledge for knowledge's sake: he was always too busy for that. He could only view the Ndebele and the Shona, as he demonstrated with his views on the civilization of Great Zimbabwe, through the prism of his political interests. In modern times this sort of approach is called geopolitics. It is for this reason that we can reduce Rhodes's attitude to the peoples of Africa to a simple formula: he divided them into the "bloodthirsty" and the "peaceful". Translated into modern terms this distinction reads: on the one hand, powerful opponents, who will probably put up serious resistance to conquest, and, on the other, weaker and therefore less dangerous opponents.

From the «White Queen» to Inkosi Lobengula

Rhodes believed that the Africans were not the only obstacle to advancement deeper into Africa. If anything, the rival European states posed a more serious threat.

The scramble for the "Black Continent" was at its height. At the Berlin Conference of 1884-1885 thirteen European states and the USA tried to define the conditions under which each successive chunk of African soil could be declared someone's sovereign territory or "sphere of influence".

After the conference the competition became only fiercer, as even the rival powers were prepared to admit. Lord Rosebery, British Prime Minister, said that the British were "pegging out claims for the future".[1]

Cecil Rhodes began advocating the seizure of the territory between the Zambezi and the Limpopo in 1887. He was not the only one in England and its South African territories to cherish these ambitions, but his role was of particular importance.

Initially he acted through Sir Hercules Robinson, the British High Commissioner for South Africa, and Sidney Shippard, Administrator of Bechuanaland since the annexation of the territory of the Tswana. Rhodes found it particularly easy to work with Shippard. They had known each other for many years, and Rhodes had nominated Shippard as his executor in his first political will in 1877.

Rhodes and his confederates understood that as the scramble for Africa intensified their plan to annexe the lands of the Ndebele and Shona would have to be advanced with great caution, stage by stage. The first stage would probably be merely to include this territory in the British "sphere of influence".

THE ORIGINS OF
THE BRITISH "SPHERE OF INFLUENCE"
A HUNDRED YEARS BEFORE

Rhodes could see that even this was no easy matter. The Zambezi-Limpopo watershed offered more than mere land. Everyone believed that it contained gold, a lot of gold.

At the same time a plan was hatched in the influential colonial circles of Germany to create a German "Mittelafrika", by linking German East Africa with German South-West Africa. Both colonies had only just been "acquired"—in 1884, but the Germans were already impatient to join them together and thus throw a belt of German territories across the entire girth of Africa.

But the Zambezi-Limpopo watershed lay between these two colonies. There could be no "Mittelafrika" until it was annexed. German agents headed for Matabeleland and Mashonaland. . .

Meanwhile, Portugal recalled its "historical rights": after all, it had been the first of the European powers to invade Africa, in the Middle Ages. Now it also dreamt of casting its hoop across the African continent—linking its territories in the west and the east, Angola and Mozambique. To achieve this it too had to gain possession of the watershed.

Portugal's designs on this area were reactivated by the Berlin Conference of 1884-1885, called to decide on the division of Africa, and by Germany's own annexation of German South-West Africa (now Namibia) in 1884. Thus, in the mid-1880s a plan was drawn up to establish a Portuguese colonial empire stretching from the Atlantic to the Indian Ocean. In 1886 and 1887 so-called "rose-coloured maps" were printed in Portugal, showing the vast areas between Angola and Mozambique in the pink colour of the Portuguese empire. At the same time Portugal was conducting talks with Germany and France, hoping to gain their consent to the implementation of its own plan. In return for such consent, which was only required in the vaguest terms, Lisbon was even prepared to make territorial concessions to Germany—on the borders of Angola and German South-West Africa, and to France—in the Gulf of Guinea.[2]

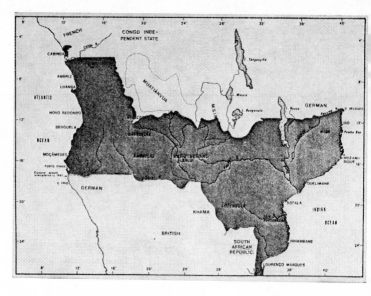

"The rose-coloured map" of Portuguese colonial claims in Africa,
published by the Portuguese Foreign Office in 1887

Then there was the Transvaal. The Transvaal government
regarded any expansion northwards as a matter of life or death
for the Afrikaner republics. Pressed by the British from the south
and the east, and after the annexation of the land of the Tswana
in 1885 from the west too, the Afrikaners were afraid of being
completely surrounded. For this reason they did their utmost to
increase their influence in the Zambezi-Limpopo area, thereby
preventing Britain from strengthening its position in the region.

Normally none of this would have bothered Rhodes much,
but he was placed on his guard by signs of a growing rapprochement between Germany and the Transvaal. It was this that
caused him to watch the actions of the Afrikaners with keen
attention.

The Afrikaners certainly gave him cause for alarm.

As long ago as 1882 Lobengula had been sent a letter by
the Commandant-General of the Transvaal army, Piet Joubert,
in which Joubert tried to turn Lobengula against the British.
He complained how hard it had been for the Transvaal to free

itself from the yoke of British domination, and wrote: "...when an Englishman once has your property in his hand, then he is like a monkey that has its hands full of pumpkin-seeds—if you don't beat him to death, he will never let go..."[3]

Such letters, for all their elaborate similes, might not have had the desired effect if the English had not demonstrated by their actions that the accusations were perfectly just. The threat of British invasion did in fact become much greater both for the Afrikaners and the Ndebele in 1884-1885, after England had annexed the territory of the Tswana, turning the south into the new dominion of British Bechuanaland, and the north, which abutted on the territory of the Ndebele, into a protectorate.

Lobengula became particularly alarmed when the British proposed marking a border between the territory of the Ndebele and that of the closest Tswana tribe, the Ngwato. Sir Sidney Shippard put his own name forward as arbitrator.

Lobengula could, of course, see that any attempt to mark out a border would inevitably lead to quarrels between the neighbours, and this was exactly what the British needed. So, sweeping aside the Ndebele's age-old differences with the Ngwato —differences such as arise between any two neighbouring peoples—he sent their chief Kgama a worried and, at the same time, friendly letter. He tried to convince his neighbour that they should resolve all internecine conflicts themselves, without admitting any interference by the Europeans.

"I heard last year from the white people that you were talking about making a boundary line. Again I hear it this year but you say nothing on the subject to me. Why don't you let me know? The white men are not your neighbours; I was your neighbour. You settle everything without consulting me. If you give your country over, and if you take in some of my ground, what will I have to say? I should like to hear answer at once... We never spoke about boundary lines. It is only now that they (i.e. the British—*A.D.*) talk about boundaries".[4]

After a long campaign of persuasion Lobengula got his way. Kgama also rejected any mediation by the British.

This displeasure with the British gave the Afrikaners their trump card. An emissary from the Transvaal, Pieter Grobler, was sent to the Tswana and the Ndebele. He took a large number of rifles for the Tswana, distributing them amongst chiefs who were unhappy about British expansion and what they regarded as Kgama's pro-British position.

The Afrikaners did not of course expect it to be easy to expel the British from the Tswana territory, they were merely hoping to obstruct the British advance northwards. Pieter Grobler then proceeded to Bulawayo. In July 1887, after painting the British threat to the Ndebele in the most alarming colours, he succeeded in concluding "a treaty on peace and amity" with Lobengula and also secured a number of privileges for the Afrikaners in Ndebele territory. He remained in Bulawayo for a long time as a sort of ambassador plenipotentiary, in order to be able to counteract British influence there on the spot.

The British were not to be outdone. Shippard at once set about intimidating the Ndebele with the threat of Afrikaner invasion. He wrote to Lobengula: ". . . I have heard a rumour that a large number of men in the Transvaal are preparing to invade Mashonaland," and added, "though I know nothing certain about this, I tell you of this report. . ."[5]

When Grobler was on his way back to the Transvaal from Bulawayo he was "accidentally" killed in Ngwato territory.

The Englishman Patterson was accidentally poisoned, the Afrikaner Grobler killed by chance. . . No one ever attacked ordinary European hunters and traders. But any tampering with international political schemes could have lethal consequences even here, in a remote part of Africa.

At this time Rhodes was applying increasing pressure on the Cape colonial authorities. It is even possible that his agents were the first to learn of Grobler's agreement with Lobengula.

At Christmas 1887 Rhodes had a meeting with Sir Hercules Robinson. It was agreed that the time had come for swifter and more vigorous action. They decided to send an official embassy to Lobengula without delay—not only to secure a treaty on "peace and amity", like that with the Afrikaners, but, more important, to ensure that the Ndebele chief did not conclude any more agreements with anyone except Britain.

We might wonder whether it was the identity of their purpose that prompted the High Commissioner for South Africa to act in unison with Rhodes and, furthermore, with an alacrity most untypical of civil servants. Or were Rhodes's powers of persuasion so strong? We have no record of their discussions, of the things that were said, and those that were implied. But it is known for a fact that shortly after this Robinson was granted 250 shares in a company set up by Rhodes for the development of the Zambezi-Limpopo area. Then later Robinson became a director of De Beers.

By now no European was trusted any more in Bulawayo. For this reason the British authorities chose as the leader of their embassy a man who would be sure to receive, if not the most trust from the Ndebele, then at any rate the least mistrust. His name was John Moffat.

John Moffat was the son of Robert Moffat, who had known Lobengula's father well. He was also David Livingstone's brother-in-law. He had been born here, in a Ngwato village, close to Ndebele territory. Later, after entering missionary service, he continued to reside in this area and had frequent meetings with Lobengula. At the end of the seventies Moffat entered the colonial service—something that happened quite often with missionaries. By 1888 he was already in middle age and it was much easier for him than for a younger man to conduct discussions with the Ndebele elders. In other words, a better emissary they could not hope to find.

Moffat's talks in Bulawayo in January-February 1888 were tense and protracted. He had to have repeated discussions with Lobengula and with the leading indunas. He tried to persuade them that the Transvaalers were deceiving the Ndebele, that the Boers interpreted their agreement with Lobengula quite differently from the way Grobler had explained it. This sounded convincing, because it was the truth. As might be expected, the Ndebele were highly indignant.

A much harder task was to convince Lobengula and his indunas that the agreement brought by Moffat was better than Grobler's. Admittedly, it did state that "peace and amity shall continue for ever between Her Britannic Majesty, her subjects and the Amandebele people". But it placed severe restrictions on the Ndebele leader: ". . .he will refrain from entering into any correspondence or treaty with any foreign state. . ."

According to the concepts of international law accepted in Europe at that time, England could consider that such an agreement placed the land of the Ndebele fairly and squarely in its "sphere of influence".

Did Lobengula see it this way, however? It is doubtful whether this can ever be ascertained now.

The Ndebele had never held, and could never have held, any of those European conceptions of exact boundaries, of territorial integrity, of the sale or concession of land. This was a people accustomed to a nomadic existence, to the constant changing of its place of abode. First Natal, then the Transvaal, now the watershed. Within each of these regions the Ndebele still did not remain constantly in one place. If there was insufficient grazing for the cattle they would move on, even if it meant moving their main settlement, their capital. The Ndebele measured their wealth in cattle, and they had only recently started to form settlements.

Besides, even a fully agricultural people, at the same stage of development as the Ndebele, could not be expected to have the same conception of frontiers and the alienability of land as the Europeans of the late nineteenth century.

We might wonder how Moffat interpreted the significance of this agreement to the Ndebele and why Lobengula and his advisers finally allowed themselves to be persuaded.

We do at least know that they did so most unwillingly. Because of this little document, consisting of no more than a few lines, Moffat was forced to extend his talks for a number of weeks. We can only presume that the Ndebele must have been trying to decide who presented the greater threat: the Afrikaners or the British?

Did Moffat succeed in intimidating the Ndebele with threats of an Afrikaner invasion? After all, the Afrikaners had already been to war once with the Ndebele and had forced them to abandon the lands on which they had settled. Had he managed somehow to dull their vigilance against the British? Or, on the contrary, did he threaten them with the anger of the "Great White Queen"? Lobengula and his councillors were forever being told of her great power.

Perhaps we will now only ascertain such facts as these when historians begin in earnest their study of oral history. It may be that the legends of the Ndebele contain the answers we seek.

What about Moffat himself? As a missionary and son of a missionary, did he not fully comprehend what he was doing? Did he realise the fate to which he was condemning an entire nation, a people he had known since his earliest childhood, and who had never done him any harm?

126

Perhaps Moffat really did believe faithfully in the good intentions of his own country. If so he might well have condoned the deceit, for the good of those deceived. As Engels had pointed out, even many scholars in the last century viewed the lives of other nations "through brothel spectacles".[6] One English missionary, when asked about the customs and morals of the "natives", replied: "customs none, manners beastly".[7]

Or was Moffat only thinking about the cosy sinecure he had been given in the colonial service? Or perhaps he did not give the matter any thought at all? He may have been a typical representative of his age; one of those who believe what is universally accepted must therefore be just.

For whatever reason Moffat carried out his assignment: on February 11, 1888 the Ndebele ruler placed his "X" at the foot of the "agreement". Moffat sealed the document with the words: "I certify the above a true copy, (signed) J. S. Moffat, Assistant Commissioner."[8] Two "witnesses" were found, who also affixed their signatures. . .

The "sphere of influence" had been created.

HOW CONCESSIONS WERE SECURED

By the international law accepted in Europe at that time Moffat's and Grobler's agreements had a more or less equal validity. But the fact of the matter was, of course, rather different. The entire might of the British Empire stood behind Moffat. From now on the territory between the Zambezi and the Limpopo would be far less accessible to rivals from Germany, Portugal and the Transvaal.

But this still did not mean that Rhodes had no more competitors in his path. He still had to reckon with his own fellow-countrymen, for whom the inclusion of this territory in the British sphere of influence was a great spur. Some of them had had their eye on the mineral wealth, and particularly the gold deposits, of the Zambezi-Limpopo area for much longer than Rhodes, from as far back as the sixties. In fact, ever since historians had first suggested this might be the site of the Biblical land of Ophir. One or two of them had even managed to secure "rights" to prospect for gold in the areas where Ndebele and Ngwato territory met.

Rhodes's main competition here came from the Gifford-Cawston Company. Lord Gifford was one of those aristocrats for whom the development of colonialism was more than a source of livelihood: he devoted himself to it body and soul. He had served in West Africa, in Australia and in Gibraltar. He fought in the Anglo-Zulu War of 1879, and even then conceived an interest in the wealth of the Zambezi-Limpopo area. We still have the text of the agreement he proposed to Lobengula. The inkosi turned it down. But Gifford's interest in the region did not abate, and in the second half of the 1880s he set about organizing a gold-prospecting company. He persuaded one George Cawston, a well-known London stockbroker, to join him in this venture. They bought a "concession" for the mining of minerals from Kgama, chief of the Ngwato, and when they heard of the conclusion of Moffat's agreement, decided to seek similar "concessions" from Lobengula too.

Gifford and Cawston lived in London, but appointed as their agents in the field efficient and energetic men. Such a one was Edward Maund. He was intimately acquainted with the region itself and with the routes leading to it, and he also knew Lobengula. In 1885, as an officer in a British unit sent to the Tswana territory, he had visited Lobengula as an official British emissary. From that day on he was haunted by the idea that the land of the Ndebele could become his Eldorado. His report on the mineral wealth of the region was published in 1886 and attracted the attention of all businessmen with an interest in the colonies.

Cawston as a denizen of the City and Gifford as a member of the aristocracy were able to count on considerable support in England itself. Their company was supported by some of London's top financiers, including the Rothschilds. These bankers, it might be remembered, were also assisting Rhodes, but were careful not to place all their eggs in one basket.

In London Cawston and Gifford had a stronger position than Rhodes. At the beginning of the scramble for the Zambezi-Limpopo area Rhodes was not well known in Britain, the very heart of the Empire. When someone mentioned Rhodes's name to the then Prime Minister, Lord Salisbury, he replied: "Rather a pro-Boer M.P. in South Africa, I fancy?"[9]

Rhodes did have certain advantages, however. He possessed

considerable capital. He could see the situation at first hand, and did not have to rely on the reports of others, however competent they might be. He was close to the colonial officials on the spot.

Gifford and Cawston decided to send Maund as their emissary to Lobengula to discuss the question of a concession. In early May 1888 Cawston wrote to the Colonial Secretary seeking his approval. The latter replied that he would have to consult officials in the area. It is to be wondered whether he realized quite what a favour he was doing Rhodes with this action. It was vital for Rhodes to steal a march on his opponents, and here he was given both a warning and time to act.

Rhodes decided without further ado to secure something from Lobengula that no one so far had managed to get: a general concession. To succeed, this operation would require not only swift implementation, but also careful preparation, circumspection, an element of surprise, and of course, total secrecy.

The diamond empire prepared its embassy to Bulawayo. Rhodes selected his emissaries. One was a businessman, the second a man who knew the language and customs of the local African peoples, and the third a lawyer, whose expertise was needed in drawing up the agreement.

Charles Rudd, Rhodes's first confederate and member of the Cape Parliament, was the businessman. The second emissary was the thirty-year-old Francis Thompson. He was chosen as an expert on "native" customs and psychology, most probably, among other things, because he had been the organizer of the "compound" system in Kimberley. Thompson had spent his childhood in the north of the Cape Colony, living close to the independent African tribes. He could speak the Tswana language. Lobengula also knew this, the language of his neighbours, and thus he and Thompson could communicate. The third emissary chosen by Rhodes was his fellow student from Oxford, James Maguire.

Now the race was on. In June Maund arrived in Cape Town from London, with instructions from Gifford and Cawston to make his way to Bulawayo and secure a "concession". In the meantime Rhodes himself had been to London. He ascertained the lie of the land and returned with a completed plan for the creation of a private company on the lines of the chartered com panies, which were granted almost unlimited rights to annex new countries in the scramble for the "division of the world".

In July Maund arrived in Kimberley and commenced his jour ney to the north. Rhodes's embassy was still not ready. It was now that Rhodes's connections with the local colonial official served their purpose. Of course, these were not casual connections: it was no coincidence that Sir Hercules Robinson, the High Commissioner for South Africa, had become a director of De Beers and shareholder in two of Rhodes's companies, while Sidney Shippard, who represented Her Majesty's government in the territory of the Tswana, was, upon his retirement a few years later, to become consultant to Rhodes's Gold Fields of South Africa, and then one of the directors of the Chartered Company set up by Rhodes.

It is hardly surprising, therefore, that Rhodes's emissaries were given a letter by Robinson in which the "White Queen's" representative in South Africa recommended them to Lobengula as "gentlemen of the utmost respectability". The letter was sealed with Robinson's seal and placed in an enormous envelope, measuring 12 by 18 inches, no doubt to make the biggest possible impression in Bulawayo.

Rhodes also gave Rudd a letter to Francis Newton, Shippard's assistant. In this letter he expressed the hope that Newton would comply with all Rudd's request. In addition Rhodes also placed great hopes in Moffat. "Your most valuable man will be Moffat," he assured Rudd, "Newton says he is thoroughly with you".[10]

Moffat did in fact do everything he possibly could. Rhodes's embassy received much assistance from the other missionaries, both along the route and in Bulawayo itself. In 1893 one of these, W. A. Elliot, received a hundred shares in the Chartered Company from Rhodes. He may not have been the only such beneficiary.

In these circumstances Maund had no chance of pipping Rhodes's emissaries to the post, even though he had practically reached the boundaries of Zambezi-Limpopo area before the others had set out on the journey.

This was in August 1888.

...That same month, in another corner of the world—Wales

—a man was born whose name today is often mentioned in one breath with that of Cecil Rhodes.

Rhodes could not have been aware of this event, of course, although he must have hoped that his work would be continued after him by other energetic men. But it could hardly have occurred to him that at the very time when he, so it seemed, was laying the foundations of the eternal might of the British Empire, the birth took place of a man destined to become one of the last idols in the history of this Empire... Thomas Edward Lawrence was his name, better known as Lawrence of Arabia. "The uncrowned king of the Arabs". A mere 35 years separated the births of these two men, one apparently at the dawn of the Empire, the other to usher in its sunset: so short are the epochs of history.

In many respects he was to become similar to Rhodes when he attained adulthood. Like Rhodes, he was not particularly fond of school. Like Rhodes, he studied at Oxford. Like Rhodes, he had an interest in history, and he even received the first prize for an essay on the "Influence of the Crusades on the Mediaeval Military Architecture of Europe". Rhodes would spend hours poring over Marcus Aurelius, and, even in the midst of the diamond rush, studied ancient Greek. Lawrence translated Homer's *Odyssey* into English. Like Rhodes he never had any great love for women, and throughout his life avoided their company, although he was not averse to making use of them when it suited his interests. They were both prone to do and say things which would have seemed outrageous to their contemporaries.

Why, it might be asked, this digression about Lawrence and comparison of him to Rhodes in this book? It is partly to give a more graphic idea of the sort of men romanticized by Kipling and other eulogists of British colonialism. But not only for this reason.

The two men had a great deal in common, despite the great differences in the historical conditions of their lives. The main thing that united them was their common goal: the consolidation of the British Empire. They both considered themselves patriots, and indeed, many of their fellow-countrymen saw them as the very embodiment of patriotism. They both operated in the outer reaches of the British Empire, among peoples regarded as backward in those days. And, for all the differences between them, the methods of the one help us to understand the methods of the other.

Rhodes's emissaries set off on August 15. Thompson, whom Rhodes had charged with preparing the expedition, had been busy since May buying two teams of mules, two wagons and provisions for three months. In Kimberley, where he made these preparations, he put it about that he was making arrangements for a big hunting expedition.

The route to the Zambezi-Limpopo highveld led across the Kalahari desert. The heat was insufferable. Men and animals were parched with thirst. The mules started to die. The wagons broke down. Then, on the borders of the Ngwato territory it transpired that chief Kgama was away and had left strict orders that no supplies were to be granted to any white men travelling north. Rhodes's emissaries, however, quickly came to terms with missionaries, and these were able to persuade the Ngwato to help them.

When they reached the Zambezi-Limpopo highveld they learned that Lobengula had instructed that no white men were to be admitted into his country without special permission. One of the Ndebele warriors set off for Lobengula's settlement with a letter from Rudd. But Rudd and his companions did not waste time waiting for a reply, and at once set off themselves for Bulawayo. More than any other white travellers before, they felt behind them the full support of the colonial authorities and of the British military units stationed in neighbouring Tswana territory. The Ndebele surmised that they had such support and were loath to resort to force.

Along the route Rhodes's emissaries were met by a warrior, bringing Lobengula's refusal to grant permission to their passage. Even this did not stop them. They arrived in Bulawayo on September 21, anticipating Maund by nearly three weeks.

The uninvited guests were given a polite reception. They were able to gain an audience with Lobengula immediately, on the evening of their arrival. He did not keep them waiting, received them very correctly, but would not discuss business. He wished them a good night.

We know these details because two members of the embassy, Thompson and Rudd, left notes about the negotiations and their stay in Bulawayo, capital of the strongest of the South African nations that still retained independence. The notes are not an entirely authentic record as neither author knew the local language. But some of the observations they make are interesting, and their treatment of events as well as their choice of topics to write about are in themselves evidence of their vision of the world, of their efforts to explain what was happening.

They wrote, of course, about Lobengula. According to Thompson he looked "every inch a king".[11] He was tall and well-built, although by that time also very stout: he weighed 120-130 kilograms.

They were also intrigued by anything "exotic". Around Lobengula's "palace"—a stone house—stood the huts of his twenty wives. All in all, the Ndebele king was reputed to have some two hundred concubines.

During their very extended stay in Bulawayo Rhodes's emissaries might have been expected to reach some understanding of, or develop some tolerance towards the people and society in whose midst destiny had placed them. But this was not to be. For example, they witnessed several executions. They never knew who was being executed, or why, yet they felt justified in deploring the brutality of the Ndebele. Their arrogance seemed to imply that no one was ever executed in England, or, if they were, they deserved the punishment. Thompson, admittedly, did recall that in ancient Rome Patricians who had gained too much wealth or power were encouraged to open their veins in a warm bath. . .

Rhodes's emissaries felt that their mission was much more perilous than it actually was. This applied particularly to Thompson, and could perhaps be attributed to the fact that his father had died in an armed clash with Africans.

Their fears proved unfounded. Thompson returned quite safely, and lived on for another forty years after his trip to Bulawayo, occupying a seat in the Cape Parliament for much of that time. But the embassy to Lobengula remained his hour of glory—it earned him for posterity the nickname Matabele Thompson.

The real danger to Rudd and his companions came not from the Africans, but from the other whites living in Bulawayo. Thompson estimated that they constituted a sizeable proportion of the ten thousand inhabitants of Bulawayo. They included not only the traders and hunters, who came and went, but also some who had made their homes here many years before and had no intention of returning to the "civilized world".

Many of them had little interest in becoming British subjects, or in retaining the British nationality they had held since birth: it was not for this, after all, that they had drifted so far from the sway of the British Empire. What sort of people were these? Some, Thompson wrote, were fugitive criminals, fleeing from the arm of the law. They made their way here from Europe as well as from South Africa. Thompson calls these "white scoundrels". They would buy captive girls from the Ndebele warriors, brought to Bulawayo after raids into neighbouring territory: ". . .they then took the girls to the borders and sold them to other white scoundrels", records Thompson.

Rhodes's emissaries also saw a man who so hated all other whites that he threatened, if he ever found himself alone in a deserted spot with another white man, he would kill him.

One of the white old-timers in Bulawayo had built himself two houses and furnished them in the European manner. According to Thompson, "he was immensely rich in cattle and other resources". He had two wives, both white women, who had once held respectable positions in society. He had died long before Thompson's arrival, but his widows refused to leave, and remained surrounded by large numbers of children, who mixed freely and played together with little black children from neighbouring households.

Thompson also describes a certain Thomas O'Connor, a Californian who had lost his way travelling in the Ndebele territory, had wandered for a long time in solitude, and had gone to the brink of insanity. The Ndebele found this half-crazed man, who had grown to resemble a large ape, and brought him to Lobengula. The king asked the local whites to take the American into their care.

It is interesting to note that at least some of the whites had formed fairly good relations with the African population of Bulawayo. In fact, this was by no means a unique occurrence in the history of South Africa. Rudd's companions noted several examples of such cordial relations.

As early as 1870, during one of the conflicts on the northern frontier of the Cape Colony a European by the name McCar-

134

hy joined the ranks of the Africans against the Cape Colonial
orces. "He was a gun mender and gunpowder maker, had been
iving for a long time among the natives, and had taken into
imself a native wife," recounts Thompson. When he was taken
risoner along with the Africans, his wife and her companions
ried to hide him. But in the end he was discovered, courtmar-
ialled and shot as a traitor.

Once Thompson himself was almost suspected of a similar act
f "treason". A less likely traitor it would be hard to imagine!
'elling the story of Thomas O'Connor, Thompson wonders: "It
vas most remarkable that the natives did not kill him."[12] Thomp-
on always expressed his disbelief—and sincere disbelief—when
escribing such cases. That there could be any good will, let
lone friendship between black and white, was absurd, even in-
redible to a man like him, brought up on the maxim "Oh,
'ast is East, and West is West, and never the twain shall
neet."

Talks about the "concession" did not begin immediately.
.obengula avoided the issue, postponing it on various pretexts.
3ut time was not working in his favour. Rhodes's emissaries tried
o scare him, telling him how the British had routed the army
f the Zulus, the people most close to the Ndebele. And Thomp-
on, to demonstrate the power of firearms, showed Lobengula
he scars of bullet wounds on his own body.

In his endeavour to avoid participating in the negotiations
imself, Lobengula dispatched Rudd and his companions to
.otje and Sekombo, the most highly placed indunas in the
Ndebele hierarchy. The local Europeans considered that Lotje
ulfilled the function of prime minister.

It is interesting to see the conditions the emissaries wished
o foist on the Ndebele. They were offered one thousand obso-
ete Martini-Henry rifles, one hundred thousand rounds of am-
nunition and a gun-boat on the Zambezi river. Lobengula and
nis heirs would be paid one hundred pounds each per
month.

In exchange the emissaries hoped to secure from the Ndebele
he right to prospect for and mine minerals, above all in the
egions inhabited by the Shona peoples. The British called this
erritory Mashonaland, as they called the Ndebele territory Ma-

tabeleland, and believed that all the Shona were tributaries of the Ndebele, which meant that Lobengula had the right to dispose of their land. In actual fact by no means all the Shona paid tribute to the Ndebele.

The talks proceeded laboriously. The two sides had great difficulty understanding each other.

Lobengula, however, comprehended perfectly the main purpose of the embassy. It was probably for this reason that Rhodes' chances of success were so slim, despite the fact that the colonial authorities of South Africa did all in their power to make the Ndebele give in. Not even John Moffat's support helped. Yet he had specially come to Bulawayo before Rudd so as to put pressure on Lobengula.

Eventually Shippard himself, the Deputy Commissioner of the Bechuanaland Protectorate, had to come to Bulawayo. When the talks started he was already standing by together with a detachment of soldiers, on the south-west frontier of Ndebele territory waiting for the signal. Runners with letters coursed regularly between him and Rudd. When Rudd saw that he would never break the resistance of the Ndebele it was decided to seek Lobengula's permission for Shippard to come to Bulawayo. "I fear the King will not do anything with us till he has seen Shippard",[13] noted Rudd in his diary.

Lobengula refused to send the deputy commissioner an invitation, but he did concede that Shippard come if he wished. He set one condition: the deputy commissioner was to bring with him no more than five soldiers, and not twenty-five as he had intended. Shippard arrived in Bulawayo on October 15 and at once called on Rudd.

The government in London was careful to conceal the participation of its officials in these talks. To this end they were even prepared to tell direct lies. When questioned on the subject in the House of Commons the Under-Secretary of State for the Colonies replied that during the period of the talks Shippard was some hundred miles from Bulawayo and that Moffat was also resident elsewhere. This explanation was given several months after the conclusion of the talks, on February 25, 1889, by which time the Colonial Office most certainly had all the information at its disposal.

Charles Helm of the London Missionary Society acted as interpreter during the most crucial phase of the talks about the "concession". He had lived for years among the Ndebele and knew their language. To a large extent he determined the sort of notion the Ndebele formed of Rudd's proposals.

Helm proved to be a most valuable find for Rhodes. Not content with the role of mere interpreter, he became Rhodes's assistant and ally, in effect, his voluntary representative in Bulawayo. He expressed the opinion to the London Missionary Society that the mining of gold in the Zambezi-Limpopo region should only be entrusted to a very powerful company, and that Rhodes and Rudd, with their company De Beers, were the men best-suited for the job. In Bulawayo itself Helm did everything possible to increase Rudd's authority, as well as that of Shippard and Moffat, in the eyes of the Ndebele.

A letter from Thompson to Helm has come down to us. In it the missionary is offered "a subsidy of £200 a year to act as our adviser and intermediary with the chief Lobengula and to hold yourself to some extent at our disposal." Apparently no documentary evidence has survived to indicate whether or not Helm accepted this offer—such documents tend not to come down to posterity. But Helm's own admission has survived: "From what I understand they would only want me to do what I have already done and should at any time be willing to do for them without remuneration"[14].

The Ndebele may not have fully comprehended the precise nature of the deceit, but they did guess or perhaps were even convinced that they were being deceived. As William Plomer records, "Sir Sidney Shippard ... was known to the Bechuana as *Marana-maka*, the Father of Lies".[15]

The mistrust of the Ndebele came fully to the fore at the end of October, when they held an indaba—a gathering of all the most influential Ndebele leaders—to discuss Rhodes's proposals. Thompson described this as the Ndebele parliament.

The indunas turned this discussion of the "concession" into a torrent of accusations against the Europeans. They openly expressed their indignation at the way British military units had been moved closer to Ndebele territory. Even the white hunters were castigated for destroying the animal life of the region.

LOBENGULA "AT HOME" - AN INDABA.

A contemporary sketch showing an indaba at Lobengula's "kraal"

Rhodes's emissaries were now forced to resort to all sorts of arguments. They threatened the Ndebele with an invasion by the Afrikaners and the Portuguese, pointing out that only Rhodes's thousand rifles could save them from total destruction. They swore to their good intentions. They had recourse to metaphors so that the Ndebele would understand them better.

"Yes," said Thompson, of himself and his companions, "there are four of us. The big one (Rhodes) is at home looking after the house, and we three have come to hunt"[16]. As for Rhodes's desire to gain the "exclusive rights" to the mining of minerals, Thompson explained that he did not want to "have two bulls in one herd of cows".

It was all to no avail. No sooner did they touch on the issue of "concessions" than the indunas would exclaim indignantly, not unlike the members of the House of Commons: "Listen, listen!".

After the indaba Rudd recorded in his diary: "It was one of the most miserable days I have ever spent as, of course, all the talking would do no good".[17]

...But then Lobengula suddenly gave in. On October 30, 1888 he placed his signature—an "X"—on the agreement about the concession, in accordance with which the Ndebele were to eceive the promised firearms, ammunition, boat and money, and Rhodes the exclusive mining rights to the entire watershed area.

Why this sudden *volte face*? How did this happen? Thompson was inclined to attribute Lobengula's sudden change of mind to his own rhetoric. He claimed to have presented Lobengula with the following irrefutable argument:

"Who gives a man an assegai if he expects to be attacked by him afterwards?"[18]

But the reason, of course, had to do with more than rhetoric. Lobengula clearly could see that his resistance was ultimately pointless.

Furthermore, Rhodes's emissaries had engaged in direct deceit. They had been assisted by the missionary Helm, who presumably saw nothing reprehensible in this dishonesty. He admitted in a letter to the London Missionary Society that during the discussions he had translated a deliberate lie by Rudd and his companions to the Ndebele. The emissaries, wrote Helm, "promised that they would not bring more than 10 white men to work in his (i. e. Lobengula's—*A. D.*) country, that they would not dig anywhere near towns etc. and that they and their people would abide by the laws of his country and in fact be as his people."

And he adds: "But these promises were not put in the concession."[19]

Indeed, there was nothing of this in the text of the treaty on the "concession". The document only stated that Lobengula would concede to Rhodes and his companions "the complete and exclusive charge over all metals and minerals" and granted them full power "to do all things that they may deem necessary to win and procure the same". But there is no mention that they would not bring more than ten men, or would abide by the laws of Lobengula's country.

Nevertheless at the end of the text we find Helm's official declaration: "I hereby certify that the accompanying document has been fully interpreted and explained by me to the Chief Lobengula and his full Council of Indunas and that all the Constitutional usages of the Matabele Nation had been complied with prior to his executing same."[20]

With this the six-week-long negotiations were concluded. Rhodes's contemporary and fellow-countryman, the economist

John Hobson, described them as a "history of competitive knavery and crime".[21]

Rhodes needed the "concession" for all sorts of reasons. Like his competitors, he wished to gain from the British government a royal charter to administer the regions of Africa lying to the north of the Transvaal. To receive such a charter he had to provide some foundation, which would give it at least the semblance of legality: a document from a well-known African ruler. The "concession" was to be this document.

Admittedly, it is clear even from its text that if it did confer any rights these were to the minerals rather than to the country itself. It was not, however, the content of the document that mattered to Rhodes, but the very fact of its existence. Let it be interpreted how people wished. At once the story was put about that with this agreement Lobengula had in essence conceded at least some if not all the lands under his rule. Newspaper articles giving this interpretation soon reached Bulawayo from Europe and "white" South Africa. The local Europeans rushed to Lobengula with these articles. The deceit was exposed.

It is easy to imagine the indignation of the Ndebele. The atmosphere in the country became highly charged. There were murmurs, almost open dissent against the inkosi—something that previously would have been an unheard-of audacity. Thousands of people converged on Bulawayo, asking whether it was true that the whites were taking their country away from them. The indunas held another indaba. They summoned Thompson and cross-questioned him. The interrogation lasted ten and a half hours. "The indunas were prepared to suspect even the king himself," wrote Thompson.[22]

In order to deflect this anger away from himself Lobengula was forced to sacrifice his "prime minister"—Lotje, just as Charles I had had to sacrifice Thomas Stafford. Lotje was indicted for giving the king the wrong advice, and executed.

Lobengula and the council of indunas summoned all the Europeans residing in Bulawayo and environs, and asked them to explain the exact import of the agreement and how it could be interpreted. The council of indunas demanded that the original of the agreement on the "concession" be presented to Lobengula, but Rudd was already on his way to Rhodes with it.

He had departed from Bulawayo in great haste as soon as he received Lobengula's "signature". The strictest instructions were issued to detain Rudd if he was still anywhere within the confines of the country.

One of those most vociferous in his protests against the "concessions" was the elder Hlesingane, one of the healers with the Ndebele army. Previously he had lived in the Cape Colony. The Zimbabwe National Archives contain a record, made by one of the Europeans, of Hlesingane's speech at the indaba of March 12, 1889.[23] He said: "O King of the country open your ears and eyes."

By agreeing to the "concession", Hlesingane argued, Lobengula had plunged the country into countless disasters; he maintained that the promises of Rhodes's emissaries that no more than ten men would be sent to prospect for gold, were not to be believed. "I have been at Kimberley Diamond Fields and one or two white men cannot work them, it takes thousands to work them. Do not those thousands want water and they also want land. It is the same with gold, once it is found the white men will come to work it, and then there will be trouble. You say you do not want any land, how can you dig for gold without it, is it not in the land? And by digging into the land is not that taking it, and do those thousands not make fires? Will that not take wood?"

The Ndebele were keen to publicize the story of this fraud as widely as possible, hoping thereby to frustrate the activities of their enemies. They were helped in this by some of the Europeans in Bulawayo, who were evidently apprehensive of Rhodes. Under dictation from Lobengula they wrote the following document in his name:

"I hear it is published in the newspapers that I have granted a Concession of the Minerals in all my country to Charles Dunell Rudd, Rochford Maguire, and Francis Robert Thompson.

"As there is a great misunderstanding about this, all action in respect of said Concession is hereby suspended pending an investigation to be made by me in my country. (Signed) *Lobengula*. Royal Kraal, Matabeleland, January 18, 1889."

This letter of warning was sent to the newspapers of "white" South Africa. It caused a sensation, and was published by the small newspaper *The Bechuanaland News* on February 14.

NOTICE.

I hear it is published in the newspapers that I have granted a Concession of the Minerals in *all* my Country to CHARLES DUNELL RUDD, ROCHFORD MAGUIRE, AND FRANCIS ROBERT THOMPSON.

As there is a great misunderstanding about this, all action in respect of said Concession is hereby suspended pending an investigation to be made by me in my country.

(Signed) LOBENGULA.

Royal Kraal,
  Matabeleland,
    18th January, 1889.

Lobengula's letter exposing Rhodes's machinations.
Below: the original, bearing Lobengula's seal; *above:* the text printed in the *Bechuanaland News*

The newspaper even included a photograph of the original with Lobengula's seal.

This was extremely unpleasant for Rhodes. His opponents decided to derive the maximum benefit from these events by proving to the British government that the "Rudd Concession" had no validity. If they had succeeded, Rhodes would never have received his charter.

As soon as he received the agreement Rhodes set sail for England. Thompson and Maguire, on the other hand, he detained with a mixture of enticements, entreaties and directives in Bulawayo, so that they would keep an eye on things and be able to neutralize their opponents on the spot. Usually extremely laconic in his letters, Rhodes gave Thompson highly detailed and totally categorical instructions.

These missives give us an opportunity to appreciate the stratagems and tactics of Rhodes the politician. He feared the whites who lived in Bulawayo, believing that they could do him a great deal of harm. For this reason they must all be propitiated, and, if possible, won over to his side. The ultimate trophy was so great that a few insignificant portions of it could happily be surrendered. "Remember," he wrote, "you have a country as big as one of the Australian colonies and if we are too greedy we may lose all".

Rhodes loved to refer to Napoléon. He wrote to Thompson that Napoléon was prepared "to share the world as long as he got Europe. Work on these lines."

It was easy for Rhodes to issue instructions from London, or even from Kimberley. But it was so much harder to carry them out in Bulawayo. The Ndebele watched Thompson and Maguire with undisguised suspicion, and not only because they refused to believe in their so-called good intentions.

Rhodes's emissaries constantly gave new grounds for this suspicion, sometimes quite unconsciously. Unfamiliar with the local customs, they sometimes performed actions which the Ndebele regarded as reprehensible, or even dangerous. Maguire once decided to have a dip and wash himself in a spring near Bulawayo. He did not know that the spring was regarded as sacred by the Ndebele, and the water from it flowed to Bulawayo. Maguire cleaned his teeth in the shrine and the water turned white... Shortly thereafter Lobengula's mother died. Naturally

Maguire was promptly accused of sorcery: taking fright, he secretly fled southwards after Rudd.

Rhodes sent despairing letters to the last of his emissaries, Thompson: "You must not leave a vacuum now... I leave all details to you, only do not leave the king alone... The thing is too big and until all whites are satisfied you cannot turn your back." "We feel it would be fatal if you left now."

Rhodes promised Thompson the earth: a house, the position of chief representative in the region. They agreed on a password, "Runnymede", which would mean: "Charter signed and sealed, position consummated". Thompson could leave Bulawayo only when he had heard this word.

Meanwhile it was becoming increasingly difficult for him to remain.

Once, after living in Bulawayo for over a year, Thompson was seized by an unaccountable fit of terror, leapt onto his horse and galloped off, losing his hat, riding without a saddle, and taking no food or water. He rode the horse into the ground, continued for another thirty or forty miles on foot, his tongue swelled up, his eyes were so bloodshot he could no longer see. Yet he managed to find water and dragged himself to a village where there was a telegraph. He sent telegrams to his wife and to Rhodes. From the latter he received an order to return at once. The same order came from the High Commissioner for South Africa.

Rhodes wrote to Thompson that he would very shortly be coming to Bulawayo himself. In actual fact he only came there after the country had been annexed, and he never met Lobengula. It is quite probable that he had no intention of ever doing so. He simply needed to play for time, somehow or other to mollify the Ndebele and the Europeans. To this end he was quite prepared to sacrifice Thompson and to promise anything under the sun. Thompson was forced to return to Bulawayo.

When the council of indunas demanded that Thompson submit the original of the "concession" agreement, Rhodes sent it, accompanied by a letter in which he warned: "I send the Concession, but do not hand it up until the knife is at your throat."[2]

This piece of paper was destined to undergo remarkable adventures. Rudd, who was carrying it to Rhodes, soon lost his way and ended up in a waterless desert. Deciding that he had met his end he buried the agreement in the sand under a bush,

vrote a note about this and pinned it to the branches. But
Rudd's coachman, an African, found his way to the Bushmen
and obtained some drinking water. Rudd returned to the desert,
dug up the agreement and finally reached Kimberley where he
handed it to Rhodes.

Then Thompson received it back from Rhodes, with instructions not to hand it over to the Ndebele. Once again the document found itself under the ground. This time it was buried
by Thompson, who placed it in a pumpkin gourd, and here the
agreement remained during Thompson's attempted flight. On his
return he dug it up and showed it to Lobengula.

It was only at the end of 1889, when Rhodes had finished
his "business", that Thompson was permitted to leave. The original of the document—that same ill-begotten piece of paper—
was taken by Thompson back to Rhodes in Kimberley.

THE NDEBELE DISCOVER EUROPE

It must not be thought that all this time the Ndebele were
sitting passively by, waiting for developments to unfold.

When he heard from the other Europeans how the English
newspapers had reported the "concession" Lobengula and his
council of indunas decided to send their own embassy . . . to London, no less. To the "White Queen" herself. They intended to
see for themselves whether she really existed, this white queen,
by whose name the colonial officials swore. They would discover
whether she was as mighty as they said, and whether Rhodes
was really her representative. Lobengula probably hoped to reach
an agreement with the queen, to persuade her to stop the flood
of her subjects into the Ndebele country.

It is not known whether the Ndebele themselves conceived the
idea of sending an embassy to London, or if it had been put
into their heads by one of the Europeans. There is no doubt,
however, but that the competition between the Europeans greatly assisted the organization of the mission. Edward Maund, representing Gifford and Cawston, was still trying to secure his concession. According to him Lobengula said to him one day: "Take
my men to England for me; and when you return, then I will
talk about that".[25]

It may even be that the idea of sending an embassy first origi-

nated with Maund, and he merely steered Lobengula impercep-
tibly towards it. However it came about, Maund agreed.

Both he himself, and those who backed him, must surely have
realised that the Ndebele mission would achieve nothing. But
they wished to use it as a trump card in the game against Rhodes.

One can only guess at what cost to themselves the Ndebele
organized this embassy. Lobengula understood that the journey
would cost a great deal of money, and he did not ask any of the
Europeans to shoulder the expenses. When he was told that at
least six hundred pounds would be required he produced a cloth
full of gold coins. He had received these coins from the numerous
concession hunters, including Rudd. In addition to money Lobengula gave his emissaries several head of cattle for the journey—as
food. Selected to go as ambassadors were two experienced and
respected indunas—Mtshete and Babayane. Maund records his
conversation with Lobengula:

"These envoys, he said, would be 'his eyes, ears, and mouth'."[26]

Babayane, according to the inkosi, possessed an excellent memory. He was related to Lobengula and in a battle had once
saved the inkosi's life. Mtshete was regarded as the finest orator
amongst the Ndebele. As their interpreter Maund took Johannes
Colenbrander, a trader from Natal.

The emissaries were to deliver a letter from Lobengula to
the "White Queen". In it the inkosi said:

"Lobengula desires to know that there is a Queen. Some of
the people who come into this land tell him there is a Queen,
some of them tell him there is not.

"Lobengula can only find out the truth by sending eyes to
see whether there is a Queen.

"The Indunas are his eyes.

"Lobengula desires, if there is a Queen, to ask her to advise
and help him, as he is much troubled by white men who come
into his country and ask to dig gold."[27]

The letter ended with a plea, which Lobengula later retracted.
It went as follows: "There is no one (i.e., of the whites—*A.D.*)
with him upon whom he can trust, and he asks that the Queen
will send someone from herself." Perhaps this request was insert-
ed by one of the local whites in the letter, and its meaning was
not explained to Lobengula? Or perhaps Maund had advised
him to ask the queen to send her own representative to Bulawayo?

The Ndebele embassy

It was probably on his prompting that Lobengula instructed his emissaries to complain to the queen about the designs of the Portuguese in the eastern part of the country—precisely the regions which most interested Maund's masters.

. . .Both emissaries were elderly men. The older, Babayane, was reckoned by the Europeans to be 75, and the younger, Mtshete, 65. Added to this Mtshete had a weak heart and suffered from elephantiasis. But they both donned their European suits without a murmur and set off for the long journey.

They travelled by coach through the Transvaal, through Pretoria and Johannesburg. President Kruger had been informed of this extraordinary embassy. But there were still problems getting tickets for the mail-coach: how could Blacks be permitted to occupy seats inside the coach?! The emissaries themselves suffered: their legs swelled up badly from the long hours of unaccustomed sitting.

Maund could not praise Babayane too highly. He called him "a charming and dear old man, always ready to do anything he was bid, pleased with everything, and one of the most unselfish men I have ever met. He gave up all his presents."[28]

Maund also had a high opinion of Mtshete, but found his character more difficult to deal with. The emissary could hardly be expected to be in constant high spirits, with his elephantiasis and weak heart, travelling through totally foreign lands, where no one understood him and he was stared at like a monster. The emissaries were totally dependent on their white guide, who anyway did not have much time for them. Added to this was the oppressive discomfort of the unfamiliar European dress, the suit of blue serge. . .

They reached Kimberley, and with it the railway line. We can imagine their anxiety at boarding the train, with its massive locomotive. Livingstone records how several members of a tribe living next to the Ndebele decided to travel to England with him. He took only one of them, called Sekwebu. Livingstone was full of praise for this man. "Sekwebu was picking up English, and becoming a favourite with both men and officers." Nevertheless, "the constant strain on his untutored mind seemed now to reach a climax". In the end, "his mind was affected," he leapt overboard and drowned. . .[29]

But Lobengula's emissaries proved equal to the task. They suffered moments of terror, but were able to suppress their fears. For example, lest he show any weakness on the train Babayane forced himself to stand for the first half hour of the journey, with his head thrust out of the window.

148

The emissaries were unexpectedly delayed in Cape Town. They waited one week, then another... Then it transpired that the delay had been engineered by Rhodes. The news of this embassy had come as a great shock to him, causing him dismay and rage.

Even without this Rhodes had more than his share of new problems. He had been harshly condemned by the missionaries, led by one of the South African bishops, for his sale of firearms to Lobengula. Nor was he helped by the assurances of his allies that the Ndebele would not be able to use the guns anyway, and that in their hands this weaponry did not pose any real danger.

But the main problem was that the Gifford-Cawston group were waging a ferocious campaign in London against Rhodes, and with some measure of success. Consequently, the Ndebele embassy was most unwelcome to him. He at once set about putting obstacles in the emissaries' path. A rumour started to circulate that these two Ndebele were not indunas and that they could not be regarded as a plenipotentiary embassy. Their companion Maund was described by John Moffat as "phenomenally untruthful".[30] This may well have been the case, but would Moffat have condemned Maund so harshly if the latter had been Rhodes's man?

It is a fact, however, that when Maund arrived in Kimberley Rhodes tried to buy him off, without first establishing whether or not he was a man of probity. Rhodes followed the simple rule that it was better to deal with a scoundrel than with an honest fool. Rhodes conducted his meeting with Maund in the customary fashion: first a proposition, then, if it was not accepted, a threat. His proposition was that if Maund abandon his London masters and join Rhodes, Rhodes would give him both money and a position. But when Maund refused Rhodes flew into a rage and declared that the High Commissioner would delay the embassy, and that the British government would not receive the indunas anyway without a recommendation from the Cape authorities.

So the emissaries were delayed in Cape Town for a long time.

Then the situation suddenly changed, and Robinson stopped putting obstacles in their way.

The truth of the matter was that a conspiracy had taken

place behind the indunas' back. The Colonial Secretary Lord Knutsford advised the Gifford-Cawston group to join forces with Rhodes. Both sides agreed. In fact, it was the only thing they could do, as their contest had reached a stalemate. Gifford and Cawston were backed by influential London circles, and Rhodes was supported by considerable forces in South Africa and England. After some reflection, the rivals decided it would be better to act in unison.

By the time the Ndebele emissaries embarked on board the *Moor*, the old vessel taking sail from Cape Town, the bargaining had already begun. The embassy was no longer a threat to Rhodes and no longer necessary to Maund.

But the indunas were not to know this. They believed nothing had changed, they hoped for the best.

This was their first sight of the ocean, as of practically everything else on their extraordinary journey. But this did not cause them any dejection of spirits: in fact, they did not even suffer from sea-sickness.

The embassy excited such interest among the passengers that even Lady Frederick Cavendish, a society hostess, deigned to converse with them. She assured them that they and their king need have no doubts about the existence of the "Great White Queen", since Lady Cavendish knew her well personally, and had kissed her hand on numerous occasions. One of the emissaries replied with dignity: "We believe it, as you say so, but we are taking our own eyes to see."

London greeted these inhabitants of the warm south with icy weather: it was mid-winter. But, as Maund records, "they bore themselves, as far as the low temperature would allow them, with ... impassive dignity".

Africans were no longer a rarity in London: they could frequently be seen in the docks. But these were a different matter, coming as they did from the "untamed" Africa of the interior, and as emissaries of the ruler of the mysterious land of Ophir. They were bound to attract the attention of the British public.

They disembarked in Southampton and boarded the train there for London. When they arrived in Waterloo they were besieged by journalists. This harassment by journalists continued throughout their stay in the Berner's Hotel.

It was probably the sensational nature of this embassy that

persuaded Queen Victoria to grant them an audience almost immediately, only two days after their arrival in London. Perhaps she was also driven by plain female curiosity.

They were escorted to Windsor Castle by top-ranking officials. Their route through the palace itself was lined by tall and impeccably turned-out guardsmen. This was sure to make a strong impression on the Ndebele emissaries.

The reception was an occasion more for ceremony than for business. The queen graciously announced: "You have come a very long way to see me; I hope the journey has been made pleasant for you, and that you did not suffer from the cold."

The emissaries proved quite at home with this exchange of pleasantries. One of them, with a respectful bow, said: "How should we feel cold in the presence of the great White Queen?", and added: "Is it not in the power of great kings and queens to make it either hot or cold?"[31]

Afterwards journalists questioned the emissaries, asking what impression the audience had had on them. But they described these impressions in the most superficial way, only recording those statements by Mtshete and Babayane which might amuse the public. For example, that the most beautiful lady in the palace was Lady Randolph Churchill, mother of the then very young Winston.

The emissaries spent the whole of March in London. They saw all the sights—from the ballet in the Alhambra Theatre to the London Zoo. They visited the Bank of England, where they were shown gold ingots and invited to try and lift sacks full of gold coins. Several dinners were held in honour of the embassy. At that held by the Aborigines Protection Society one of the guests was Rider Haggard.

The Ndebele were astounded by London, its endless rows of houses and numberless multitudes of people. When they spoke to each other on the telephone they were astounded that such a small machine could learn their language, and so quickly.

The general tendency to surprise the emissaries seemed sometimes to conceal a desire to frighten them. The Colonial Office had decided that as the indunas had arrived and their visit had to be publicized, then the officials might as well derive whatever benefit they could from this event, by instilling in the indunas a holy dread of the British.

151

In Windsor Castle they were shown, hanging on the wall, the spear of the Zulu king Cetshwayo, vanquished by the British ten years before. In Madame Tussaud's they were told that the figure they saw before them was Cetshwayo in person, punished thus for his unruliness.

The emissaries were taken to Portsmouth, the biggest naval base in England. In Aldershot they viewed the manoeuvres of ground forces—of ten thousand soldiers. They watched cavalry attacks and an artillery display. They saw the very latest weaponry and witnessed the firing of an 111-ton cannon.

The manoeuvres were commanded by General Woods. The emissaries were introduced to him, and their hosts were careful to point out that it was he who had routed the Zulu army in 1879 and had sent Queen Victoria the Zulu king's spear. At the same time the emissaries were receiving constant assurances of England's humane intentions and protestations that she would never allow anyone to cause their people any harm.

It was generally assumed that the emissaries were properly impressed with both the might and the magnanimity of England.

Two meetings were held with the Colonial Secretary, Lord Knutsford. During their final meeting he delivered Queen Victoria's answer to Lobengula's letter, an answer which consisted of several vague and quite non-commital sentences. The British government did not, of course, take any measures against the concession hunters. Only one of Lobengula's requests was complied with: that the queen send him her representative. The Colonial Office shrewdly availed itself of this naive request and a few months later a British resident in Bulawayo was appointed—none other than John Moffat.

Admittedly the misunderstanding was quickly revealed. In August 1889 Lobengula replied to the letter from the British colonial authorities: "With regard to Her Majesty's offer to send me an envoy or resident, I thank Her Majesty, but I do not need an officer to be sent. I will ask for one when I am pressed for one."[32] But such a letter from Lobengula was not reckoned with, and it was not even made public at the time.

In addition, the queen sent Lobengula and his indunas her portrait, a five-sovereign coin on a gold chain, and the indunas received bracelets as presents.

The emissaries' companions presumptiously assumed that their

152

charges had been impressed by everything European and "civilized". Maund refers to "the English clothes which they loved so well",[33] which he had told them to don. All the greater his surprise, therefore, that on their way to South Africa the emissaries steadily discarded their European apparel, piece by piece, as they drew closer to home.

Finally they arrived back in Bulawayo. On their return home they remained closeted with Lobengula for two months, giving daily accounts of their experiences. Sometimes they had as many as seventy indunas gathered around them, listening intently. Of course their discussions with Mtshete and Babayane were dominated by one topic: the white men.

It is interesting to see how "natives" reacted to the whites. Perhaps the following illustration is typical.

The white man "is constantly anxious to conceal his flesh. His body and his limbs are his flesh. Only that which is above his neck is the real person. This is how it was explained to me by one white man, who enjoyed great respect and was considered very wise. . .

"When a youth takes a maid as his wife he never knows whether or not he has been tricked, for he has never before seen her body. The girl ... conceals her body, so that no one may behold it, or delight in its appearance.

"Flesh is sin... And even the junction of our limbs to create people for the joy of this great earth is a sin."

It is for this reason that the white man's body "is shrouded from head to toe in loin-cloths, mats and skins, wrapped about so closely that no single human glance, no single ray of sunlight can penetrate them; so closely that the body beneath becomes pale and sickly".

As for European houses and cities: the white man lives like a snail in a solid house. He lives between rocks, like a scolopendra in cracks in the lava. There are rocks all round him, beside him and above him...

As for money: talk to the European about the god of Love —he pulls a face and smiles. He smiles at your naivety. But give him a shining piece of metal or a big, heavy piece of paper, and his eyes will at once light up and his mouth will start to dribble with saliva. Money is his love, money is the god he worships. He also offers his round metal and his heavy paper to us, to make

153

us lust after them. They are supposed to make us richer and happier.

As for things: the quantity of things makes the white man poor. If someone has but a few things he regards himself as poor and he grieves. There is no single European who would sing and rejoice if he had only a mat and a bowl, like each of us. Men and women from the white countries could not live in our huts; they would at once rush off to collect wood from the forest, tortoise-shells, pieces of glass, coloured stones and many other such things; they would toil from morning to night until their hut was full of things, large and small, things which easily fall apart, which can be destroyed by the least fire, by any tropical rainstorm, and then they would have to procure new ones, again and again. The hands of the European never tire of making things. It is for this reason that white men's faces are often so fatigued and sad. They wage war with one another not for virile glory or to test their strength, but for things.

As for time: the European is always short of time. Because of this he is forever worried and conducting many foolish conversations. Yet there can never be more time than fits between sunrise and sunset. One man was seen turning successively red and green in the face, and trembling in every limb, because his servant came to him one breath later than he had promised to come.

As for counting the years of their life: this searching and calculating is full of peril, for in this manner they have ascertained how many months the life of most people lasts. Each one of them now remains mindful of this and, when his allotted number of months is up he says: "Now I shall soon die." All joy departs from his life and he does soon die.

Here the author craves the reader's indulgence. Mtshete and Babayane were of course gifted and exceptional men: it was no accident that they were chosen for this most responsible mission. No doubt their account of Europe and the life of the white man was more remarkable than the extracts we have cited above. Unfortunately, however, we have no record of this account.

All that has been recorded about the Ndebele embassy, apart from a few official British documents and newspaper articles, is, in essence, the memoirs of Maund, which we have already had occasion to quote above. From them the reader can see that

Maund was primarily concerned with the exotic details of the missaries' behaviour, and did not make much effort to understand their mentality.

Seemingly only one sentence has come down to us of the accounts given by the emissaries to Lobengula. When they were describing how much gold they had seen in the Bank of England Lobengula enquired incredulously:

"Why, if the Queen has so great store of gold, do her people seek more?"

The emissaries replied:

"That is the point, they go all over the world seeking it, not only in our own country, because they are all obliged to pay tribute to her in gold."[34]

But the observations and reflections on the life of the white man quoted above come from the book *Der Papalagi*.[35] In the introduction we are told that these are the notes of a chief from the Samoan islands who visited many European countries and decided to inform his fellow-tribesmen how the white man (in Samoan—"papalagi") lives at home, in Europe. We Europeans present a woefully ridiculous aspect in these accounts... The chapter titles tell a story in themselves: "The Grave Illness of Thinking", "On the Place of the False Life and on the Many Papers". The final chapter is entitled "Papalagi Wants to Draw Us into His Darkness".

Der Papalagi was translated from the German into Russian and published in 1923. The publishing house never questioned for a moment the authenticity of the "speeches". Nor did the journal *Zori*, which published a review of the book under the heading "Naïvety or Wisdom",[36] cast any doubt on their authenticity.

It might appear strange that both the editors and reviewers could have been so easily gulled. The author of the book was, of course, the same person as its publisher—none other than Erich Scheurmann. Although this German writer had in fact once lived in Samoa and in all probability had conversed with the local chiefs, it is obvious from the style and the content of these "speeches" that they are the work of a European.

This device—passing off one's own reflections as the observations and deliberations of a simple-hearted aborigine, wise in his naivety—has been widely used by European poets, writers and philosophers. We need only recall the works of Jonathan Swift,

Voltaire's *Candide,* Oliver Goldsmith's *The Citizen of the World,* all following a tradition arguably started by Montesquieu with his *Lettres Persanes.*

It was during the lifetime of Rhodes and Lobengula, at the end of the 1880s, that Anatole France invented his Arab narrator Djeber bin-Hams and had him make fun of the French:

"There is a custom with Occidentals and particularly with the Franks to give what they call 'balls'. Remark in what this custom consists. After having rendered their wives and their daughters as seductive as possible by exposing their arms and shoulders, by putting perfume on their hair and their gowns, by spreading a fine powder over their flesh, by lading them with flowers and jewels and by instructing them to smile even when they do not feel like doing so, they repair with them to vast, warm halls, lit with a multitude of candles as numberless as the stars, and furnished with thick-piled carpets, with deep armchairs, with soft cushions. Here they drink fermented liqueurs, exchanging animated remarks and betake themselves with these women into whirling dances, at several of which I have been present. Then, when the moment comes, they assuage their carnal desires with great fury, either after having first extinguished the candles, or having arranged the carpets in a manner suitable to their designs. Thus does each take his pleasure of the lady he prefers or who has been assigned to him. I insist that it is so. Not that I have beheld it with my own eyes, my guide always having conducted me from the rooms before the orgy, but because it should be absurd and contrary to all probability that things prepared in the manner I have described could have any other issue".[37]

This device enabled the European writer to criticize his own society and fellow-countrymen. The attraction of the device, however, was not confined to this.

Beholding one's world with a new, fresh view, as it were for the first time, just as it was beheld by Lobengula's emissaries, meant to evaluate it in a new way, not from within, but from without. Its values were seen through different eyes, as was the place of one's society in the history of all mankind. This device gave at least some idea of the other societies which constitute this history, and some understanding of the "native people" to which the narrator belongs. It enabled the reader to reconstruct model of this people's way of thinking, of their view of the world.

Another interesting essay in this genre came from the pen f the Moscow writer, Yakov Svet. In his novella "An Involuntary Odyssey" he describes the fictitious journey to Europe by Columbus's interpreter, a Red Indian whom the Spanish call Diego.

Why, might we wonder, is it only writers who explore this theme? If it is so fruitful, why is it neglected by academics nd scholars?

Until very recent times academic Europe cared little what he "natives" of Africa, or anywhere else, might think of it. This s no longer the case. Today academics and scholars—historians, psychologists and ethnographers—have begun in earnest to study he formation of the notions different peoples have of one another.

So sahen sie uns. Das Bild der Weissen in der Kunst der farbigen Völker (How They Saw Us. The Image of the Whites in he Art of the Coloured Peoples)—under this title a book was published in Leipzig in 1972. A book put out in Paris in 1976 s entitled: *Noirs et Blancs. Leur image dans la littérature orale africaine* (Blacks and Whites. Their Image in African Oral Literature). The number of such studies is constantly on the increase.

It appears that writers intuitively sensed this lacuna in human knowledge before scholars and tried either to fill it or to turn it to their own advantage. It is not unusual, after all, for them to be ahead of their academic brethren. Frederick Engels maintained that he had learned more from the novels of Honoré de Balzac about French society and even about the economic details of its life, "than from all the professed historians, economists and statisticians of the period together."[38]

The Soviet Academician Mikhail Tikhomirov reproached his fellow historians in 1962: ". . . to this day no one has even attempted to describe the life of a people, its views, its festivities, its calamities and aspirations, to describe every aspect of life in another age. Only writers attempt this, as did Romain Rolland in his story about *Colas Breugnon*. Meanwhile the historians can only grumble at writers, accusing them of inaccuracies."[39]

The writers and scholars we are considering are, of course,

all Europeans. This is not to say, however, that no inhabitan
of those distant southern lands ever left any record, any mem
oirs or notes of the impression Europe made on him when h
first visited it.

Alas, we shall never know how Europe looked to the te
Red Indians whom Columbus brought with him to Spain in 149
not even to the one who became the great navigator's guide
returned to the West Indies with him and helped him "discover
Jamaica.

Folklore and legend help us see what notions the African
first formed of Europe.

The first Africans to see Europe reached its shores severa
centuries before the Ndebele indunas. There were not only slave
—whose impressions were, naturally enough, more predictabl
and easier to understand—but also those who came, like th
indunas, as official emissaries. It is remarkable to think tha
almost four hundred years before Lobengula's embassy, simila
embassies were sent to Europe by the ruler of the Congo, who
at that time had been converted to Christianity, and his son, wh
took the name Dom Henrique on his baptism and graduate
from a seminary in Portugal, was elevated to the rank of bisho
in Rome in 1518.

Another early African visitor was the West African Antor
Amo. Some two hundred and fifty years ago he was raised to th
degrees of Doctor of Philosophy and Master of Law, and taugh
at the universities of Halle, Wittenberg and Jena. He left numerous works of philosophy and theology, which have been repub-
lished in recent years in the German Democratic Republic. Bu
we do not know what Europe looked like even to a man of his
remarkable destiny.

At roughly the same time in Holland, in Leiden, another African, named Jacques Eliza Jean Captein, was studying theology
His impressions also remain lost to posterity.

Their contemporary, the Ethiopian slave brought to Russia at
the beginning of the 18th century, became known as Hannibal, or
Peter the Great's Negro, and secured still greater renown as the
grandfather of Russia's greatest poet, Alexander Pushkin. We
know that in Russia Hannibal attained a position of power and
influence unparallelled by any other African in Europe. He even
became a general-in-chief in the Russian army.

What did he think of Russia, or of France, where he had studied or many years? All that had come down to us of Hannibal's writings are his works on engineering and a very brief autobiographical essay. Yet we know he also wrote memoirs, but subsequently destroyed them all.

During the years of the scramble for the partition of the world Queen Victoria and the other European monarchs and rulers were host to emissaries from the most far-flung countries, bearing complaints from their peoples against the activities of the Europeans. If we could only learn something about their impressions much light would be shed on the complex process of the formation of the different peoples' views of one another. In turn this would assist the process of mutual understanding, which has always been so sorely lacking in the history of international relations. The problem is, how are we to ascertain this valuable information?

As we have said, it is not entirely true to say that nothing has survived of the memoirs written by Africans. There are extant memoirs, and some dating back hundreds of years. One such book excited such interest that it was almost simultaneously published in several European countries, appearing in Russian in 1794.

The Russian edition had the following title: *The Life of Olaudah Equiano, or Gustavus Vassa the African, Born in 1745, Written by his own Hand; Containing the History of His Upbringing among the African Peoples; His Capture, his Slavery; the Sufferings Endured by Him on the West Indian Plantations; the Adventures Undergone by Him in Different Parts of the World; Descriptions Both of the Different African Peoples, of Their Faith, Customs and Habitudes, and of the Many Countries Seen by Him during his Life, with Many Touching and Curious Anecdotes and with the Inclusion of His Engraved Portrait.*

One can imagine the fascination with which his European readers read of Olaudah Equiano's amazement on first beholding snow:

"It was about the beginning of 1757 when I arrived in England, and I was near twelve years of age at that time. I was very much struck with the buildings and the pavement of the streets in Falmouth, and indeed any object I saw filled me with new surprise. One morning when I got upon deck, I saw

159

it all covered over with the snow that fell overnight: as I had never seen anything of the kind before I thought it was salt, so I immediately ran down to the mate and desired him, as well as I could, to come and see how somebody in the night had thrown salt all over the deck. He, knowing what it was, desired me to bring some of it down to him: accordingly I took up a handful of it, which I found very cold indeed, and when I brought it to him he desired me to taste it. I did so, and I was surprised beyond measure ... a little after I saw the air filled with it in a heavy shower which fell down on the same day."[40]

This may not be the most important of the observations made by Equiano in Europe. It is remarkable, nonetheless, that in memoirs written some thirty years later, after so many terrible ordeals, years of slavery and humiliation, he should remember his first snow.

When the seventeen-year-old Rhodes sailed from London to Natal he had of course no idea that almost half a century before the Zulu inkosi Shaka had wished to send several of his Zulu subjects to London to study, to his "brother" King George. Nothing came of this scheme. Shaka's chosen candidates only got as far as the Cape Colony: the British authorities would let them no further.

By the time of the Ndebele embassy to London there had already been visits by Africans from South Africa to the British Isles. They did not, however, travel in the capacity that Shaka had intended: as representatives of independent nations.

The first South African black to be educated in Britain came not from the Zulu nations, but from their neighbours, the Xhosa. His name was Tiyo Soga. He was no longer alive at the time of the Ndebele embassy, having died in 1871. Tiyo Soga published a large number of articles in the South African press.

He addressed the following words to his fellow African: "White people brought us knowledge and wisdom in respect of many things. If we were willing that our young people should partake of that wealth of knowledge and wisdom, we should be lifted out of ignorance. For to the white people too, this wisdom and knowledge is not indigenous. It came at a certain time. There was a time when their progenitors were the laughing stock of their more civilized conquerors. Today, the white people laugh at us.

160

"But although they have brought many things that are bless-ings to us in this life and even in the life hereafter, there are some evil things which we wish that the white people had left behind. Even the blessings have lost their value and can no longer be praised as blessings, if we look at the work done by liquor amongst the black people. Liquor has produced abominations which were not known amongst the Xhosa peo-ple... Liquor is like a firebrand thrown into dry veld grass."[41]

This was what he wrote in his published article, naturally mak-ing due allowances for the consorious eye of the colonial authori-ties. He gives a more candid expression of his views, however, in his admonitions to children. Here he passionately defends the dignity of his own people:

"Among some white men there is a prejudice against black men; the prejudice is simply and solely on account of colour. For your own sakes never appear ashamed that your father was a Kaffir, and that you inherit some African blood."

Tiyo Soga's children were half-caste: their mother was a Scot. They were possibly the first children in South Africa to be born to the legal union of an African and a white woman. Their posi-tion in society was, of course, unusual and awkward. Their father reminded them that in America mulattos frequently passed themselves off as white and adopted a haughty attitude to the Negroes, and insisted that this was most regrettable:

"I want you, for your own future comfort, to be very careful on this point. You will ever cherish the memory of your mother as that of an upright, conscientious, thrifty, Christian Scotswom-an. You will ever be thankful for your connection by this tie to the white race. But if you wish to gain credit for yourselves—if you do not wish to feel the taunt of men, which you sometimes may be made to feel—take your place in the world as coloured, not as white men; as Kaffirs, not as Englishmen."[42]

Even in modern times problems like this are all too rarely approached with such dignity, tact and wisdom. Yet we can imagine how hard it must have been for him to reach this, the only true decision, how hard to avoid the extreme positions towards which great numbers of people in many different countries gravi-tate even today: hating either the blood which makes you an outcast, or the blood which confers privileges on others.

When we read such records we are able to see in a different

light the Africans of those years, and the Europeans, and their attitude to each other.

It is not long since the travel notes of the East African Salim bin Abakari, describing his journeys in the early and middle nineties, shortly after the Ndebele embassy to London, were published in a large edition. They are called *My Journey to Russia and Siberia,* and *My Journey to Europe—from Dar-es-Salaam to Berlin.*[43]

Salim bin Abakari's travels were very extensive: St Petersburg, Moscow, Nizhny Novgorod (now Gorky), sailing down the Volga, Samara (now Kuibyshev), Omsk, Biisk, Barnaul, Tomsk, Semipalatinsk, Tashkent, Samarkhand, Bukhara, Baku. From St Petersburg's Yevropeiskaya Hotel to the Russo-Chinese frontier. He meets Russians, Tatars, Kirghiz, Kalmyks... He describes observances and procedures, in the theatre, in trains, on steamers. Customs which strike the African as exotic such as the drinking of tea from morning to night, particularly when on the road...

Unfortunately, in his notes, this African author never compares Russia with his native country. The comparisons are always with Europe, with which he had grown very familiar by this time. As the favourite valet of a German merchant, Abakari travelled widely through Europe and came to see many things through European eyes, losing that freshness of perception which might be expected of an African travelling to this distant northern land for the first time.

The Ndebele indunas had no gradual period of acclimatization to help them. They arrived in London directly from Africa, and we can presume that their impressions were consequently more vivid, richer and more varied. For this reason too they would have been of particular interest to us.

But for the time being we know very little about them. We might wonder whether they dared to describe everything, or if they held back in places, realising that they could not possibly be believed. We can only hope that some of this may yet come to light, when the historians of Zimbabwe have collected more oral legends of their country. In fact, one leading Zimbabwean historian, Stanlake Samkange, has already manifested an interest in the Ndebele embassy to London.[44]

ENGLAND IS THE CHAMELEON
AND I AM THAT FLY

Without awaiting the return of his emissaries, on April 23, 889 Lobengula wrote to Queen Victoria again. Where in his irst letter he had complained about the conduct of the whites in general, here he exposed the fraud which had led to his concluding an agreement with Rudd.

"Some time ago a party of men came into my country, the principal one appearing to be a man named Rudd. They asked me for a place to dig for gold, and said they would give me certain things for the right to do so. I told them to bring what they vould give and I would then show them what I would give.

"A document was written and presented to me for signature. I asked what it contained and was told that in it were my words and the words of those men.

"I put my hand to it.

"About three months afterwards I heard from other sources that I had given by that document the right to all the minerals n my country.

"I called a meeting of my indunas and also of the white men, and demanded a copy of the document. It was proved to me that I *had* signed away the mineral rights of my whole country to Rudd and his friends.

"I have since had a meeting of my indunas, and they will not recognise the paper as it contains neither my words nor the words of those who got it.

"After the meeting I demanded that the original document be returned to me. It has not come yet, although it is two months since, and they promised to bring it back soon.

"The men of the party who were in my country at the time were told to remain until the document was brought back. One of them, Maguire, has now left without my knowledge and against my orders.

"I write to you that you may know the truth about this thing, and may not be deceived."[45]

The return of the emissaries from England only brought the Ndebele further disillusionment. Lobengula sent several more petitions to Queen Victoria, but their tone grew increasingly despairing. On August 10, 1889 he wrote: "...the white people are troubling me much about gold. If the Queen hears that have given away the whole country, it is not so. I do not under stand where the dispute is because I have no knowledge of writ ing."[46]

The Ndebele's true attitude to the "Great White Queen" can be judged from their treatment of her presents. Lobengula gave the gold chain and coin to one of his wives, "not caring" as *The Times* recorded, "to keep presents from the white people".[4] Mtshete and Babayane gave their bracelets to Europeans living in Bulawayo.

It was becoming increasingly clear to Lobengula that "Rhodes's people" in fact enjoyed the full support of this same "White Queen" and with her of the full force of the British colonial machine. In a conversation with the missionary Helm he graphi cally described this relationship with the following image:

"Did you ever see a chameleon catch a fly? The chameleon gets behind the fly and remains motionless for some time, then he advances very slowly and gently, first putting forward one leg and then another. At last, when well within reach, he darts out his tongue and the fly disappears. England is the chameleon and I am that fly."[48]

Setting Up His Own State

The tongue, thrown out by the chameleon to catch the territory between the Zambezi and the Limpopo, was to be the Chartered Company.

These chartered companies were described by Prime Minister Salisbury as an original method for England's participation in the dissemination of civilization and Christianity among the African peoples. The journalist Arthur White wrote: "It is, in short, necessary for the public to understand that, in Africa at least, chartered companies are absolutely essential for the promotion of what are euphemistically called British interests, and that, if they suppress those companies, it is morally and immorally certain that rival European Powers will take their place, for they, at any rate, do not hesitate to advance the national flag wherever the ground for its erection can be begged, borrowed or stolen."[1]

British politicians loved to dwell on the self-sufficiency and independence of these companies. Salisbury declared that "they conduct, according to their own fashion and with their own resources, their own lines, and, to a great extent, at their own risk, the development of the regions that have been committed to their charge."[2]

In time these companies became surrounded by a veritable aura of Romantic glamour. "How much the British Empire—I prefer that old title—owes to the enterprise and efforts of the merchant adventurers, including the chartered companies, of the City of London... the spirit of adventurous romance, which has not even yet quite deserted the City of London. It was reinforced by the invaluable spirit of private enterprise and of profit-making, one of the most respectable motives in the world."[3] This plaudit was delivered as recently as 1949, on the occasion of the sixtieth anniversary of the British South Africa Chartered Company by its then president, Dougal Malcolm.

It is worth taking a closer look at these chartered companie at the privileges their "charters" conferred and at the reasons fo their formation.

AFRICA LEASED OUT TO COMPANIES

The scramble for Africa by the European powers, which start ed in the seventies, intensified with each successive year. By th end of the eighties it had reached an exceptional peak of inten sity. The rival powers keenly scrutinized one another, on the look out for any careless move.

The seizure of new territory presented certain complications i European politics. The problem was: how to extend the empir without incurring any serious risks? The answer was found in thi new instrument for the annexation of new territory—the char tered companies.

These companies, having first secured "agreements" witl "native" leaders, would then receive a special charter from thei own government. The charter stated that the government gav its approval to these "agreements", and by the same token to th activities of the corresponding company.

In practical terms this meant that the government permitte the companies to annexe some piece of hitherto "undivided" ter ritory and to administer it. The "agreements" were only neces sary because of international law, which prevented any particula government from administering areas which did not come unde its jurisdiction. The "agreements" made it possible to get roun this stricture.

No significance whatsoever was attached to the proper formula tion of these "agreements". The government would simply endors the interpretation of the agreement offered by the company and would at once declare that this "agreement" constituted th basis for any activities the company wished to pursue. All tha anyone knew was that such-and-such a country had been give by the government to such-and-such a company.

It was in this way that the chartered companies receive mandates to annexe immense areas of the African continent The granting of a charter signified the psychological, politica and material support of the government.

Meanwhile the government itself, standing behind the chartere company, bore no direct responsibility for the latter's actions. In the event of any conflict with any rival powers the company could back down, if the worst came to the worst, without its parent country suffering any loss of face.

On the other hand, if the company treated the African populace so viciously that even the European public started to object and the situation verged on the scandalous, the government could take the position of an outside observer or even intervene as an arbitrator. The company, after all, was its own master...

In addition the annexation of new territory did not usually promise instant profit. On the contrary, the actual process of conquest, the prospecting for minerals and preparations to develop the resources of the new country, to say nothing of the suppression of uprisings and the complex process of "pacifying" the vanquished indigenous population all demanded vast sums of money.

The official levying of funds through parliament from the treasury would incur the displeasure of the tax-payer. In addition the discussion in parliament of plans to annexe some new country would provoke unnecessary conflict between the political parties and would give the rival powers the opportunity and time to take counter-measures.

But here we have a company with its own money, which seemingly has no connection with the tax-payer's pocket and leaves the government completely out of the picture.

In actual fact the government would provide the companies not only with money but also with the lives of British soldiers. As time went on this became increasingly easy to arrange. The public grew accustomed to the idea that the African countries—those in which the companies had established themselves—were in some way important and necessary to England. Their history had already been enhanced by "heroic" events, and their distant soil had been "consecrated" with British blood... In other words, the ground had been prepared. After this the government could calmly take the reins of power into its own hands.

This two-phase tactic of colonial expansion was most widely used by the British government. In a despatch to St Petersburg Russia's ambassador to London Yevgeny Staal described the British government's *modus operandi* as follows: "Where it has been unable or unwilling to operate with its own means it has granted special charters and privileges to private trading companies, which at their own expense have waged wars, secure in the knowledge that the government of their country, in the event of danger or need, would not refuse them assistance."[4]

These companies, created by financiers from the City and the captains of the mining industry, sometimes even dictated their own terms to the government. Their boards of directors usually included representatives of the aristocracy and sometimes even members of the royal family.

The idea of setting up these companies in Africa came to the British government when the scramble for the division of the world was at its most frantic. In 1886 a charter was granted to the Niger Company, in 1888 to the Imperial British East Africa Company. At that time it was common to read effusive praise of the companies in newspapers and journals, commending their energy and contrasting them to the indecision of the government. At the beginning of 1886 Otto von Bismarck had also proclaimed the idea of founding a "German commercial empire" in Africa, by creating companies with government support, and two years later the German government granted a charter to the German East Africa Company.

The main theatre of operations of these companies at that time was Africa. At the end of the nineteenth century they and several other similar associations from Britain, Germany, France and Belgium controlled some two million square miles of territory and at least fifty million inhabitants of the African continent.[5] "Africa leased directly to companies..., and Mashonaland and Natal seized by Rhodes for the stock exchange,"[6] wrote Engels at the time.

"NO OTHER CHARTERED COMPANY"

In his discussion of the chartered companies Engels only mentions one person by name: Cecil Rhodes. Indeed, the British South Africa Company founded by Rhodes was the largest of them all. "No other chartered company appealed so strongly to the cupidity of the gamblers in the stock exchange. None attracted such widespread admiration or condemnation. And no other company had a Rhodes."[7]

Rhodes was able to link this company inextricably with his

wn name, even though he was not the only one and not even
ṭe first to campaign for its creation. A mandate to conquer new
ịrritory had been the cherished dream of Gifford, Cawston and
ṃany others—in fact, of all those who dreamt of annexing the
ṇuntries lying in the interior of Africa.

Rhodes swiftly reached an agreement with Gifford and Caw-
ṣon. But he did encounter opposition from some who had no
ẉish to see such vast territories thus farmed out to a small group
f̣ tycoons. Sections of the industrial and commercial bourgeoisie
ṭrongly objected, and further objections on their behalf were
ṛaised by the London Chamber of Commerce and by the
ạlready influential Joseph Chamberlain, future Colonial Secre-
ạry. They did not want access to the wealth of Africa to be
ṃonopolized by a single company. The mouthpiece of these
ḅourgeois groups was the journal *The Economist,* which came
ụut in condemnation of Rhodes and his associates and insisted
ṭhat the government itself should undertake these annexations and
ṇot entrust such an important task to a newly-fledged company.
"If Mashonaland is worth a serious dispute with a foreign
ṣtate ... it is worth the small expenditure which direct govern-
ṃent by the Colonial Office would perhaps entail."[8]

The missionary organizations and the Aborigenes Protection
ṣociety also opposed the granting of this charter. The notorious
ṛifles—the ones Rhodes had promised Lobengula—were taken as
ṭhe target for public attacks against Rhodes. Newspapers published
ṇartoons of Ndebele warriors brandishing these firearms and
ṃassacring the British. Even the then Colonial Secretary Knuts-
ṃord joined the band of critics. He described the promise of the
ṛifles as a dangerous mistake.

We must, however, realise that all these men were talking
ạnd writing in full seriousness about some great danger, as if
ṭhey were faced with the full rearmament of a proper army,
ạnd not the dubious bartering of a thousand obsolete rifles.
Ạnyway, they knew perfectly well that the Ndebele warriors had
ṇo idea how to use firearms, nowhere to learn and no one
ṭo teach them, and that ammunition would be very hard for them
ṭo obtain...

In actual fact the rifles were, of course, a mere pretext. Rhodes
ḳnew the real cause of his difficulties: among his associates there
ẉas at that time no highly placed British official. Even he him-

169

self had not by then gained sufficient influence for his name t
lend weight and an aura of respectability to his company in th
eyes of the propertied classes. Besides, many people felt that hi
political views were decidedly suspect.

On April 30, 1889 Lord Gifford appealed to the governmen
on behalf of the company which it was hoped to set up, askin
for the "sanction and moral support of Her Majesty's Govern
ment and the recognition of such rights and interests as wer
legally acquired in the territory." Gifford referred to the suppor
of Rhodes's Gold Fields Company, of his own Bechuanalan
Exploration Company and, most notably, of Lord Rothschild, o
the prominent banker Baron Erlanger, of Cecil Rhodes and c
Charles Rudd.

The Company gave the following undertakings: "(1) to exten
the railway and telegraph northwards towards the Zambezi; (2
to encourage emigration and colonization; (3) to promote trad
and commerce; (4) to develop minerals and other concession
under one powerful organization, so as to avoid conflicts betwee
competing interests."

The Colonial Secretary supported the application since, in th
first place, the company's founders could, on the basis of the ordi
nary companies act, proceed without a charter at all, and in th
second place, through such a company Her Majesty's Govern
ment would avoid diplomatic problems and heavy expenses.

But this was not the end of the struggle for the charter. Fo
the whole of 1889 Rhodes was forced to work without respite
First of all, as a matter of urgency, he had to win over his rivals
Many of those who claimed "rights" in the watershed area, or t
the north of the Zambezi, were bought off with shares in th
future chartered company. In the process no one bothered to
check very closely whether these people did in fact have any
"agreements" or "concessions". There was no time: Rhodes was i
too great a hurry. The stakes were so high that he was quit
prepared to sacrifice a little for the sake of the main cause, to
prevent any undesirable talk, adverse gossip, letters to the news
papers and so forth, and to ensure that everything went as
smoothly and swiftly as possible.

Rhodes's main weapon was money, and he had frequen
recourse to it. He would pay out sums of money to entire politica
parties. He gave ten thousand to Parnell and another five thou-

sand to the Liberals, lest, as he himself said, they "would evacuate Egypt."

And there were politicians and journalists to be bought off, too.

Rhodes invited Lord Cecil, son of Prime Minister Lord Salisbury, to become a permanent adviser to the company. Salisbury was alarmed by the proposition, but his son did not share his opinion and accepted.

Rhodes's activities were not confined to London. There were influential people in the Cape too. By April 1890 they had also become shareholders, to the tune of thirty-four thousand shares. Nor did Rhodes overlook the Belgian king Leopold II. He could also have his uses.

Lord Rothschild played an important role in the campaign to get a charter. Just as in 1888 he had decided the outcome of the battle in the diamond industry, so now, by becoming one of the founders of the new company, was he able to assist Rhodes not only as a financier, but also as a politician.

There was one more operation that had to be carried out without delay: leading members of the aristocracy had to be brought onto the board of directors of the new company.

The veneration of titles and the aristocracy in general in Britain at that time is satirized by Bernard Shaw with his usual sardonic way, talking through one of his characters, Lord Augustus Highcastle:

"I am ever at my country's call. Whether it be the embassy in a leading European capital, a governor-generalship in the tropics... I am always ready for the sacrifice. Whilst England remains England, wherever there is a public job to be done you will find a Highcastle sticking to it."

Aristocrats often regarded their posts as mere sinecures, and approached matters of state in the same spirit as Lord Highcastle: "Just you wait, something more important will always crop up. All sorts of family matters, for example, and things like that."

Many companies tried to court aristocrats—a big name at the head of a list of directors was regarded as good window-dressing and imparted respectability, ensuring the favourable disposition of those in high places.

Rhodes and his new associates held talks with several representatives of London's society elite. Finally it was agreed that the Duke of Abercorn would be president of the company and the Duke of Fife vice-president.

The fifty-year-old Lord Abercorn, son of the Lord Lieutenant of Ireland, preferred life on his Irish and Scottish estates and was not too much concerned with the affairs of the Chartered Company. But he was a friend of the Prime Minister, Lord Salisbury, and himself an influential member of the Conservative Party, so his name on the list of directors at once lent appropriate weight to the company.

The forty-year-old Fife, an influential Liberal, was very close to the throne. Quite recently, in the summer of 1889, his engagement had been announced to the daughter of the heir to the throne, the Prince of Wales. Fife, already an earl, was now raised to duke. Just like Abercorn, he did not interfere in the affairs of the company and wasted no time reading its lengthy reports, but did receive thousands of shares in it at a price well below that quoted on the market.

The third peer cost Rhodes a little more effort. This was Albert Grey, who had not received his peerage at the time the company was being set up. He, in fact, did try to become involved in the operation of the company, but he was so indecisive that Dr Jameson, Rhodes's closest assistant, once described him as "a nice old lady, but not a genius, who does not like committing himself to any opinion."[9]

All this only goes to show how shallow the differences of opinion among the British ruling elite really were: right until the end of the spring of 1889 both Fife and Grey had campaigned against Rhodes and the granting of a charter to his company.

On Fife's insistence Horace Farquhar was later appointed to the board of directors. He was a friend of the Prince of Wales, and an aristocrat who had made his name in London society with his flair for business (he rarely refused invitations to participate in financial and commercial operations).

Of Rhodes's own group only himself and Alfred Beit went on the board, and from their main rival group—Gifford and Cawston. The aristocrats, among whom we can also number Lord Gifford, ended up in the majority.

Rhodes probably did not feel particularly comfortable amongst all these peers. As a self-made man, he was bound in his heart to regard them as nonentities, and to make matters worse, arrogant and boastful. Yet he could not help envying them. They received everything on a plate: they did not have to fight for their wealth and titles, to squander the best years of their lives overcoming endless obstacles. Whether he liked it or not, they would always remain the elite, the flower of Britain. And he, whatever heights he might scale in his career, would never be their equal.

Perhaps Rhodes simply felt flattered to move in such select company? We must remember that this was a different age, with different values.

Whatever his feelings, he certainly understood the rules of the game. And for his window-dressing he was able to secure the very top names. But for himself he reserved the most powerful position on the board: the office of managing director.

Rhodes conducted all these activities—recruiting influential allies and winning over his opponents—at the same time as holding discussions with the government. It was easy for him to come to terms with Prime Minister Salisbury: after all Rhodes had literally surrounded him on all sides. Besides, there was no real difference in their views. They both believed that it was both necessary and important not only to annexe the Zambezi basin, but also to move further north, as far as the Great African Lakes. Salisbury believed it vital to occupy the area of Lake Nyasa (now Lake Malawi), but he was hesitant about asking Parliament for funds for this purpose. Acting on behalf of his new company Rhodes took these financial commitments on himself: he undertook to give the British administration in Nyasaland ten thousand pounds a year from the moment of its establishment. This undertaking did not place any financial burden on the company: the British government subsequently reimbursed its expenses with interest.

In addition the company gave a subsidy of twenty thousand pounds and undertook to pay nine thousand pounds a year to the British African Lakes Company, which was on the edge of bankruptcy. Neither was this assistance any act of charity: it effectively enabled Rhodes's company to subjugate this company.

The scene would now appear to be set: after all these services the government was not likely to object to the granting of a charter. The public, however, was a different matter.

Even in those days the British were accustomed to begin their day with the morning papers and end it with the evening papers. In many other countries newspapers had not yet become part of people's daily life, but Kipling was able to write of his own country:

> *The Soldier may forget his Sword,*
> *The Sailorman the Sea,*
> *The Mason may forget the Word*
> *And the Priest his Litany:*
> *The Maid may forget both jewel and gem,*
> *And the Bride her wedding-dress—*
> *But the Jew shall forget Jerusalem*
> *Ere we forget the Press.*[10]

Later Bernard Shaw was to remark acerbically in one of his plays: "Even God would not be omniscient if He read the newspapers."[11]

Rhodes understood the truth of all this only too well. In order to secure the support of the press, and with it of public opinion, he frequently donated large sums of money to the *Times* correspondent Scott Keltie and to the editor of the influential journal *Fortnightly Review* John Verschoyle, and won over the leading journalist Sidney Low.

William Stead, publisher of the *Pall Mall Gazette* and of the journal *Review of Reviews*, campaigned against Rhodes until the spring of 1889. In a meeting with Stead in April 1889 Rhodes expounded his ideas to him and then offered to participate in a publishing venture started by Stead, contributing for this purpose the sum of twenty thousand pounds and promising to provide still greater financial support in the future. Stead proclaimed Rhodes as the new saviour of the British Empire. Who knows which proved more effective: Rhodes's power of persuasion or his money, but it cannot be denied that a commonality of beliefs grew up between the two men. This was to be so close that in several wills he wrote in the 1890s Rhodes named Stead as his second executor (Rothschild being his first), with the obligation, in Rhodes's behest, "to realise my ideas". Frederick Engels considered Stead to be an excellent entrepreneur.[12] It was precisely these qualities which were to prove so invaluable to Rhodes.

From the spring of 1889 panegyrics of Rhodes adorned the
pages of such influential publications as *The Times* and the *St
James's Gazette,* although the former had previously always taken
a sceptical stance, and the latter had been openly hostile. The
Fortnightly Review, The Nineteenth Century and a number of
other journals were similarly attentive to him.

Former opponents now became allies, critics turned into
apologists. Seemingly nothing could stop Rhodes now. Even the
prestigious Royal Geographical Society came out in his support.
In May 1889 it recommended commercial associations as the best
agents for the dissemination of civilization through Central
Africa.

. . .On February 25, 1889 the question was asked in the House
of Commons, whether the government knew about the Rudd concession and the assistance given by British officials to Rhodes in
bringing pressure to bear on Lobengula. The Under-Secretary
of State for the Colonies de Worms denied that officials had
been involved, and in response to the question declared that "Her
Majesty's Government do not consider it necessary to express any
opinion."[13]

On March 26 de Worms stated that, although Lobengula's
lands were "under the sphere of British influence", the government was not entitled to interfere in the internal affairs of "the
real rulers of the country." On the granting of concessions, he
said: "I do not think the Government had any power to approve
or disapprove."[14]

On April 2 the radical Henry du Pré Labouchere asked
whether the Cabinet was aware of Lobengula's assertion that he
had been deceived by their missionary interpreter. Labouchere
quoted Lobengula's statement. De Worms replied that he knew
nothing about all this and that the government did not get involved in such matters.

These answers were practically from Kipling:

Them that ask no questions isn't told a lie.[15]

On April 5 de Worms refused altogether to answer similar
questions. From the end of May the press was writing about the
granting of the charter as if it were a *fait accompli.* But government representatives were still refusing to answer questions bearing on the charter, even as late as August 24.

Flag of the British South Africa Company

The charter was signed by Queen Victoria on October 29, 1889. The Company's sphere of operations was defined as "the region of South Africa lying immediately to the north of British Bechuanaland, and to the north and west of the South African Republic (i.e., the Transvaal—*A.D.*), and to the west of the Portuguese Dominions". Within this region the Company's rights were assured to have "the full benefit of the concessions and agreements made as aforesaid, so far as they are valid". In turn the company was obliged to "preserve peace and order", to "abolish by degrees any system of slave trade or domestic servitude in the territories aforesaid", to "regulate the traffic in spirits and other intoxicating liquors within the territories aforesaid, so as, as far as practicable, to prevent the sale of any spirits or other intoxicating liquor to any natives". In addition the Company "shall not in any way interfere with the religion of any class or tribe of the peoples of the territories aforesaid or of any of the inhabitants thereof", should pay "careful regard ... to the customs and laws of the class or tribe or nation", and even to "the preservation of elephants and other game".[16]

The Company was accorded the right to organise an administrative machinery, to have its own police force, to establish banks and shareholding companies, to grant plots of land for use over a definite period or in perpetuity, to issue concessions for mining umbering, etc., and to establish settlements anywhere in the foresaid territory.

The Company had its own flag, coat-of-arms, motto, revenue stamps and postage stamps. The coat-of-arms included everything. There was a shield with oxen, ships and an elephant. It was held up on either side by antelopes. Below was the motto: Justice, Commerce, Freedom. Above all this, naturally, stood the British lion. The flag was the Union Jack with the lion in the centre and beneath it the company initials: BSAC.

Thus did the British South Africa Company come into being, with its own army and police, and even its own flag. In time this company was to become the undisputed lord and master of a territory many times larger than that of Great Britain.

Surely this was no more nor less than an "imperium in imperio"?

And if so, what are we to make of the man who controlled it all? He had no high sounding office or title which would have reflected the full extent of his power. His name was quite simple: Cecil Rhodes.

Rhodes had undivided control over the company's affairs. "He was the only director who knew what he wanted and how to carry it through," writes one of his biographers.[17] Rhodes's absolute power was officially confirmed. In May 1890 Abercorn and Fife signed a document granting "Power of Attorney of the British South Africa Company to C. J. Rhodes".[18] Its convoluted legal terminology may be quite simply translated by the one sentence: "Everything that is done by the bearer of this document is done entirely with my agreement and for the good of the State".

"We are in the dark here ... but I have the fullest confidence in the wisdom of any move which you and Jameson may agree in thinking the right one... Do whatever you think right. We will support you whatever the issue."[19] This comes from a letter written to Rhodes during one of the Company's crises by Albert Grey, the only one of the peers on the board who had made the least attempt to become involved in the Company's affairs. In effect even the British government did not exercise any control over Rhodes. Lord Abercorn was to admit later: "Mr Rhodes had received a power of attorney to do precisely what he liked without consultation with the Board, he simply notifying what was done."[20]

Seal showing the Company coat of arms

The contradictions in the charter granted to Rhodes are a
once obvious. On the one hand, even the original petition request
ed assistance only in implementing concessions and agreement
concluded with the Africans, and the charter itself repeatedl
stressed that its objective consists precisely in this. This was tan
tamount to acknowledging that any rights which the Compan
had obtained or intended to obtain in the future were based o
treaties with the African peoples and that the charter served n
other purpose than to indicate that the British government un
dertook to protect rights obtained in this way.

On the other hand the charter was concerned with establishin
the Company's administrative power over an immense area.

The sole agreement concluded by the Company by the tim

t received its charter was that with Lobengula. Even if we accept this as satisfying the charter's insistence on the "validity" of agreements, it only gave the right to prospect for minerals. There was no way it could justify the granting of administrative power to the Company.

These contradictions and ambiguities can be explained quite imply. The government wanted to bestow the most extensive and fully substantive powers on the Company, but at the same ime it feared international complications resulting from excessively unceremonious treatment of this immense and still undivided piece of Africa. For this reason, while granting Rhodes and his associates an effective mandate to rule over millions of Africans, he government referred merely to the necessity to safeguard the contractual and concessionary rights obtained from the African chiefs themselves.

It must have cost the skillful British lawyers a great deal of ime and energy to disguise the real purpose of the charter. There is something excessively contrived about the convoluted phrasing of its numerous articles, and it emphasises its concern for the Africans rather too frequently. So frequently, in fact, that one might be led to think that a charitable society was being set up.

For a long time after the proclamation of this charter questions continued to be asked in various publications about the juridical meaning of this document. Even eight years later the missionary John Mackenzie wrote: "It is first of all of importance to have a correct idea as to what was given to the Company by the Imperial Government."[21]

The charter gave the Company the possibility to become a tate within a state, but to realise this the Company had first o crush the military might of the indigenous people, to organize a system of oppression, and to create and put into effect a mechanism for the exploitation of the population and the natural resources.

All this required immense financial outlays. Added to which, he director-peers were fully entitled to expect profits from an enterprise to which they had agreed to lend the lustre of their names.

In the future they could look to the labour of the Africans. But to what could they turn in the first few years? Official mention was made of several sources of revenue. The Company was entitled to half the profits made by each prospector in the territory covered by the charter. Should any mining company or prospector sell their claim the Company received half its value. It could sell portions of land as farms and for urban construction and derive income from the operation of railways and the telegraph.

But all this was a long, drawn-out process, and for the time being the main source of funds was stock market speculation.

Immediately upon obtaining its charter the Company issued shares to the value of one million pounds, at a nominal value of one pound each, shares to suit everybody's pocket. These shares helped create an impression of the Company's democratic nature, of the participation of the masses in its affairs.

But the shares were not offered to the public at once. First, almost half a million shares were distributed among the directors and other "useful" people who received them almost gratis, at a mere three shillings for one-pound share. A further two hundred thousand shares were taken by De Beers.

As if this were not sufficient, Rhodes, Gifford and their associates, soon after gaining the charter, secretly set up another company, behind the shareholders' backs: the United Concessions Company. According to their own declaration, this company supposedly "handed over" to the Chartered Company all its "rights and concessions".[22] Rhodes, Gifford and others, now in their capacity as directors of United Concessions, were able to reserve to themselves half the profits of the Chartered Company and ninety thousand of its shares.

Even this, however, was not the end of the story. The public were subsequently informed that these "rights and concessions" did not include the Rudd concession. It remained in that case unclear what rights and concessions were meant: after all, the Rudd concession was the main one, and served as the legal basis for the obtention of the charter. Nevertheless, a further million shares were issued under the Rudd concession. Acting in the name of the Chartered Company Rhodes and his fellow directors transferred these million shares to themselves and only then placed them on the market.

Rhodes's outlay on the press was repaid a hundredfold. The sensational newspaper coverage of the new Company had the effect of boosting the price of the one-pound shares on the tock market to three, four and sometimes even nine pounds, by whipping up hopes of fabulous dividends. This brought massive profits to the founders, although no real chance could be seen of any dividends being paid for the next few years. The Company declared that for the first two years it would not pay out "a single farthing".

The Kaffir Circle (the division of South African securities on the London Stock Exchange) enjoyed the lion's share of the speculators' attention throughout 1889 and 1890. This was a trend that was to last for a very long time.

In this way the Company's management had been able from the very first to secure massive profits for the Board of Directors and for prominent representatives of the British ruling circles, one of whom was no less a figure than the Prince of Wales.

The rank-and-file shareholders who lived in England, however, were totally deprived of their rights, if only because the shareholders' meetings were held in South Africa. But the main thing that ensured the total impunity of the Company's management was the support it enjoyed from the Imperial government. The government responded to any criticism of the Company by declaring that it had no intention of interfering in its activities. Thus, when Labouchere attempted on January 27, 1891 to expose the financial machinations of the directors in the House of Commons, de Worms replied: "...Her Majesty's Government was not, when the charter was granted, and is not, aware that the facts are as stated and is not responsible for the details of the relations between the British South Africa Company and any other Company or person holding concessions within the field of its operations."[23] On other occasions government representatives parried such questions by emphasising how grateful they were to the Company for freeing the government from the onerous expense of setting up an administration in the interior of South Africa, and of building a railway and telegraph.

The forces behind the Company were so powerful, it enjoyed such obvious support and had such extensive possibilities to make further successful conquests that Lenin described the creation of the British South Africa Chartered Company as one of the major landmarks in world history after 1870.[24]

His First Military Campaign

The charter was secured, the company established and practically all the opposition in England had been overcome. Rhodes's hands were now free. Lobengula had no one to turn to with his complaints against Rhodes. British South Africa was now under Rhodes's control: in May 1890 he took office as Prime Minister of the Cape Colony and publicly declared that he had sought this position in order to speed up the occupation of the Zambezi basin. He came to power thanks to the support he enjoyed from Hofmeyr and the Cape Afrikaners. The Afrikaners might have been expected to resist the growth of British influence and Rhodes's occupation of new territory. But Rhodes had been able to play on and turn to his own advantage even those very slight contradictions which occasionally arose among the Afrikaners, in particular between the Cape Afrikaners, on the one hand, and the Transvaal Afrikaners, on the other.

It was at this time that Kruger, President of the Transvaal, resolved to build a railway line across Mozambique, in order to reduce his country's dependence on the British possessions that surrounded it. But this inevitably entailed the weakening of the Transvaal's trade and other links with the Cape Colony and to a certain extent hit at the profits of the growing Afrikaner bourgeoisie of Cape Town and the Colony as a whole.

Rhodes wasted no time in showing his sympathy with the Cape Afrikaners. In their turn they helped him secure the office of Prime Minister.

Now he was not merely rich, but also powerful. At long last, he could proceed with the annexation of that coveted territory which was so vaguely delineated in the charter. The question was: where was he to begin?

First of all Rhodes decided to send a representative of the Chartered Company to Bulawayo with full powers of attorney.

Ie needed more than a mere informant: he needed a man fully cognizant of Rhodes's own designs who could take decisions in the spot.

Rhodes's choice fell on Dr Jameson. Jameson, an exact contemporary of Rhodes, was at this time one of his closest associates. This was partly, perhaps, due to the fact that Rhodes, with his poor health, had faith in this medical man. But the main thing was that Jameson was always prepared to participate in any venture proposed by Rhodes.

In his student years, Jameson's "sensitivity to suffering made him faint at the sight of his first operation".[1] Yet when he came to South Africa, he was able to turn a blind eye even to an outbreak of small-pox among the African miners in the De Beers Company. Rumours about such an epidemic might, after all, have had an adverse effect on the value of the company shares... Later the orders of Dr Jameson led on more than one occasion to the spilling of innocent blood in South Africa.

Jameson's name is mentioned in all the history books in connection with the infamous Jameson Raid—an abortive attempt to seize the Transvaal in 1895—and the international scandal it provoked. He also earned himself a place in South African history as Rhodesia's administrator and in the beginning of the twentieth century as Prime Minister of the Cape Colony.

These were high offices, but many of his contemporaries would have foreborne to regard Jameson as a personality of any major significance. Matabele Thompson considered him Rhodes's hanger-on, a paltry figure, capitalizing on the poor health of his patron. Thompson believes it was a sorry day for Rhodes when he first made the acquaintance of this man. Admittedly Thompson had his own scores to settle with the doctor. In 1889 Jameson took his place in Bulawayo and concluded the diplomatic negotiations with Lobengula. All the glory became his, while Thompson remained in the shade.

When Rhodes dispatched Jameson to the Ndebele few people had heard of him. His political career still lay ahead of him, and we only mention him now because from this moment on all Rhodes's activities were inextricably linked with "Doctor Jim".

It was then, in late 1889, that Jameson carried out his first important assignment from Rhodes. He presented himself to Lobengula on October 17, before the official signing of the Char-

From right to left: Dr Jameson, John Moffat and the interpreter Doyle

ter, and started to seek the inkosi's consent to the entry of some of Rhodes's "gold prospectors" into his country. Lobengula already knew Jameson—he had first visited Bulawayo in April—and he greeted him with the words:

"What good is it telling me any more lies? I will not be satisfied unless I can see Rhodes himself."[2]

Through his interpreter Jameson replied that Rhodes could not come right then, but that he would definitely come at a later date. During the following months Jameson continued to seek this permission. He travelled back and forth to Bulawayo, pleading, cajoling and threatening. He tried to use his medical skills, and treated Lobengula for his gout.

As always, support was also forthcoming from the British authorities. In early February 1890 an embassy arrived in Bulawayo from Queen Victoria: three statuesque officers of the Royal Guard in their red uniforms, cuirasses and black busbies. They brought notification of the Charter, about Queen Victoria's support of the Company, and about the appointment of a British resident to Bulawayo.

But Lobengula remained stubborn. The talks dragged on into May 1890. Jameson became increasingly threatening, demanding that the Ndebele "allow the road".

"Well, King, as you will not confirm your promise and grant me the road, I shall bring my white impi and if necessary we shall fight."[3]

Lobengula's predicament is easy to appreciate. His young warriors clamoured for war. Their anger threatened to explode against the Inkosi himself. What was he to do? From the accounts of his emissaries Babayane and Mtshete, who had by now returned from London, it was evident what a formidable power stood against the Ndebele. Even without their descriptions he knew that any struggle was futile. The Zulus had been crushed ten years before and their army was much more powerful than his.

Should they retreat to the north, beyond the Zambezi River? The Ndebele had already discussed this possibility. It would be hard for them to move from their present home. They had lived here for fifty years, and their fathers only came here, to the north, after being savagely routed. How could Lobengula now order his people to leave their accustomed abode without even attempting to take up arms against these presumptuous whites—could he expect his warriors to swallow this? He himself had instilled in them a belief in their own invincibility. They would undoubtedly have rioted.

Thus Lobengula had no alternative but to trust in fortune, in what destiny would bring.

For the present he was forced to submit to Jameson. He realised that it would make precious little difference if he refused to "allow the road", anyway: in fact, it would probably only precipitate the clash.

HIS "PIONEERS"

While Jameson was still waiting for Lobengula's consent the Company was busy assembling armed units to penetrate deep into the Zambezi-Limpopo area to build forts and to consolidate their positions.

These units are believed to have been of two kinds. The Chartered Company had its own mounted police, numbering some five hundred men. In addition there were one hundred and seventy-eight "pioneers", who were to travel together with the police in the capacity of gold prospectors and prospective settlers. In actual fact there was little to distinguish the "pioneers" from the police. The rewards they were to receive were identical: during the march each man was to be given seven shillings and sixpence per day, and when they reached their destination, three thousand acres of land.

Their hopes and dreams were not, of course, pinned on this land, for all the thousands of acres they were promised. It is doubtful whether many of them planned to remain there for the rest of their lives. But Rhodes had inspired his "pioneers" with the same promise that has always been a strong lure to conquistadors: the promise of gold.

Rhodes promised each "pioneer" fifteen claims in which to prospect for gold. And who knows, maybe there beyond the Limpopo, they would find new deposits of diamonds, a new Kimberley...

The majority of these people did not have a penny of their own, but Rhodes promised them: "Stay with me, ... and I'll send you home a millionaire."[4]

Rhodes adroitly recruited men to his army, just as previously he had skilfully assembled his "window-dressing". Then he had selected aristocrats, but a different material was needed for his "pioneers", for the men who were to help divide up a foreign country, to conquer Africa and create the Empire. One writer records rapturously: "They were men such as Rhodes loved, of British blood in the main, of all classes, artisans and working miners rubbing shoulders with cadets of good families—some famous English cricketers among them—with a sprinkling of likely young Dutchmen—in the springtime of youth, and fired by the great adventure."[5] The journalist Newman described their march as "the victorious finish of a short but brilliant campaign".[6] It was only after several decades had passed that the first memoirs were published which shed any real light on the expedition.

One example is Sam Kemp's book: *Black Frontiers, Pioneer Adventures with Cecil Rhodes's Mounted Police in Africa.* I have already had occasion to quote these memoirs, with reference to the gold rush. They were published in 1932, forty-two years after the events they describe. Sam Kemp still remained a sworn admirer of Cecil Rhodes. Nevertheless, in his book the "pioeers" and their expedition are depicted in a far from idyllic light: "No questions concerning their past lives were asked of the pplicants," he writes. In other words, the same policy was followed as in the recruitment offices of the French Foreign Legion, n which any criminal could seek safe refuge. "Physical perfection alone was demanded, and man after man was refused because of some slight disability".[7] The doctors scrutinized each pplicant from their teeth to their fingernails. It is easy to imagine what sort of men these were, these men as Rhodes loved. Was t not such as these that Kipling had in mind when he wrote:

> Bear witness, once my comrades,
> What a hard-bit gang were we...[8]

Men with a not altogether untarnished past constituted a goodly portion of these "pioneer columns", at once felt quite at home and quickly came to accept one another.

Kemp himself writes that during their march the exhortation frequently rang out: "Volunteers wanted ... Please step forward."[9] But usually no one budged.

Many of those in the vanguard of the Chartered Company— Rhodes's "state"—had highly disreputable records, from the top-ranked officials to the rank-and-file "pioneers". Of course even the worst of these had not always been such scoundrels. But the men whose wanderlust sent them off from the shores of Europe in pursuit of wealth and adventure could not be expected to preserve their Romantic Visions intact for long in the rough and tumble of the South African Klondyke.

Let us take, for example, Sam Kemp. If we are to believe his book he was by no means the worst of Cecil Rhodes's acolytes. But even he can see nothing reprehensible in recalling that when he arrived in Natal as a callow youth of seventeen summers he was soon appointed overseer on the mines. The thrashing of "rebellious" black workers, and sometimes even putting them to death, was a routine matter for Kemp, and he makes no attempt to conceal it. And for all we know, even worse things went on about which he did forbear to write.

People flocked from Kimberley and Johannesburg to the assembly point in Mafeking. There they were allotted horses, guns and equipment, consisting of khaki shorts and woolen socks and a pair of thick cloth puttees to protect their legs from snakes.

Sam Kemp, a veteran of the "pioneer" trek. A photograph taken later in life

According to information first published in 1978 by the Zimbabwe historian Prof. Raymond Roberts, of the nearly two hundred "pioneers" more than half were aged between twenty and twenty-nine, the youngest was fifteen and the oldest fifty two. Of all these "pioneers" a mere 29, or 15 per cent, remained living in this area, in what was to become Rhodesia. The others died of malaria, were killed in battles or for one reason or another left the country during the next ten to twelve years.[10]

THE MARCH

When giving his consent to the entry of "gold prospectors" into the Zambezi-Limpopo territory Lobengula imposed the condition that they travel through Bulawayo. He wanted to see them with his own eyes.

This was quite unacceptable to Rhodes. This was not, of course, the handful of prospectors that Lobengula had been promised, but an entire armed troop. It comprised an armed police, "pioneers" and African labourers. Added to these were some two hundred Ngwato warriors. Their chief Kgama had been talked—or coerced—into detailing this unit to assist the "pioneers". The result was an army one thousand strong, if not stronger. Complete with cannons, machine-guns, not to mention rifles and revolvers. Directing them through Bulawayo would mean a military confrontation with the Ndebele. This would be inevitable: Lobengula would be powerless to restrain his warriors, even if he wished to.

In fact, this was Rhodes's original intention. In December 1889 he signed a contract with the Englishman Frank Johnson and the American Major Maurice Heany. They were instructed to form a unit of five hundred men for the seizure of Bulawayo. In the process they were to kill Lobengula, or at least to take him captive and with him as many indunas as possible. Rhodes believed that once he had taken hostages like these he need have no more fear of the Ndebele army.

A pretext was devised for this operation. Rhodes planned to put about a rumour that Lobengula had decided to attack the Ngwato, his neighbours, and that some preemptive strike was needed to save them.

They found a way how best to mollify public opinion—in

Britain and in the world at large. In Bulawayo Rhodes's troop were to liberate all the slaves. Johnson was informed that this step would at once shut the mouths of all the philanthropists and "put off Exeter Hall",[11] headquarters of the British Anti-Slavery Society.

Rhodes promised Johnson and Heany one hundred and fifty thousand pounds and a hundred thousand acres each. They had already begun to recruit men into their unit.

It seemed as though everything had been thought of, when suddenly Rhodes's plan collapsed. Its undoing was drunkenness. After a few drinks one day Heany spilt the beans to same missionaries, and news of the venture then reached Henry Loch, the new High Commissioner for South Africa, sent to take the place of Sir Hercules Robinson. Loch had absolutely no objections to the expansion of the British Empire, but in contrast to Robinson he had not yet become close to Rhodes and brought under his sway. Apprehensive about the excessively opportunist nature of this undertaking Loch forced Rhodes to go back on his plans, at least for the time being.

The truth about this planned escapade only came to light quite recently. Frank Johnson, whom Rhodes had charged with leading the attack on Bulawayo, decided to write his own memoirs. He called them *Great Days*. But no one was keen to publish them and they lay in manuscript in the Central African Archives in the then Rhodesia. In 1940 they were eventually published—but not in full: the chapter "I contract with Rhodes to Kidnap Lobengula" was omitted. The justification for this omission was that the Second World War was in progress: no fuel could be given to the Nazis' anti-British propaganda machine. But even after the war no one hastened to publish this chapter. Only in 1974 did a few lines from it appear in John Flint's book[12], and I myself finally came upon the full chapter in 1985, while working in the Zimbabwe National Archives.

What, we might wonder, if Frank Johnson, like most of Rhodes's accomplices, had never left any memoirs? The story would have been buried for ever, as so many other episodes of that time now lie buried in oblivion. And not only from that time...

Loch's wariness forced Rhodes to re-examine his scheme. He discussed several other possibilities with his advisers and in the end concluded that it would be better to head for Shona territory and keep away from Bulawayo. In general it would be better to show themselves as sparingly as possible to the Ndebele. They should skirt the Ndebele territory from the south and then the east, setting up military forts some two or three hundred miles to the east and north-east of Bulawayo and then, once this bridgehead had been established, further strategy could be decided.

Rhodes now appointed Frank Johnson at the head of the "pioneer" column. If he had only known then that this headstrong adventurer would later take up scribbling as a hobby! The "African Napoléon", like other politicians before and after, did not like his associates to have free tongues. He may not quite have followed the formula "Dead men tell no tales", but he was still careful not to let garrulous people get too close to him.

In accordance with this new plan the "pioneers" route was not only several hundred miles longer, but much more difficult too. The direct trail to Bulawayo had been blazed many years before, although Rudd and Matabele Thompson, as we have seen, still managed to lose their way and only survived by a miracle. But the new route which Rhodes plotted led through territory almost unknown to the whites. They were able to find some guides, however: Frederick Selous and Matabele Thompson. But even for them most of the journey was through unfamiliar territory.

The journey proved to be no mean ordeal for the "pioneers". The terrain was rough and perilous. They suffered from heat and thirst, and were attacked by a variety of diseases, known and unknown. Notable among these were blackwater fever, against which both quinine and rum proved powerless, and dysentery. Snakes were frequently encountered, including the deadly black mamba. Even the insects offered serious dangers: the ticks, bearing tickbite fever, and, as they moved nearer the Zambezi, the tsetse fly.

Everywhere they were pestered by gnats, flies and mosquitoes. For protection the pioneers set aside their razors and hairclippers, but this new growth of hair only encouraged parasites of another kind.

Their horses were attacked by lions. Once a herd of elephants trampled their camp, and the number of human casualties grew rapidly. Despite the severe prohibitions one man bathed in a river and failed to see a crocodile...

The "pioneers" also witnessed an invasion of locusts. In three days the veld for miles around was turned into desert.

In addition they had to traverse rocky terrain and ford rapid streams. Worse still, they had to haul heavily loaded wagons with them over these obstacles. The Africans who bore the brunt of this hard labour tried to run away, and the horses died of horse sickness.

For many this pursuit of possible wealth cost them their health others paid an even dearer price: their lives.

They also had to contend with the constant danger of coming face-to-face with Ndebele warriors... To Rhodes such an encounter between the "pioneers" and the Ndebele would only have meant a brief delay in the realisation of his plans. To each "pioneer", however, it meant the possibility of death. Their morale was constantly undermined by fear. Every night they outspanned, setting the wagons around their camp in a circle and erecting searchlights and machine-guns. To avoid possible outbreaks of panic the officers were careful not to talk in the presence of the others about sightings of Ndebele warriors.

Nothing could be further from the bravado with which Kipling's pioneers sing:

> *We've painted the islands vermilion,*
> *We've pearled on half-shares in the Bay,*
> *We've shouted on seven-ounce nuggets,*
> *We've starved on a Seedeboy's pay,*
> *We've laughed at the world as we found it,—*
> *Its women and cities and men—*
> *From Sayyid Burgash in a tantrum*
> *To the smoke-reddened eyes of Loben,*
>   *(Dear boys!)*
> *We've a little account with Loben.*[13]

Their "little account" with Loben—Lobengula—might have been repaid with considerable interest had not these same men, the bearers of the white man's burden, succeeded in sending the Ndebele king to an early grave.

The settling of this "account", the northwards trek and the land of the Ndebele were things the "pioneers" would never forget. The "pioneers" that survived, that is.

The fate of the "pioneers" was scarcely an enviable one. It s doubtful whether any of them did in fact become millionaires. 'ew even found simple material comfort. So much of their lives vas taken up by digging this foreign soil: almost daily, from the ery beginning of the march, they had to dig graves and then, fter they arrived, they had to erect forts and strengthen their efences.

"It took a smile from Lady Luck many times to pull one hrough. Sooner or later Lady Luck was sure to frown instead f smile, and that was the end. Burial-parties night after night— o commonplace did they become on that long trek north that hey seemed a part of routine and were ignored, forgotten in five ninutes."[14] But the Africans, the servants and those who carried he equipment, were buried on the spot, where death had over- aken them, and without any ceremony.

The hardships of the journey reduced the kit they had been ssued to rags. The feet suffered most: their boots soon fell to ieces.

A priest dying of blackwater fever told the doctor: "I want to ie with my boots on." But his modest request was not granted: omeone removed these coveted boots while he was still suffering is death agony... After describing this melancholy episode, Sam Kemp adds: "That was not to insult the poor fellow or to deny im his last wish, the troopers actually wanted his boots."[15]

Once a lieutenant disappeared—one of those many officers vhom Rhodes's agents had recruited from the British army to ake command of his police and the "pioneers". The lieutenant vas very unpopular as a pedant and martinet. Lady Luck turned he other way for a moment, and someone simply shot him during hunting expedition. The culprit was never found. Rhodes's roopers now whispered to one another: "Wonder who's got his oots?"[16] Meanwhile, in books and articles published at the ime it was stated that the trek was completed "without the loss f a single life".[17]

In fact more accidents and misfortunes probably took place nce the "pioneers" started to settle down in those parts of the ew country they had selected for their forts. This is a familiar attern: the hardships become less, people drop their defences, nd at once some lose their strength, their nerve or their health. Yet the cost of the trek is not lessened by taking into account

The "pioneers" transporting a Maxim machine-gun. A contemporary
sketch

where the men died—whether on the march or at a halt. It was a
cost measured in human life.

For his part, when Lobengula learnt what Rhodes's "small
group of 'gold prospectors'" actually comprised, he was stunned
He had of course guessed that Rhodes would send more than

the ten men he had promised, but not an entire troop, complete with artillery!... The main condition had not been met: this army was marching far from Bulawayo, careful not to show themselves to Lobengula. The inkosi exclaimed in indignation:

"Why, if you say I have given you the whole country, do you come in like thieves to steal it; if it is really yours you do not need to steal in?"[18]

In a desperate attempt to move the conscience of the British, Lobengula dispatched another embassy. Mtshete, one of the two indunas who had visited Queen Victoria, now travelled to Cape Town, to the High Commissioner Henry Loch.

Mtshete repeatedly insisted that the Rudd "concession" had been obtained by fraud. It had no legal force, all the more so since the Ndebele had refused the thousand rifles which featured in the agreement as payment for the "concession". Mtshete complained that Rhodes, not content with searching for gold in one specially assigned area, now wished to "devour" the entire nation of the Ndebele. Mtshete described John Moffat, who had been appointed British resident in Bulawayo, as Rhodes's man.

None of this had the slightest effect on Loch. He brought Rhodes himself in on the discussions with Mtshete. While the Mtshete embassy was still on the road, Loch had written to Lobengula that he, in his capacity as British High Commissioner for South Africa, had already given his approval to the dispatching of forces by the Chartered Company, "to guard your country against encroachments" and that they came as friends "who desire only your good".

When the "pioneers" reached the Macloutsie River, on the boundaries of Ndebele territory, the Ndebele were able to see at first hand how many "friends" they had. Lobengula sent the pioneer commanders a letter full of irony: "Why were so many warriors at Macloutsie? Had the King committed any fault, or had any white man been killed, or had the white men lost anything that they were looking for?"

Jameson, who was marching with the "pioneers", replied that "the soldiers were not directed against Lobengula but were merely an escort for protection on the way to Mashonaland by the road the king had approved".[19]

Lobengula denied that he had ever given any such approval.

Nevertheless he restrained his own warriors from attacking the "pioneers".

By mid-September 1890 the "pioneers" had built four forts in Shona territory, far to the east of Bulawayo. Upon entering this territory they established their first fortified base, Fort Tuli, and as they moved further ahead, they set up three more. The southernmost of these they called Fort Victoria, in honour of the Queen, the second Fort Charter, to glorify their own Chartered Company, and the northernmost Fort Salisbury, after the then British Prime Minister.

Fort Salisbury thus became the final point on the trek. Subsequently it was to be the main city and administrative centre of Rhodesia (today this is Harare, capital of the Republic of Zimbabwe). The Company's flag was first raised there on September 12, 1890. Thereafter that date was celebrated as the day of Rhodesia's foundation. When some forty-odd years later the veterans of the conquest of Rhodesia gathered together in a London restaurant to remember the days of past glory, the hero of the occasion was E. C. Tyndale Biscoe, the man who had raised the flag.

The most varied rumours began, of course, to spread among the Shona about the strangers—"white people without knees", as they were called because their knees were covered up with trousers.

A prediction attributed to the Prophet Chaminuka gained wide currency: "There shall come from the sea a race of knee-less white men who will build white houses throughout the land. They will bring with them a mighty boulder (this is what Chaminuka called the locomotive and carriages, about which they had heard—A. D.) such as had never been seen before. It will ride with such force that no-one will be able to stop it, or divert it from its course. These kneeless people will rule the land with an iron fist for many years. Be that as it may, the ancestor spirits will restore the land back into the hands of their progeny, not permitting foreigners to rule the land forever."[20]

THE NEW ELDORADO

With the "pioneer" trek the third round in the scramble for the riches of Africa had begun. First the diamond fever of

Kimberley, then the Transvaal gold rush, now the fabulous gold deposits of the Zambezi-Limpopo area. Dr Jameson, who had led the "pioneer" column into the new territory, declared for all to hear that in its wealth in gold Mashonaland was worth fifty Rands. Jameson's was a voice of authority: he was the highest representative of the Company in the region, later to become the Chief Magistrate.

This was nothing compared to the excitement of the British press. Fleet Street decorated the new territory with the most splendid metaphors, of which the "New Eldorado" was by no means the most florid. ". . .Matabeleland is like Canaan",[21] wrote *The Times*, normally so restrained. "The Land of Ophir", chorused the *Pall Mall Gazette*. It assured its readers that in a few years' time they would see the image of Queen Victoria in the gold with which Solomon had adorned his throne.

At the end of 1890 the Chartered Company published its "Memorandum of the Terms and Conditions upon which Persons are permitted to prospect for Minerals and Metals in Mashonaland".

"Any person", stated the first paragraph, "may take out a licence on binding himself in writing to obey the Laws of the Company and to assist in the defence and maintenance of Law and Order, if called upon to do so by the Company."[22] Each licence-holder, continued the memorandum, gained the right to one alluvial claim measuring one hundred and fifty feet by one hundred and fifty feet, and ten claims, each measuring one hundred and fifty by four hundred feet—in the areas where gold-bearing veins were found. He was to work each claim on a basis of parity with the Chartered Company, in other words he had to surrender half his profit. The licence fee was ten shillings per month.

Thus began the partitioning of the mineral wealth of Mashonaland. Rhodes did not dare encroach on the land inhabited by the Ndebele, presumably reasoning that everything had to be done in gradual stages.

The Company threw open the doors of this new country not only to gold prospectors but also to settlers. Rhodes declared that land for ten thousand farms had been set aside for Europeans. The Company's representatives lured colonists with talk of an abundance of "native labour" and assured them that "the reception given to the pioneers in the populous region occupied by the Mashonas and the Makalakas was excellent".[23]

The appeal to people to take up permanent residence in the depths of Africa did not have an immediate response. But the lure of gold claims worked with instantaneous effect. An entire army of prospectors seemed to rise like mushrooms from the ground, and dispersed through the land in their feverish hunt for the yellow metal.

The most colourful characters now started appearing on the roads of the region: these ranged from indigent tatterdemalions, who had never known good fortune, to swells who in the very recent past had frequented the expensive bars of Kimberley and Johannesburg, where champagne had flowed for them in rivers.

It would seem that South Africa had so recently succumbed to diamond and gold fever, yet enough time had passed for many men to taste both the sweetness of success and then the bitterness of failure and bankruptcy. Their wealth slipped away from them just as quickly as they had acquired it. "Where, indeed, are the Dicks, Toms and Harries, the fortunates and the millionaires of those days? Nobody, of course, will be able to give a complete answer; but I came across them bit by bit in Mashonaland. . . They are in flannel shirts, doing all sorts of hard work, on harder fare, and I met them at every town, almost every outspan. How it does change them!" wrote one eye-witness in 1892. In the barman of a roadside inn he recognized the former director of several companies, a once successful broker. All that survived of his erstwhile glory were the gold frames of his eyeglasses. The same author encountered another: two years before he had raised hell in the best hotel in Johannesburg because a waiter had served him champagne in a dirty goblet.

" 'You will expect me to lap dirty water out of a pannikin next', he said to the shrinking waiter, and I heard him and admired, for was he not the master of £200,000? Truly he had a right to expect his glass to be like crystal, and his table linen to vie with the driven snow!"

But in Mashonaland this same upstart *bon viveur,* who had in the meantime been overtaken by ruin, was indeed reduced to lapping dirty water out of a pannikin, and eating in a comparable fashion. He was clad in filthy rags and had not washed for six weeks. "He had had the fever, and every time he washed he had a relapse. So he gave up washing. I never saw a dirtier face. It is wonderful how the dirt hung on without flaking off".[24]

In those parts it was nothing unusual to find English peers of the realm. Not only those like Randolph Churchill, who came here on a reconnaissance mission with his mining engineer, but men who rolled up their sleeves and set to work digging in the African soil for the gold which their titled ancestors had failed to bequeath them. It is hard to imagine an English lord going barefoot, but this was how they found Lord Henry Paulet. His companion, the son of Baronet Sir John Swinburne, was just as poorly attired.

An Old Etonian served as sergeant in the Company's troop. Behind nondescript names like Johnson and Smith there were frequently concealed the scions of the most illustrious houses of Great Britain, those younger sons waiting for their lucky hour, about whom Vassily Shulgin was in such raptures.

The magnetic pull of this chimerical gold must have been immensely powerful, for men willingly subjected themselves to ordeals that far outshadowed anything endured by the diggers in the Transvaal and Kimberley. For a start it was so much harder to get here. All the main European settlements were hundreds of miles away.

"When a man has got as far as Victoria, it seems to him that he has arrived at the end of the world. Civilization is thousands of miles away..." The newcomers felt "like a Rip van Winkel or Robinson Crusoe".[25] There was nothing familiar before their eyes. Everything was strange, alien, incomprehensible—the people, the vegetation, the animals. The sun burned like a magnifying glass. There was no shelter, unless they crawled beneath their wagons. In rocky gorges or when crossing mountain rivers they had to unload and reload their wagons, beneath the blazing sun, time and time again, otherwise they would never get across.

The best part of their provisions was the tinned food. They prepared a dessert from maize meal, cocoa and sugar that, for some reason or other, they called Charlotte à la Russe. But most of them had no opportunity to enjoy such "delicacies"; their diet was little better than offal.

It was about 1700 miles to the Cape ports, and Mashonaland itself had no roads and no bridges across its many little rivers. The transport of provisions and other goods from the coast to the Company's forts cost £70 per ton, and during the rainy season—several months a year—the country was cut off altogether from the rest of the world.

For those who were ruined it was hard to get themselves out of this woe-begone territory: it was very far to the coast and transportation was desperately expensive. The Company turned this circumstance to its advantage, to cut its own costs. In 1891 the police force was almost entirely restaffed with volunteers who had come as prospectors and gone bankrupt. They had no alternative than to hire themselves out to the Company and safeguard its interests for a miserly wage.

The unaccustomed climate, the innumerable hardships and, most particularly, the fever took their toll of dozens of men. But this did not stem the flood of prospectors. By the end of 1891 there were between 1500 and 1700 whites in Shona territory. They streamed in daily, from all over the world. Americans called the territory "Cecil Rhodes's Shop".

On rare occasions Rhodes himself could be seen in the region. Clad in his inevitable pale flannel trousers, pepper-and-salt jacket and felt hat with its brim turned down, he would ride horseback behind the carriage bearing Jameson and Selous. His love of horse-riding remained with him always, although he never mastered the art of good horsemanship and was always a sloppy rider. The only thing that distinguished him from most of the prospectors was his smooth-shaven cheeks. Among the European inhabitants of this region in those days this was a clear sign of prosperity and often of a higher social class.

THE DISAPPOINTMENTS COMMENCE

We can assume that Rhodes must have been well aware of the true state of affairs in his empire. The "pioneers", however, were to suffer many disappointments. The Chartered Company boasted of its forts as major settlements, practically new centres of European civilization. At the end of 1892 an eyewitness wrote: "I, who had read the glowing accounts which have appeared in the English and South African journals, descriptive of Salisbury, xpected much. Had I not read of English, Wesleyan, Roman Catholic, and Presbyterian churches? Of great hotels, a hospital and many stores?"[26] But, as the writer found out, there were only our hundred people in Salisbury. And in Fort Charter there were only five: a lieutenant, a sergeant, two troopers and one civilian.

An idea of the first years of "pioneer" life can be gained from the exhibits in the present-day Zimbabwe National Museum—the weapons, the clothing and the household utensils. Further information can be gained from the early newspapers collected in the National Archives of Zimbabwe. There one can see the very first of these, the handwritten *Nugget*. Its first issue came out in Fort Victoria on November 11, 1890. The weekly *Mashonaland Herald,* also hand-written, started publication in Fort Salisbury on Saturday June 27, 1891. It cost one shilling, but the publisher, who distributed it himself, sometimes agreed to take marmelade or candles instead of money, and once even an old spade. Soon, in October 1892, a typographically printed newspaper started publication. It was published in Salisbury, and alongside news articles, carried a great number of classified advertisements. It was called the *Rhodesian Herald.* Thus was Rhodes's name immortalized, although the country itself only became officially known as Rhodesia three years later.

All the same these forts had little in common with citadels of culture. The troopers in the local garrisons were more interested in liquor. A bottle of whisky cost forty shillings: in comparison we can point out that a blanket, bought in Kimberley for five shillings, here served as a month's wages for an African labourer.

Any newcomer would be asked by nine out of ten old-timers in Salisbury: "Got any whisky?"

The fever raged unchecked, and quinine was in very short supply. People would pay up to a hundred pounds for a single ounce of this life-saving medicine.

Admittedly, some people could do without quinine: "My stomach won't hold guy-nyne, but it sucks up whisky like a sponge. Give me a bottle of whisky a day and I'll defy the fever".[27]

The gold-diggers did not mix with the local Africans and held the lowest opinion of them:

"Give a Mashona plenty of Kaffir beer, plenty of rice, several wives, and an odd fowl or two, and he wants nothing more".[2]

Yet how many of the prospectors themselves aspired towards the heights of culture and achievements of the intellect? For Kaffir beer, read brandy or champagne, for rice—five-course meals, for wives—mistresses, and they could be describing themselves. . .

The "pioneers" considered the Shona slow-witted and unskilful. Of course the Shona had great difficulty ascertaining what the Europeans really wanted from them. For many this was their first encounter with white men, and they understood them far less than did the Africans in the Cape and the Transvaal. We might wonder how quickly the Europeans would have understood what was required of them, if the tables had been turned, and they had been required to carry out strange and unfamiliar orders from the Shona. It is a mark of ignorance to condemn the customs and behaviour of another people—after all, this is so much easier than trying to understand them. The new settlers regarded their arrogant racism as the natural concomitant of the "high intelligence" of their race.

In actual fact this "intelligence" was usually manifested in rather mundane ways, such as their attempts to palm off matches with broken heads on Shona tribesmen in barter deals. Or by jesting, when asked to pay in shillings, that "the woman who made the shillings was dead",[29] or by making the "natives" work for an entire month for just one blanket as payment. Or by abducting young Shona girls, regarding this as the most natural thing in the world. Their reasoning was that the Shona had already been taught to accept such treatment by their neighbours the Ndebele. "The Mashonas are so long accustomed to have their women and goods taken from them by force, that if a European were to abduct a dusky maiden, her departure would be considered as rather hard lines on her husband".[30]

The men in the Company's strongholds, its forts, led a dreary garrison life. Their occupations included drinking, gambling and, occasionally, hunting. They entertained themselves with practical jokes, usually coarse and often very cruel. This went on not only in Salisbury, Charter and Victoria, but also in what should have been the most lively place—Tuli, at the entrance into the Zambezi-Limpopo highveld.

"Tuli can never be called a lively place and when I was there found that every hour had at least a hundred and twenty minutes. It is always terribly hot at Tuli, and the men there swore horribly at everything, and no wonder. They swore at the Cape brandy, at the rations, at the work, at the commanding officer, the Commissariat officer, and most of all at the Chartered Company. They had no furniture, poor food, nothing much to read, and led an uncomfortable, shiftless, aimless sort of life."[31]

Even in the comparatively populous town of Salisbury there were barely five women to the four hundred men. "It must be confessed that men by themselves do not constitute a lively community. Without the women we are very dull dogs indeed, and therefore it is that Salisbury was as dull as a rusty knife."[32]

The exotic African life is reflected in the sort of jokes and anecdotes that circulated. These included the inevitable stories about the people whose land the pioneers now occupied. About how Lobengula's wives were chosen: the girls were lined up and he selected those whose bodily profiles extended farthest both east and west. Or about how cannibal tribes were squeamish about eating the flesh of white men, regarding it as too salty.[33]

Nor was their life particularly transfigured by ennobling sentiments of camaraderie. An admired maxim with the soldiers and the Company's officers went as follows: "Every man for himself and Providence for us all".[34]

What, we might ask, did these men hold sacred? Did they have certain idols they looked up to? It would seem they did. If the blacks had their king and tyrant, Lobengula, we troopers also had ours. Cecil John Rhodes, of course. It was for him we had undertaken this long, dangerous trek, it was his name which magically held the troopers together kept them from mutinying and deserting. It was odd the feeling the troopers had for Cecil Rhodes. Many of them had never seen him and knew him only by reputation, yet they seemed to understand him as a man of heroic visions.

"Heroic visions—that was the answer. In the name of his visions, in Rhodes's dream of a great empire subdued, explored, and civilized, connected by bands of steel, we troopers found our goal. In a strange, abstract way we admired and loved that silent man ... In return, it might be noted, Cecil John Rhodes loved his troopers ..."[35]

Such are the fond reminiscences of one trooper, some fou and a half decades later. But he fails to explain why he, aft serving eighteen months with Rhodes's "beloved" troopers, le their ranks and departed forever from this new "Canaan", turnin his back on the three thousand acres granted him and on every thing he had been promised. Yet Rhodes had promised him, i person, that he would make him a millionaire.

Alas, there were many disappointments in store for those wh were seduced by the euphoric publicity in the newspapers int abandoning their own lives and businesses for an uncertain futur here, deep in the African continent.

By now there was a growing suspicion in this "land of Ophir" "England's El Dorado of Africa", that no one had in fact discov ered any gold at all. Even in the Salisbury region, at the centr of the Company's operations, where its activities should hav been most vigorous, there were no signs even of any prospecting

Something seemed to be wrong. It was not that the Compan had deceived the public with its advertising. Rhodes had pursue that mistaken policy in all good faith. But in the end he hac deceived himself. He had every ground to believe that there wa gold in the region, as attested to by the ancient mine workings and legends, going back to the Middle Ages, recorded by the Por tuguese conquistadors. It is most unlikely that Rhodes believec the "pioneers" would really find fifty times as much gold here a in the Transvaal: he let Jameson preach this to the gullible. Bu we can be sure that he did believe there was some gold in th region, and that they would certainly find considerable deposits if not a second Rand.

But very little gold was found—little by comparison not only with the ridiculous prophecies of the press, but even with the hopes of Rhodes and his associates. Matters could have turnec nasty, with a scandal flaring up through all Britain and al Europe. If there was no gold there would be accusations of bluf and fraud.

Rhodes needed a new sensation, some way of stirring up fresh excitement about his new creation. Hence his delight when he learnt that Lord Randolph Churchill had decided to visit his empire and write a large series of articles from it for the British public.

The Churchill family had developed close links with South frica, starting with Randolph (or perhaps with his wife, who upposedly had made a great impression on Lobengula's ambas-dors during their audience with Queen Victoria).

Randolph Churchill's voice was one that his fellow-Britons eeded most closely. This was thanks not so much to his politi-al authority—although he had held the high offices of Chan-ellor of the Exchequer and Secretary of State for India—as to is eccentricity. It was said that his cherished dream was the ffice which his son was to hold twice in the twentieth century: ae position of Prime Minister of Great Britain. But Randolph locked his own political advancement: while the son's eccen-icity provoked an amazement, often closely akin to respect, in he British public, the father's antics were seen only as scandal-us. Who knows: perhaps Winston learnt from his father's aistakes?

One way or another, the name Randolph Churchill always ttracted attention. It was for this reason that the London news-aper *Daily Graphic* was prepared to offer him one hundred ounds for each piece he sent from Cecil Rhodes's empire. This vorked out at 1s 9p per word—an unheard-of rate at the time. he proprietors of this influential paper hoped that Churchill vould dazzle and thrill their readers with his extravagant impres-ions and views.

Rhodes of course hoped that these articles would rebound o his benefit. He was quite justified in this hope, for Churchill vas a shareholder in the Chartered Company.

Cecil arranged a meeting with Churchill, and in February 891 in a room at a fashionable London hotel they got together o study the map of Africa and plan Randolph's route. *The Times* of February 28 carried a report that "Lord Randolph Churchill has definitely decided to visit Mashonaland in the pring"[36] and that his journey was expected to be one of the most memorable events of the entire year.

Churchill, on the other hand, hoped that this journey would assist him in his career. He agreed to an interview with the journal *South Africa*, the mouthpiece of Rhodes and other South African nillionaires, and significantly hinted that the purpose of his ourney extended far beyond the usual hunting expedition for aristocrats and sportsmen. Among other things, Randolph Chur-

205

chill cherished hopes of rectifying his own financial problems wit
this journey. His finances were in dire straits, although he wa
married to the daughter of an American millionaire. It woul
be very hard to set matters right with the honorarium from
his newspaper, for all that it was extremely generous. So Chur
chill, succumbing to the general epidemic, lugged along with h
baggage a special machine, only recently invented, for the extrac
tion of gold. In addition, he set up his own gold-prospecting an
mining company. Its members comprised, besides himself, his clos
relatives and several financiers, newspaper publishers and militar
men. It was they who subsidized Churchill's trip, giving hir
£16,000. He also took with him an expert on gold deposits, th
American mining engineer Henry Perkins.

Churchill was joined on his departure from London for South
Africa by Alfred Beit and another close associate of Rhodes's: the
engineer Charles Metcalfe. "Both, in a way, were unofficial mem
bers of the Churchill expedition", writes Brian Roberts in hi
book *Churchills in Africa,* "but nobody wished to emphasize th
Rhodes connection". Nevertheless, he continues, "that Cecil Rho
des had great hopes of Lord Randolph's visit there can be n
doubt".[37]

To be sure, Churchill sang Rhodes's praises, describing him a
a genius. Once he had established fairly close relations with Rho
des, Beit and certain other magnates of the Transvaal gol
industry, Churchill was able to find profitable ways to invest hi
own family's capital and that of his friends. He proudly wrot
from Johannesburg about this to his son, the seventeen-year-ol
Winston. It was even rumoured that he had discussed the possi
bility of finding Winston a good job in the Transvaal gold busi
ness. Indeed, why not? If the Prime Minister Lord Salisbury'
son could serve under Cecil Rhodes, was this so ignominious fo
the son of Lord Churchill?

A few years later Winston did in fact visit these parts, as di
Randolph's sister, Lady Sarah. Winston never worked in any o
Rhodes's companies, but he still assisted Rhodes's designs by
taking part in the Anglo-Boer War that Rhodes had prepared
He was a military correspondent, was taken prisoner and made
a daring escape: this was the beginning of his illustrious career
At one point his aunt also found herself in the very thick o
battle.

Thus before long the entire Churchill family had acquired a personal interest in the career of Cecil Rhodes. But his first devotee—Randolph—did Rhodes immeasurably more harm than good. This can be attributed in part to Churchill's uneven character, his lack of restraint, his extreme and ill-considered views.

It all began with his pronouncements about the Afrikaners. Things in South Africa could have turned out very differently, he asserted, if the good Lord had given the Afrikaner the tiniest bit of common sense. He once expressed a wish to see a typical Afrikaner farm. When they took him to one such homestead the farmer's wife, who had been forewarned, came out to welcome the "English Lord". The Lord's reaction was most unexpected. An eyewitness records: "Perhaps the old lady's figure was not up to his ideal of the female form divine. I do not know. Anyway one glance was enough. 'Ugh! go on, go on, get away! drive off,' shouted his Lordship, as he thumped the driver in the back. 'Awful people! drive on! get along! I won't stay here'!"[38]

It is hard to see the Afrikaners forgiving Churchill an affront like that. For many years Rhodes had laboured to win their friendship for England, only to receive such a setback. He now had to deal with the consequences of Churchill's gibes and antics, and try to mend the bridges his Lordship had destroyed.

Churchill also contrived somehow to offend certain of the gold barons. Each of them longed for marks of attention from this distinguished aristocrat, but His Lordship confused their names and, after dining with one of them, would say to him the following day:

"Let me see, have I met you before?"[39]

The newspapers of England and South Africa were full of these and similar stories, some authentic, others fictitious. Churchill proved a most fertile source of anecdotes. After his first few *faux pas* practically his every word was met with ridicule or shouts of protest.

His journey through the Zambezi-Limpopo area was no different. Churchill took with him the young South African journalist James Percy Fitzpatrick, believing that his colleague would paint the expedition in the most flattering colours. Fitzpatrick did indeed publish a small booklet, entitled *Through Masho-*

naland with Pick and Pen, but in it Churchill is savagely lampooned.

He informs his readers how Churchill sent Lobengula a special bath chair, designed to assist entry into the water. "It was a happy thought", comments Fitzpatrick, "and would complete Lord Randolph's South African education." Then, he records, Churchill wanted to return from Mashonaland via Bulawayo, but changed his mind when he recalled that Lobengula exercised "kingly rights in regard to the life and death of strangers within his gates".[40]

Horrified by the labour intensity of diamond mining in Kimberley, Churchill berated the fair sex for their vanity, as their passion for adorning themselves with jewels was the cause of this exhausting toil. In his opinion, whomever men might be descended from it is clear that women are descended from apes.

As might be expected this provoked a flood of indignant letters from his female readers.

The journey of the former Chancellor of the Exchequer was now ridiculed in music-hall songs in England. Eventually Churchill's wife had to seek the intervention of Joseph Chamberlain to suppress the most audacious of these songs.

Of course Rhodes had not expected events to take such a turn. Far from bringing the expected benefits, Churchill's expedition had in fact damaged Rhodes's cause.

As he visited the Chartered Company's forts and travelled across its domain, Churchill somehow failed to see the radiant pictures Rhodes had painted for him when they planned this journey together in London. What struck Churchill most was that everything was so expensive. In Fort Salisbury he decided to sell part of his equipment, so as not to have to haul it back with him, and was astonished to discover he could sell his cotton shirt for three and a half times as much as he had paid for it in London. The other prices were of the same order. "During this sale I realized with some regret," he notes, "that a large and well-conducted trading expedition into this country would have been a far more profitable speculation than gold prospecting."[41]

Perhaps the most important disappointment of the expedition was furnished by Churchill's mining engineer, who surveyed

he whole of Mashonaland in vain and came to the conclusion
hat there were no significant deposits of gold anywhere in the
egion. His findings seemed convincing to Churchill and he
wrote that "Mashonaland ... is neither Arcadia nor an El Dorado".[42]

Rhodes was unable to conceal his irritation. He accompanied
Churchill on his travels through Mashonaland, but when he
saw that he could not curb his Lordship's antics, he abruptly departed, leaving Churchill to make the long return journey without
him. Churchill was quite incensed, but was forced to swallow his
rage.

Admittedly he did forgive Rhodes subsequently. He even stayed
with him for a few days in Cape Town. The English Lord had
every reason to regain his good humour. Although relations between himself and the Afrikaners, and their President Kruger,
were, to put it mildly, less than cordial, he had nonetheless purchased a few gold claims on his return journey through the
Transvaal, and these claims proved to be so rich that they were
soon valued at £70,000.[43] This was the foundation for the Churchill family's close interests in South Africa.

This expedition caused Rhodes many unpleasant moments,
although Churchill's articles[44] did not have any serious influence: most often, the public looked to them for entertainment rather
than information. In addition, Churchill's political opponents
and rivals availed themselves of every opportunity to discredit
him, citing his *faux pas* and his illness, about which rumours had
started to circulate. Soon he was struck down by palsy, a consequence of syphilis, and then death. He lived less than half the
span of years allotted to his son Winston.

Of course, the Churchill expedition and its echoes were merely
one episode in the Company's early history. But it was an indica-
tive episode, and a cause of alarm for Rhodes.

The history of the Chartered Company was only beginning.
Rhodes's creation was to experience many more turns of fortune.
It was then, in the early 1890s, that it showed unmistakable signs
of its first crisis.

On the stock market faith in the enterprise began to waver.
It was well known that the trek made by the "pioneers" and
police had cost Rhodes about three hundred thousand pounds.
Added to this were the construction and maintenance of the forts,

the administration, the Company's armed forces, construction of the railway and the telegraph. By July 1891, after approximately one year, the Company's expenses had amounted to £700,000. Rhodes was forced to seek subsidies from De Beers and Gold Fields. Barnato, Beit and other colleagues in the gold and diamond business in Kimberley and the Transvaal were prepared to accommodate him, but this support had its limits. Even at the top of the Chartered Company Rhodes now came across bewilderment and anxiety on the part of the other directors.

People started to talk about Jameson's incompetence after he had taken change of the Company's administration in the Zambezi-Limpopo area in 1891. Rhodes supported him with the full weight of his authority. He would say: "Jameson never makes a mistake".

Meanwhile Rhodes telegraphed to Jameson: "Your business is to administer the country as to which I have nothing to do but merely say 'yes' if you take the trouble to ask me."[45]

Men who worked alongside Rhodes frequently praised him for his ability to concentrate on the most important thing and to leave everything else in the hands of assistants, whom he trusted to do the job without interference or petty supervision. This was precisely how he behaved with Jameson. Unfortunately, however, the doctor had had no experience in the complex matter of running an entire country. His mistakes received wide publicity, and Rhodes could not shield him altogether from criticism.

The Company's primary weakness was the ambivalence of its position. No one was entirely certain what exactly the Company possessed or what its rights were. "The position of the Chartered Company of South Africa is not very clear," admitted *The Times* in 1890.[46]

The same year that Churchill carried out his tour of inspection another event took place which to this day has never been satisfactorily explained.

In November 1891 Lobengula concluded an agreement on land rights with the German entrepreneur Eduard Lippert. It stated that for an initial payment of one thousand pounds and then five hundred pounds a year Lippert was granted for a period of a hundred years the right to establish farms in the ter ritory of the Ndebele and the Shona, to use grazing land and even to build towns.

Just like the "Rudd concession" this agreement was not a bona fide legal instrument. The signatories interpreted its text in totally different ways. The Ndebele, who had no private ownership of land, did not have the slightest comprehension about the transfer of land rights. Lobengula believed he was giving Lippert the chance to build dwellings and to graze cattle in free land, but on no account to take possession of this land.

Furthermore, Lobengula was no longer capable of checking and double-checking the possible interpretations of an agreement, as he had done with the "Rudd concession". Evidently the most important thing that mattered to him was that the Germans who concluded this agreement should act against the British. He was desperately searching for a way out of the predicament: declaration of war, he realized, was clearly a lost cause. He could not lead his people across the Zambezi. All that remained for him to do was to make repeated attempts to sow dissension in the ranks of the enemy. Of course Lobengula knew about the Anglo-German contradictions in Africa, and, like a drowning man clutching at a straw, he seized this opportunity to play on the conflict.

But Lobengula's plans to deal Rhodes this blow foundered, as had his embassy to the "White Queen" and many other undertakings. It was hard, virtually impossible in fact, for him to understand the workings of European colonial politics: only chance, a miracle, could help him and his people now. But Rhodes and the British authorities carefully preempted any such undesirable "miracles".

The British government, learning of this new threat to the Chartered Company, swiftly came to its assistance. The Colonial Secretary, Lord Knutsford, telegraphed the High Commissioner for South Africa, Loch, that the Lippert agreement was not to be recognized, and that Lippert himself was to be arrested if he set foot in Mashonaland.

In those days, and for a long time thereafter, it was generally accepted that Lippert had zealously tried to secure the support of the German government, but to no avail. The German press, above all Bismarck's *Neueste Nachrichten* and the *Hamburgischer*

Correspondent criticized Chancellor Caprivi's government for this lapse.

But Lippert himself must have realized right from the start that he would never be able to use the agreement, and he made a deal with Rhodes's group. He decided to resell the agreement to Lord Rothschild, and Lord Rothschild ceded the right to buy it to the Chartered Company. All this took place before November 17—the date of the signing ceremony between Lobengula and Lippert. In other words, when the inkosi placed his "X" on the document, the concession had already been sold to Rhodes. The Colonial Secretary Knutsford and the High Commissioner Loch gave their approval to the re-sale of this new "concession".

One of the newspapers published a caricature: bending over Rhodes and Lippert, Loch gives them his blessing.

When he placed his "X" on the "concession" Lobengula could not have suspected that he was delivering yet another powerful weapon into the hands of his most dangerous enemy.

All this is reasonably clear. What is not so clear is whether the entire story of the Lippert concession had not been planned in advance by Rhodes. Lippert's action came at a most opportune moment. Rhodes's critics were instantly deprived of their major argument—that if Rhodes did have any rights these extended only to the natural resources below the ground, and not to the land itself.

Rhodes himself had no hopes of acquiring these "rights" from Lobengula. The inkosi had only agreed to grant them to Lippert because the German posed as Cecil Rhodes's sworn enemy.

Does this not suggest that the entire affair was orchestrated by Rhodes? All the more so when we realize that Lippert was a first cousin to Beit, Cecil Rhodes's close friend, associate and main adviser. Historians have already posed this question, but as yet it remains unanswered. Rhodes took the secret with him to the grave, along with a number of others, even more important.

The acquisition of this "land concession" was equated by Rhodes to increasing the capital of the Chartered Company by a million pounds. He issued more shares for this immense sum and acquired the opportunity to engage in new speculative ventures on the stock market and yet again to defraud his rank-and-file shareholders.

There was a danger of all these machinations inflating the scandal that had already grown up around the Chartered Company. A radical way out had to be found. In other words, Rhodes could waste no time with the next stage in consolidating his hold on the Zambezi-Limpopo highveld.

And the First War

It is safe to assume that a war against the Ndebele had figured in Rhodes's designs for a long time. Rhodes's policies should have indicated this quite clearly. Nonetheless, many participants in those events only realised much later how inevitable this step was. It often happens in history that contemporary observers are blind to what hindsight makes obvious.

One of the "pioneers" wrote: "In the final analysis we troopers of Cecil Rhodes's Mounted Police were merely stage-setters for the Matabele wars. In the course of our scene-shifting we trekked almost a thousand miles and lost almost one-half of our men. For a back drop we had the African veld and jungles and forests; against it we erected the flimsy, almost make-believe forts of Tuli, Victoria, Charter and Salisbury—scenes for various acts of the drama.

"Already the actors were rehearsing."[1]

The word "drama" is aptly chosen. One act followed the other. But when the Ndebele, Shona and English soldiers died in battle, they were not acting and there was nothing stagey about their deaths.

The rehearsals were bloody.

For the "pioneers" these rehearsals consisted of attacks on Shona settlements. The pretext for these attacks was easy to find. One "pioneer" missed a few possessions. Another was killed by an unknown assailant... In punitive raids dozens of Africans were slaughtered, cattle confiscated and villages burnt to the ground.

In May 1892, with a delay of six months, the Ndebele finally found out about the re-sale of the "Lippert concession". This quickly inflamed passions and led to impassioned calls to expel the intruders. The question of future relations with the British so electrified the situation in the country that many warriors, particularly the younger ones, as

vell as many indunas started to give almost public expression
o their dissatisfaction with their inkosi.

Unfortunately, to date historians have been able to draw most
of their information about the situation in Ndebele territory
almost exclusively from British sources. Now that independence
has been achieved in Zimbabwe, historians there have started
heir own inquiries, oral historical tradition is being collected, the
memories of old people recorded, and inevitably, many things
vill appear in a different light.

But from the evidence gathered by the British we gain the
mpression that Lobengula knew of this conspiracy designed to
change his policies and leading to immediate war with the Brit-
sh. He, however, continued to regard such war as fatal for his
people and tried to postpone it with every means at his disposal.

"READ LUKE XIV:31"

In 1974 the British historian John Flint, whose name we have
already mentioned more than once in the pages of this book,
wrote that "neither Jameson nor Lobengula wanted war"[2].

This is hard to believe. While Lobengula may indeed not have
wanted it—he regarded such war as a catastrophe, Jameson,
and Rhodes standing behind him, thought differently. To them
war might only have been undesirable from a tactical point
of view, until a certain time—until they had made thorough preparation for it.

Among Rhodes's supporters there were some who had wanted
war as early as 1890, during the "pioneer" trek, when Rhodes
and Major Frank Johnson, one of the commanders on the march,
secretly plotted Lobengula's overthrow. But at that time Rhodes
had answered the "hotheads" among his followers:

". . . I shall certainly some day be pressed to do as you want
me to do, but you must remember that I have only the right
to dig gold in that land; so long, therefore, as the Matabele
do not molest my people, I cannot declare war against them and
deprive them of their country, but as soon as they interfere with
our rights I shall end their game."[3]

It is clear from these words that absolutely anything could
serve as a pretext for starting this future war. The "rights" of
the Company were still so vague that any action by the Ndebele

215

could be interpreted by Rhodes as a "violation" of Company rights.

In mid-1893 a situation developed which was particularly favourable for the initiation of hostilities. That year De Beers profits were the highest ever in the history of the company. In consequence, Rhodes's group was able to assign considerable funds for a war.

If we are to accept the British accounts the event which served as a pretext for starting the war looked like this. In May 1893 a group of Shona near Fort Victoria stole 45 metres of copper wire, which the employees of the Chartered Company had brought for the telegraph line. It was never explained why the Shona needed this wire.

The Company administrators complained to Lobengula. A Shona village, whose inhabitants may or may not have been connected with the theft of this wire, decided to make amends to the Company with a gift of cattle, but Lobengula considered that this cattle belonged to the Ndebele, not the Shona. He sent a large detachment of warriors to the area of Fort Victoria—to investigate the matter on the spot and punish the culprits. On June 29 he sent Jameson a letter, assuring him that the detachment had been ordered not to touch the white settlers.

The complex nature of relations between the Ndebele and the group of Shona peoples was never fully comprehended by the Europeans. For a long time it was believed that the "bloodthirsty" Ndebele were bent on exterminating the "peaceloving" Shona, and that they treated the Shona worse than the Spartans treated the Helots. Current research being carried out by historians who are themselves of Shona or Ndebele nationality will shed much-needed light on the history of the mutual relationship of these peoples. It is in any case quite evident that the warlike Ndebele regarded the contiguous groups of Shona people as their tributaries, and considered any interference in their affairs by the Europeans as violating the stability of this relationship.

It is hard to say how much credence should be accorded to British accounts of the extreme cruelty displayed by the Ndebele detachment in their treatment of the Shona living near Fort Victoria. Lobengula was probably anxious to demonstrate to the Shona that his authority still extended over this region, de-

pite the arrival of the "pioneers" and the construction of a British
ort. Be that as it may, the arrival of this detachment of Ndebele
gave Jameson his pretext to start war. This was a perfect oppor-
unity to set the Company up as the protector of the
Shona.

On July 10 Jameson wrote to Lobengula demanding that
he forbid his warriors to cross the "border". In itself this demand
was a provocation, for no such border even existed. There was
no mention of any border in any of the documents which the
Company might adduce in their support: neither in the "Rudd
concession", nor in the "Lippert agreement". Even if we suppose,
for argument's sake, that these documents had legal force, the
first talked of the right to mine minerals, and the second about
the right to build dwellings and settlements. These agreements
did not confer any sovereignty over any territory.

Anyway the Ndebele would not even have understood this view
of the situation. It was not admitted by their norms of law, and
did not mesh with their sense of justice.

What, we might ask, did Jameson refer to as a "border"?
Probably the region marking the division between territory inhabited predominantly by the Shona peoples and that inhabited
by the Ndebele. In other words, Jameson wished it to seem that
Lobengula's authority only extended over Ndebele territory while
the Company exercised control over the Shona territory.

After sending his letter to Lobengula Jameson summoned to
Fort Victoria the indunas commanding the Ndebele detachment.
In compliance with Lobengula's strict instructions that they
should avoid any conflict with the Company, the indunas went
to see Jameson. He then declared that he would only talk with
one of them, Manyewu, and set them the ultimatum to retreat
with their detachment to beyond the "border line", otherwise
he, Jameson, would give them short shrift.

When asked where this border was, Jameson replied that the
Ndebele knew perfectly well.

It is a mark of the discipline of the Ndebele and their unques-
tioning obedience to Lobengula that even this insolent behaviour by Jameson did not provoke them to take up arms there
and then, by Fort Victoria.

Jameson, however, had decided that such an armed conflict
would take place. He set the ultimatum by the sun. Only about

Ndebele warrior

one hour remained, but they had some thirty miles to cover to the area which he regarded as the "border".[4]

This ultimatum took the Ndebele completely by surprise. No doubt, Jameson had reckoned on this. All this took place on July 18, only a few days after Jameson's letter was dispatched

Lobengula, and Jameson could be almost certain that Lobengula would not have envisaged giving precise instructions in the
event of such an ultimatum. Or if he had, the indunas would
not yet have received them.

The Ndebele started to retreat in the direction pointed by
Jameson. But after one and a half hours he sent thirty-eight mounted men after them, under the command of Captain Lendy. It was
not particularly hard to catch up with the Ndebele footsoldiers,
particularly the rearguard group, in which there was one sick
man who had to be carried. The horsemen opened fire on this
rearguard, killing between thirty and fifty warriors. Even here,
in obedience to Lobengula's order, the Ndebele put up no resistance.

Captain Lendy, on whose orders the men opened fire, is
described by John Flint as "a brutal man".[5] But this is a matter of more than just the brutality of one captain. Lendy only
did what Jameson expected of him. Meanwhile Jameson, in his
report to High Commissioner Loch later that day, declared
that the Ndebele had opened fire on Lendy's detachment first.

In his message to the Company directors, however, Jameson,
in essence, openly proposes that war be initiated: "Three years
of negotiations has only induced them (the Matabele—*A. D.*)
to encroach more". Of his own actions Jameson proudly reports
that he "ordered them to cross the border at once, giving a
short time to obey, and telling them I would drive them out
if they did not"[6].

In his report to the Colonial Office, High Commissioner Loch
totally supported the Company and justified Jameson's actions.

It was Rhodes who had to make the decision. And he gave
the order: not, admittedly, in so many words, but by citing
the Gospel. Answering Jameson's request for further instructions Rhodes telegraphed: "Read Luke fourteen thirty-one".
When he opened the New Testament at this place, Jameson read:
"Or what king going to make war against another king, sitteth
not down first and consulteth whether he be able with ten thous-
and to meet him that cometh against him with twenty thous-
and?" In other words, Rhodes was asking: "Do you have enough
forces to initiate military action?" Jameson telegraphed back:
"All right. Have read Luke fourteen thirty-one."[7]

Rhodes's telegram meant war. But the war did not begin

immediately. The Company still had to make its final militar
preparations... Public opinion in England had to be prepared
too.

THE WORLD LEARNS ABOUT THE MAXIM GUN

In order to stir up a war hysteria Jameson constantly in
formed the public at large about the preparations for war bein
made by the Ndebele, about the approach of their troops t
the Company forts, and about their assaults on the Shona an
on the Europeans. In fact every one of these reports was pur
fiction. Reconnaissance patrols sent into the areas in questio
found no Ndebele warriors there. The number of these repor
continued to increase, however, and the ordinary Englishma
must have gained the impression that the Ndebele were real
poised to attack.

In Parliament these fictions were repeated from one sittin
to the next, and decisive action was demanded from the gov
ernment. In the House of Commons Ellis Ashmead-Bartlett
representing the interests of the industrialists in the town c
Sheffield, demanded "whether Her Majesty's Government wil
now give the responsible authorities in Mashonaland a free han
in dealing with the Matabele attack."[8]

The Ndebele were described as cannibals. This antagonisn
enabled the government to make it appear that it was forced—
contrary to its own peaceableness—to comply with public opi
nion. Without the backing of the government it would have bee
hard to carry out a successful war, although Rhodes had stated
that his Company "ask for nothing and want nothing."[9]

The government gave its backing, and in a most substan
tial way. The British military unit stationed in Bechuanalanc
started to make preparations for war in early August and it
commanding officer discussed with Jameson the best way o
joining forces, in the event of an outbreak of hostilities.

The British government gave the Company permission t
increase extensively the size of its own armed forces, and Prim
Minister Gladstone, to the noisy applause of many of the members
relayed to the House of Commons Rhodes's words that the
Company could quickly deploy another thousand armed horsemer
in the region of the forts. As for the batch of rifles already bought

y Lobengula, the British authorities saw fit to detain these
a Bechuanaland.

The possible weak spot was likely to be communications.
t was difficult to organize supply lines, via Cape Town, the
Cape Colony, the Afrikaner republics and the Kalahari desert.

It was for this reason that Rhodes speeded up construction
f the railways, a project to which he had always accorded
immense importance. One railway was to be built from the
outh, from Cape Town, and another, not so long, to the east,
o the Indian Ocean and the port of Beira in the Portuguese
olony of Mozambique.

In September the first section of the line, extending some one
hundred and twenty kilometres from Beira, was finally open-
d. By this time the Company's military preparations were, in
he main, completed.

Each Company volunteer was promised after the war six thous-
nd acres of farmland, fifteen to twenty mining and five alluvial
claims. The Ndebele's communal herds were also shared out in
dvance: half to the Company and half to the volunteers. With
uch inducements it was not very difficult to recruit troops. Almost all the male Europeans who were then residing within the
Company's "possessions" took up arms. Together they constituted
. force of one thousand, excellently armed, mounted troops.
The Company also had its own artillery, and sufficient supplies
f ammunition. "Natives" were enlisted in this army to serve as
porters and for all auxiliary services.

The British troops stationed in neighbouring Bechuanaland were
placed on combat alert, and the Ngwato chief, Kgama, under-
ook to mobilize between two thousand and three thousand of
his own warriors against the Ndebele.

As might be expected, Lobengula and his people knew, if
not all, then at least enough, about these preparations. Immediately after Jameson's massacre of the Ndebele near Fort Victo-
ia, a section of the Ndebele army stationed on the north bank of
he Zambezi was summoned back to Bulawayo. Lobengula also
gave orders for sentry units to be posted along the roads leading
nto his country from the south. The British newspapers called
his incontrovertible proof of his aggressive intentions.

Europeans living in Bulawayo reported at that time: "the
King is angry, but ... his attitude is not apparently warlike".[10]

221

He refused to accept any payment from the Company for th
Rudd and Lippert concessions, describing this as "bloody-mo
ney".[11] But he still tried to avoid war. Even Graham Bowe
Imperial Secretary of the Cape Colony, wrote in an official di
patch on August 17, 1893: "The chief Lobengula, who is appa
ently anxious for peace, seems to be doing his best to restrain h
people, and to protect the lives of the Europeans who are res
dent at Bulawayo."[12]

When, in their preparations for the war, the British autho
ities instructed all the Europeans that they should leave Bula
wayo, Lobengula gave them guides and assured their safety o
the journey. In his letters to Queen Victoria and the Britis
colonial officials Lobengula accused the "whites" of perfid
denied the existence of any "border" and at every point stresse
his own aspiration for peace.

"I ask you what was the reason, why your people quarrelle
with mine?" he asked. "...What did they do that your peop
should fight with them? It they had been sent to fight the
would have fought...

"Your white men don't know how to tell the truth. The
speak like this to make an excuse for having killed my peopl
How many white men were killed?

"I have asked Dr Jameson this, and also what things m
people took, but he does not tell me.

"Perhaps they have let you know and you may tell me."[13]

It was in such terms that Lobengula appealed to the Britis
High Commissioner for South Africa. He also wrote to Quee
Victoria on August 19, referring to her own suggestion that h
inform her of any conflicts arising with the Company.

"...They told my people that the white men had bought th
country and the people who live in it.

"Your Majesty, what I want to know from you is if peopl
can be bought at any price?...

"My impi was told to leave their arms coming into camp
Their disarming them was a clever trick to attack them arm
less. Further they stated that I do not allow them (European
—Tr.) to enter my kraal with arms; neither do I.

"Your Majesty, allow me to ask by disarming whom did
mislead first and then kill?

"Also they state I made a line between them at Shashi an

222

Mnyati rivers of which I am ignorant. With whom did I agree to make this line which my people are not allowed to cross into Mashonaland? ... Why do your people kill me?"[14]

Loch forwarded this letter from Lobengula to London by post, so that it only arrived on October 24, over two months later, when the war was already in full swing, while incomparably less important documents were sent on by telegraph. Yet this unusual tardiness on the High Commissioner's part did not occasion any criticism from the Colonial Secretary. In his turn the latter also waited a few weeks before writing to Loch that, in view of the changed situation, he believed it was "not advisable to send any reply to Lobengula at present in name of Her Majesty the Queen".[15]

The Ndebele decided to send to the "White Queen" another embassy, headed by Mtshete, who had visited her three years before. This embassy arrived in Cape Town on September 26. One of Rhodes's colleagues predicted that the High Commissioner would not on any account allow the emissaries to proceed to London, and would send them back to Bulawayo after three days or so. His prediction proved correct: the emissaries had to return empty-handed. Only they were detained not three but ten days in Cape Town.

But the height of Loch's hypocrisy was the message he sent to the Colonial Secretary: "I cannot conceal myself peace becomes every day more doubtful. Lobengula not sending reply to my friendly message."[16]

Contemporaries believed that there was no love lost between Cecil Rhodes and Henry Loch—unlike the relations between Rhodes and Loch's predecessor Sir Hercules Robinson. Perhaps this was so, which only goes to show that Henry Loch acted as he was intended, and knew his job well.

In this way everything possible was done to ensure that the convenient moment to start the war would not be missed. The moment Rhodes and Jameson chose was indeed convenient. Furthermore, the Ndebele army was severely weakened by an ill-starred military expedition to the land north of the Zambezi, a campaign occupying their best units, between six and eight thousand men, i. e. nearly half the army. These units had come into contact with a smallpox epidemic, and Lobengula detained them in the north of the country lest they spread the terrible disease among his people. In September the threat of war forced Lobengula to lift the quarantine prematurely, but the battle worthiness of these troops had been undermined.

Rhodes and Jameson knew about all this from the British missionaries, traders, hunters and gold-prospectors resident in Bulawayo. In addition, with the assistance of these people—or at least some of them—Jameson was able to keep Lobengula disoriented until the very last minute, giving him the impression that war could still be avoided. The hunter Johannes Colenbrander, who had accompanied the Ndebele embassy to London as interpreter, now received secret instructions directly from Rhodes. Lobengula trusted Colenbrander perhaps more than the other whites. Meanwhile Colenbrander, having promised to bring Lobengula weapons from the Transvaal, instead went to see Jameson and gave him a full report on the state of the Ndebele army. When war broke out he used his knowledge of the region to guide one of the British columns to Bulawayo

The exact date of the outbreak of war—or, to be more precise, of what was then commonly referred to as war—is not all that easy to establish.

Even in Europe wars were not always "declared", and here, in a remote part of Africa, it would not even have occurred to Rhodes to declare war against a lot of "savages".

On September 24, 1893 High Commissioner Loch asked Jameson to inform him by telegraph when the Company's forces, stationed in Forts Charter and Victoria and any other centres, would be ready for action.

But Loch needed a plausible pretext if he was to send British troops from Bechuanaland to assist Rhodes. Loch wrote to Jameson on October 2: "It must, however, be evident that the Matabele have hostile intentions ... before I sanction an aggressive advance on Bulawayo."[17]

After everything else Jameson had done it was not hard for him to organize such "evidence". A day later, October 4, he informed Loch that, according to his intelligence, seven or eight thousand Ndebele warriors had been concentrated near Fort Victoria. And on October 5 it transpired that the Ndebele had opened fire on a British patrol. . .

That very same day, October 5, after sending Mtshete's

mbassy back to Bulawayo, the High Commissioner permitted
ameson to drive the Ndebele away, and on October 6 he sought
ie Colonial Secretary's sanction to increase the British force
ationed in Bechuanaland.

This time he used the telegraph—unlike with Lobengula's
iessages—and the Colonial Secretary's reply arrived later the
ime day. It read: "As fighting has begun, emergencies may arise
iddenly which require immediate action without previous refer-
ice to me. You are, therefore, authorised to take such steps
s you may consider advisable to meet contingencies as they
ccur."[18] The Secretary authorized the Commissioner to use
iy ammunition available in the British colonies in South Afri-
i. That very day, October 6, Loch sent a telegram to John
loffat to be handed to Lobengula. This, presumably, was in-
:nded to serve as a declaration of war. But this telegram,
hich was deliberately vague, did not mention war. In any
/ent, it is not certain that it was ever delivered to Loben-
ula.

Meanwhile two columns of troops set off in the direction
[Bulawayo, one from Fort Victoria, numbering more than three
undred Europeans and nearly as many Africans, and the other
·om Fort Salisbury, of almost three hundred Europeans and
iree hundred Africans. About four hundred men more were
:anding at the ready in Fort Charter. Two thousand Ngwato
/arriors led by Kgama, Lobengula's old enemy, were march-
ig from Bechuanaland. And in Bechuanaland itself five hundred
!ritish men and officers had been placed on alert.

We might wonder what Rhodes's "pioneers" felt at this time.
\fter all, it was them and not Rhodes, who were destined to
:e Ndebele spears thrust at them, and to come face-to-face
/ith these enraged warriors, fiercely protecting their country
.nd their people and ready to fight to the death.

One thing they did not have to fear was bullets. They knew
hat Lobengula had amassed an entire arsenal of rifles, but
hey also realised that in the hands of the Ndebele warriors
hese weapons presented no great threat. Without the necessary
kills of marksmanship they were virtually useless, and these
kills were not to be found here, deep inside Africa. There
vere no instructors. Some people even used to joke that the
Ndebele had a belief: the higher you point the barrel the fur-

ther the bullet would go. It is certainly true that they had more faith in their trusty spears.

Thus Rhodes's troops were essentially only threatened by spears. Although they were armed with rifles and artillery, they still knew how lethal a skilfully wielded spear can be and remembered the death of the dynastic Prince of France, Napoléon's son, who had gone to war against the Zulus as if on a pleasant excursion. He was dispatched by just such a spear, as were another fifteen hundred men in the battle of Isandhlwana.

They recalled the accounts of the few survivors of that battle: "The Zulus came on like the waves on the ocean shore —never stopped, never shouted or said a word, till our fellows ... were surrounded, then they gave a shout and dashed at the camp, and in five minutes there was not a man left".[19]

What was true of the Zulus was true of the Ndebele. Everything in their army came from the Zulus: their weapons, their tactics, even their courage. The men themselves, the many thousand warriors of this army, the most powerful in all South Africa, were, in the final analysis, also Zulus.

This must have preyed on the minds of even the most headstrong and reckless soldiers. The bravest among them must have wondered if this was not to be a second Isandhlwana.

But they nourished a secret hope. As often in history, this hope resided in a new weapon. Not rifles, nor cannon—they had had these at Isandhlwana—but something altogether new.

Their hopes were linked with the first automatic weapon in the history of mankind. Not many people had even heard of it by this time, and its power had not yet been properly tested in battle conditions.

This weapon was the Maxim machine-gun. It was this weapon, used in many wars since then, that was destined to undergo one of its first field tests in the battle with the Ndebele. It had been invented as long before as 1883 by an American engineer, Hiram Maxim, but there were few wars in progress at the time where it could be properly tested. Perhaps the only place it might have been used was in the skirmishes in Uganda, in 1891. But then not many people even knew about these...

Rhodes's "African Empire" was also hardly a testing ground which would be entirely acceptable to the War Offices of the great powers. The special conditions here were very different from those in Europe. Nevertheless, news of Rhodes's exploits spread quicker and further in Europe than did rumours about events, for example, in Uganda.

In addition, fire would be opened not from one or two machine-guns, but from eight. And the opposition was also quite considerable, affording thousands of live targets.

BAYETE!

The fictitiousness of the pretext for war was evident at once. For several days the columns, which advanced fairly quickly, did not see a single Ndebele warrior. There was no one to "chase away". But by this stage very few people were concerned about a pretext for war.

Still anxious to avoid war, Lobengula now sent a new embassy to the "White Queen", consisting of three indunas, one of whom was his own brother. Lobengula asked the English trader James Dawson to accompany them as interpreter. The embassy set off on October 16 and a day later arrived at the first village inside the British protectorate of Bechuanaland.

Here a comedy was played out with a tragic issue. Dawson met up with his old friends and went drinking with them. In his absence the local British Resident, pretending not to know who these Ndebele visitors were, gave orders for their arrest.

One induna was killed "resisting arrest", another in "his endeavour to escape".[20] Nevertheless, Lobengula's letter was still delivered to the High Commissioner. He, in turn, informed the Colonial Secretary: "Lobengula sends message denying he has any impi on borders; offers to send anyone I may appoint to see; says he hears of the advance on part of whites, and that he sees they want to fight, and asks why they do not say so."

For his own part, the High Commissioner nonchalantly added:

"I do not think it is now of any use to send any messages in reply; the columns are out of reach of telegraph and until events have taken more definite shape further negotiations would be useless, and even prejudicial."[21]

The British Resident in the north of Bechuanaland, having dealt so savagely with Lobengula's embassy, the next day gave his soldiers the signal to move. A column of British soldiers and **volunteers** set off to assist the Chartered Company, and en route seized cattle belonging to the Ndebele. At the same time the columns from Fort Victoria and Salisbury were swiftly approaching Bulawayo, also seizing cattle and burning down villages on the way.

The first major battle took place on October 24 on the Shangani River. According to British calculations, there were about five thousand Ndebele. It is easy to predict the issue of this battle, even without knowing specific details. As Hilaire Belloc was to write subsequently:

> *Whatever happens we have got*
> *The Maxim Gun, and they have not.*

Fifteen years before a Zulu army had been able, albeit at terrible cost to their own number, to gain the British positions and engage the enemy in hand-to-hand combat, where bayonet and spear were almost equally effective.

The Ndebele suffered a different fate. Hailing their inkosi for the last time with the traditional Zulu battle cry "Bayete!" they advanced on the enemy, and when the fighting started, surged forward in the same formidable waves as their Zulu cousins. But suddenly machine-gun fire broke out. This was nothing like rifle fire, or even artillery bombardment. With those a few men, even if only every second, third or fourth man, still managed to reach the enemy. But this fusillade mowed everyone down, without mercy or exception. Hundreds of warriors were struck down immediately, and their comrades could not understand what was happening. They had never even heard of anything like this—indeed, where should they have?

One of the indunas later recalled that, as he led his warriors forward, he suddenly saw them falling, mowed down by machine-gun fire, like scythed maize stalks.

Despite the hail of machine-gun bullets, they fought courageously. Their first attack was only repulsed after twenty minutes. The British calculated that about five hundred Ndebele warriors were killed and wounded.

The British themselves lost only a few men, but the losses of the "native legion", which they threw into battle first, and in the most dangerous sections, were considerable.

The second major battle took place on November 1 on the

A skirmish between the Ndebele and the "pioneers"

Bembezi River, 48 kilometres from Bulawayo. Seven regiments—
between five and seven thousand warriors—attacked the British. The battle lasted for two hours. The Ndebele lost about
one thousand men. Two regiments were almost completely annihilated.

The third battle was on November 2, on the Ramaqwabane
River. The Ndebele attacked a column of British government
troops. These were advancing from Bechuanaland, together with
Kgama's army. This battle lasted three and a half hours. At
particularly dangerous moments the British withdrew their soldiers from the fighting, sending Kgama's units in to take their
place. The machine-gun fire served its purpose here too, but
Kgama's units still suffered large losses and, objecting indignantly to the role they were being forced to play by the British,
headed back to Bechuanaland.

The Ndebele lament for those who died in the battles is
reflected in many songs and poems. Here is one by the poet
Mayford Sibanda, in his own English translation:

> *Now the shadows fall,*
> *Night approaches.*
> *May she not hasten her steps.*
> *Let it not dawn.*
> *May the night cover me forever.*

I fear the breaking forth of day;
It will uncover the battlefield, on which
Lie the mighty men of valour,
Dliso and others remain there.

The milk pails are dry,
The cattle folds are desolate,
No more wedding dances are performed therein.
Bulawayo's dance spaces are forever silent,
The dust of the dancing joyous regiments
Will rise there no more.
You maidens, weep for Lobengula, the King of the
AmaWaba Regiments,
He adorned you with copper ornaments,
Perfumed you with the inkiza scent
And anointed your faces with oil.

The glory of yesterday has lifted like the mist of the
valley,
The sun has chased it away, and the wind carried it
to realms unknown.
May the night swallow me forever.
Because this day is cursed.[22]

On November 4, units of the Chartered Company occupied Bulawayo. To be more precise, they occupied the site of Bulawayo, for as the Ndebele retreated from their capital they set fire to their houses. The only people left to greet the victors were two English traders, who had not been so much as touched by the "bloodthirsty" Ndebele.

A number of articles and books have been written in Britain on the so-called "Matabele War". Yet this campaign hardly merits the title "war". It was more like wholesale slaughter of people, virtually unarmed, since they were unable to use their weapons in battle.

Over the years Rhodes had repeatedly conveyed to Lobengula his wish for a meeting. In his turn Lobengula had more than once demanded such a meeting, exasperated by the interminable shenanigans of Rhodes's emissaries. But this meeting never actually took place.

Now Rhodes was able to set forth for the newly-conquered land by the safest route—from the east, via the Mozambican port of Beira.

Meanwhile Lobengula and the remnants of his army, after leaving Bulawayo, marched northwards, towards the mighty Zambezi. The going was tough. The men were exhausted by the difficult, unpopulated terrain, and demoralized by the awareness of their own desperate predicament. In their despondency they decided that the gods and the spirits of their ancestors had abandoned them, that they were entering a terrible time, the age of suffering that every nation is destined to pass through.

Using Ndebele warriors as messengers, Jameson sent Lobengula a letter demanding that he surrender and threatening to send troops in pursuit. Lobengula's reply came back immediately. He recalled how all the messengers he had sent to the British seemed to disappear without trace. If these messengers could be shown to him alive, he would then agree to appear before the British in person.

Then he sent his son Nyamanda and another runner to the British. The message they carried—a verbal one, as he now had no European secretaries—was that he accepted defeat and asked for his people to be given the possibility to retreat to the north. The inkosi gave these runners all the gold in his possession and said that this was the only thing that could buy freedom from the whites. So much for the white man's reputation throughout Africa.

But along the way this gold was stolen by two whites, when the emissaries stopped to ask them how to find Jameson. Then the Company representatives refused to conduct any discussion, citing as their reason that the runners had no letter or written documents with them. With this they dashed Lobengula's final attempt to make peace.

Jameson sent a posse in pursuit of Lobengula, three hundred men with four machine-guns and a cannon. Thirty five of them—Major Allan Wilson's detachment—came upon Lobengula's tracks. Encountering groups of retreating Ndebele Wilson assured them that he went with proposals of peace. But once he caught up with the inkosi's wagon he demanded that everyone present surrender. It seems that Lobengula himself was not in the wagon at the time. Realising the Englishmen's real intentions, the Ndebele killed them all.

In England the death of Wilson and his men at once grew into a legend, a process assisted, naturally, by Rhodes. Newspapers reported that at the moment of death they sang "God save the Queen". Wilson became a national hero. The tragedy was even dramatized in *Wilson's Last Stand*, which played in the theatres of England.

They never did catch up with Lobengula. Shortly after, in January 1894, he died. A few weeks after his death the management of the Chartered Company announced, quoting as their source the indunas who had accompanied Lobengula, that he had died of smallpox. But it was rumoured that he had never contracted the disease at all, but had taken his own life together with one of his closest associates.[23]

The circumstances of the final weeks of Lobengula life are still surrounded in mystery. Nothing certain about the cause of death, the date or the place. But for many years the rumour circulated among the Ndebele that he was still alive, and at any moment would reappear to lead his people against the British.

Here is one of the songs the Ndebele sang then. Its text is from the private collection of Caleb Dube of the University of Zimbabwe. I reproduce it here with his kind permission.

> *Kekho okwaziyo ukuthi wena Lobhengula,*
> *Mnfanenkosi watshonaphi*
> *Okwaziwayo yikuthi wena kaNdaba wanyamalala,*
> *Kawufanga.*[24]

Lobengula's death proved very opportune for Cecil Rhodes. At once steps were taken to ensure that the inkosi's power, which had united the Ndebele, had been crushed for ever. Rhodes took three of Lobengula's sons away with him to the Cape Colony, one of these being Njube, regarded as heir to the throne.

In 1986 an essay was published in Manchester on the fate of Peter Lobengula, one of the sons of Lobengula or so, at least, he claimed. He lived about one and a half decades in Britain, working for a long time in the coal mines of Lancashire, and died in poverty on November 24, 1913.[25]

Lobengula's death was an immense blow for the Ndebele. Having lost the power that held them united, the indunas started to surrender one after another. The last of them surrendered in April 1894.

In his examination of the policies of the European powers which went to war in 1914, Lenin gives the following description of a war like Cecil Rhodes's first war: "Take the history of the little wars they waged before the big war—'little' because few Europeans died in those wars, whereas hundreds of thousands of people belonging to the nations they were subjugating died in them, nations which from their point of view could not be regarded as nations at all (you couldn't very well call those Asians and Africans nations!); the wars waged against these nations were wars against unarmed people, who were simply shot down, machine-gunned."[26]

THE REACTION IN ENGLAND

No country in the world was better supplied with news at that time than England. Nevertheless, it is doubtful that the British received objective reports of this war. The press obtained its information from employees of the Chartered Company or from other people equally under Rhodes's control. Even the British journalist Newman, an ardent supporter of Rhodes, admitted: "Unfortunately throughout the whole campaign very little correct news had reached the public."[27] These are the words of a man who worked in the land of the Ndebele and the Shona as a war correspondent, and who regarded the war itself as a "brilliant campaign".[28]

This is not to say, however, that the British press gave little attention to the war. Quite the reverse. But its reports were almost all of the same kind, in the same key and at the same pitch. Such examples are the article of Rider Haggard in *The Pall Mall Gazette* in which he writes that the campaign served to "break up a bloody and odious tyranny, and to advance the cause of civilization in Africa",[29] and an article in *The Times*, which declares that "the destruction of the Matabele military system will be almost as great a blessing to the Matabele themselves as to the Mashonas and other peoples whom they plun dered".[30]

The press described the battles won by machine-gun bombard ment as grandiose. Jameson was hailed as a great commander For months on end newspapers and magazines were filled with portraits and biographies of the "heroes" of the war.

Rhodes's own pronouncements attracted particular attention As we have seen, he was a man of few words, but at a celebratory banquet given by the mayor of Cape Town found it appropriate to declare:

"There never would be on record a campaign conducted with such a small expenditure of money and human life, and, at the same time, with such great humanity."[31]

Declarations like this increased Rhodes's popularity. It is true that the losses suffered by his own troops were indeed small In the Chartered Company's balance sheet the outlay on the war amounted to a paltry £113,500.[32] The ordinary English man was impressed by this "thriftiness". What the Company at tempted to conceal from him was that the funds for this war also came from his own pocket: after all, the soldiers were not only "pioneers", but also units of the British army. Even those mem bers of the public who did discover this did not take the news too close to heart. In truth, the expense had not been very great.

Cecil Rhodes's first war was typical for the age of the "par tition of the world". Its only untypical features were the skilful manner in which it had been prepared and precision with which it was conducted. Rhodes's actions were even met with approval by England's rivals, the French, some of whom saw his war as an example to emulate.

The French writer Leroy-Beaulieu expressed this approval with particular clarity: ". . .Cecil Rhodes initiated the war with the Matabele for the simple purpose of seizing their territory. But after all, he develops this territory, where the previous owners have done nothing; true, he profits by it, but his country profits too, and it is his Chartered Company which takes on itself all the trouble and risks inevitable at the beginning of any process of colonization, while the British Empire will take possession of these territories when civilization has already penetrated them and tran- quility has been secured in them".[33]

At the turn of the century such views about Europe's civilizing mission were not compromised, as they are today.

Five years after the war against the Ndebele the American President McKinley justified the conquest of the Philippines in the following terms:

"I walked the floor of the White House night after night until midnight; and I am not ashamed to tell you, gentlemen, that I went down on my knees and prayed Almighty God for light and guidance more than one night. And one night late it came to me this way—I don't know how it was, but it came... That there was nothing left for us to do but to take them all, and to educate the Filipinos, and uplift and civilize and Christianize them as our fellowmen for whom Christ also died".[34]

It was natural to think like this in Europe and North America. Lenin commented on this more than once: "...Domination over hundreds of millions of people in the colonies by the European nations was sustained only through constant, incessant, interminable wars, which we Europeans do not regard as wars at all, since all too often they resembled, not wars, but brutal massacres, the wholesale slaughter of unarmed peoples."[35]

To the honour of the British people it must be said that these jingoistic attitudes were by no means universal. England has always been renowned for its ability to produce men and women ahead of their time and prepared to speak their minds to the government and to the people.

In 1894 in Cambridge a pamphlet was published with the title: "The Matabele—Scandal and Its Consequences".[36] The author lashes out against the British public and government:

"The British Tiger has tasted blood, and returns to the banquet of blood, as usual, under the mask of the highest benevolence... If any other European State ventures to annex a region in Asia, Africa, or Oceania, there is an outburst of pious indignation on the part of the British Public: to Great Britain alone is reserved the right of invasion, confiscation, and annexation... The device of Chartered Companies is an ingenious one: it is to supply a kind of buffer of crime ... how can a Company have a conscience, when it has no soul to be saved, and no backside to be kicked?...

"It is no new idea, no brand-new conception of Mr Rho des's fertile genius, to kill out as vermin so-called inferior rac for the sake of their land and their gold. . .

"The British Matron, reading her paper at the breakfast tabl remarks that two thousand more savages have been killed. ' rise of ten per cent in Mine Shares', is the rejoinder of Pate Familias."

The author realizes that he cannot expect to make muc impact on public opinion, but he endeavours to kindle a spar in the conscience of at least a few. His words are all the mor admirable for this: "My pamphlet will perish, as it deserves One or two copies may survive on the shelves of the Librar of the British Museum, and the two great Universities, to recor the fact that there were a few voices in 1894 crying in the wilder ness to denounce crime, even when committed by their ow countrymen."

The author of the pamphlet calls himself "One Who (1) Re members the Punishment which fell upon Cain for Killing hi Brother, and (2) is jealous of the Honour of Great Britain" He does not give his name. It may well have been the work o several people, even an entire group.

There were also some outspoken English critics, who did giv their names. Such, for example, as the Social Democrats, th members of the Social-Democratic Federation. In their weekl publication *Justice* they wrote: "The British nation is once mor pledged to assist a gang of plundering adventurers to rob a nativ population of their territory and freedom."[37] "Unless we wan the name of Englishmen to become synonymous with moder piracy we ought immediately to call for prompt Governmenta interference."[38]

A group of radicals led by the M. P. Henry Labouchere als protested publicly, in the press and in Parliament. In the journa *Truth* and in the *Daily Chronicle* Labouchere railed agains "these filibustering and massacring expeditions . . . of Mr Rhode and his pernicious company, a wretched, rotten, bankrupt se of marauders and murderers."[39]

Labouchere demanded that the government prosecute th crimes of this war. Another M.P., the radical H.W. Paul quote the cynical statements of representatives of the Chartered Compan and demanded that the government express its attitude to thes

atements. The M.P. A.C. Morton enquired in the House of
ommons:

"I should like to ask ... whether the Government approve
f this murder of 3,000, or even 500 men, for the purpose of
lundering and stealing their land."[40]

An appeal was launched among the Britons in South Africa
o set up units of volunteers to fight on the Ndebele side against
heir fellow-Britons. This appeal issued from members of the
rades union movement. Naturally, there was no chance of such
nits coming into existence: the British colonial authorities would
ot have permitted a single person to depart for the war with
his aim. Nevertheless, the appeal is remarkable in itself—in
latant defiance not only of the authorities, but of the most
idely-held, bigoted attitudes.

This courageous defiance was applauded by the Social Demo-
rats in England. The weekly *Justice* promptly congratulated the
outh Africa Labour organization (referring to the trades union
rganizations which were campaigning to establish a Labour
arty) on having had "the courage to start an agitation for
olunteers to aid the Matabele in their unequal struggle for
iberty".[41] The Social Democrats realised that it was effectively
mpossible to set up such volunteer units at that time, but in itself
his fine undertaking was seen as exceptionally important and
ital in their drive to educate the British workers. By contrast,
he press which supported Rhodes reported the idea of helping
he Ndebele with indescribable indignation. In *The Pall Mall
Gazette* the Vice-President of the Labour Union of Johannesburg,
who had allegedly made the appeal, was described as "a wretched
reature".[42]

The voices of protest raised against this war proved to be so
nsistent that the British government was forced to open an
nquiry into its causes. Unfortunately, essentially only one fact
vas subjected to scrutiny: who opened fire first in July 1893,
when Jameson announced the violation of the "border" and sent
Captain Lendy in pursuit of the retreating Ndebele. Even this
nquiry only took place in mid-1894, a full year after the events
hemselves, by which time the participants had already forgotten
much and many of them could not be found.

Some of the evidence adduced had in fact appeared earlier
n the press. Such, for example, was a letter from a soldier in

Lendy's troop, who compared the fighting with deer-hunting. H‍
describes how the troops fired at the retreating Ndebele at point
blank range, so that every victim took in no less than four o‍
five bullets. Or the letter from a missionary describing ho‍
Lendy opened fire on the Ndebele rearguard, who were marchin‍
peacefully forward, only to be shot at close range, at a distanc‍
of five or six yards, utterly without quarter. The inquiry onl‍
confirmed all this. Those participants who could be found an‍
who were prepared to give evidence, usually said: "Immediatel‍
they were sighted, Captain Lendy gave the order to commenc‍
firing."[43]

The English official Newton, charged with conducting the in‍
quiry, tried to reject the claim that Lendy had given no quarte‍
to the Ndebele. But he used a very strange argument: he collecte‍
a mass of evidence that the Ndebele themselves never asked fo‍
quarter from anyone. The findings of the inquiry clearly incrim‍
inated the Company, but this did not in the least deter the‍
Colonial Secretary, who reached the following conclusion: ". . .I‍
has given me sincere satisfaction to find that the result of a‍
inquiry so exhaustive and impartial has been clearly to exonerat‍
Dr Jameson and the officers of the British South Africa Compan‍
generally from the serious charges which have been made agains‍
them in connection with these occurrences."[44]

The Idol of His Day

The Ndebele were crushed, Lobengula was no more. The way was now open for the implementation of other designs.

Rhodes had entered his fifth decade, he was now in his forty-first year. Later in life, as he looked back over his career, he must have seen the years 1894 and 1895 as his zenith. Many were the strings he held in his hand—and these were not mere strings, but ropes! Head of the De Beers diamond mining company, of the Gold Fields of South Africa, master of the Chartered Company and of its immense territories—by whatever names they were known. From 1895 the name "Rhodesia" was officially confirmed —with Rhodes's own assistance, of course. From 1890 he was Prime Minister of the Cape Colony. And in early 1895 he joined the top officials of the British Empire in the Queen's Privy Council.

The conquest of the lands of the Ndebele and the Shona had been Rhodes's most arduous project, but theirs was by no means the only country he annexed. He gradually extended the frontiers of his "empire" northwards, to include the countries north of the Zambezi.

He was able to foist one of his agreements on Lewanika, ruler of the large Lozi nation. Until the war against the Ndebele, this agreement might have been dismissed as a mere piece of paper, with no particular significance. But now, after Rhodes's troops had established themselves so firmly on the south bank of the Zambezi, his ambitions to occupy areas to the north of this great river became reality. Of course, for the time being any influx of "pioneers" was out of the question, but there was no doubt in anyone's mind that the left bank of the Zambezi was also part of Rhodes's "empire". The area inhabited by the Lozi and the contiguous territories started to be called North-Eastern Rhodesia.

As they moved nearer the Great African Lakes Rhodes's emissaries announced the creation of a third Rhodesia—North-Western.

Admittedly no real power was established there by the Chartered Company until several years later, and even at the turn of the century this part of Africa was not subjected to anything like the "opening up" of the lands of the Ndebele and the Shona, but two more Rhodesias did soon appear on the map (they were united into one—Northern Rhodesia—in 1911).

Rhodes also tried to seize Katanga, today the Zairean province of Shaba, which even at that time was believed to be rich in minerals. But the Belgian king Leopold II, availing himself of the complex nature of European international politics, was able to prevent Rhodes's incursion into Katanga. In the east, the process of defining the borders between the Chartered Company's possessions and the Portuguese colony of Mozambique became so fraught with tension that armed conflicts erupted.

Even further to the north the extensive territory along Lake Nyasa, which today has become the Republic of Malawi, was transformed with Rhodes's active assistance into the British protectorate of Nyasaland. The post of Administrator of the Chartered Company in the vast territory of Northern Rhodesia and the post of government administrator of the British protectorate of Nyasaland were held in the first half of the eighteen-nineties by one and the same man: Harry Johnston.

Meanwhile, in his capacity as Prime Minister of the Cape Colony, Rhodes prepared and effected the annexation to the Cape of the lands of the Tswana in the north-west, and of the Pondo and Tonga in the east.

Historians have calculated that Rhodes added 291,000 square miles to the British empire overseas—an area larger than that of France, Belgium, the Netherlands and Switzerland combined.[1] He controlled the destinies of millions of people and determined the way of life in lands whose territory was many times as large as that of his own country, Great Britain.

It seemed Rhodes was now sailing free. In England Lord Rosebery, who came to power as Prime Minister in 1894, not only sympathised with Rhodes's policies but also had an unconcealed personal regard for him. In 1895 Rosebery's cabinet fell and Lord Salisbury returned to power.

For Rhodes this was a change from good to better. The most influential figure in Salisbury's cabinet was to be "Colonial Joe" —Colonial Secretary Joseph Chamberlain. Once he had been mistrustful of Rhodes, but those days were now past. On taking up his portfolio, he wrote to Rhodes: "As far as I understand your main lines of policy I believe that I am in general agreement with you, and if we ever differ on points of detail I hope that as sensible men of business we shall be able to give and take, and so come to an understanding."[2] This was said à propos of a particular issue, but could easily be applied to the relations between these politicians in general.

To make things even easier for Rhodes, Salisbury and Chamberlain recalled Lord Loch from Cape Town. Hercules Robinson, who was once again appointed High Commissioner for South Africa, was now at Rhodes's beck and call.

BACK AT HOME

To industrialists, merchants and financiers Cecil Rhodes was both a guiding star and someone on whom they pinned their hopes.

Since the 1880s the manufactured products of Great Britain, which had long been regarded as the "workshop of the world", had been encountering increasing competition, primarily from the German industry. The British government was forced to set up a special commission to identify obstacles in the path of England's overseas trade. The Birmingham merchants who appeared before the commission on October 28, 1885, bitterly complained that they were being ruined by competition from abroad. Their complaints filled five thick "Blue Books"—the result of the special commission's work.

This lent the colonies a new attraction. Half-way through the nineteenth century Palmerston had said that a gentleman was not obliged to own all the roadside inns between the town and his estate—in other words, England did not have to own all the countries between it and its main overseas possession— India. Now, at the end of the century, the opposite idea was growing in popularity. People now spoke of "Commerce following the flag". A country's trade would only be protected in those countries over which its own flag flew.

The Birmingham industrialists, led by Chamberlain, reached the conclusion that new markets should be sought in the colonies and that colonialism should be combined with the expansion of trade. The merchants, manufacturers and bankers of London Manchester and Sheffield also turned their eyes in that direction Stanley was able to play on these feelings when he told the Manchester Chamber of Commerce in 1884:

"There are forty millions of people beyond the gateway of the Congo, and the cotton spinners of Manchester are waiting to clothe them. Birmingham foundries are glowing with the red metal that will presently be made into ironwork for them and the trinkets that shall adorn those dusky bosoms, and the ministers of Christ are zealous to bring them, the poor benighted heathen into the Christian fold."[3]

Other journalists, less famous than Stanley, were equally adept in inflaming the imagination of the industrialists. For instance Elihu Buritt, as quoted by the Russian journalist Shklovsk (Dioneo), observed: "The Arabian Sheikh eats his pilau with a spoon made in Birmingham; the Egyptian pasha drinks his sherbet from a goblet fashioned in Birmingham, illuminates his harem with a Birmingham crystal candelabrum and adorns the prow of his boat with Birmingham-made ornaments. The redskin, continues Buritt, hunts and makes war with a Birmingham rifle in his hands; the rich Hindu adorns his chambers with Birmingham crystal. Birmingham sends spurs and stirrups to the pampas for the gauchos, and shining buttons for their leggings. It sends axes hatchets and sugar-cane presses to the blacks in the tropical colonies. The tin cans, containing the Australian prospector's supplies of meat and vegetables, bear the impress of their Birmingham manufacturer."[4]

Now there were plans to build a railway line all the way from Cape Town to Cairo! A telegraph line across the entire continent! This meant thousands of miles of rails, enough wire to encircle the world, millions of nails, oceans of pitch. Provision and merchandise for the construction workers... This was enough to thrill the heart of any entrepreneur, and not just English ones. The American consul in Cape Town reported back to his government, that the great influx of immigrants resulting from the occupation of the Zambezi regions would soon open up an extensive market for US-made industrial, agricultural

nd mining machinery, and that the native peoples, whose needs
vould quickly increase thanks to their contracts with the white
ace, would immensely increase the volume of trade, of which
le expected the United States to receive a large share.[5]

All this is firmly linked to the name of one man: Cecil Rhodes.
Rhodes had been the initiator of more than one war in his life,
)ut he still loved to repeat that "rails cost less than bullets and
arry farther".[6]

The imagination was seized by the very scale of the Cape-to-
Cairo project, the most ambitious of any plan yet conceived in
Europe for the opening-up of Africa.

Several of the European powers dreamt of embracing the
entire length or breadth of Africa with their dominions. The
French wished to cast their hoop across Africa from Senegal in
he west to the shores of the Red Sea in the east. Germany looked
ower down, from German East Africa to German Southwest
Africa. The Portuguese aimed for a swathe of colonies stretching
rom Angola to Mozambique.

The British northward thrust along the Cape-Cairo axis cut
across all these horizontal swathes, and in the end it was only
his longitudinal band of possessions that was achieved. There
vas a time, albeit a short one, when an uninterrupted line of
British colonies and dependencies stretched the entire length of
Africa, from north to south.

The list of men who were connected with this grand design
luring the many years of its implementation is a long one.
Some are now forgotten, like the journalist Edwin Arnold or the
engineer James Sivewright. Others are remembered to this day,
uch as William Gladstone, leader of the British Liberals, or
Harry Johnston, one of the "empire-builders".

As early as 1876 Arnold had published a pamphlet in which
le advanced the Cape-to-Cairo idea. Sivewright promptly de-
nonstrated the necessity for a telegraph line to be laid the entire
ength of the railway.

In 1877 Gladstone wrote: ". . .Our first site in Egypt, . . . will
)e the almost certain egg of a North African Empire, that will
grow and grow . . . till we finally join hands across the Equator
vith Natal and Cape Town. . ."[7]

A decade later Johnston was feeding the hopes of the respectable readers of *The Times:* if the government would decide

to be more active in the Great African Lakes region, which lay on the Cape-to-Cairo line, then one day the British possession in South Africa would be joined in a single long chain of British dominions with the British sphere of influence in East Africa and the Egyptian Sudan.

This idea was one that appealed to the Prime Minister Lord Salisbury, too. Johnston's article in *The Times* received his personal commendation.

But, as Anatole France was to say, an idea does not belong to him who has it first, but to him who establishes it firmly in the minds of men.

Rhodes wrote no books, nor pamphlets, nor even any newspaper or magazine articles. The propagation of his ideas in the press was the work of others. Thus, in the spring of 1889 an article by Charles Metcalfe appeared in *The Fortnightly Review*, a London journal. In it Metcalfe wrote of a railway that would ultimately link the Cape with Cairo, and carry civilization through the heart of the Black Continent. Charles Metcalfe was not writing from a general point of view, but as one with a close knowledge of the business. At the time he was busy working on the construction of the railway line from the diamond fields to the north, to the interior of the continent. He was building it on Rhodes's instructions.

It was in fact the Cape-to-Cairo idea that formed the basis for Rhodes's acquaintance with Lord Salisbury. In spring 1889 Rhodes had a meeting with Harry Johnston, who was agitating for the expansion of the British possessions in the Great African Lakes region. They met at a dinner hosted by John Verschoyle, at that time deputy editor of *The Fortnightly Review*. At their meeting they discussed the Cape-to-Cairo scheme and Johnston told Rhodes of Lord Salisbury's sympathy with it. To this Rhodes replied:

"You are to see Lord Salisbury, at once, tell him who I am, give Lord Rothschild as my reference. . . Say that if money is the only hindrance to our striking north from the Zambezi to the headwaters of the Nile, I will find the money."[8]

He at once gave Johnston a cheque for two thousand pounds and promised that he would give the government ten thousand pounds a year towards the cost of administering this region. But he set one condition: that his company be given the royal charter

Soon a meeting took place between Rhodes and Salisbury and the agreement Rhodes sought was granted. This marked the beginning of a long cooperation between these three men. It is interesting to note that the journalist Verschoyle also had long links with Rhodes. In 1900 (under a pseudonym "Vindex") he published a large volume of speeches and statements by Rhodes.

Rhodes adopted a highly practical approach to the Cape-to-Cairo scheme, availing himself of every opportunity to extend the band of British possessions, to lay more miles of railway line and to sink new posts for the telegraph cable.

> *By the might of our cable tow (Take hands!),*
> *From the Orkneys to the Horn*
> *All round the world (and a little loop to pull it by),*
> *All round the world (and a little strap to buckle it)...*[9]

Rhodes ensured that the Cape-to-Cairo idea was inseparably linked with his name. In his own lifetime there remained only one country along the entire length of this projected line that was not annexed by the British: German East Africa (the Union Jack was only raised over it, or at least over most of it, in 1918).

Rhodes did all he could to occupy the countries on this line, which in the British Empire came to be known as Bechuanaland, Southern Rhodesia, Northern Rhodesia, Nyasaland, Uganda. In 1893 he visited Cairo, to see the projected Cape-to-Cairo route from the northern end. He first promised, then provided extensive support in this region to General Kitchener, commander of the British troops.

In the matter of the railway line and the telegraph Rhodes also matched his words with action. The telegraph was easier to lay, but by the end of 1894 the railway line, too, had reached Mafeking, and was well on the way to Rhodesia itself.

Thus Rhodes did not merely arouse the hopes of British industrialists, merchants and financiers. He also fulfilled these hopes.

> *To the grist of the slow-ground ages,*
> *To the gain that is yours and mine—*
> *To the Bank of the Open Credit,*
> *To the power-house of the Line!*[10]

An extensive analysis of the project published just before th Second World War under the title: *The Cape-to-Cairo Dream. A Study in British Imperialism*, begins with a portrait of Rhode and with his words, and reaches the conclusion that Rhode played a leading role in the British expansion in Africa, but tha he was, "likewise, a wirepuller behind the scenes."[11]

The idea of "uniting" the whole of South Africa beneat the British flag also first appeared long before Rhodes's day, whe the Afrikaners retreated from the territory seized by the British t establish their own republics beyond the Vaal River—the Sout African Republic (commonly known as the Transvaal) and o the Orange River—the Orange Free State. The moment thes republics came into existence the British authorities started effort to "unite" them with the Cape Colony and Natal into a Sout African federal union—beneath the British flag, of course.

Many proponents of British colonial politics had already en deavoured to put such a plan into effect. Amongst these wa Lord Carnarvon (perhaps this is why Rhodes once named hir as executor of his will). This plan promised rich benefits to th British capital: the continued development of mining, an impetu to the development of towns, ports and everything else that w now describe as the infra-structure. And, of course, a continuou supply of cheap labour.

In the final analysis, this plan too became associated not wit Carnarvon, nor with anyone else, but with Rhodes.

Plans for the "partition of the world" could be associated wit the names of many men. But Rhodes was more candid than th others. "The world is nearly all parcelled out, and what there i left of it is being divided up, conquered, and colonized. To thin of these stars that you see overhead at night, these vast world which we can never reach. I would annex the planets if I could I often think of that. It makes me sad to see them so clear and ye so far."[12] Not many men would have dared write this, not even those who shared his views. If today Rhodes's name has come t be most closely associated with the plans of colonial expansion it is because he dared to speak out.

But, more important, it is also because he was able to mak his "imperialist dreams" reality in world politics. His beliefs di not remain mere exhortations, delivered from a rostrum, empty slogans trapped in the smoke-filled halls of "patriotic assemblies" r the interminable discussions and deliberations conducted in he curtained tranquility of ministerial offices.

Rhodes was able to stir the hearts of people of different classes vith his social ideas. He loved to repeat that the seizure of colonies was of greatest benefit to the ordinary people of his country. It benefited them because in these colonies the surplus population of Great Britain could find a use for its skills.

In giving expression to ideas which were also held by many bourgeois politicians, Rhodes was able to formulate these ideas with greater force and clarity, perhaps even in a cruder and more intelligible way. He always kept pace with the age, and some people believed he was even ahead of his age.

Tens of millions of people in Britain and many other European countries were seriously contemplating leaving their native lands, and departing from Europe for ever. Many of them took the plunge. It is reckoned that between 1881 and 1915 32.1 million people emigrated from Europe—almost one million a year.[13] Many of them must have been particularly impressed by Rhodes's persuasive talk of colonizing distant lands.

Indeed, his claim that imperialism would better the lot of the ordinary man was believed by many in Britain itself, and it is very likely that most of these were themselves ordinary men, uninitiated in the ways of politics.

It was them that Rhodes was addressing when he said that every factory hand had to realize that until he controlled the world markets he would live from hand to mouth, and that the working man had to understand that if he wished to survive he had to hold the world and world trade in his hands, and the moment he allowed the world to slip out of his hands he was finished.[14]

In this way he taught the ordinary man to believe that the idea "expansion is everything" was vital precisely to him, the ordinary man. His teaching met with considerable success. Countless numbers of politicians through all the ages have speculated on people's patriotic feelings, but few of them were as successful in this as Cecil Rhodes. Thousands of people gathered at the shareholders' meetings of his Chartered Company, and, although he paid no dividends and did not even promise to pay any in the near future, he received wild ovations. All this derived from

247

This was how British aristocrats saw Rhodes. A portrait by the
Duchess of Rutland

his consummate skill in whipping up extreme patriotic sentiments bordering on chauvinism. He cast his spell on all: the rich,
the workers, and above all the petty bourgeoisie. The social
conditions at that time were such that the petty bourgeoisie, as
Lenin points out, "owing to their economic position, are more
patriotic than the bourgeoisie or the proletariat."[15]

It was hardly difficult for Rhodes to convince his countrymen f the civilizing mission of the British Empire. After all, at the beginning of our century even Mahatma Gandhi, an Indian, believed that this empire would bring benefit to the entire world.

Rhodes became the idol of the London streets. On sighting his baggy figure shopkeepers, cabmen, omnibus owners and ordinary workmen and soldiers loudly hailed him. We might wonder how many of them had the slightest idea exactly what benefit his ideas would bring them.

> Walk wide o' the Widow at Windsor,
>   For 'alf o' Creation she owns:
> We 'ave bought 'er the same with the sword an' the flame,
>   An' we've salted it down with our bones.
>   (Poor beggars!—it's blue with our bones!)[16]

What is really astonishing, however, is the way he was able to gain such influence in London's highest circles, with members of the British aristocracy. The *nouveaux riches* were regarded in Victorian England with a certain disdain: this was not America. Yet Rhodes was himself one of these *nouveaux riches*.

Nevertheless, not only was Rhodes able to secure solid connections in the top aristocratic circles, he even earned among them a regard that bordered on adulation. The royal family bestowed their favours upon him, duchesses vied with one another to win his attention.

The following exchange is typical of Rhodes's conversations with Queen Victoria: " 'What have you been doing since I last saw you, Mr Rhodes?' says the Queen. 'I have added two provinces to Your Majesty's dominions.' 'Ah,' rejoins his Sovereign, 'I wish some of my Ministers, who take away my provinces, would do as much.' "[17]

Whenever he visited London—and, as Mark Twain commented, "he is the only unroyal outsider whose arrival in London can compete for attention with an eclipse"[18]—all Britain's top nobility gathered at the dinners in his honour, even those who were enemies, and for years had avoided encountering one another.

Lord Salisbury, a politician who, it might be thought, would have long been inured to any sort of surprise, wrote with puzzlement to Queen Victoria about a dinner at the house of her granddaughter, the Duchess of Fife: "There was an odd dinner at the Duke of Fife's to celebrate the arrival of Mr Rhodes. The Prince of Wales sat between Mr Gladstone and Lord Salisbury and the Duke of Fife—between Lord Hartington and Lord Gran ville".[19] Lord Salisbury, himself a scion of England's most blue blooded families, publicly sang Rhodes's praises. He described Cecil Rhodes as "a very considerable man, a man of very many remarkable powers, and remarkable resolution and will".[20]

Even Queen Victoria gave a dinner in Rhodes's honour. The newspapers noted with amazement how politicians and public figures who had avoided meeting one another for years gathered together round the Queen's table when Rhodes's was the guest of the evening.

There were innumerable articles about Rhodes in the British press. A typical encomium declared how the work done by Mr Rhodes and his assistants would stand out in history as one of the finest examples of the pioneering and colonizing genius of the British race.[21]

Rhodes's own fanatical belief in the "pioneering and coloniz ing genius of the British race" largely explains his popularity among the different sections of the then British society, from the man-in-the-street to the aristocracy.

At that time, as the nineteenth century drew to its close, the European powers were making more and more use of propagan da, through the press, through education at school and university, to inculcate nationalism and chauvinism. The ideas of national Messianism were being discussed everywhere in Europe. In 1893 the prominent Russian historian Vassily Klyuchevsky wrote in his diary à propos of a congress of historians in Munich: "Nowa days they have started more and more often to prescribe the tasks and directions of the teaching of history... The general goals of teaching are being replaced by local and specific goals, the self-awareness of man by German political awareness, the moral feeling by the national feeling, and humanity by patriotism."[22]

Another interesting observation came from an elder contem porary of Rhodes, the Russian satirist Mikhail Saltykov-Shched rin. He was writing of his own country, but his words are appli cable to all countries and probably to all ages: "Man is anyway prone to instilling in himself a feeling of nationality, more than any other feeling, and, in consequence, to inflame this feeling in him to a greater extent that he would voluntarily admit, if left o his own devices, means that one is no longer acting on his patriotism, but on dark feelings of exclusiveness and isolation."[23]

Similar sober warnings were also sounded, of course, in England.

Suffice it to recall the sagacious and ironic Jerome K. Jerome, another contemporary of Cecil Rhodes. He wrote:

"It is the idea of the moment that size spells happiness. The bigger the country the better one is for living there. The happiest Frenchman cannot possibly be as happy as the most wretched Britisher, for the reason that Britain owns many more thousands of square miles than France possesses. The Swiss peasant, compared with the Russian serf, must, when he looks at the map of Europe and Asia, feel himself to be a miserable creature...

"The happy Londoner on foggy days can warm himself with the reflection that the sun never sets on the British Empire. He does not often see the sun, but that is a mere detail. He regards himself as the owner of the sun; the sun begins his little day in the British Empire, ends his little day in the British Empire: for all practical purposes the sun is part of the British Empire...

"I cannot get it into my unpatriotic head that size is the only thing worth worrying about."

Unfortunately, in Rhodes's and Jerome's day, as at so many other times in the history of mankind, such views were unfashionable. Jerome understood this only too well. He wistfully concludes: "My views on this subject are, I know, heretical".[24]

As one reads the newspapers and journals of England of that time one involuntarily recalls a well-known story by Voltaire. No sooner has the satrap opened his mouth to speak than his confidant cries: "He will be right". In his day Cecil Rhodes was not unlike this satrap.

This is how things were in England.

AND IN AFRICA?

It is easy to imagine that many or even most of the emigrants from England must have supported Rhodes. It was from their ranks that Rhodes recruited his "pioneers", volunteers and the administrative cadres of the colonies. It was among them that he distributed shares, calling upon them to play their part in his grand designs and to receive their share of the profits.

Yet, surprising though it may seem, it was the Afrikaners and their party the Afrikaner Bond which made him Prime Minister of the Cape Colony in 1890.

He appealed to the Afrikaners primarily because of his measures to develop farming. He opened up new possibilities for them to grow rich, showing them how to transform their patriarchal farms into profitable enterprises. To improve fruit production he invited experts from California. He ordered birds from America, which kept the citrus trees free of insects. After a visit to the Ottoman Sultan in Istamboul in 1894 he arranged for angora goats to be shipped from the Sublime Porte. He explained how the development of industry and the construction of railways facilitated the marketing of agricultural produce.

Besides, he offered the Afrikaners a system of dues that was clearly to their advantage, admittedly at the same time trying to secure their support for a similar alteration of tariffs on the export of diamonds.

He also assured the Afrikaners that British expansion into the interior of the continent would bring benefits to them too.

Skillfully playing on growing bourgeois attitudes among the Cape Afrikaners Rhodes endeavoured to drive a wedge between them and the people in the patriarchal Transvaal. Kruger, meanwhile, was trying to weaken the British influence, and thus placed all sorts of obstacles in the way of trade with the Cape Colony. In 1894 construction work was completed on the railway line from the Transvaal to Delagoa Bay on the Mozambican coast of the Indian Ocean. The line had been built, contrary to Rhodes's wishes, with the assistance of the Germans, and all his attempts to buy it were rejected by Kruger. Once this line was opened Transvaal's dependence on the Cape Colony was considerably diminished, and Kruger promptly increased the tariffs on the Cape-Transvaal border. This aroused the indignation of many of the Cape Afrikaners and prompted a new rapprochement with Rhodes.

In his effort to create a bond between the Cape Afrikaners and the British Empire Rhodes sent Jan Hofmeyr, leader of the Afrikaner Bond, to represent the Cape Colony at an imperial conference in Ottawa in 1894.

Applying all these measures, yet without trusting in them exclusively, Rhodes also attempted to bribe members of the Afrikaner press and distributed shares in his Company among Afrikaner politicians in the Cape Colony.

The Afrikaners in his cabinet of ministers were closer to Rhodes than the few Englishmen who were regarded as liberals. In his anxiety to maintain a firm, one-party government, which would accept its Prime Minister's view without any beating around the bush, Rhodes often had less difficulty finding a common language with the Afrikaner members of the cabinet, than with his liberal countrymen.

The stumbling stone proved to be the "native policy".

In the Cape Colony the franchise was given to anyone who had immovable property worth twenty-five pounds. In 1892 Rhodes sharply increased this qualification. Now it was necessary to own property worth seventy-five pounds or to receive a salary of fifty pounds a year and to have a rudimentary ability to read and write English. This measure further reduced the already small number of African voters.

But Rhodes went much further still. He elaborated a bill, which he called a "law for Africa". Initially the law was intended to apply only in the Glen Grey district in the east of the Cape, hence its name: the Glen Grey Act. The law stipulated that the Africans were to be allotted plots of land, each family receiving eight acres. But the families were large and the farming methods extremely primitive, with the result that these plots did not by any means satisfy everyone. In addition the district was considered to be overpopulated and there were not enough plots to go round. A tax was introduced for men who possessed no land—of ten shillings a year. Rhodes described this as "a gentle stimulus to these people to make them go on working".[25]

Racial segregation was so extensively applied in this district that its inhabitants now lost the right to vote to the Cape Parliament. As if by way of compensation their own local elective organs were set up. The district was declared African territory and Europeans were no longer permitted to reside in it.

In this law we can already see features of the policies which are followed in South Africa today and which go under the name of "apartheid". Rhodes's "reforms" turned the Glen Grey district into a forerunner of today's bantustans.

When this law was debated in Parliament Rhodes insisted that he aimed to extend the Glen Grey experiment to all the "native" areas.

"I hope we shall have one native policy in South Africa," he affirmed.[26]

Speaking in the Cape Parliament on July 30, 1894, Rhodes justified the need for this law by referring to the laziness of the Africans. "Their present life is very similar to that of the young European about town, who lounges about the Club during the day and dresses himself for a tea-party in the afternoon, and in the evening drinks too much, and probably finishes up with immorality".

He added: "Now, I say the natives are children. They are just emerging from barbarism".[27] Thus Rhodes came to the conclusion that the natives had to be forced to work, to do manual labour, and that this would be the best possible way of life for them. (It is revealing that the editors of the journal *New Rhodesia*, quoting these remarks by Rhodes fifty years after his death, should see in them a concern for the happiness and welfare of the Africans).

The liberals described this as the introduction of forced slave labour. Not without a touch of irony Rhodes compared the life-style of the Africans with the behaviour of the most frivolous circles of British aristocratic youth. As he saw it, the African and the young gentleman were equally idle and useless. He informed the members in a parliamentary debate:

"I was much more of a slave than any of those natives could easily be. . . for nine mortal years of my life; and it was compulsory slavery too . . . six years at school I had to work five hours during the day and prepare work for the next day for three hours in the evening, while at College I was compounded in the evenings and not allowed out after 9 o'clock."

One of the liberals sarcastically enquired: "And you never went out, I suppose?"[28]

Rhodes's ideas were echoed by Lord Grey, who wrote that work was foreign to the Africans. Harry Johnston also believed that unless the natives worked, under European supervision, on the development of the rich resources of Tropical Africa—where they had led useless, unproductive, baboons' lives—then, by virtue of existing circumstances and under pressure from the impatient, hungry and dissatisfied human race, the combined energies of Europe and Asia would plunge them back into slavery which in the coming struggle would be an alternative of complete elimination.

Yet all the while Rhodes insisted that he was not proceeding from a racist position, not from any belief in the racial inferiority of Africans. "I could never accept the position that we should disqualify a human being on account of his colour," he asserted.[29]

Rhodes's views rested on the belief that by virtue of its historical development European civilization had stolen a march of two thousand years on Africa. "In fact," he insisted, "it is not a question of colour at all ... I think we have been extremely liberal in granting barbarism of forty or fifty years training what we have ourselves obtained only after many hundreds of years of civilization."[30]

It would be wrong to imagine that this line of argument led Rhodes to conclude that the Africans should be introduced to European civilization as quickly as possible. On the contrary, Rhodes believed that the Africans in the Glen Grey district and other "native reserves" "should be apart from white men."[31]

Neither was he in favour of encouraging European-style education for the Africans. He sounded a warning against "over-educating" the Africans:

"I ... have found some excellent establishments where the natives are taught Latin and Greek. They are turning out Kaffir parsons, most excellent individuals but the thing is overdone. I find that these people cannot find congregations for them. There are Kaffir parsons everywhere—these institutions are turning them out by the dozen. They are turning out a dangerous class. They are excellent so long as the supply is limited but the country is overstocked with them. These people will not go back and work and that is why I say that the regulations of these industrial schools should be framed by the Government; otherwise these Kaffir parsons would develop into agitators against the Government."[32]

Rhodes also supported the bill brought in by the Afrikaner Bond, on the introduction of corporal punishment for "disobedient" African labourers. This bill was one of the main causes

Rhodes on his journey through Rhodesia

of the estrangement of the more progressive members of the English community in the Cape Colony from Rhodes. This breach did not occur immediately.

There had been a time when Rhodes had cast his spell over these people too. Olive Schreiner herself once described him as "the only great man and man of genius South Africa possesses".[33] The opinion of this woman carried considerable weight. Her novel *The Story of an African Farm* was highly regarded in England, America, Germany and Russia, where it had been translated in 1893. Olive Schreiner was a friend of Karl Marx' daughters and was closely acquainted with leading socialist thinkers in Western Europe at the time. Her stories were translated into many foreign languages. Today her name is featured in the programme of the South African Communist Party. In this document Olive Schreiner's views are described as socialist and her convictions as revolutionary.

That Cecil Rhodes was able for a time to bring even Olive Schreiner under his sway is an indication of his remarkable ability to influence people. Schreiner later admitted that she suffered one of the gravest disillusionments of her life when he finally saw Rhodes in his true colours. In her next story he describes Rhodes as deadly for Blacks.[34]

In the end the liberal group in Parliament was able to get he corporal punishment bill thrown out.

In May 1893 Rhodes purged from his cabinet those members who had objected to his "native policy" and who refused to turn blind eye to the corrupt activities of one of the ministers. Rhodes called on the entire government to resign, and at once formed a new cabinet, this time without the dissenting members. These latter began to form a new party, called the Progressive Party. But so long as Rhodes enjoyed the support of the Afrikaner Bond their activities posed no threat.

In this way a paradoxical situation arose: it was precisely the Afrikaner politicians in the Cape government and parliament who ensured the stability of Rhodes's position. Then in the 1894 parliamentary elections Rhodes's supporters gained two thirds of the seats. The universal adulation accorded Cecil Rhodes inevitably started to tell on his behaviour and the manner of his life.

His language became increasingly bombastic: "That is my thought". "My thought" was one of his favourite expressions.

In Cape Town Rhodes bought for what was then a fabulous sum—£60,000—an area of land measuring fifteen hundred acres, in which stood a number of old buildings known in Dutch as Groote Schuur—the Big Barns. The buildings dated back in the times when the Cape Colony belonged to the Dutch East India Company. Rhodes decided to build there a house that would serve not only as a mansion for himself and his retinue but also as the official residence of the Prime Minister of the Cape Colony and the premier of the future "united" South Africa.

Engaging the services of an excellent architect Rhodes did in fact erect a remarkably fine house, and not a vulgar, *nouveau riche* monstrosity. The house was built in the old Dutch style. In it he set up a large library. At the turn of this century this was probably one of the best libraries in Africa. The book list is still extant[35]—I have seen it myself at Rhodes House in Oxford.

A considerable part of the library consisted of books, atlases and maps on Africa, beginning with the seventeenth century. Works on South Africa are selected with particular care. Among

Groote Shuur, Rhodes's mansion in Cape Town

them were the books of George McCall Theal, an unlucky pros
pector who suffered a fiasco with the diamond mines, but the
became the first professional South African historian.

Aristotle, Plato, Tacitus, Titus Livy, Pliny, Virgil, the whol
of Ovid, sixteen editions of Cicero and books about him. . . .Bein
interested in Ancient authors, Rhodes hired linguists to tran:
late Ancient Greek and Latin works for him.

Nor were the works of John Ruskin, Voltaire or Rousseau fo.
gotten, of course. The classic research by the English ethnographe
Edward B. Tylor *Primitive Culture*, which is still published toda:
a book with the fashionable title *The Yellow Danger*; one :
Winston Churchill's first books; biographies of famous people; te
books on Napoléon, including *Napoleon's System of Educatio:*

An important, if not the most important part of the libra:
consisted of books on state and civil law. There were dozens :
books on labour legislation, on the agrarian question, on Roma
law; on the constitutional system of the United States of Am:
rica, Canada, Australia and Switzerland. The shelves also he:
Problems of Poverty by John A. Hobson, the economist who w:
one of the harshest critics of Rhodes and his policy.

Rhodes's obvious interest in the ideas of socialism can b
judged from the presence of books by Frederick Engels *Socialis:*

Utopian and Scientific) and Edward B. Aveling *The Students' Marx*, as well as, apparently, Dr A. Shaffle's *Quintessence of Socialism*.

The richness of the library may be judged from the books Russia, a country that might seem to have been rather remote om Rhodes's direct interests: six books by Lev Tolstoy; three oks on Peter the Great; *Underground Russia, Russia under the ars* and other books by the Narodnik Sergius Stepniak-Kravinsky, who spent the last years of his life (1884-1895) in London; a book by the well-known American traveller George Ken n on the harsh conditions endured by the exiles in Siberia; book translated from the Russian *A Russian Province of the orth* by A. Engelhardt. There were several books on the politi s of czarist Russia: *Russian Politics* by Herbert M. Thompson, *ussia in Central Asia* by George Curzon, *The War in Crimea* E. Hameley, and *England and Russia* by W. C. Baxter.

The presence of these books at Rhodes's house (many of em, moreover, in the billiard room) in no way means, of course, at Rhodes had read them all. The choice of books does, wever, reflect his interests and tastes.

In the last years of his life, Rhodes, in the words of one his secretaries, liked to read half a dozen books at a time, tting down one and picking up another. His favourite reading s still Marcus Aurelius, Plutarch's *Lives*, Edward Gibbon's *he Decline and Fall of the Roman Empire*, a number of well-itten biographies, *England in Egypt* by Alfred Milner, and the en famous book by Admiral Mehan on the role of military ght.

Rhodes also had a notebook in which he wrote down the otes he liked most, the vast majority of these being the thoughts Gibbon.

Rhodes was less fond of belles lettres, though the library d contain, for example, almost all of Balzac and works of Omar hayyam. Rhodes explained his dislike of Dickens in that he vas not interested in the class of people that Dickens wrote out".[36] He hardly read any poetry, but had all Kipling's works the library.

Most of Rhodes' domestic staff were Africans. They included obengula's two sons, whom Rhodes loved to show off to his ests.

Among the celebrated guests who stayed in Rhodes's new ma
sion were the Prince of Wales—the future King Edward V]
Rudyard Kipling and the young Winston Churchill. Touri
and ordinary citizens—provided they were white, of course—we
also allowed to relax on the steps of the mansion and to picr
under the trees in the grounds. This greatly boosted the populari
of the hospitable householder.

Rhodes's domination over all areas of life in South Afri
is succinctly captured by Mark Twain: "In the opinion of ma
people Mr Rhodes is South Africa; others think he is only
large part of it."

This influence also spread into the boundless British Empi
According to Twain, "he is the only colonial in the British don
nions whose goings and comings are chronicled and discuss
under all the globe's meridians, and whose speeches, unclippe
are cabled from all the ends of the earth".[37]

Even beyond the bounds of British Empire—in France,
Germany, in Italy, despite their condemnation of his activiti
the ruling circles still saw in him an example to emulate.
Rhodes's ascent they saw a symbol of the age.

The Afrikaners are laying their arms. Fr
Johannes Meintjes's book *De Boerenoorlog
Beeld Fibula,* Haarlem, 1978.

INSTIGATOR
of the Boer War

The Conspiracy Against the Afrikaners

One day at the very beginning of 1896 *The Times* publish
a letter which at once caught the attention of all its reade
The author of the letter was a household name: Lady Warwic
The celebrated Daisy, fabled society beauty and inamorata
the Prince of Wales.

It is inconceivable that any reader, after seeing her name at t
foot of the letter, would not have cast his eye over the conten

Warwick Cas
Jan. 4, 18

"Sir,

"It passes belief that today the English Press is so far forge
ful of its bright traditions as to discuss, in cold blood, the pr
pective shooting or hanging of Englishmen by the Boers. . .

"Sir, would any Englishman worthy of the name and t
nation have failed to act exactly as Dr Jameson and his galla
companions have done? He is appealed to by the leading residen
of Johannesburg to come to the assistance of their women an
children at a moment when a revolution is seen to be inevitab
On his way to succour his countrymen with a force of mount
police, and after having disclaimed every intention of hostili
to the Boers, he is apparently attacked by their armed forc
Further than this we as yet know nothing.

"But, whatever may have been his fate, there is not an Englis
woman of us all whose heart does not go out in gratitude an
sympathy to these brave men. They did their duty, and if th
have gone to their death, even in a fair fight, so much the wor
for the Boers. But if they have been taken prisoners, to l
afterwards done to death in cold blood, then there is no long
room in South Africa for a 'Republic' administered by their mu
derers. Neither German nor French jealousy can weigh in t
balance at such a moment. . .

"Are we, in short, so stranded in the shallows of diplomacy and of German intrigues that it is a crime for our kinsfolk to succour their kinsfolk in a mining camp in South Africa! Had Dr Jameson, on the contrary, turned a deaf ear to the appeal of these of our race..."

The letter is long. It must have been strange for her contemporaries to see the radiant Daisy suddenly talking about Hottentots and Bushmen, and describing how these wretched creatures had been persecuted by the repulsive Boers. It was so much more in character for her to recall how the Boers had been abused by the recently deceased Randolph Churchill. Or in note, with reference to those English gentlemen taken prisoner by the Afrikaners, that they were "personally known to many of us".

Her letter made a profound impression on its readers. Twenty-five years later Margot Asquith, wife of the British politician Lord Herbert Asquith, begins a volume of her memoirs by reproducing the full text of this letter.[1]

At much the same time as publishing this letter, January 1896, *The Times* printed a considerable number of letters similar in content and attitude. Despite the low-key presentation of letters in *The Times*'s correspondence page, and the sober and staid appearance of the newspaper in general, with no photographs or drawings, these letters created a sensation. They were remarkable for their highly emotional tone, most uncharacteristic of *The Times*, and the lists of prominent names that stood beneath them.

A few days after Daisy's letter to *The Times* the poet Alfred Austin published his poem "Jameson's Ride". The following stanzas are typical of the poem:

> *Let lawyers and statesmen addle*
> *Their pates over points of law:*
> *If sound be our sword, and saddle,*
> *And gun-gear, who cares one straw?*
> *When men of our own blood pray us*
> *To ride to their kinsfolk's aid,*
> *Not Heaven itself shall stay us*
> *From the rescue they call a raid.*

> *There are girls in the gold-reef city,*
>   *There are mothers and children too!*
> *And they cry, "Hurry up! for pity!"*
>   *So what can a brave man do?*
> *If even we win, they'll blame us:*
>   *If we fail, they will howl and hiss.*
> *But there's many a man lives famous*
>   *For daring a wrong like this!*

For this ode Austin was not only paid a fee of twenty-five guineas: it was largely thanks to "Jameson's Ride" that he received the highest accolade accorded to a poet in England: he was appointed Poet Laureate as successor to Tennyson, who had died four years before.

The publication of these letters and verses marked the beginning of a newspaper war between England and Germany, in the course of which there were numerous other memorable events.

But the reason for all these developments was Cecil Rhodes's new war—his second, not counting minor armed clashes with the Portuguese and some African peoples.

LIKE A BOLT OF LIGHTNING

Exactly a week before Daisy's letter, on December 29, 1895, in the tiny village of Pitsani Potluko, in Tswana territory, the sound was heard of army bugles calling assembly. At that time the main military units of the Chartered Company were stationed there, beside the Transvaal frontier, having been transferred there from Rhodesia. With them was the Company Administrator: Dr Jameson.

The end of December is mid-summer in Southern Africa. On that day, a Sunday, the men and officers were idly waiting for the heat to abate so they could play sport, or cards, or go drinking. Suddenly they received orders to fall in by three p.m.

Jameson informed them that he had received an extremely important letter from Johannesburg, requesting them to go to the assistance of the British population of the city, who were being subjected to intolerable harassment from the Afrikaner authorities. He read the letter out to the assembled troops.

It stated that Kruger was oppressing the British in the Transvaal, and all foreigners in general—or Uitlanders, as they are called in Dutch. The taxes paid by Uitlanders gave the Afrikaner treasury its main source of income—gold mining, together with all other industry and commerce, was in the hands of the Uitlanders, while the Afrikaners continued, as of old, to live on their farms. It was on these Uitlanders that the country's entire modern economy rested, yet they were denied the right to vote in elections for the Volksraad (Parliament)—the Afrikaner parliament, since the government regarded them as temporary residents. A petition was addresed to the Transvaal government by forty thousand Uitlanders, seeking full civil rights, but their request was turned down. An extremely tense situation developed.

"The government (i.e. of the Transvaal—*Tr.*) riles the national sense of Englishmen at every turn. What will be the condition of things here in the event of conflict? Thousands of unarmed men, women, and children of our race will be at the mercy of well-armed Boers, while property of enormous value will be in great peril... The circumstances are so extreme that we cannot but believe that you and the men under you will not fail to come to the rescue of people who will be so situated."[2]

This highly emotional appeal ended with a very business-like promise to reimburse all expenses incurred.

The text was followed by five signatures: the inner circle of Rhodes's and his associate Alfred Beit's entourage. These were Rhodes's elder brother, Colonel Francis Rhodes; the mining engineer John Hays Hammond, whose expertise and support Rhodes valued so highly that he poached him from Barnato by offering a fabulous salary—the equivalent of 75,000 dollars per year plus a share of the profits; Lionel Phillips, who, despite being President of the Transvaal Chamber of Mines, was still totally dependent on Beit, like the remaining two signatories: the gold moghul George Farrar and the lawyer Charles Leonard, chairman of the Transvaal National Union, an Uitlander organization that had been petitioning since 1892 for electoral rights.

There was of course something strange about the content of this letter. The lamentation about the wretched position of the "unarmed men, women and children" was not substantiated anywhere in the letter. As for their being denied the right to vote in the Transvaal: many people regarded this as quite normal.

President Kruger of the Transvaal was always adamant that the Uitlanders had only come to the Transvaal for a limited time, to make money. He pointed out that none of them were prepared to renounce their own citizenship, and only wished to acquire that of the Transvaal in addition to their first, their main citizenship. There was considerable truth in Kruger's assertions. It is quite another matter that many of the Uitlanders subsequently put down roots in the Transvaal and remained there permanently; this often came about quite independently and contrary to their original intentions.

This was all quite evident to anyone who bothered to give the least thought to the real situation of the Uitlanders. But Cecil Rhodes's soldiers and officers were not distinguished for their ability or proclivity to reflect on such issues, which they regarded anyway as too general and somewhat abstract.

The following year, 1897, Olive Schreiner published her story "Trooper Peter Halket of Mashonaland". In Halket she depicts a typical soldier in the Chartered Company's detachments: ". . .the jaws were hard set, and the thin lips of the large mouth were those of a man who could strongly desire the material good of life, and enjoy it when it came his way".

A few pages later she continues: "Then Trooper Peter Halket fell to thinking. It was not often that he thought. . . Peter Halket had never been given to much thinking. . . As a rule he lived in the world immediately about him, and let the things of the moment impinge on him and fall off again as they would, without much reflection".

When he did reflect, his thoughts turned on subjects such as this: "All men made money when they came to South Africa —Barney Barnato, Rhodes,—they all made money out of the country—eight millions, twelve millions, twenty-six millions, forty millions: why should not he?"[3]

It is a vicious portrait, but in many respects it seems quite just.

The ranks of soldiers and officers, to whom Jameson read this letter from Johannesburg, contained many Peter Halkets. Jameson added his own view, that they should answer this appeal for help without delay.

His words were greeted with universal delight. That same evening a cavalry column set out in the direction of the Transvaal border. It was very close: only three and a half miles away.

An'a drop into nothin' beneath you
as straight as a beggar can spit...[4]

...They crossed the border with light hearts. This was partly because of Jameson's assurances that he did not expect any armed clashes and that they would only have to fight in the event of an Afrikaner attack. According to him the one and only purpose of the expedition was to defend the peace-loving inhabitants of Johannesburg.

Today we cannot but marvel at the blind obedience with which these men followed Jameson. Anything must have seemed better than the tedium of the camp in those barren parts on the edge of the Kalahari desert, beneath the blazing sun.

Here they had a chance to visit the "City of Gold", to seize their share of the fun, and, who knows, maybe of the riches too!

What could be more natural than to celebrate the occasion with a few drinks? As a result, the two soldiers Jameson sent to cut the telegraph wires linking the border posts with Pretoria, cut the wrong wires.

About four hundred men and officers of the Mashonaland Mounted Police crossed the border, together with one hundred and fifty Africans—bearers and servants. They had with them eight Maxim machine guns, three artillery guns, six hundred and forty horses and one hundred and fifty eight mules. They were under the command of Colonel John Willoughby. They marched all night. By morning they had covered thirty-nine of the one hundred and fifty miles that separated them from Johannesburg, and they joined forces with a second unit that had crossed the border further to the south. This comprised one hundred and twenty-two men and officers of the Bechuanaland Border Police.

Together they constituted an impressive force for a surprise invasion. They felt assured of the element of surprise, since they knew the telegraph lines had been cut. In happy ignorance they pressed on towards Johannesburg.

The Afrikaners maintained no border posts. But on Monday morning, December 30, the government in Pretoria received a telegram from an official in a small settlement near the western border: "British troops have entered republic from Mafeking, cut telegraph wires, and are on the march toward Johannesburg."[5] Soon they received information about the size of the force, and their armaments. Kruger at once dispatched orders to all the adjacent districts: the Afrikaners home guard was to assemble and surround the British.

A messenger was sent to Jameson to ask what he had in mind and to demand that he and his men turn back at once. In reply Jameson repeated what he had said to his own soldiers.

Then, when they had covered another third of the journey, they met another messenger bringing an appeal to them to turn back, this time not from the Afrikaners but from the British High Commissioner Sir Hercules Robinson.

Robinson learnt of all this from Rhodes. Rhodes knew about the expedition almost immediately, on Sunday evening. He at once summoned one of the officials of the British Imperial Secretary and announced in his presence: "Jameson has taken the bit between his teeth and gone into Transvaal!"[6]

Rhodes, however, only conveyed the news to Robinson the following morning, by which time Jameson's troops had already penetrated deep into Afrikaner territory. Thus by the time Robinson's messenger reached Jameson he had covered two thirds of the distance.

Jameson and Colonel Willoughby refused to obey Robinson's order. Willoughby explained that retreat was out of the question: they would not be able to find sufficient provisions and fodder on the territory they had covered. In addition, the horses were tired, it would take several days to return, and armed units of Afrikaners had by then assembled behind them. They only had one option: to press forward, to the friends waiting for them in Johannesburg and its environs.

Meanwhile in Johannesburg an old conspiracy had come to light. The very same people who had appealed to Jameson for help had set up a Reform Committee in Johannesburg itself. They drew up a list of demands, supposedly put forward by all the Uitlanders, appointed a deputation to Kruger and launched a call for a massive meeting to support these demands.

On December 30 successive editions of the Johannesburg newspaper, the *Star*, hit the streets every few hours. The third edition, which came out at five p.m., told its readers: "Forces making for Johannesburg. Conflict lamentably imminent. Suspense at an end. Immeasurable gravity in the situation".[7]

For a while it seemed as though the suspense which had gripped the town for the last few weeks was indeed at an end. A "Proclamation to the Men of Johannesburg" was drawn up, in the name of the Provisional Government of the Uitlanders' Republic. It was signed by about sixty men, led by Charles Leonard and Lionel Phillips, President and Vice-President respectively of the newly-declared republic.

The rebels swiftly unpacked the crates containing weapons smuggled in earlier and hidden in mine-shafts. An announcement was even made appealing for volunteers to join a medical corps. The main centre of rebel operations was the administrative offices of Rhodes's Gold Fields company.

But it almost at once became clear that the conspiracy had been very poorly prepared. For a start, by no means all the Rand mine-owners—the "Randlords"—had been drawn in. But far worse, the instigators themselves had not obtained the broad support of the Uitlanders on which they had been reckoning. Insufficient thought had been given to the rebellion's organization. The conspirators vacillated, now giving out arms, now issuing appeals for law and order. Everything was fraught with uncertainty, indecision and fear. This became apparent in the very first hours, and particularly during the early hours of Tuesday, when the entire city kept an uneasy vigil. Everyone was frozen in anticipation, and very few dared take up their arms. And when the shout was raised in the streets: "We've licked the Dutchmen", a few heads appeared in windows for a moment, but things went no further. The citizens were biding their time. It was this that decided the fate of the town.

In the end the "Proclamation to the Men of Johannesburg" was never published. The editor of the *Star*, in which it was to be printed, was so alarmed when he saw the composed plates that he at once destroyed them. Very few printed copies remained.

By the morning of December 31 the Reform Committee was itself addressing the following appeal through this same newspaper: "The committee earnestly desires that the inhabitants refrain from taking any action which can be construed as an overt act of hostility against the government."

The engineer Hammond, one of the leaders of the Reform Committee, took fright and raised the four-colored flag of the Transvaal above the Gold Fields Company building, despite the

269

fact that he had signed the Proclamation, which firmly declared that a new republic was being set up with its own flag. The Transvaal officials refused to give Hammond a Transvaal flag, fearing that it would be dishonoured. So Hammond and his friends were forced to find four strips of coloured material—red, white, blue and green, stitch them together into the Transvaal flag and raise it in full view of an immense crowd, who quite rightly saw this as an act of capitulation.[8]

The general confusion mounted by the hour. No one knew exactly what was going on, and the most contradictory rumours flew around. The men swiftly dispatched their wives and children to Cape Town. They took the trains by storm, packing people into the carriages like sardines. One woman gave birth on the train, the child died, and she remained where she was, pressed on all sides, clutching its little body.

For three days—December 30 and 31 and January 1—the situation was constantly changing. One thing was clear, however: the Uitlander rebellion against Kruger had not taken place. It had fizzled out, without ever really flaring up.

...But Jameson and his soldiers did not know this. They continued their march forward, although their pace slowed as they became increasingly exhausted. En route they saw in the New Year. More and more frequently they glimpsed the silhouettes of Afrikaner horsemen on the horizon: these were gathering themselves into units and trying to surround the British troops. But the Afrikaners had no artillery or machine-guns, and therefore initially kept at a respectful distance.

On January 1 there were several exchanges of fire. The British were forced to use their machine-guns and artillery.

Added to all this, Jameson was let down by the local inhabitants that he had recruited as guides, to lead his troops past the main Afrikaner forces. These guides, perhaps deliberately, led the British by a route that was less than fortunate for them.

On January 1 Jameson received another message from Robinson instructing them to leave the Transvaal. Did Jameson not believe that Robinson's orders were serious? Or did he feel it was simply too late to go back?

Most probably he decided the British authorities were sending these orders as a blind, when in actual fact they were counting on the success of his expedition. The main thing was that he felt Rhodes's support behind him. He believed in victory, and victors are not put on trial. So he doggedly continued what he had begun.

But their chances of success dissipated even before they ever reached Johannesburg. Near the village of Krugersdorp, with only one day's march left to Johannesburg, the detachment fell into an ambush. At various points behind the range of hills and behind boulders the sunlight glinted on Afrikaner rifles. By now Jameson's soldiers were on their last legs. With only short halts they had been on the march for four days and nights. This last day they had had practically nothing to eat. Men and horses were collapsing with exhaustion.

From behind their cover the Afrikaners were able to pick the British soldiers off one by one. This they proceeded to do. The soldiers rushed for cover, but they were completely surrounded. The nightmare started on the evening of January 1, and was renewed at dawn the following day.

Only one course of action lay open to them: surrender. Jameson had not foreseen this. The soldiers did not even have a white rag they could use as a flag. A woman from a neighbouring farm came to the rescue: they raised her apron aloft on a wagon shaft. This was in the morning of January 2, when Jameson's casualties, dead and wounded, numbered seventy-three men.

> *Soldier, soldier come from the wars,*
> *I'll up an' tend to my true love!'*
> *'E's lying on the dead with a bullet through 'is 'ead,*
> *An' you'd best go look for a new love.*[9]

After feeding the English soldiers, who were dropping with exhaustion, the Afrikaners at once led them, crushed and crestfallen, into their capital. That same evening the gates of Pretoria's town jail clanged shut behind Jameson and his men. Here they were finally united with the Johannesburg conspirators.

AND THE PEALS OF THUNDER

Jameson's "ride", or the "Jameson Raid", lasted three and a half days. The attempted rebellion in Johannesburg was of even shorter duration. But just as thunder does not roll at the same moment as lightning strikes, the rumbles in "big politics" only started after the events in the Transvaal itself were already over.

Properly speaking, the uproar in the European capitals had in fact started on December 31, when news of the incursion into the Transvaal reached Europe. The top officials in the German foreign ministry and the colonial department, cancelling all engagements, gathered in Potsdam in Kaiser Wilhelm II's palace and resolved to take two measures without delay: first, to send a detachment of marines to the Transvaal, and second, to make a harsh presentation to the British government.

In the execution of the first of these measures the captain of the cruiser "Seeadler", positioned off the coast of Portuguese Mozambique, was ordered to set ashore a detachment of troops and dispatch them to Pretoria—ostensibly for the protection of German subjects. Meanwhile, Paul Graf von Hatzfeldt-Wildenburg, the ambassador in London, was instructed to inquire of the British government whether or not it condoned Jameson's actions, and to call for his credentials should the answer prove unsatisfactory.

The ambassador called on Lord Salisbury on January 1. The prime minister at once counselled him not to say a single word in connection with this matter, which could be interpreted as a threat, and then assured him that he did not condone Jameson's actions.[10] The ambassador did not ask for his credentials. But the following day he received even stricter instructions from Berlin: to hand Britain a note declaring that Germany would not permit any changes in the Transvaal. This ultimatum was delivered on January 2. By that evening it had become clear, however, that the situation in the Transvaal had been defused, and Hatzfeldt was able to recover his note in the morning of January 3, discovering to his relief that the British had not even got round to opening it.

The German ambassador in London could see something that was not apparent to Kaiser Wilhelm and his closest associates. An atmosphere of extraordinary excitement prevailed in London. A considerable proportion of the British population regarded the victory of the "Boer bumpkins" over famed Jameson as an insult to British national pride. And the ambassador realised that any peremptory action by the Germans could provoke a violent storm in England.

Back in Potsdam, however, Kaiser Wilhelm continued to rage. Gathering the inner circle of his government in the morning of anuary 3 he proposed that they place their marine force on lert, declare a protectorate over the Transvaal and send in German troops. This adventurist proposal horrified his listeners: uch action could only be taken once war with Britain had been lecided on. But Wilhelm had no navy, and his scheme to create a block of European states against Britain was quite unrealistic.

His ministers exhorted him to reconsider and then waited or him to cool down. Finally they persuaded him to limit himself o sending a bombastic telegram to Kruger. In it he declared: 'I express to you my sincere congratulations that you and your people, without appealing to the help of friendly powers, have ucceeded, by your own energetic action against the armed bands which invaded your country as disturbers of the peace, in restoring peace and in maintaining the independence of the country against attacks from without."[11]

On the day before Wilhelm had written to Czar Nicholas II n a more bellicose mood: "I hope that all will come right, but ome what may, I never shall allow the British to stamp out the Transvaal."[12] But the letter to the Czar was private and did not appear in the press, while his telegram to Kruger at once became a newspaper sensation. It had been intended to be just that.

This telegram became the first peal in that roll of thunder which was to be heard throughout the entire world. "Without appealing to the help of friendly powers", the Kaiser had written. In other words, Germany considered itself fully entitled to take up arms and join the scramble in Southern Africa—at least that was how his words were interpreted in England. It is easy to imagine the storm of indignation this caused. Daisy's letter was one of the first reproofs delivered to Wilhelm, but by no means the most strongly worded.

This precipitated a whole series of developments. The German government first sounded out the Portuguese, to see whether Lisbon would permit a German expeditionary corps to march through Mozambique to the Transvaal. At the same time the Pan-Germanic Union, the Colonial Union and other chauvinist German organizations, which began campaigning under the slogan "Hands off!", decided to make use of this anti-British fervour to push forward programmes for the accelerated construction of a German navy in preparation for war with Britain.

Even in England matters were not confined to a newspaper

The colonial division of Africa gave African woodcarvers new ideas for their work: here, Kaiser Wilhelm and Queen Victoria

war. On January 8 the government announced that it had set up a so-called flying squadron. British companies severed relations with their German counterparts. London mobs smashed the windows of German shops and beat up German sailors. Ambassador Hatzfeldt reported to Berlin that if the British government had decided to declare war they would have done so with the full support of public opinion.[13] The English journal *The Speaker* observed that on this occasion the riff-raff and street rabble had joined forces with "society".

The squabbling was mostly between England and Germany, but other governments, parties and organizations also joined in to some extent or another. Public opinion practically everywhere supported the Afrikaners, as the weaker side. To this day the Transvaal Museum in Pretoria has on display the gifts sent at the time to Jameson's victor, the Afrikaner general P. A. Cronje. Among them is a sword, decorated with a picture of an Afrikaner defeating a crowned lion. This gift came from France.

THE SECRETS ARE REVEALED

The cost of this sabre-rattling campaign, which marked a new stage in the arms race of that time, was to be borne by tens of millions of tax-payers in Britain, Germany and the Transvaal.

At this stage we should consider who the real instigators were, and, since we are primarily concerned with Rhodes, what role he played in the conflict. And what, in fact, was the British government's role in it?

A great number of years passed before historians got to the bottom of all this. It was a very difficult process bringing each new document to light, while those privy to the truth were most unwilling to divulge their knowledge.

This, of course, applies to the conspiracy itself, rather than to Rhodes's mere aspiration to include the Transvaal in a "federation" of Southern African states under the British flag.

Rhodes never made any secret of this cherished dream. By virtue of its economic role and even of its geographical position the Transvaal was so important, that without it any "federation" would have been quite out of the question. Until the end of 1894 Rhodes still hoped that he would achieve this without an armed conflict, by economic means, by applying pressure behind the scenes, forming secret compacts and bribing key officials.

But in his pursuit of this dream Rhodes kept on encountering new obstacles. He was inclined to personify these, and to see the figure of Kruger behind them all. In his view, all opposition to his plans was rooted in Kruger's narrow-mindedness, in the President's inability to understand the advantages the Transvaal would derive from its incorporation in the British Empire.

A man in his seventies, Kruger was without doubt a representative of the old school. His youth and manhood had been closely associated with the Great Trek of the Afrikaners north from the Cape Colony and with the first decades of the Transvaal's existence, long before the gold rush. In those days the Transvaal was almost totally insulated from the influence of European civilization. The Afrikaners lived on isolated farms, far apart. Many of them were illiterate and if they did read it tended to be from only one book: the large family Bible, the contents of which were interpreted quite literally, as their ancestors the Calvinists had interpreted it when they left the shores of Europe in the seventeenth century.

Of course, Kruger was out alone in bearing the burden of the Afrikaner past. After a visit to South Africa in the year of 1896, during which he observed the patriarchal life of the Afrikaners, Mark Twain commented in his characteristic manner: "Summed up—according to the information thus gained—this is the Boer:

"He is deeply religious, profoundly ignorant, dull, obstinate, bigoted, uncleanly in his habits, hospitable, honest in his dealings with the whites, a hard master to his black servant, lazy, a good shot, good horseman, addicted to the chase, a lover of political independence, a good husband and father . . . until latterly he had no schools, and taught his children nothing; news is a term which has no meaning to him, and the thing itself he cares nothing about."[14]

Elsewhere Twain subjects the Afrikaners to still more savage ridicule. His derision was shared by the British, whose newspapers abounded with scurrilous anecdotes about "Oom (Uncle) Kruger".

But Kruger was anything but a senile old man. However patriarchal his views may have been, he was always able to find his bearings in the most complex developments of international politics. Without this skill he would not have been able to retain the office of president. He was in no position to rule by brute force: his country was not a great power and anyway his citizens by nature were a truculent breed.

At the same time, the problems he faced grew more complicated every year. First came the "gold fever", then the massive influx of foreigners. By the mid-nineties these almost outnumbered the Afrikaners themselves, and were certainly more numerous than the adult Afrikaner population. If the Uitlanders had been given the vote they would have installed their own government! There was only one course of action open to him: he had constantly to find new excuses, to play for time and to manoeuvre.

In exactly the same way he manoeuvred between the great powers, Britain and Germany, constantly endeavouring to play one off against the other. He never made any secret of this and even declared at a banquet given in honour of Kaiser Wilhelm II's birthday: "Our small republic is still only crawling about beneath the great powers, and we can feel that when the one is about to step on our foot the other tries to prevent this."[15]

In 1894 construction work on the railway—quite independent of the British and giving the Transvaal its own gateway to the ocean through Portuguese Mozambique—was finished at last. This boosted Kruger's confidence, and he started to obstruct the British wherever possible—he raised the duties on the railway line leading into British territory, and on his orders other routes through the Transvaal were closed to them altogether.

In this wily old man Rhodes had a formidable opponent. Rhodes was growing ever wealthier and more powerful—but the same was true of Kruger, too. The gold mining industry prospered, the mine-owners grew rich, but the Kruger government taxed them and all the Uitlanders so heavily that the Transvaal had long since ceased to be a destitute republic, permanently on the verge of bankruptcy. Over the nine or ten years since the opening of the first gold mines the revenue of the Transvaal treasury had multiplied more than eleven times. And although the Afrikaner republic was almost completely surrounded by British possessions, it started to receive the most up-to-date arms, which were accompanied by instructors, from Europe, primarily Germany.

Was Rhodes to try and outlast Kruger, to wait him out, in the meantime acting stealthily and surreptitiously? But, in the first place, Rhodes knew that he himself did not have all that long to live, and perhaps less even than the elderly president. Secondly, as he proceeded from one triumph to the next, Rhodes became convinced that he was destined always to succeed. He became imperious, extremely self-confident, and intolerant of any criticism. The success of each risky venture impelled him to engage in new escapades.

From the end of 1894 he started preparations for a coup d'état in the Transvaal. In this, as in all his projects, he was not the originator of the idea.

The idea of seizing the Transvaal had already occurred to the High Commissioner Henry Loch. In July 1894, when Loch visited Johannesburg, the Uitlanders unharnessed the horses from the carriage in which he rode together with Kruger, and pulled the carriage forward themselves, throwing an enormous British flag over it, much to Kruger's fury. This episode deeply impressed Loch: it taught him to believe in the Uitlanders and he started asking Lionel Phillips, president of the Chamber of Mines, how many guns they had and whether they would be able to hold the town for six days until reinforcements arrived.

On his return to Cape Town Loch posted a detachment of soldiers in Tswana territory, right by the Transvaal frontier. It was this detachment that later marched into the Transvaal with Jameson. In addition Loch asked the then Colonial Secretary Lord Ripon to send another five thousand soldiers to the Cape Colony and even to give his authorisation to an invasion of the Transvaal.

Rhodes knew all about Loch's plan, but he believed the coup should be carried out primarily by local forces—the Uitlanders and those amongst the "pioneers" and volunteers who had settled in South Africa, while the British government itself should keep strictly behind the scenes.

At the end of 1895 Rhodes, accompanied by Jameson, visited the Transvaal and met Kruger. As before, they failed to find a common language, and then Rhodes did start discussing the possibility of a conspiracy and coup d'état with some of the Uitlander leaders.

The plan which misfired so badly in December 1895 had, in all essential features, been worked out by Rhodes a year before, in December 1894.

Naturally enough, it had been kept a deep secret, as had Loch's plan. But from documents which have since come to light it is clear that a full year before the Jameson Raid Rhodes had decided to make his company, the Gold Fields of South Africa, the centre of the conspiracy. The company was to finance the activities of the secret Reform Committee, which was also composed of Rhodes's employees and his closest confederates. Rhodes's other company, De Beers, was to be responsible for organizing the transport of arms from Kimberley to Johannesburg.

Rhodes also earmarked funds to reward anyone who would agree on the decisive day to take up arms to overthrow the Transvaal government in Johannesburg and to hand over power to the Reform Committee. Jameson, standing on alert at the border, would then charge into the Transvaal. After this the British High Commissioner would act as "mediator", and the Transvaal would be "annexed", as had happened once before, in 1877,

Rhodes recruited only one of the gold-mining moguls into the conspiracy: Alfred Beit, who had been Rhodes's partner in De Beers and in the Chartered Company, but had his own gold-mining company.

There were various reasons for Rhodes's reluctance to draw others in. On a personal level he was hostile to some of his fellow industrialists. Furthermore, at that time, from 1894 practically to the end of 1895, the gold-mining industry was experiencing a boom, bringing in fabulous profits, despite the high taxation imposed by the Transvaal authorities. Consequently, the idea of a coup would have appalled many of the gold-mining magnates, who would have been terrified that some unforeseen turn of events would undermine their profits.

There was another side to all this, too. Hammond, Rhodes's adviser on mining matters, had predicted that he would now have to start looking at much deeper seams, as the seams nearer the surface would soon be exhausted. Rhodes's Gold Fields Company was the first to start sinking deep shafts. But this entailed much greater expenditure: on dynamite, equipment and labour. All three of these were expensive, and on top of everything there were the hefty taxes levied on them by Kruger's government.

Later it was deep seams that were to provide the main source of gold in the Transvaal, but at that time production from them did not seem very efficient. The majority of the mine-owners had yet to come up against the problem, but it affected Rhodes keenly. Beit, in his turn, knew it through Rhodes's experience.

Mining costs had somehow to be cut. This meant that taxes had to be reduced, and the only way to do this was by eliminating the system introduced by Kruger.

The conspiracy took shape in October 1895. Troops of the Chartered Company were moved from Rhodesia to Bechuanaland, to the Transvaal's western border. At the end of October Rhodes gathered together in his palatial mansion in Cape Town the men he had decided to make the ringleaders of the plot: his brother Frank, Hays Hammond, Lionel Phillips—the president of the Chamber of Mines, and Charles Leonard, Chairman of the Transvaal National Union, the Uitlander organization.

The first three unanimously shared Rhodes's views, but Leonard had to be persuaded. In fact, Rhodes never expected to

get much use out of this National Union. The Union's politica
activities were limited to the compilation of petitions, and i
was unlikely to provide the real force behind an armed coup
But the inclusion of its chairman would give the impressio
that the conspiracy was widely supported.

Last but not least, Rhodes needed the might of the Britis
government and the representative of this government in Sout
Africa, the High Commissioner. In early 1895 Rhodes, on a visi
to London, confided his plan in the then Prime Minister, Lore
Rosebery. The Prime Minister gave his approval, but insiste
that Jameson's invasion must be preceded by an uprising i
Johannesburg.

To carry out his plan Rhodes really needed Robinson as Higl
Commissioner, and not Loch. Loch might have views of hi
own, while Robinson had long been in Rhodes's pocket. In orde
to accommodate Rhodes, Loch was replaced by Robinson.

In June 1895 the Liberal government fell and the Conservative
returned to power. Salisbury was Prime Minister again, an
Joseph Chamberlain became Colonial Secretary. But their atti
tude to Rhodes's plan was the same.

On October 2 Chamberlain sent a secret inquiry to Robinson
in Cape Town: were changes going to take place in the Transvaal, and how soon? On November 4 Robinson answered in a
long letter, which, of course, was also secret. He wrote tha
the adult male population of the Transvaal Afrikaners wa
already outnumbered four to one by the Uitlanders. This wa
an exaggeration, but it was not the main point of his letter
Robinson wrote that ". . .the capitalists have now abandoned all
hope of a peaceful settlement of their grievances and contemp-
late taking the law into their own hands".

He then goes on to write directly about the conspiracy and
even about its possible outcome. "Immediately on news being
received of a rising at Johannesburg and the establishment there
of a provisional government, the High Commissioner, as the
representative of the paramount power in South Africa, should
issue a proclamation, directing both parties to desist from hostilities and to submit to his arbitration."[16] In other words, the
British High Commissioner himself would resolve the quarrel
between Rhodes's protégés and Kruger's government.

Thus both Chamberlain and Robinson not only knew about

the conspiracy: they had even determined exactly at which moment and in which manner Great Britain itself would enter the stage. On November 6 Chamberlain, acting on Rhodes's insistence, handed over a long strip of land in the British protectorate of Bechuanaland, along the Transvaal border, to the Chartered Company, on the pretext that Rhodes was constructing his railway on it.

To be sure, Rhodes had designs on the whole of Bechuanaland. But three Tswana chiefs had travelled to London to protest, much like the Ndebele emissaries six years before. Their whole affair attracted undesirable public interest, and Rhodes did not get as much as he had wanted. In a fit of rage he wrote to Fife that it was sinful and criminal to leave the immense territory of Bechuanaland to the Tswana.

Nonetheless, Rhodes gained a bridgehead for his assault on the Transvaal. At the same time Chamberlain disbanded the British Bechuanaland Police, and ordered that its weaponry be sold to the Chartered Company. In addition, many of the men and officers of this police force joined the service of the Chartered Company, boosting Jameson's forces.

On November 19 Jameson travelled to Johannesburg and held meetings with the conspirators. Together they determined the date of the uprising: December 28. It was Charles Leonard who wrote, to Jameson's dictation, the now notorious "invitation letter" from the "women and children" of Johannesburg, which Jameson subsequently read aloud to his troops when giving the order to invade the Transvaal. No date was given on the letter. Jameson took it with him, so as to be able to produce it at the right moment, put the date on it and pass it off as a call for help, hot from Johannesburg.

But by the appointed date it had become clear that the plot had been badly prepared. Far fewer arms had been smuggled into Johannesburg than had been intended. No volunteers could be found among the Uitlanders, even for generous remuneration, to attack the Afrikaner arsenals. The leakage of information was so bad that the conspiracy soon ceased to be a secret at all. It was even discussed in the Cape Town and London newspapers. Jameson himself only had six hundred armed men instead of the intended fifteen hundred.

By December 26 the conspirators in the Transvaal had changed their plan of action. The Transvaal National Union had drawn up a new petition calling for reforms and they decided to present it to Kruger on January 6. In this way the rising, planned for December 28, had to be postponed for an indefinite period, if not abandoned altogether. The conspirators did everything they could to inform Jameson and prevent him from crossing the border. Two officers were sent to warn Jameson and Hammond sent a telegram.

But Jameson, as we have seen, had ears for only one man: Rhodes. Knowing this, Frank sent his brother a telegram, and Charles Leonard went in person to Cape Town to see him.

Moreover, Chamberlain telegraphed Rhodes on December 27 that Jameson was not to proceed if there was no rising in Johannesburg.

But Rhodes did not stop Jameson. Why not? Was it his belief in his own unfailing good fortune, in his lucky star? The temptation was too great for him, and with it the hope that the appearance of Jameson in the Transvaal might galvanize those confounded, vacillating conspirators into action, and cause them to rise up after all—indeed, by now they had nothing to lose.

In any event Jameson received daily dispatches from Rhodes, bearing the signature of F. Rutherfoord Harris, his closest aide, on December 26, 27 and 28. The message of each was the same: Jameson was to stand firmly by the decisions that had already been taken.

On the 28, the final day, Jameson telegraphed to Harris that he and his men were going to proceed, unless they received orders to the contrary immediately. No such orders were given.

It is true that on December 29 Rhodes did send Jameson another telegram. But this was sent so late that Jameson had no chance of receiving it, and it was couched in such ambiguous terms that even if Jameson had received it he would hardly have interpreted it as countermanding the invasion. This dispatch could only have been intended for one purpose: in the event that the conspiracy failed it would provide some sort of alibi for Rhodes. And that only after a most favourable reading of its text.

Of course Jameson knew, without any telegrams, what Rhodes really wanted. These men understood each other perfectly. Kiplıg even maintained that there was a telepathic link between ıem. But Jameson had a mind of his own, and we may wonder ow he dared to proceed with the invasion if he knew that the ısing in Johannesburg had been called off and that his own ɔrces were three times smaller in number than were needed.

In the first place, it is clear that he must have underestimated is opponent—the Afrikaners. Secondly, he overestimated the lement of surprise of his own invasion and, to a still greater xtent, the role of his Maxim guns. He had seen their effective-ıess in battles with the Ndebele, he knew that the Afrikaners ıad no machine-guns, and he said: "You do not know the Maxim gun. I shall draw a zone of lead a mile each side of my ɔlumn and no Boer will be able to live in it".[17]

But the most important factor, of course, was Jameson's in-ıate adventurism. This was perhaps the most salient feature ɔf his character.

The outcome we have already seen. . . The Afrikaners took ıp positions where machine-guns were useless against them. The rising in Johannesburg, which flared up for an instant with he news of Jameson's invasion, at once died out. . .

Rhodes probably realised it was all over the moment he ɩaw that he no longer had any control over events. In short, ɩe had missed his last chance.

Had he been more able to view himself and his own actions ʻrom the side he might have recalled the words ascribed to Tal-ɩeyrand: "Should you engage in any chicanery, then you must ɩry your damnedest to ensure it succeeds: remember that the chicanery of unsuccessful people is never pardoned!"

But, to judge by his character, Rhodes would not have re-garded his actions as chicanery.

It is interesting to see Rhodes's reaction to the news that Jameson had crossed into the Transvaal. It is recorded for us by William Schreiner, one of the Cape ministers. On Monday December 30, he brought these tidings to Rhodes. "The moment I saw him . . . I saw a man I had never seen before. His appear-ance was utterly dejected and different. Before I could say a word, he said: 'Yes, yes, it is true. Old Jameson has upset my apple-cart.'"

At that moment he must have understood, or at least sensed,

that his political career was seriously damaged, if not totall
ruined. To think that only a few hours before he had bee
in full control. . .

It was Schreiner's impression that "Mr Rhodes was reall
broken down. He was broken down. . . He was absolutely broke
down in spirit, ruined. . ."[18] Yet it was only his political caree
that was imperilled. His millions were not in the least threa
tened, nor was his life. The fate suffered by those he ha
dragged into this sorry business was far worse. And that applie
not only to the men killed by the Afrikaners in battle.

An uncertain fate also awaited the luckless Johannesbur
rebels, particularly after the Afrikaners had found in Jameson'
saddle-bag the notorious "invitation letter" calling for the salva
tion of the women and children. More incriminating evidenc
would be hard to imagine: they had signed it themselves in
premeditated attempt to overthrow the government throug
armed rebellion. A crime punishable by death.

They all wound up in prison, awaiting this sentence, wit
the exception of Charles Leonard, who fled to Cape Tow
dressed as a woman. A number of conspirators were tried an
the ringleaders, those who had signed the appeal to Jameson
were indeed sentenced to be hanged.

In the end their sentences were commuted to fines—£25,00
each. Historians usually write that this was only to be expected
Kruger would never have dared put to death the citizens o
Great Britain and the United States. On sober reflection it i
quite natural to reach this conclusion, particularly for the histo
rian contemplating all this in his tranquil office, in anothe
place and another time.

But to those sitting in the deck and hearing themselves sen
to the gallows sober reflection does not come easily. They had
already endured their fill of fear. One of them even took his
own life.

As for Jameson himself, in the end he got off very lightly.
The British government promised Kruger that it would try Jameson, his officers and men, and punish them as its own subjects.
But when they arrived in Britain the soldiers were exonerated
of any responsibility—they had only carried out orders, after
all. Only Jameson and five officers went before the judge. The
officers received sentences of five to seven months imprison-

nent each, and Jameson fifteen months. He was released long
before the end of his term on the pretext of poor health.

Nonetheless, he had had to stare into the eyes of his own
death. First in battle, then later, when he fell into the hands
of the incensed Afrikaners, he must have expected the very worst.

The assault on the Transvaal cost Rhodes dear. In financial
terms it was not a great deal for a man of his fortune:
£400,000. This includes the fines imposed by the court on the
rebels. But on January 5 he was forced to resign the post of
Prime Minister of the Cape Colony. This was the biggest blow
of all.

By the beginning of February Rhodes was already in England.
First he conducted discussions with Chamberlain through inter-
mediaries, then on February 6 they met and talked for two hours.
They had to coordinate their lines of action, particularly in connection with the setting up by the British parliament of a
special commission of inquiry into the Jameson raid—in common parlance, the "Rhodes Commission".

Each of the two men, Rhodes and Chamberlain, was equally
anxious to screen himself. They were not even above a little
mutual blackmail. It was essential to shield the British government—this was Chamberlain's trump card, as its minister. By
shielding his government, he *ipso facto* saved himself.

Rhodes understood that he would not be able to get off scot-
free, but he was nonetheless anxious not to become the whipping
boy for the whole fiasco. He needed an opportunity to shift the
main burden of guilt onto Jameson's shoulders. He was similarly anxious that the government would not take its cue from the
Chartered Company's critics—whose number had increased
radically after the Jameson Raid—and reduce the prerogatives
of this, Rhodes's most cherished creation.

It was of course no easy task for the two men to work out
a common line of action. They laboured over this for a long time
to come.

But it was evidently at that time, in the weeks immediately
following the raid, that they reached a fundamental agreement,
deciding by a process of concealment and deceit to create the
tangled mass of fact and fiction that it has taken historians
so long to unravel.

Rhodesia Against Rhodes

For the first two and a half months after the ill-starred raid into the Transvaal Rhodes was almost continuously on the move. On January 10 he set off from Cape Town for Kimberley, perhaps anxious to feel the support of his most faithful vassals. He did indeed arrive to an enthusiastic reception. Then he returned at once to Cape Town and set sail for England on January 15. But he stayed only for four days, before leaving London on February 10, travelling through the Mediterranean to Mozambique, from where he made his way to Rhodesia.

The route he selected was not the shortest. As a retired prime minister he probably did not want to be subjected to the endless questioning, to listen to people's condolences and to suspect his well-wishers of secret gloating. He did not want to be besieged by reporters. In London and Cape Town this would have been inevitable, but a long sea-voyage provided a convenient means of escape.

Once in Rhodesia, on his own territory, he could keep himself aloof. Here he would be free to seek his own company, in a country which no one could now take away from him. He would be able to sit out the furore.

But events took a different turn.

On March 20, the day when Rhodes came ashore in Mozambique, a skirmish took place in Bulawayo between a unit of police and a group of Ndebele. News of this incident may not particularly have alarmed the Company authorities, who were still swallowing the consequences of the Jameson Raid, sweeping aside any traces which could still be concealed. But on March 23 several Europeans were killed, including one of the "commissioners on native affairs". These killings were carried out by Ndebele policemen, who had been recruited by the Company

The Secretary of State for the Colonies Joseph Chamberlain asks Cecil Rhodes and John Bull whether either of them will pay the costs of suppressing the Ndebele rising. John Bull is most indignant: he feels it's bad enough that he should have to fight for Rhodes. Cartoon from *The Labour Leader* of April 11, 1896

They were supported by the inhabitants of several villages, and were led by a brother of Lobengula.

During the following two days risings took place in several districts, and by the end of March the entire country was in revolt. The Europeans hastened from all over the country to Bulawayo and two other fortified centres. By mid-April the entire Ndebele country, with the exception of these three points, was in the hands of the insurgents.

Thus 1896 brought another great setback to Cecil Rhodes who had previously never experienced defeat.

Once the rising had begun many people realised how inevitable it had actually been. Since the end of 1895 Rhodesia had been without its chief administrator, Dr Jameson, and most of his police units, which had gone to the Transvaal with him. The company's armed forces had left the country in full view of the Ndebele, who had also been fully aware of the absence of the familiar figure of Dr Jim. They decided to avail themselves of this comparatively favourable moment.

In a lecture delivered as early as January 1896 the Czech naturalist Emil Holub predicted that after the débacle of the Jameson Raid "a rising would take place among the Matabele". In a letter received by the Vienna correspondent of *The Times* on March 30, 1896, Holub stated: "It is now nine years since I have left South Africa, but I was absolutely sure of a rising of the Matabele from the moment when I first heard of Dr Jameson's achievements."[1] Any strategist was bound to consider the possible consequences of the failure of the assault on the Transvaal, but it is doubtful whether Jameson envisaged a Matabele rising. Giving this view, Holub substantiates it with reference to Jameson's extreme self-assurance, a self-assurance which, according to Holub, was fuelled by the universal acclaim and adulation which surrounded Jameson in London.

Be that as it may, the fact remains that Rhodes and Jameson were really caught unawares by the rising. Their attention had been taken up first with the organization of the raid, and then with its failure.

It is also possible, of course, that the rising would have taken place even if Jameson had not taken his soldiers out of the country. Perhaps it was inevitable. A great deal of discontent had already built up in Southern Rhodesia, the country which now formed the central region of Rhodes's empire—between the gold and diamond kingdom to the south and the other Rhodesias to the north.

LIFE IN THE CENTRE OF HIS EMPIRE

Rhodes was keen to quickly change the traditional way of life in the Zambezi-Limpopo territory and to organize everything anew, in accordance with his own model. His aim, it must be remembered, was not merely to seize new territories, but to colonize them, and that meant creating a large and stable white community.

He imagined that he would gather here the sort of young Britons of whom he had written in his wills: people wholeheartedly committed to the idea of the greatness of their nation and their empire. Men who wished to achieve and were capable of achieving: prospectors, farmers, traders, engineers. Men of action. He wanted people with initiative who would also be blindly subservient to him—and he hoped to find these utterly incompatible qualities in the same people. This illusion was one he shared, in fact, with many historical leaders, both before and after him.

Following his lead, the British press sought to persuade its readers that the colonization of Rhodesia was a matter of British colonial pride. Rhodes's "pioneers" were held up as examples to emulate. Even *The Times* laid its colours on thick: "...Energetic, stalwart, bronzed, keen of eye, these pioneers of Matabeleland were the very pick of Anglo-Saxon manhood."[2]

Rhodes hoped that the settlers would establish the sort of farms, towns, mining industry and commerce that would make the country which bore his name a vital part of the British Empire, and perhaps of the world as a whole. He also intended Rhodesia to become the springboard for the further expansion of British dominion in Africa, for the realisation of his Cape-to-Cairo scheme—for both the telegraph line and the railway—and, in the final analysis, for the creation of a broad, continuous and stable swathe of British possessions. With his characteristic energy he set about implementing these plans.

To the amazement of the Ndebele and the Shona, increasing numbers of white men were arriving from the south. They came on horseback and in wagons, and the poorest among them often covered part of the journey on foot, many of them perishing on the way from sickness and privation.

In 1895 the European population of the country had grown to 3600. A new Bulawayo swiftly arose on a site five kilometres to the south of the devastated Ndebele capital. The streets of the new town were very broad—broad enough for a full team of oxen—usually 12 pairs, but sometimes as many as 24—to pass

Joseph Chamberlain beams like the sun as he watches Rhodes's reprisals against the Ndebele. Cartoon from *The Labour Leader* of May 23, 1896. The newspaper lampoons Chamberlain's words: "It is to such men as Cecil Rhodes that England is indebted for her Imperial greatness"

in two-way traffic. Quick-growing trees were planted. Rhodes appealed to his "pioneers" to build as many houses and as quickly as possible. The town very quickly took shape.

Brick and stone buildings rose on the site of the old corrugated-iron shacks. Cricket pitches were laid and even a racecourse, not to mention the retail shops and bars. By March 1895—slightly more than a year after the war with Lobengula—the population of Bulawayo numbered more than fifteen hundred Europeans, and that of Salisbury, more than seven hundred.

The man who gave the country its name wished to develop private enterprise as swiftly as possible, to instil in people "the spirit of Cecil Rhodes". He vigorously encouraged in the "pioneers" the belief that Bulawayo and the other towns of Rhodesia would become new Johannesburgs and Kimberleys. He even hand-picked thirty young men in Kimberley who most closely corresponded to his idea of a colonist, and dispatched them to Rhodesia.

But life in this new country was arduous. Whenever Rhodes visited Rhodesia the settlers would start complaining of the hardships and privation, and asking for money. Of the thirty hand-picked young men from Kimberley only two remained in Rhodesia by 1896. The others, as Rhodes's secretary later admitted, either died or left the country after their health was ruined.[3]

The main setback was the final collapse of any hope of gold. This hope, after all, had been the main attraction for the colonists. At the beginning of the nineties it became clear that here was very little gold in the land of the Shona, and now it emerged that the potential of Ndebele territory was no better. In 1894 John Hammond was sent by Rhodes on an exploratory tour of the country. He was then regarded as perhaps the world's leading expert on gold: on mining methods and on the discovery of deposits. If Rhodes still retained any illusions these were quickly dispelled by Hammond. There was very little gold.

This meant still more emphasis had to be placed on the development of farms and consequently on the plunder of the Africans.

The development of the country, as Rhodes saw it, was closely connected with the plunder of the Africans. Rhodes, like most Europeans of that time, regarded this as only natural. The Chartered Company saw all the arable land and pastures of Rhodesia as its own property. The process of appropriating land went ahead so fast that when the Ndebele who had retreated northwards in the final stages of the war in 1893 started to return, much of their land had already been handed over to Europeans.

Rhodes decided to round up most of the African population in reserves. To do this he set up the Land Commission. In its report[4] it proposed setting aside for "the Matabele nation and their slaves..." (i.e., the Shona living in Ndebele territory) two reserves of a total area of 10,500 square kilometres. Not only did this deprive the Africans of most of their land, what little they were left was anyway very poor. The Commission worked with such haste that it did not even inspect one of the reserves.

As for the Shona, they were not even allocated any territory with definite borders of their own. The Chartered Company felt perfectly entitled to sell the colonists any land they wished in any region. Settlements of Shona were only allowed to stay on plots of land that had thus been sold with the consent of their new "owners", and these latter only gave this consent on condition the chiefs and headmen would assign labourers to them.

A particularly crippling measure for the Africans was the mass requisition of their cattle. The Chartered Company considered livestock to be one of the spoils of war. By the beginning of 1896 the herd owned by the Ndebele numbered a mere 40,000 head, a sixth of its size before the 1893 war.

Soon after the end of hostilities, in early 1894, Jameson as chief administrator had gathered together the indunas and informed them that their tribesmen would have to work in the mines and on the farms.

There were various methods of making them work. In the first place, a hut-tax was introduced. In European terms it was no great sum. But the Africans had no way of getting even this small amount of money, other than by working for the whites. In fact the introduction of this tax was a complicated process: first a census had to be taken. This had still not been completed when the uprising started.

Secondly, the establishment of reserves created a reservoir of labour for hire. There was less land in the reserves, it was of poor quality, and it was harder to scratch out a living from it. The alternative was to seek work outside. But here too it was some time before the entire mechanism had begun to function.

The third method was the most natural and required no special administrative measures. The Africans were encountering for the first time European-made artefacts—axes, knives, hoes, etc. They could see their advantages and they wished to acquire them for themselves. To do this they needed money, and this meant working for the whites. But even this method only brought results with time.

So the Company took the simplest and, seemingly, most effective path: coercion. The commissioners for native affairs ordered the chiefs, indunas and headmen to send young men to work in the mines and to perform other heavy manual labour for two to three months a year. Since these orders were only carried out with great reluctance by both the chiefs and the rank-and-file villagers, police units were sent to recruit workers.

Nor did Rhodes's administrators draw the line at corporal punishment. One eye-witness, Thompson, records how "...the word 'twenty-five' said in English to any of the boys (i.e. Africans—A.D.) was sufficient to make them grin in a sickly way—they quite understood what is meant".[5] What every African knew was that the standard punishment was 25 lashes with the sjambok.

The British government did not object in the least to these observances. Speaking in the Commons, Chamberlain gave them his firm seal of approval:

"When you say to a savage people, who have hitherto found their chief employment, occupation, and profit in war, 'You shall no longer go to war; tribal war is forbidden', you have to bring about some means by which they may earn their living in place of it, and you have to induce them, sooner or later, to adopt the ordinary methods of earning a livelihood by the sweat of their brow. But with a race of this kind I doubt very much whether you can do it merely by preaching. I think that something in the nature of inducement, stimulus, or pressure is absolutely necessary if you are to secure a result which is desirable in the interests of humanity and civilization".[6]

Readers of *The Times* were assured: "The natives are quite

contented with the new regime, and are willing to work for the settlers".[7]

But the Ndebele themselves told another story: "Our country is gone, our cattle have gone, our people are scattered, we have nothing to live for ... we are the slaves of the white man, we are nobody, and we have no rights or laws of any kind."[8]

A COUNTRY IN REVOLT

In the Republic of Zimbabwe a massive programme is under-way to record and process the oral historical tradition: folk legends and oral narratives. After a thorough study and compa-rison of these materials the historian will be able to see the African uprisings from within, through the eyes of the Africans themselves. But for the time being we are forced to rely predom-inantly on accounts by Europeans—those who were either on the other side of the barricades, or somewhere outside the conflict altogether, and who therefore saw far from everything, and un-derstood even less than they saw.

Nevertheless, it is possible to state without any doubt that the Ndebele rising was very carefully prepared. This applied not just to a few isolated regions, but to everywhere, or almost everywhere. It was prepared by the entire nation. Its organiza-tion was seen to by many of the most respected men: indunas and Lobengula's relatives. An important role was played by priests of the M'limo cult. The spirit of M'limo performed much the same function for the Ndebele as the oracle of Delphi for the ancient Greeks.

Later, at the height of the rising, the hunter Selous recalled how Umlugulu, one of Lobengula's kinsmen, had come to see him and tried surreptitiously to find out the strength of the Company's troops, and how many men had gone with Jameson. The engineer Hammond noted that the town sentries had detained a woman discovered smuggling assegais in a bundle of firewood to other members of her tribe in Bulawayo.

Among the Ndebele themselves a rumour had arisen in Feb-ruary 1886 that M'limo had decided to put an end to the rule of the white men. The full eclipse of the moon which took place in that month was taken as the augury for this. It was also rumoured that Lobengula was not dead, but far away to the

294

north, where he was assembling an army to march against the British.

The time of year was not favourable for the uprising. The rains had ended, and the dry season had commenced, the roads hardened and became easily passable for the British troops. Furthermore, the harvest had begun in May, and it could not be abandoned: this would mean famine.

All the same, the advantages resulting from Jameson's departure with a considerable number of his troops, outweighed all the other considerations. An additional significant factor was the outbreak of a mass epidemic of rinderpest, with the resulting death of cattle. The authorities of the Chartered Company ordered the wholesale slaughter of cattle, to prevent the spread of the disease. This drove people to desperation. It was then that they decided to act swiftly and drive out the British before the main harvest work began.

A highly credible account of the insurgents' plan was given subsequently by Robert Baden-Powell. Later he was to rise to the rank of general, and became famous by founding the Boy Scout movement. But at that time, in 1896, he had come to help Rhodes put down the rising. According to his information, the rising was planned to start at the time of the new moon, on March 30-31. The Ndebele were supposed to march on Bulawayo, surround it on three sides, expel the foreigners, and then, breaking up into small detachments, to liberate the entire country.

In fact the first skirmish took place some ten days earlier, quite spontaneously, as often happens when tensions reach their peak. But subsequently events proceeded more or less according to plan.

During those first days the priest of the M'limo held an indaba—a gathering of the indunas. Here the plan of action was definitively agreed on. The Matopo hills were to be the centre of the rising, as this was the least accessible region of the country for the British troops.

Detachments of warriors moved in an organized manner towards Bulawayo, advanced close to the town, and took up positions on three sides, leaving the southwest clear. According to calculations by the British, possibly exaggerated, magnified by fear, by the fourth week in April the insurgents' forces numbered some fourteen or fifteen thousand, and they were less than three miles from the town.

Thus it was that even here Cecil Rhodes's achievements were threatened with total failure. It was not merely a question of whether Bulawayo would stand or fall: the insurgents, for all their large numbers, would hardly have been able to overcome artillery and machine-gun bombardments. But this was certainly a mortification after all the bragging about a new Eldorado, about a country expected to prosper. News of this scandal, this humiliation, would spread to all the corners of the globe, especially coming, as it did, hard on the heels of the Jameson Raid...

The insurgents did not attempt to take Bulawayo. Having surrounded it on three sides and closed off all the lines of communication, they left the main road to the southwest, to the British possessions open, as if inviting the British to leave of their own free will. Throughout the entire period of the rising not a single carriage was detained on this road, nor a single European killed, although large numbers of warriors were stationed near the road.

It is evident that the Ndebele leaders did not want great bloodshed and naïvely imagined that the Europeans, once they felt the common will of the entire nation, would take fright and leave of their own will. To complicate matters, there was no unity among the leaders of the rising. They could not decide among themselves whom to elect as Lobengula's successor.

Even when it transpired that the white men would not leave Bulawayo by the route made available to them and instead were fortifying the town, further differences of opinion arose. Some proposed that they storm the town, while others insisted that this would be a recipe for disaster.

In the meantime the British had recovered from their initial shock. While they were elaborating their plan of action public opinion was also being prepared. In the first dispatches the people of Britain read about terrible carnage, about the countless corpses of their countrymen, about the savage murder of a white girl. In Bulawayo, six and a half thousand women and children, whom a similar fate awaited, were appealing for salvation, reported *The Times*.[9] In actual fact there were only

1547 people in Bulawayo at the time, of whom 915 were men of call-up age and all excellently armed.[10] The entire European population of the areas of the country affected by the uprising was half the number of women and children reported by *The Times* to be endangered in Bulawayo.

But the propaganda had its desired effect: it helped Rhodes teach the Africans a "lesson" he believed would last forever. It was apparent in the very first weeks of the rising how he intended to do this. Rhodes's men were still in no position to take on thousands of warriors, but the reprisals began with those Africans who were working as servants and were unable to leave Bulawayo. They were accused of spying and were hanged outside the town fortifications, in full view of the insurgents.

In the meantime army units were being formed and officers appointed. The British authorities at once made available ten Maxim guns of the very latest model. The gold mine owners announced that they were setting up a detachment of volunteers at their own expense. The offspring of some of Britain's most aristocratic families, including sons of Lord Grey and Lord Gifford, set out for Southern Rhodesia. The British government did not conceal the fact that English soldiers would shed blood for the Chartered Company. When Chamberlain was asked in Parliament who would have to stand the expense of suppressing the rising—Rhodes's Company or the treasury, he said that he was "in doubt".

The British did use the road left clear for them by the Ndebele, but not for the purposes of retreat. On the contrary, it served as their supply route for reinforcements. Lord Grey arrived in Bulawayo to take Jameson's place as Administrator of Southern Rhodesia. He held a parade of the troops on May 3 and announced that "Bulawayo was now as safe as London."[11]

By early June all the main British reinforcements had reached the town and there were three thousand British soldiers, armed volunteers and police of the Chartered Company. Extensive operations were commenced to the north of Bulawayo.

The British burnt down villages, drove away the cattle that the Africans still had, destroyed their crops and stores of food. Special detachments were set up charged with the destruction of grain. Dynamite was used to blow up the Ndebele people's "fortifications"—simple caves.

Echoes of these reprisals reached England and the government was forced to answer inquiries in the Commons. Their answers were marked by total intransigence. When asked whether the rules for the conduct of war permitted the destruction of dwellings with fire and dynamite, Chamberlain replied:

"The burning of the kraals of a native enemy is in accordance with the usages of South African warfare".[12]

When asked about the destruction of foodstocks, he responded:

"I presume that grain is only destroyed by our forces when it is impossible to carry it away for the consumption of our own people."[13]

He fenced the question about the starvation of the Ndebele by assuring the members that he fully trusted the officials on the spot and had no intention of interfering with their sphere of competence.

These replies were delivered by Chamberlain to the applause of a large number of the members.

During June and the first half of July the British laid waste the country north of Bulawayo. But the main stronghold of the rising was in the south, in the Matopo hills. The units of insurgents who had initially surrounded Bulawayo had retreated to the safety of these hills, and the main British forces now set out after them.

It soon transpired that the British could not count on a swift victory here, in the Matopos. Of course, in hunger they had a powerful ally. But the Ndebele had managed to store a certain amount, albeit limited, of food in the hills. The main advantage was that the rocky terrain enabled the Ndebele troops to defend themselves for a long time.

The British dispatches reported that the Ndebele fought with the utmost ferocity. Having been reduced to desperation by the destruction of their villages and extermination of their families, they now started attacking the enemy. On the night of July 19 they assaulted a detachment of four hundred and seventy men. After the battle, which lasted for six hours, the British casualties numbered thirteen dead and gravely wounded. This figure was uncommonly high for a single encounter in a colonial war.

The following day the British tried to mount an assault

gainst Babayane's regiment. This induna, one of Lobengula's missaries to Queen Victoria, was now, in his old age, one of the leaders of the rising. His warriors made skilful use of the natural fortifications of the rocky outcrop, and the British had to be content with having blown up a few caves housing peaceful inhabitants. An official telegram to London lamented the unsatisfactory results of the offensive. It noted that enemy losses were very slight, apparently 50 men, that the effect of the battle on morale was doubtful.

I do not recall whether Kipling, who has been quoted so often in the pages of this book, ever wrote specifically about the Ndebele warriors. But his lines about the Sudanese rebels fighting the British at this same time on another section of the Cape-to-Cairo strip could apply equally to the Ndebele:

Then 'ere's to you, Fuzzy-Wuzzy, an' the missis and the kid;
Our orders was to break you, an' of course we went an' did.
We sloshed you with Martinis, an' it wasn't 'ardly fair;
But for all the odds agin you, Fuzzy-Wuz, you broke the
square.

So 'ere's to you, Fuzzy-Wuzzy, at your 'ome in the Sudan;
You're a pore benighted 'eathen but a first-class fightin' man;
An' 'ere's to you, Fuzzy-Wuzzy, with your 'ayrick 'ead of
'air—
You big black boundin' beggar—for you broke a British
square![14]

On this occasion Rhodes needed no dispatches to provide his information about the fighting with the Ndebele. He now led his own detachment of two hundred and fifty men. He was not considered to be a brave man, and it must have cost him a great deal of effort to subject himself to the relatively small risk of being killed in a skirmish.

In May, an hour before his detachment set off for Bulawayo, he sent a letter to Sir William Harcourt, the presiding judge in the Jameson Raid trial. This letter is very sentimental in tone, and must have seemed strange coming from a 43-year-old man, particularly someone as ruthless as Rhodes. He wants Harcourt to understand: "I have tried to unite South Africa, and no sordid motive has influenced me."[15] Rhodes

asks him to burn the letter if Rhodes survives the war. If no
however, he asks Harcourt to remember Rhodes's last words a
the judge sits smoking in his drawing room.

Are we to conclude from this that Rhodes really did liv
those days in expectation of his own death? Or was this merely ;
ploy, by which he hoped to touch the heart of the old judge
In general we might wonder what business he had writing t
Harcourt in the first place? This may be because Harcourt wa
largely responsible for pronouncing, if not a verdict, then a
least a moral assessment of Rhodes's actions. There was alway
a danger that Harcourt would not shield Rhodes to the exten
which Rhodes wished. Harcourt had, after all, described him a
"capable but not honest"![16]

In early May Chamberlain had asked Rhodes and Beit t
resign from the board of directors of the Chartered Company
Rhodes replied in a telegram: "Let resignations wait—we figh
Matabele tomorrow".[17]

Rhodes spent two days writing his letter to Harcourt, Ma
13 and 14. Perhaps it took too long to reach Harcourt, o
perhaps it failed to stir the heart of the old judge, who had
heard all sorts of pleas in his time. At any rate Harcour
wrote to Chamberlain on June 21, 1896: "As long as Rhode
remains as Managing Director there can be no peace in Sout
Africa".[18]

On June 26 Rhodes was dismissed from the board of th
Chartered Company, the company that was his most cherished
creation.

. . .It was during these same days in June 1896 that the
Shona rising started, in the eastern districts of Southern Rhode
sia. "The whole country round Salisbury has risen," read ;
dispatch from Salisbury on June 23.[19]

With this event Rhodes was to lose another mainstay. The
entire world knew from his words that by conquering Rhodesia
and overthrowing the "bloody tyranny" of Lobengula he had
saved the "peace-loving" Shona from the "bloodthirsty" Ndebele.
And here the Shona were following the Ndebele in rising up
against their own benefactor!

If the Ndebele and Shona rising became too protracted shares
in the Chartered Company would collapse and this massive
stock-exchange bubble would burst. Rhodes would be reminded

f his own declarations that it was no general sent from England, nor any officers of the Queen's army who had commanded the operations to suppress the rising, but he, Rhodes. If he had been in command he would have no one to use as scapegoat.

In Cape Town he was awaited by a committee of inquiry into the Jameson Raid, and in London by a parliamentary inquiry. He would have to stand trial!

The Deputy High Commissioner to South Africa had even come to Rhodesia to investigate the situation.

Yet the thing he probably feared most was that the memory of his own name, the word "Rhodesia", which had only just appeared on the maps, would not survive... He anxiously protested: "They can't take that away. They can't change the name. Did you ever hear of a country's name being changed?"[20]

By now Rhodes had experienced the full truth of the King's words in Hamlet: "When sorrows come, they come not single spies, but in battalions". To add to his woes, he seemed unable to throw off his malaria. Periodically he would shake with attacks of fever. His heart also gave occasional murmurs. He had virtually none of his closest friends with him. After the ill-starred raid they were all in prison, awaiting trial... One of his biographers records that thoughts of suicide even entered his mind.[21] This is probably a bit of an exaggeration: he still had his protectors, his followers, and, most important, his money.

Nevertheless, to save what he considered his life's work, he had to take emergency action. The question was: what action?

WERE THESE REALLY MOMENTS IN LIFE THAT MAKE IT WORTH LIVING?

Should he open talks with the Ndebele? This was very difficult! They remembered only too well the 1893 war, when one after another Lobengula's emissaries disappeared, shot "by mistake" by Rhodes's "pioneers".

Attempts were made to establish some sort of contact. Finally Rhodes's emissaries managed to have a meeting with a few indunas. When it was suggested that they cease resistance the indunas replied:

"Why should we surrender? We have held our own and driven the whites back each time they have attacked us here... If

the whites are tired of fighting they can come and surrende
to us here."[22]

Rhodes's emissaries had used the wrong approach. Every
thing had to be started again.

At last, in these hills they came upon an ancient crone. She
was one of the wives of Mzilikazi, Lobengula's father. It was
through her that they established their first contacts with the
leaders of the insurgents. After lengthy discussions the leaders
declared that they were prepared to meet Rhodes, so long as
he came to them accompanied by no more than three men
After all the harm done to the Ndebele by Rhodes and his
emissaries this stipulation was perfectly understandable.

The meeting and discussions—or, to give them their Ndebele name, indaba—took place on August 21. Rhodes took Colenbrander with him as his interpreter—he had already performed this function for Lobengula's emissaries in London. His
other two companions were an old friend, and a correspondent
from *The Times*. The correspondent was invited so that he might
immortalize this great event. Rhodes took every opportunity to
emphasize the solemnity of the occasion. As they rode up to the
appointed meeting place he declared that this was "one of
those moments in life that make it worth living."[23]

Before them stood five or six of the more distinguished indunas, with a large number of insurgents assembled around
them. None of them threatened Rhodes's life, but they unleashed
a storm of accusations against him. He was forced to hear
what atrocities had been committed by his Native Commissioners, his "pioneers" and his police. He heard how women and
even children had been killed, how the most respected elders
were "treated as dogs" and how land and cattle had been taken
away from the Africans.

These were indictments of Rhodes himself: the system had
been created by him, after all. The treatment meted out by the
settlers to the Africans reflected his own views and his motto
that land was more important to him than the natives were. But
at those negotiations he insisted, of course, that there had been
abuses carried out against his will.

At a certain point Rhodes walked away from his companions
and sat among the Ndebele, wishing to emphasize by this action
that he was entirely on their side. Now he started to talk of

302

This is how Rhodes's negotiations with the insurgents were depicted in a British text-book for Rhodesia

concessions. He declared that he, Rhodes, was on the Africans' side. That he would personally undertake the reorganization of the running of the country. All these abuses, he said, were a thing of the past, finished with. They would not recur.[24] The indunas would suffer no retribution for the rising, and they would be returned the full extent of powers which they had enjoyed during Lobengula's reign.

The meeting lasted four hours, and Rhodes got his way in the end: it was agreed to continue the talks.

The world was instantly told—and in the most colourful detail —the legend of Rhodes's feat in the Matopo hills, how he entered the den of his enemies and, at constant risk to his own life, secured the cessation of this bloody war. The great empire-builder had stepped unarmed into the camp of savages whose hands were stained with the blood of white women and children—for many decades to come the British public recalled this scene with a certain pleasant sensation.

To himself Rhodes must have seemed like Napoléon on the

bridge at Arcole when, a century before, in 1796, the Corsica had charged forward bearing a banner in his hands. From a the evidence it would seem that Rhodes greatly exaggerate the threat to his life. His mind was perfectly capable of conceiving of the Africans as black savages whose actions were controlled by stimuli totally incomprehensible to the white man This was the stereotype of the African widespread in Europe and the one which would have fuelled Rhodes's worst fears a this time. Like so many politicians, he was a slave to the ver stereotypes which he had created through his own endeav ours.

In actual fact the Ndebele were not such savages, as w have remarked on numerous occasions above. Their rising was carefully considered act. Each of the warriors knew his ow duties and rights, knew what he could and could not do. How ever loathsome a figure Rhodes may have been to them the realised that an entire army stood behind him. They understood that these peaceful talks were necessary to them, the Ndebele and they could see that in hunger the British had a formidabl ally.

Is it therefore so surprising that Rhodes was not killed? No one so much as touched a hair on his head, even though nex to the indunas stood young warriors regarded as impulsive and hot-headed.

Rhodes was probably being quite sincere when he declared that this was "one of those moments in life that make it worth living", but there was not nearly as much risk and danger in this moment as he imagined.

We might wonder what made this moment so magnificent for Rhodes. Was it the haggling with people around whose necks he had drawn a noose of famine? And at whom he had pointed the muzzles of his guns?

Rhodes saw all this in a different light, of course. For the rest of his life he was to regard the indaba in the Matopo hills as his hour of glory.

The old matriarch, Mzilikazi's widow, who had helped Rhodes organize this first meeting with the indunas, had been of such assistance to Rhodes that he had her portrait painted and hung it in his bedroom. This was the only female portrait which ever adorned any home of Cecil Rhodes, unless one counts the

The indunas with Ndebele warriors in Bulawayo after the 1896 rising

painting of Sir Joshua Reynolds, which he had been so fond of since childhood.

Discovery of the grave of Mzilikazi, Lobengula's father, led Rhodes to another idea. During the indaba some of Rhodes's volunteers discovered a skeleton in one of the caves. The objects around it clearly indicated that this was a holy shrine. The reckless "pioneers" plundered and defiled the tomb, scattering the skeleton. The indunas complained to Rhodes, who gave orders that the tomb be restored as far as possible to its original state. Then, at a later date, he directed in his will that he be buried in the same area, not far from Mzilikazi, at the site of his talks with the indunas.

A week later, on August 28, a second meeting was held. This proved to be noisier than the first indaba. The indunas Dhliso and Babayane listed injustice upon injustice perpetrated against their people by the British. The situation was rendered particularly tense by the shouts and brief verbal assaults by the young warriors.

One of them asked Rhodes: "Where are we to live when it is over? The white man claims all the land."

To which Rhodes replied:

"We will give you settlements. We will set apart location for you: we will give you land."

The young chief shouted angrily:

"You will give us land in our own country! That's good of you!"

Rhodes then objected to talking to the young warrior while he still had his rifle in his hand; the young chief said:

"You will have to talk to me with my rifle in my hand. I find if I talk with my rifle in my hand the white man pays more attention to what I say. Once I put my rifle down I am nothing. I am just a dog to be kicked."

The speakers at this meeting included one of Lobengula's secretaries, a comparatively young man, whom *The Times* correspondent called Karl Kumalo. Kumalo informed his listeners how he had been arrested in Bulawayo. He said that the only evidence adduced of his participation in the rising—evidence regarded as conclusive proof—was that he was "an educated native". He was shot through the head "while attempting to escape". But the head wound proved not to be fatal, and he crawled away, went into hiding, and thereafter did indeed join the insurgents.[25]

Kumalo's speech and his "resurrection", as the British press called it, were most inconvenient for Rhodes, not only because of the young man's understandable resentment, but also because he was well acquainted with the situation in the English camp, with all its conflicts and clashes. He even knew that the High Commissioner's office was preparing an inquiry into the activities of Rhodes's administration and that Sir Richard Martin had been appointed to conduct it. Kumalo insisted that Martin have a meeting with the insurgents.

Karl Kumalo was supported by Babayane. He pointed out that, according to a rumour, the "White Queen" had sent her induna into the country to investigate matters. This was a good thing, he concluded, for now, at long last, efforts to hide the truth would cease.

They eventually made the acquaintance of the "Queen's induna" on September 9, at the third meeting. This time Rhodes's team had been joined by the new administrator of Rhodesia Lord Grey and the "Queen's induna" Richard Martin.

It is unlikely, however, that the meeting with Martin jus-

A Shona village

tified the hopes of the Ndebele. In contrast to Rhodes, who usually patiently heard them out, Martin delivered an immensely long lecture to the Ndebele. He was particularly hard on Babayane. He said that the British government failed to understand how such a man as Babayane, who had visited England and seen the might of the queen with his own eyes, could still have decided to rise up. Could he not understand the futility of his actions, and was he not aware that the queen did not allow such acts to go unpunished? But the queen was merciful, she would pardon everyone who had fought in battle. Only those who had attacked and assassinated peaceful settlers would be put on trial.

The final indaba was held on October 13, attended by all, or nearly all, the indunas: those who had risen up, and those who had not joined the insurgents. This indaba marked the end of the Ndebele rising.

It might be wondered how Rhodes managed to achieve this.

On his way to the talks and, to a still greater extent, while they were in progress Rhodes understood, perhaps for the first time, that the Africans were people to be reckoned with. As he listened to the indunas he applied to them his favourite maxim: every man has his price. He had to buy off the indunas, at any rate the more influential among them. The indunas were promised that their former rights would be restored. Rhodes divided the Ndebele country into twelve districts and proposed appointing one of the indunas in charge of each of these (although their authority was, of course, not intended to cover the whites). The indunas were also promised a salary. As an example all this was at once granted to those who had not taken an active part in the rising.

In this way Rhodes laid the foundations of a tradition: the buying off of the African nobility—the cornerstone of the "native policy" on which the colonial system was maintained in Rhodesia for more than eighty years.

It should be stated that with this measure Rhodes did not earn the approbation of the "pioneers". Many of these, if not the majority, took a much harder line than their leader, and were far more conservative and pig-headed than him. Not all of them could understand exactly why any concessions had to be granted at all. The journal *Bulawayo Sketch* declared on October 17: "The iron hand must now be felt beneath its glove covering".

When the indunas came into Bulawayo on October 24, at

Rhodes's invitation, the settlers greeted them with ferocious irony.[26]

Thus Rhodes's actions, strange though it may seem to us today, were seen by some as free-thinking, almost revolutionary high-handedness.

Rhodes could not, of course, limit matters to the granting of a few concessions to the indunas. He was also forced to forego any widescale reprisals against the insurgents, and to promise many village communities that they would retain the lands they had had in Lobengula's time. Finally, because of the famine, relief supplies had to be distributed.

Once he was satisfied that the agreements he had sought had come into effect, Rhodes left Bulawayo for Cape Town. This was in December 1896.

Rhodes did not believe it was necessary to hold any talks with the Shona people, who did not have the same military organization. They were forced into capitulation by the harshest punitive measures. These were already being carried out during the Ndebele rising, and were conducted on a broader scale after it ended, when the British could pit all their forces against the Shona.

We shall never know exactly how many villages and clans disappeared then. They further increase the already long list of ethnic groups and entire tribes that were wiped from the face of South Africa.

In Shona territory crops were burnt down and caves in which the inhabitants of mutinous villages had taken refuge were bombarded with artillery fire, and blown up with dynamite. After the explosions it was impossible even to approach the caves for a long time, so strong was the stench from the putrid corpses. General Frederick Carrington, who commanded these operations, described them as police work.

The fight against the recalcitrant Shona was waged across the entire country, consisting of hundreds of punitive operations. One of them was carried out against the village of Shaungwe.

The village was situated on the brow of a steep hill, some eight hundred feet high. In the past the Ndebele had repeatedly laid siege to it, but had had to withdraw empty-handed. The civilized British took a course of action at which the Nde-

"Two Rhodeses". A cartoon from the Rhodesia journal *The Nugget* of June 12, 1897. Trying to pacify the Ndebele, Rhodes throws them crumbs, while all the Shona get is explosions of dynamite

Kagubi, one of the leaders of the Shona rising, in captivity, and
Charwe, the spirit medium of Nehanda

bele had drawn the line, even though it must surely have occurred to them too. They cut off the insurgents' water-supply.
They set up machine-gun posts on all the slopes of the hill. The
besieged villagers found themselves in a desperate situation.
Nevertheless, only twelve of them surrendered immediately, the
others preferring to try and burrow their way through the
machine-gun fire. Ninety of these were killed and the rest got

through. Two hundred women surrendered, exhausted and broken by the long siege. Eye-witnesses praised their composure. "The self-restraint shown by the women when they were brought into the camp was extraordinary. They had been many days without water, and their thirst must have been terrible; yet they sat quietly in a circle, and when water was brought showed no unseemly eagerness to drink. There was no struggling; each woman took a sip from the calabash, and handed it on to her neighbour; their stoical composure was astonishing."[27]

The "pacification" of the Shona continued for a long time after Rhodes's agreement with the Ndebele. The last strongholds of rebellion were not suppressed until much later.

Discontent continued to ferment among the Ndebele too, to whom Rhodes had made so many promises—years before, through Matabele Thompson in the discussions with Lobengula, and subsequently in person. . .

In his memoirs Matabele Thompson recounts how he revisited Rhodesia in 1904, after the completion of the railway, and on a station platform he met an induna he had known before. The induna said to him: "Oh Thompson, how have you treated us, after all promises which we believed?"

"I had no answer," writes Thompson.[28]

The risings of the Shona and Ndebele peoples were among the largest of their kind in Africa in the nineteenth century. They have remained in the memories of these peoples as the Chimurenga, which in Shona means liberation struggle. The names of its heroes, like the *mhondoro* (mediums) Kagubi and Nehanda with the Shona, and Mkwati with the Ndebele, are surrounded with glory in present-day Zimbabwe.

The history of the Shona and Ndebele risings is a large and important topic. The present author has done extensive research into the history of these movements, and thirty years ago, in 1958, published a book entitled, in Russian, *The Matabele and the Shona in the Struggle against British Colonialization, 1888-1897*.[29] This was one of the first, if not the very first, study in historical literature of the resistance mounted by the Shona and the Ndebele to colonial conquest.

Since that time a great number of documents and other materials have come to light. In the course of the last few years

Zimbabwean historians have made an immense contribution to the study of these events.[30] The present author, after his own perusal of the materials collected in the Zimbabwean National Archives and after studying the findings of his Zimbabwean colleagues intends to return to this vital theme.

In this book, *Cecil Rhodes and His Time*, however, the Shona and Ndebele risings will only be discussed with reference to Rhodes himself.

Mere Setback
or Utter Debacle?

Rhodes's talks with the indunas and the results they brought helped him to regain some of his lost stature, both in his own eyes, and in the opinion of many of his countrymen. Yet this achievement could not, of course, entirely erase the damage inflicted on his prestige by the failed rebellion in the Transvaal and the Shona and Ndebele risings in Rhodesia.

Of course only faint echoes of the machine-gun fire and dynamite explosions in those remote Shona villages reached the outside world. Nonetheless, at least they were heard. . .

People's eyes were only properly opened to the harsh reprisals against the Ndebele and the Shona by a work of literature, and not the military dispatches or the reports filed by journalists. Olive Schreiner published her story "Trooper Peter Halket of Mashonaland" in 1897.[1] It became so well-known that the Russian translation was published almost immediately, in 1898, and was reissued a number of times. Printed next to the title page of the first English edition was a photograph depicting, in a Rhodesian landscape, a tree, from which three Africans hung by their necks, and standing around it a group of Rhodes's "pioneers", striking arrogant, self-satisfied poses.

Later, during the years of the Nazi aggression and the Second World War, such pictures became common-place. But at that time, at the end of the nineteenth century, the photograph left a profound impression on the book's readers.

This was a shock for the British aristocratic ladies who admired Cecil Rhodes and his "pioneers". Admittedly, the hanged men were only blacks, but this kind of thing just would not do. . .

Rhodes's position now was an unenviable one. And to think that he had so recently been at the very peak of his career. . .

He racked his brains, wondering if he would ever achieve

The photograph used as frontispiece to Olive Schreiner's *Trooper Halket of Mashonaland*

anything more in his life. But to judge by his character he must have been convinced that somehow, once again he would harness the elusive and capricious Lady Luck to his chariot. It would take time, years, even. The question was: did he have these years? At night he would sometimes feel the cold hand of Death reaching towards him.

Time and again he would draw up the balance sheet of his life.

He had undoubtedly received a number of terrible blows, one after another. When, to cap it all, his elegant mansion Groote Schuur in Cape Town caught fire and was burnt to ashes, Rhodes was unable to suppress a groan of despair.

"What with the Raid, rebellion, famine, rinderpest, and now my house burnt, I feel like Job, all but the boils."[2]

Rhodes still had a long way to go to attain the depths of misfortune suffered by Job. But he had lost forever the aura of a man whom Lady Luck never cheats, that aura that had won for him the adulation both of ordinary men, and also of those who shaped the destinies of England and Europe, of people who, it might be thought, had lost faith in everything. It was for this reason that people of very modest means had invested their hard-earned money in his one-pound shares, and entrusted their destinies to him, secure in the faith that Rhodes would not fail them. The aristocrats who so readily added their names to the lists of founding members of his company alongside the magnetic word "Rhodes" had no fear of any ignominy. . .

But how different it was now. Even the Leviathans of the British press, who had always lauded Rhodes, were no longer entirely with him. And most remarkable: William Stead, in whom Rhodes had confided so much, whom he had tried so hard to infect with his ideas, and to convert wholly to his own way of thinking, was somehow different now, after the Jameson Raid. Some closeness remained, but his former faith in Rhodes was gone.

As for the politicians, they now played a waiting game. Not all, perhaps, but many of them. Asquith, for example, was invited to join the parliamentary Committee of Inquiry into the raid (the "Rhodes Commission"). Chamberlain himself went to see him, and tried to persuade him, but Asquith refused. He preferred not to tie his hands, and to see, first which way the wind was blowing.

Later Margot Asquith was to recall in her memoirs her husband's reaction to Chamberlain's propositions.

"I asked him why he had refused, to which he answered: 'Do you take me for a fool?' "[3]

As for the aristocrats that Rhodes had tried to win over with gifts of shares and directorships in his companies, they must now have felt that they had supported Rhodes far more than he even deserved.

In his turn he, quite naturally, saw most of them as traitors. What else could be expected of such men, who had preferred to bank up the fire through the efforts of another, of Rhodes? Reared in "high society", that school for scandal, they were adept only at making caustic remarks and capable of ruining a man's reputation with two or three venomous sentences. Like Lord Illingworth or Lord Goring in the plays of Oscar Wilde, who had just become fashionable on stage. Perhaps some of Wilde's celebrity was due to the scandalous trial in which he was given two years imprisonment for homosexuality, literally on the eve of the Jameson Raid. Although he was certainly a writer of extraordinary talents, displayed even in his most recent play: *The Importance of Being Earnest*. This vied with the Jameson Raid for the public's attention.

The public laughed at the jokes of Wilde's lords. Yet the object of their mirth should have been the lords themselves: with their vain and futile lives, their inability to act. Whatever talents they may have had were squandered on idle chatter. Men such as these were able to turn their backs on Rhodes with the greatest of ease, as someone quite outside their circle and certainly unworthy of their attention.

In South Africa itself there was now no figure more loathsome to the Transvaal Afrikaners than Cecil Rhodes.

In the Orange Free State, "Groot" Adriaan De la Rey must now have been regretting that he ever asked Rhodes to stand godfather to his grandson.

And to think how he had toiled to overcome the suspicion and mistrust of the Cape Afrikaners. But he had succeeded in the end! They had voted for him, believed in him, and helped him become Prime Minister. Now all that effort had come to nothing.

His most faithful helpers and his friends or those who were almost friends had all been on trial, had been thrown into Afrikaner prisons as conspirators. Some, like Jameson, had been taken captive. Their names were now dragged through the dirt by the press all over the world. Their every step was now eagerly watched by the public. . . This would not continue indefinitely, of course, but it was unpleasant enough while it lasted.

Worse still, Rhodes was no longer able to act on the political stage in the capacity of an official statesman. He had lost the office of premier. All that remained was for him to act behind the scenes, trying to persuade others. But they would now look behind them, and be afraid to proceed.

Yet this was perhaps still not the worst aspect of it all.

These blows could not fail to affect his health, his nerves and mental stability. Previously he had been able to keep full control of himself, and he owed much of his success to this ability. But now he became increasingly irritable and unbalanced. This was plain for all to see.

Barney Barnato, Rhodes's rival and, subsequently, associate

Added to this was the death of Barney Barnato, a man who had for twenty-five years featured prominently in Rhodes's life, initially as his main rival, and then as his main associate.

On June 14, 1897 Barnato leapt from the railings of the ocean liner *Scot* into the Indian Ocean. The alarm was given: "Man overboard!" A rescue party was mounted and his body was found: but it was too late.

This was a most astounding and unexpected event. Barnato

ad been on his way from South Africa, where he shared the
hrone of the diamond kingdom with Rhodes. In the world gold
narket he even outranked Rhodes.

Details of his life were published as far afield as St Peters-
urg, Moscow, and Siberia. The journal *Russkoye Bogatstvo*
(The Wealth of Russia) informed its readers:

"Every word uttered by Barney Barnato was eagerly seized
ke the wisest saying of an oracle... After all, he was czar of
he stock exchange, a man who possessed hundreds of millions,
nd who, by merely twitching his eyebrows, could make or break
ortunes—in a word: 'Our Barney!' ...There can be no doubt
ut that in the near future 'our Barney' would have taken his
lace on the crimson benches in the House of Lords. For already
eated there are the noble 'Knights of the Bottle': the whisky
ukes, the beer barons, the gin viscounts, so why, for goodness'
ake, should they not give a seat to this clown too, since he has
s much money as all the 'Knights of the Bottle' taken together?"[4]

Barnato was then, in June 1897, on his way to London, to
ttend the festivities on the occasion of the sixtieth year of
Queen Victoria's reign. These had been arranged with unprece-
ented pomp, to celebrate the triumph of Britain, and of the
British flag, which now flew over one quarter of the surface of
he earth. Delegations from all over the immense British Empire
vere gathering in London to take part in the festivities, due to
egin on June 20. Barnato's fellow-passengers on the luxury liner
ncluded some of the highest ranking officials in Cape Town.

They were passing Madeira. England lay only four days
istant. Barnato was engaged in leisurely conversation with
ohn Gordon Sprigg, Rhodes's successor as Prime Minister of
he Cape. They were probably discussing the Kimberley dia-
nonds Barnato and Rhodes intended to shower at the feet of
heir queen—this was to be one of the richest gifts presented
t this most opulent of celebrations. Then Barnato turned to his
ephew to ask the time. The latter had barely had time to
nswer that by his watch it was thirteen minutes past three
vhen he observed that his uncle was no longer on deck. Barnato
ad thrown himself overboard.[5]

Barnato's death was bound to be a shock for Rhodes.

With Barnato's departure Rhodes lost a mighty ally, a rock
f support. They had never been friends, and in company with

many others Rhodes was not above making fun of the uncouth Barnato: he was a man almost completely without education who had probably never read a single book in his life. But once they had amalgamated their diamond companies, in 1888 Rhodes could hardly have grounds to bear Barnato a grudge The former clown did not understand Rhodes's ambitious de signs, was bewildered by them and perhaps even chaffed Rhodes about them, just as Rhodes made fun of his Jewish accent, but he did not prevent his associate from making polit ical gambles, not even when such activities threatened the prestige of their joint business ventures. Presumably he thought it a harmless enough pastime for his partner to indulge in.

And when Rhodes was in trouble—after the Jameson Raid Barnato did everything in his power to help him, even though he himself had no direct interest in doing so.

It must have been a severe blow to Rhodes to lose such an ally.

Inevitably comparisons were made between the two men. They were exact contemporaries, each 44 years old.

In health they were very different: Barnato had retained the acrobat's agility from his years in the circus. He had always loved sport, and had only given up boxing a few years before his death. With his strong heart and lungs he was more than a match for the sickly Rhodes.

The same was true for his mental state. Unlike his soli tary partner, he was a family man. On board the ship they celeb rated the third birthday of his son. Barnato showed the ship' crew his son's present: a little bicycle.

Unlike Rhodes again, he was very close to his relatives. He intended to leave some of his businesses to his nephew.

Was it that his energy had run out? This, too, was un likely. He had a mass of new plans, and although he was build ing himself a luxury mansion in London he had no intention of retiring.

What could it have been? Perhaps some secret disease, which no one knew about?

It was evident that in recent years Barnato had become much more excitable and highly strung. He had started to drink It took at least a bottle of liquor for a man of his vigour to deaden his mind, to suppress the awareness of something that was constantly tormenting him. He complained of hallucinations.

As Rhodes shifted through all this in his memory his own worries must have increased: after all, he himself had long suffered from hallucinations.

To the rest of the world it seemed as though Rhodes and Barnato had acquired their wealth as easily as Aladdin with his lamp. But they had no genie to help them. They made their way ahead in fierce competition with thousands of others: and to do so they had to devote themselves body and soul to the pursuit of this one goal.

Napoléon is reputed to have said that everything in life must be paid for. Indeed, he is hardly the first man in history to have seen this truth.

Now Barnato, too, had paid the price.

For long after Rhodes would be unable to recall the death of his erstwhile partner without a feeling of dread...

But unlike Barnato Rhodes was alive, and a man cannot live permanently in the memory of his sorrows, or in premonitions of disaster. Man lives in hope: particularly such an energetic man as Rhodes.

Life succoured these hopes. The original source of his influence—his money—was still with him. This was a not insignificant advantage.

Rhodes spent almost the whole of 1896 in Rhodesia. He only departed shortly before Christmas for the Cape Colony, first for Port Elizabeth, and then for Cape Town on December 27. The city fathers gave a dinner in his honour for five hundred persons, at which Rhodes delivered a speech.

"If I may put to you a thought, it is that the man who is continuously prosperous does not know himself, his own mind or character. It is a good thing to have a period of adversity. You then find out who are your real friends."[6]

These words already tell us that Rhodes had not entirely given up hope. As he continued his speech became increasingly confident. He assured the guests that, whatever mistakes he may have made in the past, he would not now deviate from his goals, and above all from the "uniting" of South Africa. On December 28 Rhodes was back in Kimberley and there he received an even more rapturous welcome.

Rhodes at once immersed himself in a ferment of activity. He busied himself with the construction of the railway: in 1897 the trains started plying between Cape Town and Bulawayo, and further still, as far as the village of Umtali in the eastern part of Rhodesia. He also devoted his efforts to the development of the sugar industry in Natal and the expansion of fruit production on Afrikaner farms on the Cape of Good Hope.

If all this would not regain for him the Afrikaner vote at the next election and would not reconcile the Afrikaner Bond, he was prepared to form a new party. Finally this is what he did: in 1898 he founded the Progressive Party.

Gradually he recovered, if not all, at least most of the positions he had lost as a result of the Jameson Raid. After his travels round South Africa in 1896 and his reflections on the trip in 1897 Mark Twain wrote about Rhodes: "The whole South African world seemed to stand in a kind of shuddering awe of him, friend and enemy alike. It was as if he were deputy-God on the one side, deputy-Satan on the other, proprietor of the people, able to make them or ruin them by his breath, worshipped by many, hated by many, but blasphemed by none among the judicious, and even by the indiscreet in guarded whispers only."[7]

But this was all in South Africa. The same was not entirely true of England, the centre of the Empire. Prim Victorian England needed time to forgive failure, even to a favourite child such as Rhodes. But gradually this forgiveness was granted.

On February 16, 1897 Rhodes appeared before the House of Commons' Committee of Inquiry into the Jameson Raid—"the Rhodes Commission". But Rhodes himself appeared as a witness, and not the accused.

The inquiry was conducted in such a leisurely fashion that Rhodes was the first witness to be questioned. More than a year had elapsed since the scandalous raid, passions had long since cooled not only in England, but everywhere in the world. Countless more recent events had eclipsed the ill-starred conspiracy against the Transvaal, such as news of the Khodynka disaster, which stunned the entire world: at the coronation of Czar Nicholas II the crowd stampeded, leaving one and a half thousand dead and as many crippled. General Kitchener had started the war in the Sudan. At the same time the French officer Jean Baptiste Marchand had begun his campaign to establish a belt of French colonies across the entire breadth of Africa. France seized Madagascar, Ethiopian forces routed the Italian army which had invaded their country. In Athens the first modern Olympic Games were held, revived after a hiatus of over 1500 years...

Both inside and outside Parliament it was generally accepted that the culprits of the Jameson Raid had in fact already been punished. Moreover, it seemed pointless to accommodate the Transvaal government, when throughout this past year Kruger had acted in a positively defiant manner towards Britain.

Cecil Rhodes's interrogation took place at the commission's first public sitting. A large number of M. P. s, lawyers, journalists and others, lucky enough to obtain passes, gathered in the hall. Among those present was the Prince of Wales. He had no fear of compromising himself, even though his close connections with Rhodes and Jameson were common knowledge.

At this sitting of the parliamentary committee Rhodes was treated not like the main culprit, which in fact he was, and not even as someone suspected of complicity, but as a great empire-builder and defender of the rights of the citizens of Britain.

Initially he was nervous and agitated, answering some questions with a certain amount of hesitation, particularly when asked whether the Colonial Secretary Chamberlain and the High Commissioner for South Africa Hercules Robinson had known about the preparations for an invasion of the Transvaal.

But he quickly recovered his customary composure. When he was asked in which of his capacities he had thought that he had a right to assemble troops on the border with the Transvaal he replied: "In my capacity as myself, because I thought I was doing the best in the interests of South Africa and of my country. That is my answer."

Then he delivered a detailed exposition of his "federation" policy, and literally cried out: "You will remember these words... I felt, rightly or wrongly, that the time had come to bring about the change that must come ... it is a pure question of time ... ten years hence we shall say ... as certain as we are sitting here."[8]

The main thrust of Rhodes's testimony can be summarized as follows.

Of course, he had great sympathy for the Uitlanders: they

were suffering badly from Kruger's oppression. He, Rhodes, used his authority to move the troops of the Chartered Company to the Transvaal border, but the other directors of the Company and the official British authorities both in South Africa and in Britain were not informed of this. As for the actual invasion of the Transvaal, he himself was not notified of this. Jameson wilfully took it upon himself to cross the border, and therefore Rhodes could not take any responsibility for the action.

During the subsequent proceedings of the parliamentary committee one of the lawyers quoted someone's comment on Rhodes's testimony, to this effect: whatever Rhodes's views on politics and actions might be, it had to be admitted that his testimony appeared to be exhaustive, clear, sincere and substantial. It was undoubtedly true that the testimony he presented before the committee was of great historical significance.[9]

The parliamentary committee concluded its work in June 1897. Rhodes was not summoned again. Hercules Robinson was not summoned at all—he was ill and died in October 1897. Joseph Chamberlain was himself a member of the committee. The question of the complicity of these two was never even raised. Rhodes's guilt was seen to comprise only what he had himself admitted. Jameson, the leading actor in the drama, was already at liberty, together with the other members of the cast.

For several decades after, the historians debated who had really been guilty, and to what extent. Gradually, one after the other documents came to light which had been concealed at the time of the inquiry. It transpired that an official called Captain Graham Bower had placed a time bomb beneath the entire affair: an account of the true history of the Jameson Raid which he had left with instructions that it was only to be opened after an interval of fifty years. He revealed that Chamberlain had visited Jameson *incognito* in prison, in order to coordinate the public testimony. Certain "missing telegrams" were found... But by this time neither Rhodes and Jameson, nor Chamberlain and Robinson, were still alive.

But at the time, when the parliamentary committee concluded its work, Rhodes was able to breathe more freely... The confounded inquiry was over. All his confederates were at liberty. Neither he nor they would again be subjected to the interrogation and questioning, nor witness the humiliating fuss made of all this in the European press.

Later that same year the name "Rhodesia" was officially confirmed by a special royal decree. Then in April 1898 Rhodes was officially restored to the position of Managing Director of the Chartered Company. In actual fact he had been able to continue managing the affairs of the Company even during his darkest hours. But the official recognition of his position still meant a great deal to him.

More important, the aura which had previously surrounded his name in the eyes of the British public may have dimmed slightly, but it still remained. He was greatly helped here by the excitement aroused by his appearance before the Ndebele rebels in the Matopo hills.

Some of his acquaintances in Britain were now more guarded with him, but at the same time he had acquired new supporters, and most of his old devotees had stuck firmly by his side.

Much has already been written about Rhodes's contacts with the world of finance and business in general, starting with his most powerful patron, Lord Nathaniel Rothschild. His ties with the highest echelon of government, with Lord Salisbury, Rosebery, Chamberlain, are also well recorded. His relations with the British colonial authorities have similarly not been overlooked.

It should also be remembered, however, that Rhodes was supported, even in his most difficult times, by people who had immense influence in shaping the attitudes of the British and in determining the way they thought, even though these people owned neither banks nor factories, nor did they hold high office.

Not least of these figures was the writer Rudyard Kipling. His close relations with Rhodes date back to the early months of 1898, when he spent a long time in Southern Africa. He took the train to Rhodesia, rode on a bicycle round Bulawayo and its surroundings. He closely observed the Afrikaners, and finally departed from Southern Africa, to quote Kingsley Amis's book on Kipling, "a convinced though not violent anti-Boer".[10]

Rhodes placed a small house in the grounds of his Cape Town estate at Kipling's disposal, and Kipling stayed there for long periods at a time. Every year from 1900 to 1907 he avoided the London winter by travelling south, and enjoying instead the summer weather of Cape Town.

Although he was *par excellence* the singer of England's great-ness Kipling was in fact born and reared in India, married to an American and at one time he even tried to make America his home. For all these reasons he was bound to feel slightly out of place in England. Rhodes and he had two things in com-mon: they both believed in the special historical mission of "Great" Britain and they were both men who had spent many years far away from the British Isles.

In a letter to Rhodes Kipling was able to share his melan-cholic thoughts about how England was really no more nor less than a small and stagnant scrap of land—both from a spiritual and a physical point of view. At the same time it must have been through his long conversations with Rhodes that Kipling's idea about the great Pax Britannica and in general about the mission of the white man were brought to fruition. One of his most famous poems, "The White Man's Burden", was written during the period of his friendship with Rhodes and was published in *The Times* on February 4, 1899.

This poem is remarkably reminiscent of Rhodes's idea—the one with which this book begins—that the younger sons should be put to work disseminating the might of the Anglo-Saxon race. We need only listen carefully to the exhortations of these lines:

> *Take up the White Man's burden—*
> *Send forth the best ye breed—*
> *Go bind your sons to exile*
> *To serve your captives' need:*
> *To wait in heavy harness,*
> *On fluttered folk and wild—*
> *Your new-caught, sullen peoples,*
> *Half-devil and half-child.*[11]

It is no surprise to see Kipling described, in one of the earliest British studies of his work, published in 1900, as "the Cecil Rhodes of literature".[12]

Kipling's fellow-feeling for Rhodes was so great that in his brief autobiography, the little book entitled *Something on My-self,* he finds space to return time and again to Rhodes, to discuss his ideas and plans, to quote his words, to recount his conver-sations and to describe the customs and habits which dominated life in his elegant residence at Groote Schuur.

He even recalls their first encounter in a small Cape Town restaurant in 1891 when Kipling was told that a man sitting near him was Cecil Rhodes.

His first talk with Rhodes, in 1897, had such a profound impression on Kipling that he gives a detailed report of it. Kipling reckoned that Rhodes looked like a Roman emperor. Following his habit of disconcerting his interlocutor with an unexpected question, Rhodes asked him:

"What's your dream?"

Kipling answered that Rhodes was part of this dream. He probably felt it his duty to glorify Rhodes. At any rate, he indignantly repudiated the rumour that he had received royalties for his verses on Rhodes and South Africa which were published in *The Times*.

In October 1898 the British press published an interview with Kipling devoted to the subject of Cecil Rhodes. Kipling was answering questions put to him by the editor of the *Liverpool Daily Post,* and the interview was at once reprinted in the journal *The African Review*, under the heading "Great Man on a Great Man". Today this interview has been almost totally forgotten, and I think it worthwhile quoting some of its more important remarks.

The editor rephrased his questions and Kipling's answers thus:

"His beau idéal, or at all events his present day idol, was Mr Rhodes. What did he think of him? The greatest of living men. Wasn't it a rather sordid sort of greatness, all having to do with the making of money. Sordid? A man worth millions who didn't spend more than £600 a year on himself? There he lived in a poor, never-finished place, keeping free and easy open house. Anybody could stay with him and enjoy his simple hospitality—had but to walk in. Mr Rhodes never presided at table—never spent long at table. The guest who had been there longest sat at the top; that was all. Was Mr Rhodes accessible? To everybody, and without introduction. Walking about in his verandah you see a poor, seedy woman come up to him with frowsy papers and a tale of woe. A few sharp questions sufficed. Then a brief hastily-written memorandum. 'Take that to so-and-so; that will put you all right.' And his sort of one-man extempore government went on in that homely tumble-down verandah all day.

"Of course, Rhodes values his milions. He knows the power of money. He knows—or knows not—what his millions may some day have to do in the making of his Empire. But as to caring for money—he's the last man in the world.

" 'Is it true that any inhumanity can justly be charged against Mr Rhodes?' Well, judge for yourself. Men—natives—formerly in his employment in the diamond mines, and who have been dispersed, come long and trying and labourious journeys to be employed by him again, and when taken on they are virtually imprisoned, and do not get out more than once in three months. Yet they are happy and contented. This does not look as if they were ill-used.

"My next question: Has Mr Rhodes, in a public sense, any morals? 'Tut!' says the other great man; 'he's making an empire.' "

All the same Kipling asked the editor to explain what he meant by morals. When informed that the interviewer had in mind high ideals, the poet reacted with vehemence:

"The best ideal is to spread civilization, and make an empire in doing it."

The editor, who clearly viewed both these "great men" in a somewhat critical light, now touched on the question of religion. He pointed out that it was widely believed that the rules of religion followed in private life also applied to public life. Here too Kipling's answer was curt:

" 'Religion has no influence on conduct.' "

He added that the fanatically religious Afrikaners were in favour of everything benighted, and Mr Rhodes was in favour of everything progressive.

When the editor asked him about the Afrikaners and their politics Kipling accused the Afrikaners of an inhuman attitude to the Africans. He was quite indignant:

" 'What nonsense to compare the grand programme of Rhodes, which included every element of advance you could ask questions about, with the stick-in-the-mud policy of these brutal Boers!' "

The editor cautiously put the question about slavery. Was there not some whiff of this in Rhodes's empire? This question provoked a strongly-worded rebuttal from Kipling:

" 'There was none and would be none, but there might be

compulsory labour, and in communities at a primitive degree of progress this would be a good thing too.' "

Kipling expressed his absolute conviction that ultimately Rhodes would get rid of the Afrikaners and make his empire.

Then the editor asked a few more slanted questions. The last so enraged Kipling that he mounted his bicycle and rode off. This was the question about the Jameson Raid: if Rhodes was so great a man and made such excellent plans, and carried them out so perfectly, how did he allow such a disaster as the Jameson Raid?

Said Kipling, " 'You have now asked a question which will probably not be answered till the day of judgement.' "[13]

It is quite evident that Kipling gives a very one-sided picture of Rhodes, and some of the facts he cites are, to put it mildly, far from exact. This is even true of what he has to say about Rhodes's hospitality. We have the following account by Arthur Holland, a man who knew Rhodes personally: "Rhodes although he often threw his house open to the public, was very shy of seeing any of them if he happened to be at home. He was even known to climb out of the kitchen window to escape and go for a ride."[14]

Nevertheless, the interview with Kipling is of great interest to us.[15] After all, a great many of Rhodes's contemporaries, above all his own countrymen, held precisely this view of him.

Of course this apologetic could not have impressed all without exception—not everyone is so gullible. What follows is a striking illustration of a contrary view, referring to events some one or two years after the interview—already during the Anglo-Boer War.

At this time Kipling was in South Africa working on the newspaper *The Friend,* published in the capital of the Orange Free State, Bloemfontein, which had fallen to the British. The ideas which Kipling addressed to the Afrikaners from the pages of this newspaper were the same as those we have seen in the above interview. A South African journalist of British parentage who also worked on *The Friend* described Kipling's activities and concluded his account thus:

"I travelled to England in the same ship (R.M.S. Briton) as Rudyard Kipling, but did not speak to him. 'I'd had him,' as the Yanks say.

"Before I met Kipling I was one of his greatest admirers and read all his works—since, I've never opened a Kipling book. In the main I looked upon him as an English jingo who came to South Africa and did the English South Africans and the British Empire incalculable harm."[16]

All the same it is easy to imagine how much support Rhodes must have enjoyed from such an admirer as Kipling. The poet's influence on British public opinion must have been quite significant. The Soviet poetess Novella Matveyeva has given the following opinion of Kipling's ageless verse:

> *Such power,*
> *Such strength*
> *There was in his song!*
> *Such life ... to honour the grave!*
> *Such truth—for a lie!*
>
> *Listen!*
> *What have you done?*
> *Heedlessly smearing your*
> *Ageless colours*
> *On time's moth-eaten canvases!*

The inner affinities between Kipling and Rhodes have persuaded us to quote so much of Kipling's verse here, on the pages of this book. His poems convey, both more succinctly and more exactly than any of the discussions by contemporaries or historians, the spirit of Rhodes's politics and that atmosphere which Rhodes and Kipling considered their own, an inherent feature of their age.

Kipling had immense admiration not only for Rhodes and his deeds, but also for Rhodes's own followers. He became friendly with Jameson and undoubtedly saw in the doctor an older mentor, a man who had carried out in practice the ideas which Kipling had hailed in his verse.

Perhaps the best-known and most-often quoted of all Kipling's poems is "If—":

> *If you can keep your head when all about you*
> *Are losing theirs and blaming it on you,*
> *If you can trust yourself when all men doubt you,*
> *But make allowance for their doubting too;*

If you can wait and not be tired by waiting,
  Or being lied about, don't deal in lies,
Or being hated, don't give way to hating,
  And yet don't look too good, nor talk too wise...[17]

Even in the Russian language there are numerous transla-
ons of "If—", including those by such outstanding poets and
anslators as Mikhail Lozinsky and Samuil Marshak.

It is easy to guess who inspired Kipling to write this poem.
e was, of course, prompted by the experiences of Jameson,
e raid, imprisonment, trial and the subsequent events.

In his autobiography Kipling wrote that "If—" was in-
uenced by features of Jameson's character. This fact is often
called today, too. Thus even the authors of the *Concise
Illustrated South African Encyclopaedia,* published in 1981, felt
necessary to point out that one of Kipling's "most-quoted
oems, 'If', is said to have been written about Leander Starr
ameson."[18]

Kipling saw Jameson in quite a different light to that in
hich he was regarded by the Afrikaners of the Transvaal. Or
y the Shona and the Ndebele. To him Jameson was a zealot, a
an who had blazed the trail for Britain into "unknown
nds", who was prepared to risk even his own life and who,
ter being taken prisoner and facing the threat of the death
ntence, and having been denounced even by many of his fel-
w-countrymen, took upon himself the full burden of respon-
bility both for what he had tried to accomplish and for his
ailure. Nor did he try and hide behind the backs of those who
a fact bore a bigger share of the guilt...

Admittedly, "If—" does not read as a poem dedicated to any
articular individual. But we know Kipling was thinking of
ameson when we come to the lines:

If you can bear to hear the truth you've spoken
  Twisted by knaves to make a trap for fools,
Or watch the things you gave your life to, broken,
  And stoop and build 'em up with worn-out tools.

This, more or less, was also how Rider Haggard thought of
hodes, of his deeds and his followers. The support of this popu-
ar writer also helped bolster Rhodes's image with the British
ublic.

In addition to being one of the most popular writers of hi
time Rider Haggard was also a public figure. His speeches in
the Aborigines Protection Society and his letters to the paper
were widely discussed.

Haggard was believed to be most competent in precisely
the sphere which the public invariably linked with the name of
Cecil Rhodes. At the end of the seventies and the beginning of
the '80s Haggard actually lived in South Africa. He served in
the colonial service in the Transvaal during the short period
when the Transvaal was controlled by Britain. After his retire
ment Haggard tried his hand at farming in South Africa.

On his return to Britain he became a writer, devoting mos
of his novels and stories, starting with *King Solomon's Mines*
to life in South Africa.

Haggard vigorously supported Rhodes from the pages of hi
journal *The African Review*, of which he was the editor. It wa
this same journal that published the interview with Kipling
about Rhodes quoted above.

In 1896 a book was published in London entitled *Monomotapa
(Rhodesia). Its Monuments, and Its History from the Most An
cient Times to the Present Century*. The author of the book, the
historian Alexander Wilmot, endeavoured to show that the an
cient civilization in the area between the Zambezi and the Lim
popo was in fact the remains of the Biblical land of Ophir, o
the mines of King Solomon. Over the last two thousand year
"its Emperors became transformed into Kafir Chiefs," he writes
with obvious contempt for the latter.[19]

To reach this conclusion Wilmot had worked in the Vatican
in Lisbon, in the archives of many countries. He was particu
larly grateful to the Jesuits for the material they made available
to him. All Wilmot's research was conducted on funds provided
by Rhodes and in accordance with his instructions. The author
begins his book with a dedication to Rhodes.

This dedication is followed by a preface by Rider Haggard
In it he declares that South Africa is not a country without a
past. Its past was Ophir, the glorious Biblical age. Later, alas
the barbarians came...

Wilmot's book came out at a most difficult time for Rhodes
after the Jameson Raid. Its publication was, however, a mos
opportune event: in a way it helped deflect public attention

om Rhodes's crimes and malefactions and it showed him in
et another favourable role—a Maecenas, patron of the arts and
cience, champion of research into the great epochs of human
istory.

Haggard made his own contribution to all this.

Rider Haggard also wrote a literary account of Rhodes's
pioneers" in the war against the Ndebele, entitled *Major Wil-
on's Last Fight.*

Later, after Rhodes's death Haggard visited his grave. There
e recalled their last meeting in the Burlington Hotel in Lon-
on. He reflected what a great man Cecil Rhodes had in fact
een, despite his various mistakes. But of Lobengula he wrote:
Doubtless this savage King deserved his fate." But Haggard
till expressed his regret at Lobengula's death, remembering how
he Ndebele leader had extended his patronage and protection
o European traders.

Nor should we overlook such an influential admirer of Cecil
Rhodes as Arthur Conan Doyle. He did not devote any of his
writings to Rhodes, but in the final analysis he possibly did
nore for him than either Kipling or Haggard. Admittedly this
only became apparent several years later, during the Anglo-Boer
War.

At the time Conan Doyle wrote a book with the title *The
Great Boer War.* Between 1900 and 1902 it came out in seven-
een successive editions. The final, seventeenth edition was
described on its title page as the "complete" edition. Despite
ts massive size—770 pages—it came out in a printing that was
exceptionally large for the time: 63 thousand copies. This for
the final, "complete" edition only.[20]

In this book Conan Doyle essentially defends Cecil Rhodes's
policies, although Rhodes is not always named.

The same holds true for another book by Conan Doyle: *The
War in South Africa. Its Causes and Conduct.*[21] In 1902 it was
published not only in Britain and in English, but in a number
of different European countries and languages. In Germany the
print-run was twenty thousand, in France and Belgium the same,
in Spain ten thousand, in Hungary eight, in Holland, Italy and
the Scandinavian countries—five, in Russia also five and in
Portugal three thousand copies.

Rhodes's idea about the federation of South Africa beneath

the British flag received a great stimulus from this book—both in Britain itself and far beyond its borders. Suffice it to recall that it was for writing these same books—and not for his celebrated Sherlock Holmes—that Conan Doyle received his knighthood.

Conan Doyle's adulation of Cecil Rhodes was so intense that, shortly before his own death he too, like Rider Haggard, made the pilgrimage to Rhodes's grave, although the journey to the Matopo hills in the Zambezi-Limpopo area was long and arduous. Conan Doyle was an adherent of spiritualism, and on various occasions he summoned the spirit of Cecil Rhodes and talked with him. Their conversation is published in a special appendix to his last book *Our African Winter*.

In this same book Conan Doyle summarizes his attitude to Cecil Rhodes, whom he describes as "...that strange but very great man, Cecil Rhodes, a mighty leader, a man of broad vision, too big to be selfish but too determined not to be unscrupulous—a difficult man to appraise with our little human yardsticks".[22]

Even among Rhodes's most devoted acolytes it would be hard to find one who delivered such an impassioned opinion of him as does Sherlock Holmes's creator in this book:

"Just as some souls are heaven-sent upon the spiritual side, the Buddhas and Christs of the world, so others are sent from on high with special practical missions, the Joan of Arc, the Napoléons, the history-makers of all sorts. Heaven-sent was Cecil Rhodes, and heaven-guarded above all human institutions is that British Empire which he did so much to extend."[23]

Besides those we have mentioned there were many others too, men of considerable popularity in Britain, who supported Rhodes.

Rhodes himself was also helped by the praise that was heaped on his "pioneers". Here is one of countless examples of this glorification; it comes from an article about Benjamin Wilson, who, like Francis Thompson before him, was given the nickname "Matabele". This article, which was published in the London journal *South Africa* on March 18, 1899, begins as follows:

"A visit from 'Matabele' Wilson is like a breath from the veld. Upon the ordinary British barbarian, with his flabby flesh and is flabbier morals, such a man exercises a healthful and stimulating influence. He is a sort of moral 'sou'-easter', blowing the desert ozone into lungs which seldom dare to expand in the heavy atmosphere of 'civilized' life."[24]

One of the volunteers in Rhodes's army, the American Frederick Burnham, went on to publish his memoirs, and he put as his epigraph the following remark by General Charles Gordon: "England was never made by her statesmen; England was made by her adventurers".[25] This assertion gained great currency in those years—and in its turn it also strengthened Rhodes's position, particularly since it was common knowledge that Gordon had high regard for Rhodes.

...Rhodes also became friendly with General Kitchener. The latter had not yet reached the zenith of his military career, he was not yet Secretary of State for War, the position he held in the First World War, during which he died, on his way to Russia on a cruiser which hit a German mine. He was not yet Field Marshall, not Earl of Khartoum.

But it was probably then, at the end of the nineties, that he reached the very peak of his fame. It was believed that by utterly destroying the Mahdist state in the Sudan he had wiped a shameful spot from the reputation of the British army: in 1885 the Mahdists had defeated the British army at Khartoum, killing General Gordon.

Kitchener acquired even greater popularity through his confrontation with a French detachment at the Sudanese village of Fashoda. If the French plan had succeeded any hope of putting into practice the Cape-to-Cairo idea would have been completely shattered. Behind Kitchener stood England, and behind the officer Jean Baptiste Marchand stood France. Marchand was forced to bow down.

It is easy to imagine what a kinship of thought Rhodes and Kitchener must have felt at that time. Once Rhodes had discussed his designs with General Gordon. When in 1899 he found himself in England at the same time as Kitchener he grew to cherish their conversations in London parks, during their morning rides.

In June 1899 Rhodes and Kitchener were together awarded honorary doctorates at Oxford University. The ceremony was conducted with its customary pomp. "All London" travelled up to Oxford for the occasion. Rhodes and Kitchener walked side-by-side through the rows of spectators, as it were embodying the greatness and glory of the British Empire. They were photographed and accorded an enthusiastic ovation.

Rhodes also recovered the esteem of high society (in fact we might wonder if he had ever really lost it). Lady Asquith was to recall afterwards how at a London reception she could not even get near to Rhodes, so dense was the circle of fashionable ladies crouching at his feet, while he sat among them "like a great bronze gong".[26]

But what about Rhodes's closest acolyte of all: Jameson? Here once again, is Lady Asquith's opinion:

"Dr Jim had personal magnetism, and could do what he liked with my sex. He was one of those men who, if he had been a quack, could have made a vast fortune, either as a doctor, a thought-reader, a faith-healer or a medium; but he was without quackery of any kind."

Kitchener also extolled Jameson—as a man altogether free of avarice: "Doctor Jim was the only one of the lot who could have made a fortune, but never owned a shilling! He was a really fine fellow".[27]

The new High Commissioner for South Africa in 1897 was Alfred Milner, a man resolute and unyielding in the pursuit of his policies. The line he followed in South African affairs was the same as Rhodes's. This soon became clear for all to see.

Rhodes inflamed imperialist passions not only with his triumphs but also with his failures. The anti-British campaign in Germany and the Transvaal did not dampen these feelings: quite the contrary.

It often happens that an outbreak of nationalism on one side engenders an outbreak of nationalism on another. Chauvinism engenders chauvinism. They then grow, feeding one another and becoming increasingly malevolent until a vicious conflict erupts, to be followed by slaughter and then by disaster, perhaps greater or lesser, but inevitable for both sides.

It is unlikely that Rhodes ever considered such a disaster. He was delighted to see that the time of his ideas had not yet passed. In other words, his own time.

Once he had recovered from the fiasco of the Jameson Raid

Rhodes directed increasingly bitter philippics against Kruger and Krugerism". Chamberlain and Milner delivered speeches in much the same vein.

The British government became increasingly insistent in its demands that the Transvaal grant voting rights to the Uitlanders. Speaking in Parliament Chamberlain even threatened Kruger with war and appealed to the people of England "to support us, if the necessity should arise, in any measures we may think it necessary to take to secure justice to the British subjects in the Transvaal".[28]

These demands were backed up with military preparations. The Transvaal was threatened with war with precisely the same objective in mind for which Rhodes had organized the Jameson Raid and the rebellion in Johannesburg.

«Terug na Die Ou Transvaal» («Back to the Old Transvaal»)

Reports and rumours about the Anglo-Boer War spread through countless countries on all the world's continents. This continued for two and a half years, from October 1899 until May 1902.

And thereafter, memories of the war lived on for several generations. It has had a most varied legacy.

For example, there is a superstition among smokers that one should not light three cigarettes with a single match. This belief, apparently, dates back to the war: when the match is struck and the first cigarette is lit the Afrikaner takes up his rifle; when the second man lights up the Afrikaner takes aim; when the third cigarette is lit he shoots—and rarely misses.

When we read about Winston Churchill, Lloyd George, the South African Prime Minister Jan Smuts, or Field Marshal Kitchener, we are invariably informed that they made their name in this war. Biographies of Mahatma Gandhi will tell us that he served in the British auxiliary forces, as a stretcher bearer. Those writing about the founder of the Boy Scout movement, Lord Baden-Powell, will tell us that the first boy scouts were the young lads he sent as runners from Mafeking during its siege by Afrikaner forces. About Conan Doyle—that he worked as a doctor in a South African field hospital. About Edgar Wallace or Rudyard Kipling—that they travelled to Southern Africa as war correspondents. It was in this war that the famous poem "Boots" was born, which later became a song.

"We're foot-slog-slog-slog-slogging' over Africa..." No doubt, other relics of the war have survived in our collective memory. Nonetheless, it is hard for us now, after two world wars, to appreciate how the world was shaken by this first major war of our century. By modern standards it seems relatively minor and, as wars go, not particularly horrific.

But at the turn of the century the war was a significant event in the world. Many people believed that in its way the Boer War marked the end of one century and the beginning of another: the modern age.

The outbreak of this war came as a particular shock because there had not been any military conflicts on such a scale for almost a quarter of a century—since the Franco-Prussian and the Russo-Turkish wars. Here on the side of the British alone, forces numbering several hundred thousand were deployed. Armadas of British ships were coursing up and down the Atlantic, ferrying countless numbers of troops and with them moutains of weaponry and gun-powder.

The Anglo-Boer War also saw the introduction of novel military strategies and tactics, and the new military hardware invented over the last twenty or thirty years here received its baptism of fire. The general staffs of many different countries at once dispatched their representatives to the battlefields of the Boer War, anxious not to miss anything of value.

In fact there were a great number of inventions and innovations. It is perhaps not widely known that the now ubiquitous khaki, the protective colour of military uniforms, first appeared in this war, as did many other forms of camouflage. Or that this was the first time smokeless gunpowder was used in battle conditions, the first time automatic weapons and machine-guns were used on a mass scale, as were shrapnel, dumdum bullets, the explosive Lyddite; this was the first war in which the field telegraph was used, and the cinema camera.

Changes were introduced in the battle order, too: the old method of attack in closed columns lost its effectiveness and was superseded by the open order formation.

Today trenches and barbed wire seem an almost inevitable concomitant of warfare. But the Afrikaners were the first ever to use barbed wire.

The concentration camp system, which later in the 20th century became so widespread, also originated during the Anglo-Boer War. Of course the South African camps were far exceeded in scale by those of the Second World War, but the death of more than twenty thousand Afrikaner women and children in the British camps was still a tragedy of shocking proportions, especially for that time.

It is astonishing how few lessons the European general staffs actually derived from the Boer War. This should surely have taught the world the significance of machine-guns, yet the truth still did not strike home. It took a world war to really demonstrate the power of machine-gun fire.

It seemed that, after the Transvaal battles, there could never be another traditional cavalry attack by troops resplendent in heavy suits of armour. But in his memoirs entitled *Fifty Years in the Ranks*, the Russian general Alexei Ignatiev records how on August 3, 1914, on the day war was declared, he happened to be in Paris and when he looked out of his window he "could not believe his eyes". Beneath him, along the road marched curassiers, horsemen "clad in mediaeval breastplates and Napoleonic helmets with steel crests, from beneath which long black tails of horsehair flew across the riders' backs". Admittedly the helmets and breastplates were covered in canvas, for the purposes of camouflage.

It is startling to imagine knights in armour like this and bursts of machine-gun fire in the same encounter—yet that very evening machine-guns could be heard firing at the German Zeppelin above Paris.

"The fate of this unfortunate regiment," wrote Ignatiev, "was of course a foregone conclusion."[1] This regiment of French horse-guards was sent forward to attack the German positions; the men and horses were mown down just as remorselessly as the Ndebele had been in 1893. The same tragedy overtook the most privileged Russian horse-guards regiments: in August 1914 they galloped into attack against German machine-guns and artillery. After the ensuing slaughter many an aristocratic family in Russia donned its suits of mourning.

Europe needed its own experience, its own tragedies, and only after this would it change its cavalry tactics and re-attire its horsemen in khaki uniforms, like the rest of the army.

Rhodes's biographers love to assert that at that time, at the end of the last century, he supposedly did not expect a war, did not believe that it would begin. Lewis Michell writes that, although a few months before the outbreak of hostilities "a vast majority of Colonists now believed war to be inevitable ... it has always been an unexplained problem why Rhodes himself continued to express a contrary view".[2]

But even the information Michell adduces indicates that Rhodes's behaviour was in fact quite understandable. Take for example this telegram from Rhodes to Alfred Beit in London: "Remember that Kruger, if the Home Government are firm, will in the end give way. All they need to do is to continue preparations as openly as possible. Nothing will make Kruger fire a shot."[3]

To one of the British ministers Rhodes said: "How much longer are you men (meaning the Cabinet of which I was a member) going to allow Kruger to humbug you? He is only bluffing, and if you were to employ your troops you could undoubtedly bring him to subjection."[4]

Loath though we may be to admit it, it is hard not to see in this an act of direct provocation.

Perhaps Rhodes still believed that there would be no bloody confrontation. That all that was necessary was to give the Afrikaners a fright and they would at once surrender? Yet it was Rhodes who had repeatedly drawn the attention of the British government to the Transvaal's defensive preparations, to the fact that Kruger had been secretly importing Krupp cannons and Mauser rifles from Germany. From the transportation of each batch of weaponry to the Transvaal Rhodes drew ammunition for his anti-Transvaal campaign and for his calls to increase the British military contingent in Southern Africa. Yet how can he have failed to suspect that these Krupp guns would one day be fired by the Afrikaner gunners? Or that in response to Britain's categorical demands Kruger might—as indeed he did on October 9, 1899—give his own ultimatum, that Britain should cease its own military preparations?

As was demonstrated by the war which broke out after Kruger's ultimatum, all Great Britain—the government, the army, and the general public—underestimated the Afrikaners, underestimated their determination and ability to uphold their independence. The incompetence and criminal irresponsibility of the authorities and the generals were paid for in the end, and as always, with the blood of ordinary people.

But a particular burden of guilt rests on Rhodes's shoulders. After all, he should have known the Afrikaners better: the Jameson Raid had been a very good lesson. . .

Yet the most important fact is that he was the main initiator

341

of this war. Even if Rhodes had done nothing during the last months, or the last year before it broke out, the war was still the result of his policies. These were policies not of a few months, but of many years, policies aimed at incorporating the whole of South Africa into the British Empire.

In fact, Rhodes's last important action before the outbreak of hostilities was directed precisely at ensuring that proper preparations were made for this war.

THE GATHERING STORM

It is puzzling that although the whole of Europe erupted in a frenzy of indignation against England from the very outbreak of the war, not one single European government actually did anything substantial about it. Things proceeded no further than denunciations in the press.

This was most surprising in the case of Germany. Less than four years had elapsed since Kaiser Wilhelm's telegram to Kruger and the row it had caused. At that time the Kaiser had made it quite clear that he was prepared to intervene if the Afrikaners were unable to cope. Yet now, with the war already into its second month, the Kaiser was on his way to visit one of the warring countries. This was not his adored Transvaal; in fact, his destination was detested England.

Nor was the Kaiser impelled by a sudden accession of grand-filial affection for his maternal grandmother, Queen Victoria. We would also be wrong to imagine that the bellicose German emperor had succumbed at last to the ideals of the Hague Conference, the first ever international conference on disarmament, which had recently ended, in the summer of 1899.

No, that was not the reason. The conference had been called, the speeches delivered, but the Kaiser had still written—albeit not for the press: "But in my own practice I shall continue to rely only on God and on my sharp sword! And I ... on all these resolutions!"[5]

Then did this mean that the Kaiser, tugging at his moustaches and rattling his sabre, had decided personally to intercede on the Afrikaners' behalf?

No, not that either. The Kaiser had come on a different mat-

r altogether. It had not even occurred to him and his govern-
ent to defend the Transvaal.

The reasons for this are complex.

...On March 11, 1899, precisely seven months before the
utbreak of the Anglo-Boer War, Rhodes had a meeting in Berlin
ith Kaiser Wilhelm and the Reichskanzler Bernhard von Bülow.
irst an audience, followed by dinner. The justification for invit-
ig Rhodes to Berlin was the question of laying telegraph and
ailway lines from Cape Town to Cairo. These lines could run
cross British possessions for practically their entire length, but
i one section they were forced to cut across German East
.frica. Rhodes was eager to secure Wilhelm's consent.

This, however, was only the pretext for the meeting. Rhodes
poke of far-reaching issues of world politics, trying as hard as
ossible to turn the Kaiser's attention away from South Africa,
nd from Africa as a whole. To do this he waxed lyrical to the
Vilhelm about the richness and beauty of Asia Minor, or the
Near East and of the Pacific islands.

Historians have left very divergent accounts of this meeting.
This is the view of George W. F. Hallgarten, perhaps the lead-
ig West German expert on the pre-First World War history
f German imperialism.

"...Rhodes the politician was dead. The champagne and
vhisky-sodas had bloated the face of this man, who to his Ber-
in hosts seemed like a colonial farmer gone to seed, or, at best,
ike an excesively slovenly English eccentric, and they held it
gainst him that contrary to protocol he presented himself to
ie Kaiser in a plain cutaway."[6]

This is what Academician Fyodor Rotshtein in Moscow wrote
bout him: a "brilliant reception" was held for Rhodes. "Both
he Kaiser and Bülow received him extremely warmly, and the
ormer was quite in raptures about him." Rotshtein compares
he Kaiser's attitude to Rhodes with the way he treated the
hen Russian foreign minister, Mikhail Muravyov. In June 1899,
hree months after Rhodes's visit, Muravyov informed Berlin
n a letter that "Russia would reconcile itself" with Germany's
ncreased influence in Asia Minor, if for its part Germany "une-
|uivocally recognized Russia's historical rights to the Bosphorus."
Beside the words "Russia would reconcile itself with" the Kaiser
ad written: "...Confound it, this won't work with me! Click

your heels and stand to attention, Mr Muravyov, when you talk to the German Kaiser!"[7]

"How different in tone to the way he addresses Rhodes," remarks Rotshtein. With Rhodes it is: "My dear Mr Rhodes, you have correctly divined my thoughts!"[8]

Hallgarten and Rotshtein draw from roughly the same sources, so it is not immediately obvious which of them is more accurate.

Let us turn to their main source, Chancellor Bülow. He leaves the following account of Rhodes: "Cecil Rhodes was bound to make a great impression on every unprejudiced person. There was nothing ostentatious about him, he was all calmness and strength. He behaved naturally, with no affectation. He stood respectfully before the Kaiser, but without any agitation or even awkwardness. In broad strokes he outlined to His Majesty his project for the British-built Cape-to-Cairo railway. The Kaiser's eyes lit up. . ."[9]

The young Kaiser's eyes must indeed have lit up at hearing such sweeping global designs, and from such a man as Cecil Rhodes. Apparently, Wilhelm could see in Rhodes a successful fellow-imperialist.

We should note here the way Rhodes sought to win over the Kaiser with a rather peculiar joke. When Wilhelm asked his opinion about his, Wilhelm's, telegram to Kruger in connection with the Jameson Raid, Rhodes replied:

"I will tell you, Your Majesty, in a very few words. It was the greatest mistake you ever made in your life, but you did me the best turn one man ever did another. You see, I was a naughty boy, and you tried to whip me. Now, my people were quite ready to whip me for being a naughty boy, but directly you did it, they said, 'No, if this is anybody's business, it is ours.' The result was that Your Majesty got yourself very much disliked by the English people, and I never got whipped at all!"[10]

It was these words that the South African poet and journalist William Plomer had in mind when he commented: "It is a little saddening to think that vast power over mankind was wielded by a man who could describe himself in such terms."[11]

Yet it seemed that Rhodes's approach pleased the Kaiser. He pardoned Rhodes his quite inadmissible dress: he had not even put on a morning coat, but appeared simply in his usual flannel suit. Nor did he take offense at Rhodes's seemingly unthinkable behaviour. It is reported that Rhodes looked at his watch and announced: "Well, good-bye. I have to go now. I have some people coming to dinner."[12]

Nevertheless (or perhaps for precisely this reason?) Wilhelm then pronounced the words which were to be quoted so often: "I wish I had a minister like you,"[13] and added that then he would be the greatest sovereign in the world.

Rhodes also took to the Kaiser. In his final will Rhodes left five Oxford scholarships to the Kaiser's personal discretion.

Leaving aside these personal impressions gained by the Kaiser and his Reichskanzler, Hallgarten's appraisal is in any case refuted by the very fact that Rhodes was invited to Berlin. This invitation was issued after he had been officially denounced by the whole of Germany for the Jameson Raid. A mere three years had passed, and here was the Kaiser receiving him as if nothing had happened, Furthermore, Rhodes travelled in a thoroughly unofficial capacity, carrying no credentials from any government and speaking entirely on his own behalf.

Obviously, the Kaiser's enthusiasm could also be partly attributed to his own character, and partly to the fact that there was much in Rhodes that was bound to impress him, such as the global scope of Rhodes's designs, and to a great extent, his racist approach to world politics. For when discussing the domination of a superior race over the world, Rhodes frequently called this race "Anglo-Teutonic".

The Kaiser could see that Rhodes was not alone in espousing these ideas. They enjoyed support in England—a support that was sometimes silent, but at other times very vocal. After the outbreak of the Boer War, on November 30, 1899, Joseph Chamberlain publicly declared: "...the character, the main character of the Teutonic race differs very slightly from the character of the Anglo-Saxon ... and if the union between England and America is a powerful factor in the cause of peace, a new Triple Alliance between the Teutonic race and the two great branches of the Anglo-Saxon race, will be a still more potent influence in the future of the world".[14]

Discussions of racial superiority were sweet to Wilhelm's ear. The notion of the "yellow peril" was at that time closely connected with his name, although this same idea was expressed in different ways by other politicians, ideologists and philosophers of turn-of-the-century Europe.

As early as 1895 Wilhelm had commissioned the German artist Hermann Knackfuss to paint an allegorical picture to his own design. As the Kaiser explained, the picture was intended to promote the idea of a Europe united to repel the "yellow peril", to protect Christianity from the advance of Buddhism, paganism and barbarity. Personified as women were the figures of Germany, France, Russia, Austria, England and Italy. They are gazing at a fiery horizon, from which the obese form of Buddha, mounted on a dragon, is bearing down upon them, striking fear into the hearts of his beholders with his inscrutable appearance. Even several decades later a prominent American historian wrote that "the picture was lurid enough to stir even the most immovable".[15]

Wilhelm needed the idea of the "yellow peril" to justify conquests in China. But he had another specific objective. He had several copies made of the painting and sent the first of these to Nicholas II. There was a very good reason for this: just as Rhodes had tried to draw Wilhelm's attention to the Near East, so now Wilhelm was trying to deflect the Czar with the Far East. In general, however, the idea of the confrontation of races was just as integral to the Kaiser's way of thinking as it was to Rhodes's. Incidentally, Rhodes often declared that he would never admit Chinese immigrants to his Rhodesia.

Nevertheless, this still does not explain the splendour of the reception accorded Rhodes in Berlin, or the neutralization of Germany in the approaching Anglo-Boer war.

The real reason behind all this is to be found in the noticeable changes which occured in German policy at that time.

Of course, Berlin continued to regard South Africa as a tasty morsel. By the middle of the year 1899 German capital investments in that country had reached 900,000,000 marks. The South African mining industry was partly financed by the Darmstadt Bank, one of whose clients was the Kaiser himself.

But it was becoming increasingly manifest to the German government that it was impossible to take part in any major conflicts in remote parts of the world without a large navy and that their influence in such distant parts as South Africa could

Cecil Rhodes (centre): "My friend the Kaiser". Kruger says: "I thought he was *my* friend". A caricature from the *Westminster Gazette,* reprinted in the journal *South Africa* of May 18, 1899

only be maintained, not to mention increased, by avoiding any open conflict with Britain. The telegram sent by Wilhelm to Kruger in 1896, hinting at the possibility of military support for the Afrikaners, was a risky venture.

Now, three years later, the Kaiser acted with greater prudence. When he detected in a letter from the Russian minister Sergei Witte a suggestion that he should harden his policies towards Britain, he wrote: "Now that England is mobilized, prepared, armed for combat and stronger than ever before—he wants to organize an anti-English league... Too late Sir! Now I do not want it."[16] He wrote this less than three months before his meeting with Rhodes.

Still more significant was the fact that by this time German plans for expansion in the Near East were increasingly taking shape. Wilhelm had recently, at the end of 1898, returned from a visit to Istanbul and Jerusalem. In Damascus he had visited

Saladin's tomb and proclaimed himself, like many politicians after him, a great friend of the Muslims. He said, "...the 300 million Muslims the world over can be sure that the German Kaiser shall always be their friend."[17]

It was for this reason that the Kaiser's eyes lit up when Rhodes told him that the future of Germany was Mesopotamia, the Tigris and Euphrates, and Baghdad, the city of the Caliphs. Wilhelm detected that he was being offered a deal. If he agreed not to interfere with the construction of the Cape-to-Cairo telegraph and railway lines the British would not create any major obstacles to the implementation of his plans for a Berlin-Baghdad railway. And they would also let Germany gain a firm foothold on the Samoan archipelago in the Pacific Ocean.

It might be wondered whether Rhodes in fact had the authority to offer such a deal. He held no credentials, but then the Germans did not ask for any. Among the groupings of British capital—which for argument's sake we can call South African, Near Eastern and Chinese—connected with colonial policies, the South African contingent was by far the most influential. Rhodes had on his side such figures as Rothschild, overlord of the City, and Chamberlain, the most influential of the ministers.

But it was not only a question of the South African grouping of British capital. However influential it may have been, what was still of more importance was the increasingly significant role played by Transvaal gold in determining Britain's financial position. Thanks to this gold Britain had been able to avoid any repetition of the severe monetary crisis which rocked the nation in 1890. At that time, faced by financial catastrophe, the Bank of England had been forced to adopt an extreme measure: to seek a loan from the Bank of France. Thanks to the Transvaal gold, however, in the first half of the eighteen-nineties Britain was able nearly to double its gold reserves.

It is therefore understandable why Britain's ruling circles should have been prepared to make far-reaching concessions, in order to safeguard this source of gold from any unforeseen eventualities. Thus there was nothing accidental about the preparations to seize the Transvaal. Nor, in fact, did Britain make much secret of its determination. The British authorities made sure the other powers knew this so there would be no danger of them stepping on Britain's pet corn.

Thus the Kaiser and his Reichskanzler did not need any credentials from Rhodes in order to understand all this.

On his return to London Rhodes had several meetings with Prime Minister Salisbury and with the first lord of the Treasury, Arthur Balfour, a man of great influence in the government and in parliament.

Rhodes's verbal accords were sanctioned a few months later as official agreements. The British government ceded to Germany two islands, so coveted by the Kaiser, in the Samoan archipelago. In turn the German authorities concluded agreements with Rhodes's companies about the laying of telegraph and railway lines on the Cape-to-Cairo route across the territory of German East Africa.

The question of the Near East was of course much more intricate. No such concrete agreements were concluded on this issue. Under the influence of Rhodes's group the British press started publishing articles about how worthwhile it was for Britain and Germany to cooperate in Mesopotamia. Some German historians believe, however, that Rhodes promised Wilhelm more than he was able to deliver.

The main result for Rhodes must have been the instruction issued to the German press by Reichskanzler Bülow on September 20, 1899, three weeks prior to the Anglo-Boer War. In his instruction he recommended that Britain should not be set off against Germany. "With regard to the Transvaal crisis our press should cultivate a calm, matter-of-fact and cool language".[18]

Rhodes had every ground for his announcement at the extraordinary general meeting of shareholders of the Chartered Company on May 2, 1899 that Wilhelm had received him in the best imaginable way and had given him every possible support through his ministers. In gratitude Rhodes described the Kaiser as a man of great significance.

It is in this way that Rhodes sought German neutrality in the event of war breaking out. Bülow wrote: "Just as the stormy petrel announces the gathering storm, so did Cecil Rhodes appear in Berlin in March 1899".[19]

This was Rhodes's triumph. But it was to be the last such triumph of his life.

THE CONSEQUENCES OF HIS POLICIES

For almost half a century, since the Crimean War, Britain had not engaged in any hostilities entailing really significant losses. For two or three generations the people of Britain had grown accustomed to the idea that only a few of their countrymen might lose their lives in distant battlefields. Not many people suspected that a war against a raggle-taggle mob of Boers would transform all this.

With the declaration of war on October 11, 1899 the London stock-market held a noisy demonstration. This started with a strident declaration that President Kruger was a bankrupt debtor and with the hanging of his effigy over the entrance. Then the national anthem was sung and the jingoistic "Soldiers of the Queen". After this it was decided that one of the companies was not behaving in a sufficiently patriotic way and when its representative appeared, he was greeted with jeering and whistling by the other brokers, who then surrounded him and started beating him up. After this a general fracas broke out.

John Galsworthy was a contemporary of these events, and he conveys the spirit that prevailed in the land at the time with remarkable perception from the moment when Soames Forsyte hears the newspaper boys shouting on Trafalgar Square:

"Payper! Special! Ultimatum by Krooger! Declaration of war!" With this "the 'Change"—the Forsyte family stock-exchange—hastily convene to deliberate the matter:

"It was the ingratitude of the Boers that was so dreadful, after everything had been done for them—Dr Jameson imprisoned, and he was so nice, Mrs MacAnder had always said. And Sir Alfred Milner sent out to talk to them—such a clever man! She didn't know what they wanted."

"We've just been saying how dreadful it is about these Boers! And what an impudent thing of that old Kruger!"

Only June, an out-and-out nonconformist, dares to object:

"Impudent! . . . I think, he's quite right! What business have we to meddle with them? If he turned out all those wretched Uitlanders it would serve them right. They're only after money."

But June is at once rebuffed:

"What! Are you pro-Boer?"

James, the eldest of the Forsytes. normaly so cautious in business matters, now takes an ominous delight in Britain's decision to go to war.

"Ah!. . . I was afraid they'd cut and run like old Gladstone. We shall finish with them this time."

In another scene Soames, sitting in a restaurant, overhears some diners, apparantly writers or actors, sympathizing with the Afrikaners and blaming the British government. Despite his usual reticence, he grumbles: "You have some queer customers."

In general the Forsytes' stance is pro-war: their attitude to the Afrikaners is bellicose in the extreme.

"En avant, the Forsytes! Roll, bowl, or pitch!"

In Oxford two young scions of this respectable family come to blows because one calls the other pro-Boer—he reckons the latter did not respond with sufficient enthusiasm to the toast: "Buller and damnation to the Boers!"

Subsequently they are both goaded by each other and the general fever of patriotism into enlisting as volunteers. In their imagination they are to gallop across the expanses of the Transvaal, taking Afrikaners in the sights of their rifles and picking them off like rabbits. The reality, however, is to be quite different. One of them does not even survive to the first battle, succumbing to an attack of dysentery.

The Forsytes' butler has a somewhat different view of the Boers: ". . .well, Sir, they 'aven't a chance, of course; but I'm told they're very good shots. I've got a son in the Inniskillings. . . . I expect he'll be going out".[20]

The butler's fears were not ill-founded. Thousands upon thousands of young Englishmen were to go to their deaths in that distant land. Perhaps the remains of the Forsytes' young relative would have been accorded a decent burial, although it is unlikely: decent burials were not the order of the day in the Transvaal. As to the fate of thousands of other young men, one could recall the fate of Hardy's Drummer Hodge:

> *They throw in Drummer Hodge, to rest*
> *Uncoffined—just as found:*
> *His landmark is a kopje-crest*
> *That breaks the veldt around;*
> *And foreign constellations west*
> *Each night above his mound.*[21]

Boer soldiers

The war turned out quite differently to the way many of the British expected. There was the "black week" when the British troops suffered defeats on all fronts. In general the first months of the war were a history of continuous defeat. The military confrontations were taking place not in the territory of the Afrikaner republics, but in the British possessions: the Afrikaners had penetrated into the Cape Colony into Natal and even into Bechuanaland.

It transpired that the Afrikaners, those "uncouth bumpkins", even had better rifles than the British. Kruger had secretly bought Mauser rifles from Germany and a mass of other superior weaponry. The British Lee-Metford rifles were markedly inferior in combat conditions to the arms wielded by the Afrikaners. What was particularly galling to the British public was that Kruger had bought his guns with British money—raised in taxes from the Uitlanders.

The Afrikaners promptly surrounded three towns in different parts of South Africa—Kimberley, Ladysmith and Mafeking. The siege lasted for many months.

Britain was forced to drink deep from the cup of humiliation. For month after month this "filthy band of yokels" held Englishmen under siege, and Her Majesty's forces were unable to break through! There were women and children in the besieged towns... It had been many years since the British had heard of their fellow countrymen in such a plight.

> *If blood be the price of admiralty,*
> *If blood be the price of admiralty,*
> *If blood be the price of admiralty,*
> *Lord God, we ha' bought it fair!*[22]

But their humiliation was as nothing compared to the jubilation when eventually the siege was broken.

When news broke of the relief of one of the besieged towns the stock-brokers not only drank their health and whooped for joy, they climbed on one another's shoulders and gallopped "horseback" all over the London Stock Exchange to the singing "Soldiers of the Queen". The festivities were so unrestrained that the following day one of the jobbers awoke in a strange house, another in a kennel on the outskirts of the town, convinced that it was his own bedroom. A third managed to crawl home, but found an assortment of strange objects in his pockets, including a pair of lady's stockings, a baby's rattle, a tuft of hair, most probably from someone's beard, and even a soup ladle. All this is described for the benefit of subsequent generations in a history of the Stock Exchange, published in London.

Galsworthy also describes the events of those days. Soames steps outside and finds himself in "the most amazing crowd he had ever seen: a shrieking, whistling, dancing, jostling, grotesque, and formidably jovial crowd, with false noses and mouthorgans, penny whistles and long feathers, every appanage of idiocy..."

In essence the mood of these people differed little from that of Soames himself. Perhaps it is precisely this that so irritate him, offends his dignity:

"Mafeking! Of course, it had been relieved! Good! But wa that an excuse? Who were these people, what were they, wher had they come from into the West End? His face was ticklec his ears whistled into. . . A youth so knocked off his top-hat tha he recovered it with difficulty. Crackers were exploding beneat his nose, between his feet. He was   bewildered, exasperated offended. This stream of people came from every quarter, as i impulse had unlocked flood-gates, let flow waters of whose exis tence he had heard perhaps, but believed in never."

Paradoxical though it may seem, it is perhaps precisely her during these revelries, that Forsyte finally realises how alien repulsive and hideous the common people—any common people anywhere—are to him. Even those who serve his own interests

"This, then, was the populace, the innumerable living negation of gentility and Forsyteism. This was—egad—Democracy! I stank, yelled, was hideous? In, the East End, or even Soho, per haps—but here in Regent Street, in Piccadilly! What were the police about! In 1900, Soames, with his Forsyte thousands, hac never seen the cauldron with the lid off; and now looking intc it, could hardly believe his scorching eyes. The whole thing wa unspeakable! These people had no restraint, they seemed tc think him funny; such swarms of them, rude, coarse, laughing— and what laughter! Nothing sacred to them! He shouldn't bc surprised if they began to break windows."[23]

. . .But the war did not end with the relief of the thre besieged towns. Nor did it end on June 5, 1900, when Pretoria, capital of the Transvaal, finally fell. Gradually turning intc a guerrilla struggle which increasingly wore out the British army, it dragged on for a further two years, until May 1902.

> *Only a wave to our troopers,*
> *Only our flanks swinging past,*
> *Only a dozen voorloopers,*
> *Only we've learned it at last!*[24]

. . .Britain, that great and proud state, longed only for one thing: for these people, whose farms had long since been burnt, whose wives and children had long since been banished to concentration camps, to agree to a truce! The Afrikaners had to be won over with the most honourable conditions.

In Britain itself the fever of jingoistic patriotism, which had seemed so inexhaustible, gradually subsided. Throughout the country there was mounting discontent with the war. Public scepticism was expressed in pamphlets with titles like: "Are We in the Right?", "Shall I Slay My Brother Boer?"[25]

But other books were published too. The moment the war ended an absurdly chauvinistic collection of soldiers' letters was published with the long and pretentious title: "The Epistles of Atkins. Being some of the lights on human nature in the ordeal of war, which illumine the letters of the common soldier, written from South Africa to his people at home; and so an answer to the question, 'How does it feel to be in battle?' "[26]

This is not to say that the letters were fabricated by the compiler of this hefty volume. They may well have been perfectly authentic: there were great numbers of British soldiers—whose letters never made it into any such collection—who cursed the war! Even Rhodes's friend, a man who shared his views, Rudyard Kipling could not ignore this in his verse.

> *What man can weigh or size another's woe?*
> *There are some things too bitter 'ard to bear.*
> *Suffice it we 'ave finished—Domino!*
> *As we can testify, for we are there,*
> *In the side-world where 'wilful-missings' go.*[27]

The men of Victorian England, the mores of Victorian England, the pride of Victorian England—all this was slipping away —and with no fanfare to accompany it. Even Queen Victoria herself—the "widow" as Kipling dubbed her—died during the Boer War.

"The whole of this lengthy reign, which had represented an almost unbroken chain of triumphs for England in all spheres, came to such a dismal end. It must have been a cause of suffering to the queen, to observe how in an atmosphere of universal disapproval of an unjust war Great Britain's moral attraction declined and how its political prestige collapsed in the defeats of its troops."[28] This comes from a dispatch sent from London by a Russian diplomat at the time.

The reason for this decline was the thousands of "fell i
action" notices from Southern Africa.

For half my company's lying still
Where the Widow gave the party.[29]

The entire world followed the course of the war in Souther
Africa with concern.

Europe sympathized with the Afrikaners, with this little Davi
heroically pitting himself against the might of Goliath. The Afrik
aners were pardoned everything, even their ignorance, so colou
fully described by Mark Twain, was forgotten. Nor was it recalle
that they themselves oppressed other people, the Africans. It wa
not yet customary to think of Africans as people.

By and large only one thing could be seen: the big man attacl
ing the little and the little fighting back for all he was wort
The Afrikaners became a symbol of the love of freedom, of cou
age, of self-sacrifice.

In many different countries committees were set up to assi
the Afrikaners. Romain Rolland devoted his play *Le temp*
viendra to the Boer War. Anatole France expressed his condem
nation of both Rhodes and Chamberlain.

Sympathy for the Afrikaners led to condemnation of Britain i
self. The world was almost united in its condemnation. But th
worst censure was reserved for Cecil Rhodes. The war was regarc
ed as the triumph of his policies and he himself as its primar
instigator.

Wilhelm Liebknecht, August Bebel, Jean Léon Jaurès, Va
Cole and other leaders of the western social-democratic move
ment campaigned against this British aggression, supporting th
arduous struggle of British socialists who publicly condemne
their own government.

Volunteers travelled to the Transvaal from France, German
Russia, Italy, Holland, America, Bulgaria and other countrie

In some cases, sympathy for the Afrikaners was more a cons
quence of an antipathy for the British and the British system
Some governments even played of these sympathies, hoping t
divert the attention of their people from their own sorrows an
hardships by reminding them of the misfortunes of a foreig
nation.

In this context we feel bound to refer once again to Mar

Twain. He lived for several years in England, and three years before the war he travelled round South Africa, visiting the Boer republics as well as the British colonies. He subjected British colonialism to impassioned criticism, but at the same time was sincerely grieved to observe the catastrophic decline in Britain's prestige. In one of his letters he gives the following expression to these feelings of regret: "Poor as it is (our civilization—*Tr.*) .. it is better than real savagery, therefore we must stand by it, extend it, and (in public) praise it. And so we must not utter any hateful word about England in these days, nor fail to hope that she will win in this war, for her defeat and fall would be an irremediable disaster for the mangy human race. Naturally, then, I am for England; but she is profoundly in the wrong, Joe, and no (instructed) Englishman doubts it."[30]

The instructed Englishmen bore out Mark Twain's hopes; these included not only socialists, radicals and pacifists, but also quite ordinary honest people too, who did not allow themselves to become intoxicated with chauvinism... Sir William Harcourt, described by André Maurois as the last of the Liberal giants of the 1880s, said that while the Crimean War was a mistake, the Boer war would be a crime.

This venerable old politician also commented of Rhodes, who had tried so hard to win his compassion during the Jameson Raid trial, that he should be given a cocked hat, a pair of plain trousers and sent to St Helena.[31]

HIS WAR?

News of Kruger's ultimatum reached Rhodes in Cape Town. But that same evening, October 9, he slipped out of his house and, hoping not to be recognized, took train for Kimberley.

None of Rhodes's biographers have satisfactorily explained this strange subterfuge, in fact none of them seem to have given it much thought. One author has written that Rhodes announced a few days earlier, before war broke out, that he was travelling to Kimberley on some business or other. Others are of the opinion that it was the proper thing for Rhodes to be in the capital of his diamond kingdom during the war. "But Rhodes knew his place. His mines were in Kimberley."[32]

But Rhodes had more than one such kingdom, and many more

mines. Why should he have chosen Kimberley in particular?

Let us assume that he did not suspect he would fall into a trap. Nevertheless, once he left Cape Town he left the centre of events. All decisions by the British side in this war had to be taken in Cape Town, or at least, if they were taken in London, had to travel through Cape Town. Yet Rhodes at once, and quite deliberately, put himself in a position from which he could have no influence on the course of events. And he was such a man of action!

Perhaps he made the journey in order to show that no extraneous events, not even war, could deflect him from his chosen path. But even for Rhodes this would have been an excessively ridiculous demonstration.

Did he perhaps believe that the war would not last more than a few days? This is possible, but still unlikely.

Perhaps he was afraid that he would not be listened to in Cape Town as attentively as he might wish, and that this would be a constant insult to his pride. For this reason, as Caesar had realized, he had rather be first in a village than second at Rome.

Or did he secretly hope that his absence would be at once felt, they would realize that they could not manage without him?

We can only speculate as to his reasons. In any event he can hardly have predicted how events were to unfold. Indeed, everyone, not only Rhodes, was taken unawares by the Afrikaners' marked superiority throughout the first period of the war.

The train which Rhodes boarded was to be the last to arrive in Kimberley. The Afrikaners promptly cut off and surrounded the town.

Rhodes's arrival was no source of joy to the inhabitants of Kimberley. He was anathema to the Afrikaners and his presence in the town only increased the perilous situation in which the town already found itself. It could only aggravate the Afrikaners and harden their resolve to seize this diamond capital, already so obnoxious to them as a symbol of British greed.

As early as October 4, when the approach of war was imminent, the mayor of Kimberley, on behalf of the townspeople, sent Rhodes a telegram asking him to postpone his journey. One of the inhabitants of Kimberley had addressed the same equest to Rhodes still earlier, on October 1, writing: "You now the Boers say everything ill that happens you are the cause f, and the coming war is put down to your account."[33]

Rhodes was blockaded in Kimberley for a period of 124 days, more than four months. Admittedly, Jameson was blockaded in Ladysmith for even longer, as in Mafeking was Colonel Baden-Powell, who had been of such assistance to Rhodes during the Ndebele and Shona rising.

In Kimberley everything belonged to the all-powerful De Beers Company. The units of volunteers who defended the town, consisted of De Beers workers and employees. The stores of provisions, the horses, the wagons—everything was the property of De Beers. The women and children took refuge from the Afrikaner shells in the De Beers mine-shafts. One of the engineers from this company even managed, while the siege was on, to build a large artillery gun. It was christened "Long Cecil", and it fired shells at the Afrikaners "with C. J. Rhodes's compliments".

Rhodes's sojourn in the beleaguered city did not earn him any laurels. Regarding himself as the lord and master of Kimberley, he behaved accordingly. He publicly snubbed the garrison commander, Lieutenant Colonel Kekewich, violated his instructions and offended him. Ignorant himself of military matters, in many ways he hindered organization of the defence.

Rhodes's character became increasingly marked by irritability, even irascibility, and impatience. He wrote abrupt letters to the British generals, castigating them for, apparently, dragging their feet in liberating Kimberley. Matters reached such a head that Kekewich was forced to complain to his supreme command and to threaten Rhodes with arrest.

...On February 15, 1900, British troops finally forced the Afrikaners to withdraw from Kimberley.

We can imagine what a hero Rhodes now felt! He must have left Kimberley confident in the expectation of honours, esteem and admiration due to him both as a man who had withstood a 124-day siege, and as a politician who saw in this entire war the end-product of his life's work.

But during the siege he had been cut off from the world for a period of four tempestuous months, months in which the attitude both of Britain and of the world itself towards this war had finally been determined. He did not know that England's prestige had reached an unprecedented low, and that in Britain itself the war had become extremely unpopular.

Rhodes could not have known all this in his besieged diamond city. Anyway, it would not have been easily swallowed by a man of his character, his philosophy and egotism. And it was still harder for him to imagine the obloquy and accusations that were now being heaped on his head.

Yet the French satirical journal *Le Rire* published caricatures showing Rhodes striding with a triumphant mien between mountains of corpses of British soldiers.

Even the Cape Town papers, *S. A. News, The Cape Argus* and others, received letters from January 1900 in which Rhodes was accused of being the culprit behind all the countless deaths in the war. In these letters Rhodes was compared to Nero, the war was described as his terrible triumph, and it was even asked whether the organizer of these horrors was not to become the next Prime Minister of Great Britain. They did not only appear in the newspapers, but were also published separately in a brochure which, admittedly, gave no date or place of publication, but carried the title: "Rhodes Triumphant: England's Future Premier."

The English social-democrats reminded the public that even before the Anglo-Boer War they had constantly denounced Cecil Rhodes's activities and that in their journal *The Social Democrat* Edward Aveling, husband of one of the daughters of Karl Marx, had published an article entitled: "Filibuster Cecil Rhodes and his Chartered Company".

A little later, when Conan Doyle started defending Rhodes's actions in his books, he at once received a reproof in the brochure, published in London, *Blood and Gold in South Africa. An Answer to Dr. Conan Doyle. Being an Examination of his Account of the "Cause and Conduct" of the South African War.*

It must have been difficult for Rhodes to see that even the rulers of Britain were forced to heed this general mood and were thus unable to openly demonstrate their close association with him.

Rhodes saw everything in a different light. In Kimberley he felt as if he had been locked in a cage. Instead of controlling the course of the war, issuing instructions to field marshals, he had been reduced to wrangling with some obscure lieutenant colonel, director of the small local garrison.

Now finally the town had been relieved. The long-awaited moment had come, when the Khaki-clad British soldiers, by their courage and their blood, had forced the Afrikaners to lift the siege. His elation at once gave way to a disillusionment that was both abrupt and cruel.

...He was not admitted to the commanding circles of the war. No commissions were entrusted to him, no one needed his help.

How unjust this must have seemed to Rhodes! This was his war they were fighting, a war directed towards achieving the goals of his life. And yet they had dispensed with his services. The left-wing newspapers even wrote that others were being forced to lie on the bed which he had made. He was reminded of his earlier utterances and deeds, but in a way that seemed false, unfair, even twisted.

It took Rhodes some time to comprehend his new position. Initially he tried to get into the mainstream of political life. The siege of Kimberley was lifted on February 15, and only a week later, on February 23, he delivered a programmatic speech to a meeting of De Beers shareholders. He described the future of South Africa, as he saw it, united under the British flag after the conclusion of the war.

From this speech it is clear that he was again launching himself energetically onto the political stage, eager to win new supporters.

On this same occasion Rhodes coined a phrase which has been quoted ever since, right up to the present day, more often than anything else he ever said. What is more, it was to become the credo for all British colonial politics and as such was, for many years, printed on the covers of innumerable colonial journals and other publications in South Africa, Rhodesia and Britain itself.

To this day people claim to see in this phrase evidence of the liberal nature of British colonialism, an indication that the patriarch of this colonialism even at the end of the last century regarded it as his goal to civilize all Africans and non-whites in general, and then, once they had attained civilization, to grant them full civil rights. The British authorities set this statement by Rhodes against the so-called narrow-minded chauvinism of the Afrikaners.

The phrase is frequently quoted in the following form: "Equal rights for every civilized man south of the Zambezi". It was subsequently interpreted up in a more extensive way, as the motto of British colonial politics: "Equal rights for every civilized man" not only in South Africa, but everywhere. It was even dubbed "the Cecil Rhodes principle".

These words contradict everything that Cecil Rhodes did. They even contradict what he said. Not many years before he had expressed his view of educated Africans with extreme clarity: "There are Kaffir parsons everywhere—these institutions are turning them out by the dozen. They are turning out a dangerous class."

How could a man who regarded "Kaffir parsons" with such contempt have changed his mind so radically?

Political slogans often have a most complex evolutionary history, and it sometimes happens that their meaning changes under the influence of changing circumstances. This is what happened here. In the speech which Rhodes delivered on February 23, 1900, the phrase about equal rights was actually quite different, although British writers subsequently were reluctant to recall this fact.

On that occasion Rhodes talked not of "civilized" men, but of "white" men. Change one word and the meaning of the entire phrase is quite different. The phrase was directed at the Afrikaners: Rhodes hoped to win over at least a part of the Afrikaner community. Once again he started courting the Afrikaners, seeking to win their trust, which he had always coveted, and which he himself had violated, first with the Jameson Raid, and then with this terrible war.

But the phrasing—restricting equal rights to whites—aroused the indignation of the coloured community of the Cape Colony. For at this time, under the shadow of the Boer War, the British authorities were laying particular stress on the liberalism and democratism of their colonial policies, and contrasting them in every way with the flagrant racism of the Boer republics. They maintained that Britain was fighting for the human rights of the non-whites, which had been flouted by the Afrikaners.

An association of coloured voters sent Rhodes a copy of the

newspaper *Eastern Province Herald* quoting his speech, and they asked him how they were to interpret the words about rights. It was now that Rhodes altered his original slogan. He sent back the newspaper, having written on the margin: "My Motto is—Equal Rights for every civilized man south of the Zambezi. What is a civilized man? A man, whether white or black, who has sufficient education to write his name, has some property, or works. In fact, is not a loafer."

Ten years later this entire story was reproduced in the Cape Town newspaper *APO*, published by the coloured community.[34] One of Rhodes's biographers, after recounting the real story of the "equal rights" motto, comments: "It is sad to discover that Rhodes was capable of juggling with so important a statement simply in order to catch votes."[35]

Ironically, Rhodes only started to earn political capital from this declaration after his death. During his lifetime even this fairly adroit move did not help him recover his lost prestige in official circles.

Naturally enough, he still received certain marks of attention. Such as speeches of welcome, including one, even, from the Muslim community of Kimberley.

But this was not what he had had in mind.

Rhodes became increasingly restive. Having returned from Kimberley to Cape Town, he immediately took ship for England, and from there returned almost at once to Africa, yet not to the countries engaged in the war and to which, one might have thought, he would have yearned to go. Instead he set off for Rhodesia, spending several months travelling around the country. In June, when a government crisis arose in the Cape Colony and there was a split between ministers who had once been Rhodes's protégés, he even made sure to keep well away from the telegraph in Rhodesia, in order not to have to hear any unpleasant news.

But in October 1900 he returned to Cape Town after all, and delivered another speech. It was probable that by then he had realized that the entire world regarded him as the primary initiator of this war, which had proved to be so bloody. This must be why he addressed his audience with the words:

"You have heard that so-and-so, and so-and-so, was the cause of the war. I will tell you the cause of the war."[36]

He then proceeded to attribute the blame to a few members of the Cape Parliament.

By this stage it seemed that Rhodes had abandoned any hopes of high political office. His ambition had been irreparably damaged, and this in turn had a deleterious effect on his health. It is this same process that causes more sickness and indisposition in a retreating army than in a victorious one.

A friend and executor of Rhodes's will wrote: "He was under no illusions. His life's work was practically done."[37]

The following year, 1901, Rhodes spent in various unexpected and particularly fruitful journeys: to Kimberley, Bulawayo, Mafeking, Kimberley again. Then England, Italy, Egypt. In early 1902 he returned to England and almost immediately came back to Cape Town.

Everything around him must have seemed quite unjust, even incomprehensible. A turning point had come in the war. Even the Afrikaners, for all the stubbornness, would be forced eventually to negotiate for peace. Peace would mean union of the Afrikaner republics with the British colonies, the creation of a South African federation forming part of the British Empire. The very thing towards which Rhodes had strived for so many years, for which he had lived and worked. His enemies remembered this and would not forgive him.

Even Britain, his own country, showed him no gratitude, despite all he had done to earn it. Nor was he accorded the role in the war which he felt was his by rights.

There was another injustice too. There had been so many episodes in which Rhodes had not personally been involved, had not risked his life, had not shared the ordeals of others, and yet these events had still become associated with his name and he had been hailed as their hero. This happened with the Ndebele War in 1893, for example, and with the "pioneer" trek in 1890.

But now he had spent four months under siege, with shells exploding all around him. And to think that if Kimberley had fallen, the Afrikaners could quite simply have torn him asunder. Surely now his image should be surrounded by an even more dazzling aura of heroism, and his name revered more than ever before.

But this was not to be.

Some people saw as the true heroes of this war the Afrikaner generals. Louis Botha, the new commander-in-chief of the Transvaal, successor to Rhodes's old enemy Piet Joubert. Or Christian De Wet, of the Orange Free State, whose photographs were displayed in newspapers the world over. Or "Groot" Jacobus De la Rey, who is credited with inventing the trench, in which the soldiers could take refuge from shrapnel. Rhodes and he had almost been friends once, and Rhodes stood godfather to his grandsons... But all this was before the ill-starred raid. It was because of De la Rey and other men like him that Dr Jim had been captured in that expedition...

Kruger was another. His army had been routed, his capital seized, he was forced to flee to Europe, yet he was hailed as a hero. At least Kaiser Wilhelm had not let him into Germany. But then France, of all countries, had! Not only did they let him in, but the whole of Marseilles turned out to welcome him. They held a banquet for four hundred people. All the talk everywhere was of Kruger, his fine, manly beard, his black frockcoat, his pipe always between his teeth. It was even remarked that he always carried a Bible in his hand. For some reason everyone thought he had a kindly face.

Yet what did these people really know about the Afrikaners? Practically nothing. When a party of Madagascans came to the Paris exhibition the crowd greeted them with shouts of "Vivent les Boers!"

Nonetheless Kruger's speeches in Marseilles were received with thunderous applause. He enjoyed the same success in Lyons, and then in Dijon. His triumph was even compared to that of Napoléon, who, on his return from Elba, had landed in the south and marched in triumph through France.

The centre of attention at the Paris exhibition of 1900 was the exhibit of an Afrikaner farm. The Parisians all asked one another: "As-tu vu la ferme?" And some scribbler by the name of Edmond Rostand, a native of Marseilles and apparently famous although still a young man, had even written a poem entitled "Hymne à Kruger":

> *Oh, quand tu débarquas dans ma ville natale,*
> *Vaincu qu'on reçois en vainqueur,*

> *Il me semble, Vieillard, et je deviens tout pâle,*
> *Que tu débarquais dans mon coeur.*

But what a torrent of ridicule France now heaped upon England and upon Rhodes personally. In the journal *Le Rire* John Bull is depicted telling him: "Les affaires, c'est le sang des autres" ("Great deeds mean the shedding of other people's blood").[38]

Still, what more could be expected of people who bore no love for England, and who supported the Afrikaners?

So what about the others, his own countrymen: who had they singled out as their heroes?

Lord Roberts, for one. Nicknamed Bobs. The British Field Marshall and commander...

> *There's a little red-faced man,*
> *Which is Bobs,*
> *An' we'll follow 'im to 'ell—*
> *Won't we Bobs?*[39]

Well, he was not without merit in his profession. Yet he was careful always to choose massive horses: mounted, he cut a magnificent figure! On horseback no one noticed how small he was, or that he was already pushing seventy.

Or Kitchener... His ice-cold eyes were greatly admired, and it was not obvious how often his face wore an expression of disgust. Of course he had been chief of staff under Roberts himself, and after a while took Roberts's place... How he had enjoyed their early morning rides together, Rhodes and Kitchener, in the London parks... How recently that was! And yet how long ago...

But Kitchener, like Roberts, in his dazzling military career had previously only fought Africans and Asians. Admittedly Kitchener had also participated in the Franco-Prussian War, but that was as a lad of twenty and only as a volunteer on the French side...

It remained to be seen whether they would be able to bring matters to a conclusion in this, their first war fought against white men... Of course, they did have under their command units which had fought in the Crimean campaign, at Balaclava,

Left: Boer notice offering a reward for the recapture of Winston Churchill. *Right:* The young Winston in the Transvaal

but then much water had passed under the bridge since that war.

As for Kipling, the amount that was written about him! How he had set up a detachment of volunteers, how he had visited the wounded, how he had collected money for soldiers' families and how he had donated to the war the royalties from his poems! The newspapers spared no ink in singing the praise of all these people...

And what a fuss they made of Baden-Powell—well, perhaps the old boy had earned it after all. He had been under siege for a hundred days longer than Rhodes in Kimberley. The Afrikaners had bombarded his little Mafeking with no less than twenty thousand shells! Good luck to him...

Or what about that callow reporter, Churchill, son of the duffer who had travelled round Rhodesia in 1891? All right, so he did escape from captivity. And the Afrikaners did put a price of £25 on his head. Not much of a price, at that. But the moment this youngster got back to London he found himself the lion of the season and was promptly elected to parliament.

Even his aunt Lady Sarah was now surrounded with glory and all because she had managed to make her way through the blockade into Mafeking, to join her officer husband inside.

Yet it never so much as occurred to anyone to regard Rhodes as a hero of this war!

The true state of affairs was, of course, not quite what it seemed to the offended Rhodes, or perhaps not like this at all. The rulers of Great Britain were not planning to use Rhodes as their scapegoat. But at the same time it was awkward for them to celebrate him as a hero of the war: too many people regarded him as the instigator of its terrible bloodshed.

To make matters worse, Rhodes put himself in the firing line. The stories in circulation about his altercations with military officers during the Kimberley siege did nothing to enhance his reputation.

Added to this was the scandal about the bill presented by his company De Beers to the British treasury. It referred to the losses sustained by the company during the siege, and was for an amount of £300,000. It even included such items as: "... £19 10s. for a wreath for a staff officer's grave, £70 for cab hire for a newspaper correspondent connected with the company, £788 in respect of native runners to bring up newspapers to Mr Rhodes from Modder River, and £25, being the expenses incurred by Mr Rhodes in getting a private letter sent to Mafeking."[40]

The government returned the bill implying that Rhodes should be ashamed to present it. But the company did not abandon its claim, it merely reduced the amount to £54,641 4s. 9p.

One of the Irish members of the House asked a question about this bill and read out what he regarded as the company's outrageous demands.

This could hardly have increased Rhodes's popularity. He had always been so sensitive to the public mood, yet now he had seriously damaged his own image.

A few years earlier he would have been only too well aware that such acts are quite inadmissible, at least not until the war had ended and passions had cooled. Now he could no longer see it. Perhaps he had persuaded himself that Kimberley was defended by the volunteers whom he himself had recruited, and that if this was the case perhaps his action was justifiable...

But people now saw things in a different light. He was quite unable to comprehend this and even more unwilling to accept it.

Fading Away

Southern Africa was in the grip of a war considered by the entire world to be Rhodes's war. Yet he could not find any place any employment for himself in it. What was it, we might wonder, that caused him to cast about in this way? Was it really his specific, concrete failures? Or was it perhaps something more oppressive: some unfathomable *Angst*, some sense of unease with the world and with himself?

Perhaps he was now starting to review his life, to make his final reckoning. To assess how many of his dreams he had managed to make reality.

> *And some we got by purchase,*
> *And some we had by trade,*
> *And some we found by courtesy*
> *of pike and carronade*[1]

But no, this was not it either. The "end to all wars", of which Rhodes had written so naively in his first political will, had not come. And the British themselves, the nation for whom Rhodes had prepared such a brilliant future, had hardly justified his hopes.

He did of course experience the anguish of unfulfilled ambitions. Perhaps his thoughts also started to turn on other aspects of life, besides business and politics? We might wonder whether Rhodes suffered from what is known as *Weltschmerz*. Perhaps he was visited by the thoughts described here by the Russian writer and contemporary of Rhodes, Saltykov-Shchedrin: "I once, my good sir, knew a man: so long as he did not understand he prospered, but when he understood, he hanged himself!"

Rhodes had reached the twilight of his career, and of his life too, from the comparatively early age of forty-three—the time of the Jameson Raid. Realization of this only came to him later, and must have caused him to look back and evaluate his own past.

We get the impression that it was very hard for Rhodes not only to rise above his political activities, but even to view them from the side. No Talleyrand or Fouché would have emerged from him, nor anyone such as the Byzantine Procopius of Caesarea, who, at the same time as maintaining the official political dogma, secretly wrote his *Historia arcana*.

Many of Rhodes's biographers describe him as an integral personality, putting stress on the fact that he was never tormented by doubts. We might ask, though, whether this is to be admired. Since antiquity it has been accepted that man is composed of contradictions and that it is precisely through his inner struggle he acquires spiritual worth.

The impression is formed that Rhodes did indeed adhere to roughly the same views throughout his conscious life. Even in his very last years and months he never seriously reappraised any of his ideas, he never paused to reconsider his own role, he never seriously repented any of his deeds. Unless perhaps such fateful episodes as the Jameson Raid, although even here he did not repent the deed itself, he merely lamented its failure.

He was forced to abandon such ideas as the creation of a special order for the expansion of the British Empire. Even this renunciation only came about by force of circumstances, and not because of any second thoughts about his ideas.

In fact, reality did not often cause him to substantially revise his views. Not only were his ideas not rejected by the British government, they were even systematically put into effect.

By this time, however, this was no longer being done by his own hand, and he no longer felt that he was the real controller of events. This sense of rejection caused him to become increasingly resentful and grouchy.

Rhodes, erstwhile Prime Minister of the Cape and member of the Queen's Privy Council, was now forced against his will to assume the posture of a man who had perhaps been unjustly passed over and insulted, yet who would not further humiliate himself by lodging complaints or bickering.

Or being hated, don't give way to hating.
And yet don't look to good, nor talk too wise...[2]

Kipling's "commandments", as set out in "If—", were soon to appear. They were to be universally applied, by those in the right and those in the wrong. They were composed in such a way that they would be applicable to everyone. Yet it must have seemed to Rhodes that they were aimed specifically at him. For whatever anyone might say, Kipling was his admirer, a frequent guest in his house, and a man who shared his views on just about all things.

Until about a year or so before his death Rhodes still felt reasonably fit, and assured many people of his physical health, which was anyway attested to by his extensive travels during this period. But this health was gradually being undermined by the malaise of a man who found himself without proper employment. Of course, he had his diamond mines, his gold mines, his Rhodesia. But all these offered him insufficient scope for his ambitions. . .

The final blow came from a totally unexpected quarter.

WOMAN INVADES HIS LIFE

Rhodes was no friend of the fair sex and avoided the company of women. In this he parted company with Kipling, who speaks for most men in his lines:

> *A fool there was and he made his prayer*
> *(Even as you and I!)*
> *To a rag and bone and a hank of hair*
> *(We called her the woman who did not care)*
> *But the fool he called her his lady fair—*
> *(Even as you and I!)*[3]

Nevertheless, a woman eventually managed to thrust her way even into his, Rhodes's, life. She forced him to squander his time, money and nervous energy, to dash about the world and in return offered no warmth, no comfort, no joy. Yet Rhodes, who had always been able to deal so skilfully and ruthlessly with others, succumbed to her wiles, when she invaded his life.

This was no ordinary woman who now stood in Rhodes's path. Her name: Princess Catherine Radziwill, a Polish noblewoman and native of St Petersburg. Sergei Vitte, who had known her in her youth, wrote: "I met a very interesting person—the Priness Radziwill: this Princess Radziwill was a lady of great beauty... Later she proved to be a great adventuress."[4] She was even able to impress the young Winston Churchill, then a twenty-year-old lieutenant of Hussars, although she was sixteen years older than him. Churchill found her quite enchanting and at the same time extremely eccentric.

The princess was able to recruit to her circle of admirers men of middle age who had considerable influence. Vitte describes her liaison with the Adjutant-General Cherevin, who was not only commander of the Royal Guard of Czar Alexander III but also one of his closest courtiers. "...She had simply seduced Cherevin, and in that way was able to exercise a certain influence in St Petersburg society, since this Cherevin was himself a man of influence, and as a result Princess Radziwill acquired some influence herself. After Cherevin's death it was found that her business dealings were not entirely aboveboard, and she moved to England." Vitte also connected her name with Ivan Vyshnegradsky, the Minister of Finance.[5]

The possibility cannot be discounted that Vitte got his facts wrong here, as he does elsewhere, when he ascribes to the princess a romantic entanglement with Rhodes. Rhodes was far away, but on the domestic scene, when commenting on St Petersburg matters, Vitte usually hit the mark. As far as the "not entirely above-board business dealings" are concerned, the princess certainly had her share of these. She was forced to leave the Russian capital, the "Palmyra of the North", when it was discovered that criminals had set up shop in the cellar of her house, and apparently not without her knowledge, and were there engaged in all sorts of forgery.

The princess made Rhodes's acquaintance in 1896, when she was already thirty-eight. They met in London, at a dinner given by the editor of *The Times*. The impoverished noblewoman resolved to get her hands on Rhodes's millions: to make him marry her, or fall in love with her—it did not matter which, so long as she achieved her end. Admittedly, most of her charms had fled with her youth. On the other hand, she had acquired experience, and the princess set her cap for the bachelor millionaire with skill and great vigour. She began with a rapturous letter—how remarkably Rhodes had conducted himself in the Raid Committee! Then she sought his advice as to how to invest her capital, saying that she was so incompetent in business matters... Admittedly, the capital she had to invest in fact amounted to nothing, of her original wealth practically nothing was left.

This was 1899, and the threat of war hung over Southern Africa. On July 1 Rhodes embarked on a ship sailing from London to Cape Town. What a strange coincidence awaited him: the princess was on the same ship and from the very first day had herself seated at Rhodes's table in the dining saloon.

She took the opportunity at dinner to complain bitterly of the cruelty and insults of her husband, and managed to let slip that she was already divorced, although in actual fact the divorce was only finalized several years later... One day, as they promenaded on deck, she fell decoratively onto Rhodes's chest.

No matter how hard the princess plied her suit, it was to no avail. By the end of the long voyage all she had managed to secure was an invitation to visit Groote Schuur. But she managed to derive maximum benefit from this and soon became quite at home in Rhodes's mansion.

Nonetheless, their relationship cannot be construed as a romance. Such an interpretation is contradicted by everything in Rhodes's life and personality. It would seem that the princess's trump card was her ability to discuss in an informed way the thing that most interested and excited Rhodes: politics. She painted a picture of such dedication to Rhodes's ideas that she was able to win his confidence. She skilfully flattered him, and never missed an opportunity to mention her connections with the noble houses of all Europe. At the same time she hinted that these same connections were now available to Rhodes.

The princess most certainly did have a wide circle of acquaintances. A person with the surname Radziwill could not fail to be well-connected: the Radziwills' relatives even included the Stuart house, the line of the British kings. Admittedly the princess carried this distinguished surname, and her title, thanks to her husband, Prince Wilhelm Radziwill, the Prussian army officer whom she had married as a fifteen-year-old girl. But even her maiden name—Rzewuska—opened many doors in its own right.

Her father, Adam Rzewuski, was aide-de-camp to Nicholas I, a general and at one time military commandant of St Petersburg. His first wife, née Lopukhina, was the favourite of Alexander I. His brother, Henryk, lived in Poland and was to ecome a famous writer. Adam's sister, widow to Count Hanski, ved in the Ukraine and married the French writer Honoré e Balzac (or, as it is stated in the church register of the town f Berdichev, where the marriage was celebrated, to "the land-wner and Frenchman Honorat Balzac, a youth of 50 years, urnished with the proper consent of his mother to enter into his matrimony with Ewa Hanska, née Rzewuska").

In Pushkin's day the Rzewuski home in Odessa housed the alon of Karolina Sobanska. Pushkin was a frequent guest here, ell in love with Mme Sobanska and dedicated to her some of is lyrics.

This noble pedigree opened up immense fertile pastures to the young Catherine. Whether in St Petersburg, Berlin, Vienna or London, she was equally at home in the cosmopolitan aristo-cratic society of these cities.

The princess had yet another talent which might have struck Rhodes as particularly useful. She wielded a skilful pen. Admit-edly, at the time she made Rhodes's acquaintance this skill had not yet been displayed in all its brilliance: it was only years later that she started to flood the European book market with a deluge of her writings on the Russian and other European courts.

To many readers in the West, for example, she was the author-ity on the life of the last of the Romanovs. Her fat volumes on the subject are not outstanding for their authenticity, and not surprisingly so. The princess was not, to put it mildly, particularly welcome at the court of Nicholas II: over the years she had acquired too scandalous a reputation. Her "recollections" are based not on her own experiences, but on second- and third-hand gossip. When it came to choosing titles for her books she certainly did not lack imagination. *The Intimate Life of the Last Tsarina; Behind the Veil at the Russian Court; Russia's Decline and Fall. The Secret History of the Great Debacle; Nicholas II, the Last of the Czars; Rasputin and the Russian Revolution.*

The princess lived for a number of years in Berlin, and sure enough, she put pen to paper and came out with: *The Disillusionment of the Crown Princess, being the Story of the Courtship and Married Life of Cecil, Ex-Crown Princess of Germany,* and *Germany under Three Emperors.* She travelled to Vienna, and there ensued *The Austrian Court from Within*; to France—*France from behind the Veil*. The books were published in English, French, German, even Swedish.

All this happened later, although by the time of her first meeting with Rhodes one of her literary exercises had already created quite a stir in Europe. In October 1883 a sketch about Berlin high society appeared in the French journal *La Nouvelle Revue*.[6] It ridiculed the upper circles of this society, starting with the Kaiser, the Reichskanzler and the court. The young princess, who by that stage had not yet managed to compromise herself completely, was still admitted to the court of Kaiser Wilhelm I and therefore she could describe it with an inside familiarity. The Berlin *monde* was alarmed. Friedrich Holstein, one of the leading German diplomats, took umbrage at the "venomous" nature of the article and tried to guess the identity of its author.

Even in *Holstein und Hohenlohe*, published many years later, in 1957, the well-known West German historian Helmuth Rogge records that the true identity of the author of this sensational article, which was published subsequently in book-form under the pseudonym Comte Paul Vassili, has not to this day been established.[7]

Yet this was the pseudonym of Princess Radziwill. She used it for a great number of her books and articles. It is remarkable to think that this entire furore in Berlin was created by the princess at the tender age of twenty-five.

She was quite prepared to place her literary skills at the disposal of Cecil Rhodes. Furthermore, she promtly made the acquaintance of leading South African politicians, such as Jan Hofmeyr, the British High Commissioner Milner and others. It was now that she started to display to Rhodes her greatest talent of all: her ability to weave intrigues. She clearly wished to place this talent at his disposal as well.

The objective of all this was to reawaken Rhodes's ambition, and persuade him to campaign once again for the position of Prime Minister. At the same time she would convince him that victory would be possible only with her assistance.

Then war broke out. While Rhodes was blockaded in Kimberley the princess remained in Cape Town, and did not let the grass grow under her feet. She was unrelenting in her atten-

376

tions to the Cape politicians, and wrote a stream of letters to London, to well-known journalists and M.P.s. She cajoled, persuaded and exhorted everyone she came into contact with, that it was essential for the prosperity of the British nation to put Rhodes in power in South Africa as soon as the war ended.

One might have thought all this would have been most agreeable to Rhodes. This, however, was not the case. Even before the war began he had started to avoid the princess's company. No doubt, her importunate behaviour put him on his guard, and possibly even irritated him. He appears to have realized quite quickly that she was attempting to spin a web around him and to ensnare him with her wiles.

When Rhodes returned to Cape Town after the siege of Kimberley the princess once again became an almost daily visitor for breakfast at Groote Schuur. It was partly due to her importunity that Rhodes so soon departed for England, spending only a month in Cape Town. The princess was on the point of following him, but he got wind of this in London and at once returned to South Africa.

The princess was in a calamitous position: her money was exhausted, and she had no more creditors.

But the wily adventuress knew what to do. Even here she was able to make contact with counterfeiters, and had false copies made of her diamonds. The real diamonds she pawned. She took to wearing the counterfeit stones and then one day reported them stolen to the police. They were valued at £50,000 —an immense sum of money in those days. If the swindle had come off the princess would have earned at least a temporary reprieve from bankruptcy. But all was revealed. She then announced that she was betrothed to Rhodes and that he was even helping her secure a divorce from her husband so that he could marry her himself. The police suppresed the case. The proprietor of her hotel, however, was less obliging, and he threw the pedigreed mischief-maker out. In the meantime the diamonds were auctioned off and bought by her son-in-law, Prince Blücher.

Princess Radziwill now resigned herself to waiting for Rhodes's return from Rhodesia. Strangely enough, when he arrived back in Cape Town in November 1900, Rhodes did give her financial assistance. He continued with this help for about six months. Admittedly, a portion of this money went towards setting up the journal *Greater Britain*. The princess did in fact publish such a journal, although it did not last very long—from June to August 1901.

It is still puzzling why Rhodes should have lent her money. She was clearly unpopular with him. Perhaps the answer lay once again in the princess's political machinations: no sooner was she back on her feet financially than she set about her old ways, flattering, scheming, canvassing supporters, trying to prompt Rhodes to restore his former ties with Hofmeyr and other leaders of the Cape Afrikaners, in order that he could secure their support in his fight for the position of Prime Minister of a future "federated South Africa".

For limited periods she probably did succeed in reawakening his ambitions. But it was no longer possible for such dreams to hold him in thrall for very long: his spirit was broken and with it his health.

Soon the police discovered that some acquaintance of the princess, a man who had already served time for forgery, was now sending her letters which deliberately referred to her supposed fabulous wealth in Russia. The princess had been displaying these letters to Rhodes as proof of her credit-worthiness.

It is a curious fact that the princess did indeed have property in Russia, even at the times when she was in direct financial straits. No mendacious letters were necessary to prove this: all one had to do was to take the directory *Ves' Peterburg* (All St Petersburg) for the beginning of this century. It states that the house at No. 3 Dmitrovsky Pereulok in the centre of St Petersburg is owned by the princess Catherine Radziwill. This fairly large building, incidentally, is still standing today, although the street and the adjacent roads suffered badly from bombing at the end of 1941. It is quite probable that the princess had other property too, but, as one of Rhodes's biographers has already remarked, for some reason her estates were difficult to realize in cash.[8]

More and more antics by the princess were revealed. Her references to her friendship with the British Prime Minister Lord Salisbury and with other influential British politicians with whom, at best, she might have been barely acquainted, were hardly meant as a harmless pleasantry. She even backed these claims with fake telegrams from her so-called "friends".

378

Her next venture was to get this same criminal friend to forge Rhodes's signature on fairly large promissory notes. In August 1901 the newspaper *Cape Argus,* of which Rhodes was a shareholder, was forced to warn its readers against accepting these forged notes bearing his signature.

The princess now tried her hand at blackmail: she let it be known that she was in possession of certain documents which compromised Rhodes, Milner and Chamberlain. Rhodes was more alarmed than the others, and it is at any rate clear that he pressed charges against the princess.

She still had sufficient energy for a new effort at blackmail. She wrote to Milner that Rhodes had apparently agreed to drop the charges if she handed over to him her correspondence with Milner. This undertaking backfired badly. On Milner's orders the princess's rooms were searched and all documents connected with Rhodes were seized. She continued her blackmail, declaring that she had other documents stored in a secure place—with the German chancellor. . . This did not help her either.

South Africa most famous sleuth—Inspector George Easton— headed the investigation into the forged promissory notes, and his conduct of the investigation subsequently became a textbook case for the training of young detectives.[9] The princess was charged on twenty-four counts of forgery and other machinations. She was arrested on November 20, 1901, and she managed to be released on bail. The first thing she did was to announce that she had other documents which compromised Rhodes. She tried to pass off some of her own forgeries as the work of the doctor Scholtz, who was a frequent visitor at Groote Schuur, and she accused his wife of being Rhodes's mistress. The doctor's nerves proved weaker than the princess's, and he soon died, hastened into the grave by this scandal.

In early 1902 Rhodes was summoned to appear as a witness in her trial. At this time he was in London. He was in poor health, and Southern Africa was in the grip of an exhaustingly hot summer. He was able, if he wished, to give his testimony in London instead, but he still set off for Cape Town. In the end he never had to appear in court as a witness: he gave his evidence in bed, no longer even able to rise. He did not hear the verdict, dying a month before it was reached.

In April 1902 the princess was sentenced to two years

imprisonment. As soon as she was released she started making money out of Rhodes again—it mattered nothing to her that in the meantime he had died. She devoted a chapter of her memoirs to him, and these were published in 1904, to be followed by an entire book, entitled *Cecil Rhodes*.

These memoirs enjoyed a period of notoriety at the time. They also attracted the interest of Vitte, who only vaguely remembered Rhodes's name and confused all the peripeteia in his life, but was still convinced that the princess had had a liaison with some Englishman who owned gold mines in Africa. "Then this Englishman died. It appears that he died so unexpectedly that he left her nothing substantial. Then, out of the blue a promissory note came to light made out by this same crooked banker for a very large sum in the name Radziwill. The note was presented before the court, but it was proved that it was a forgery and in the end princess Radziwill was thrown in prison, where she served her full sentence. On her release from prison she described everything connected with this matter in her memoirs. These memoirs created quite a stir for a little while—a week, but now, of course, they are quite forgotten."

The machinations of this genteel lady would by now have been utterly erased from our memories, if she had not been mentioned by one of the most respected authors of this century: André Maurois. Because of her he was forced to write an appendix to his famous novel *Prométhée ou la vie de Balzac*. What had happened was this: some twenty years after Rhodes's death she perpetrated a particularly successful literary forgery, *The Unpublished Letters of Mme Hanska*. Furthermore, she announced that there was an entire archive of materials relating to Balzac's wife and that this would be published in 1957. She caused Balzac scholars considerable labours and her forgery cost Maurois a great deal of time and effort. He was forced to investigate her forgeries. In this appendix he spared her no abuse, dubbing her "la terrible Cathérine". He revealed one fabrication after the other.

"To dupe the Balzac scholars of America the princess Radziwill presents herself as 'having spent her childhood and youth under the roof and protection of Mme de Balzac'. This is also inexact. Catherine Rzewuska, born in St Petersburg on March

30, 1858, entered the world at a time when her aunt had most definitely emigrated."

Maurois came to the conclusion that the failure of the princess's designs to make good at Rhodes's expense prompted her to apply her counterfeiter's guile to Balzac scholarship. After the trial and her imprisonment in Cape Town her husband finally divorced her. "Rejected by her own family, discredited in Europe, dishonoured in South Africa, the impetuous Catherine tried her luck in North America. She discovered that there was an entire tribe of Balzac scholars in the USA and resolved to make capital out of her prestigious Rzewuski origins."

In his book on Rhodes, published in 1953, Maurois only vouchsafes the princess a fleeting mention. In his book on Balzac, however, he recalls her associations with Rhodes: "For the purposes of revenge and enrichment ... she endeavoured, with a diabolical patience, to imitate Rhodes's handwriting... The adventuress, already used to forging Cecil Rhodes's signature, was certainly capable of writing the *Unpublished Letters of Mme Hanska*."[10]

But despite these ruinous exposures, forgeries by this adventuress continued to appear in various books and journals. Even in our time, the *Spectator*, regarded as a very respectable publication, informed its readers in 1979 that "Wilhelm Radziwill's wife Kasia ... had been brought up by Balzac's widow Madame Hanska".[11]

Maurois himself was taken in by some things, although he was well aware that Princess Radziwill's life was nothing but fiction and fabrication. In *Prométhée*... he smugly informs his readers that the address of her last residence is mentioned in the *Gotha Almanach* published in 1929 as 63, Ligovka, Leningrad.

The address, of course, is a false one. We do not know whether she misinformed the *Gotha* compilers, or if this was their own error, but the simple fact of the matter is that this lady was, of course, not welcome in the USSR. She died in New York, where she had been earning her living by teaching Americans the rules of "*bon ton*". In fact she almost made it to her appointed year of 1957.

It is remarkable that even in her death she succeeded in confusing the historians. Different handbooks and historical stu-

dies give different dates for her death: one South African biographical dictionary gives the year as 1930, another puts May
1941, and a very respectable work on the genealogy of the aristocratic houses of Europe, published in Britain in 1971, even
puts it at May 12, 1945.[12]

...It seems fair to assume that the princess's own unfulfilled
life caused her to squander her energies on intrigues and blackmail. She never really had a family of her own. It is evident
that she was not ideally suited to be a wife and mother. Even
her husband, as Vitte records, "was the most contemptible of
people". She bore this husband several children, but her character was such that these children never occupied an important
place in her life. She had lovers, who were increasingly aged as
she herself advanced in years, and to judge from all the evidence
it was not love that drove her into their arms.

The intrigues, the scandals and gossip, this counterfeit life
must have taken the place of something real, something which
she, like any woman, would have longed to have. Or did she
not even want that?

...Why, for example, did Rhodes, even after he had grown
wise to her, continue to correspond with her for so long, and
give her money? And even risk his life by returning from England to attend her trial?

Today we know that she had nothing to blackmail him with.
If she did have in her possession certain documents with which
she attempted to scare him, these would surely have come to
light by now. After all, the princess had countless opportunities
to publish them: she outlived Rhodes by no less than forty three
years. An entire lifetime. And of course, if she had had in her
possession secret materials about him she would have published
these during some of her frequent periods of penury.

What was it, we wonder, that Rhodes feared? Perhaps to
this day something important about Rhodes and Catherine Radziwill's relationship remains undiscovered, although a great deal
has been written about them: in 1969 an entire book, even, was
published in London with the title: *Cecil Rhodes and the Princess*.[13] Not all of Princess Radziwill's papers in the Rhodes
archive in Oxford were put at the researchers' disposal. In the
first half of the 1970s, the historian John Flint complained
about this.[14] At the end of 1986 I had an opportunity to see

these papers.[15] Unfortunately, however, they are of more than dubious value. Even the Princess's diaries consist of notes on meetings and conversations that never actually took place—evidently she intended showing them to someone...

Perhaps Rhodes merely thought that the princess might have found something, during her frequent visit to Groote Schuur, when she shamelessly wandered through the house, entering his personal rooms, usually closed to visitors. Or he might have feared that somehow or other she had gained possession of secret documents relating to the Jameson Raid. After all, blackmail does not need any grounds, or documents. All that is needed is an ability to threaten: whether with revelations, hints of liaisons, allegations, it matters little which.

It is quite possible that Rhodes had grounds for his fear. His nerve had already started to weaken. He was no longer the man he had once been, and anyway he was used to having men as his adversaries. Faced by a woman, who drew the line at nothing in her assault, he lost his head.

The material for this book often came to light from quite unexpected quarters. Once, as I sat with an older friend, the writer Vladislav Glinka, in his grand apartments in Khalturin Street beside the Winter Palace in Leningrad, I recounted to him the story of Rhodes and Catherine Radziwill. The omniscient Glinka patiently heard me out and then slyly asked:

"And do you know who once owned this house, Khalturin No. 11, in which we are sitting? You don't? Well, its proprietress was Mme Zherebtsova, the second wife of Adam Rzewuski and step-mother to this same princess of yours. So who knows, perhaps the journey which took this princess of rogues to Cecil Rhodes began right here."

I was forced once again to marvel at the extraordinary coincidences with which the people's destinies are so cunningly woven together, one of which had so unexpectedly joined together this street, once the fashionable Millionnaya of St Petersburg, and the Cape Town mansion of Cecil Rhodes.

Consulting an old edition of the directory *Ves' Petersburg* I ascertained exactly which house had belonged to this woman, who had hastened the death of Rhodes, and then I went to see it, in Dmitrovsky Pereulok. In my own childhood I had lived nearby, and in November 1941, during the blockade of Leningrad, I had once waited out an air-raid in the gateway of this building. At that time I could never have guessed that one day I might hunt out the name of its former proprietress in a tatty old directory.

In Warsaw I met Princess Isabella Radziwill and I asked her about her notorious relation. At the same time I learnt much of interest about the Radziwill family in general and about those who had become related through marriage, reaching as far afield as Jackie Kennedy-Onassis. I was amazed to learn that my interlocutor and her own immediate family had also been cast by the vagaries of fate into the Transvaal, after the Second World War, to a suburb of the City of Gold, Johannesburg, where Rhodes and Jameson had once tried to raise a rebellion, and to places where "la terrible Cathérine" had once pursued her quarry Rhodes.

HIS LAST WILL

Rhodes's voyage to attend the princess's trial was to be his last. At the relatively young age of forty-eight he was already old and infirm. On the ship he suffered from asphyxia even in his luxury cabin. To ease his breathing they made up a bed for him on a table in the ship's chart house, but during a storm he fell off the table and was badly bruised.

When he arrived in Cape Town his friends could hardly recognize him. His eyes had lost their sparkle, his face was misshapen and repulsively puffy, his skin flaccid and his grey hair unkempt and matted. It was evident that he himself felt his lifeblood ebbing away. It must have been satisfying for him to recall how not so long ago, a mere year or two before, he had endeavoured to immortalize himself for posterity, sitting for hours on end for portrait painters, striking the majestic poses of Roman patricians.

It is possible that Rhodes already felt the approach of his death. At any rate, on February 4 he wrote to Sir James Rose Innes, a political opponent of long standing: "As one gets older I feel how foolish I am—little odds and ends are allowed to separate us."[16]

February 1902—towards the end of the South African sumner—proved to be a particularly hot month in Cape Town. Rhodes was constantly short of air, and found each breath increasingly hard to take. His condition got so bad that it was impossible for him to remain in Groote Shuur and he moved to his little cottage in Muizenberg, where fresh breezes blew in constantly from the sea. Even here he had a wall knocked down, so that there would be no obstruction to the sea-breezes, and had large quantities of ice laid down to cool the air. For two weeks his servants stood prepared to harness up the horses: Rhodes was planning to set off for the Drakensberg where it was much cooler, but in the end the order never came. Instead Rhodes decided to return to England where spring had broken. His departure was fixed for March 26. This was the day on which he died.

Of how many people do we remark: for the first half of his life he spent his health, making money, and for the second he spent his money trying to preserve what little health he had left. In Rhodes's case the irony is even more pronounced: in his early years he dreamt of world domination, at the end of his life he dreamt only of a mouthful of air. To quote the Soviet poet Tkhorzhevsky:

> *I asked God for an easy life:*
> *Would I had asked for an easy death.*

His doctors and everyone around him could see his days were numbered and his death was expected from one day to the next.

Afterwards a legend arose that Rhodes's last words had been: "So little done, so much to do..." In actual fact, it appears he acquitted himself in a far less pompous and more natural way for a dying man, asking: "Turn me over."

He asked that he be buried in Rhodesia, in the Matopos, where once he had held his talks with the leaders of the Ndebele rising. He called this place the "View of the World", because of the extensive vistas that opened out before the beholder.

Of his decision to be buried there he said: "This is no new idea, as I am simply copying Mosilikatze. I found him sitting in his cave looking over the wide Matopos."[17] Mosilikatze, or as we spell it today, Mzilikazi, was Lobengula's father, who died in 1868.

As he had asked his tomb was placed here. His tombstone bears the epitaph he requested in his will: "Here lie the remains of Cecil John Rhodes". Nothing more, not even his date of birth or death. Rhodes considered these superfluous: he said that he would be remembered for another four thousand years.

The contemporary British press recorded that thousands of Ndebele participated in his funeral procession: they marched behind the coffin which was borne on a gun carriage and greeted Rhodes's body with the traditional Zulu salutation: "Bayete!" Perhaps, indeed, they did: stranger things have happened in history.

In Britain the journalist William Stead expressed the opinion of many when he wrote: "When Mr Rhodes died, the most conspicuous figure left in the English-speaking race since the death of Queen Victoria disappeared."

Stead made a comment which was singularly perspicacious for the time. He wrote that while there had been wealthier men than Rhodes—Carnegie, Rockefeller, Astor, these had used their wealth primarily for strictly financial purposes. Rhodes, on the other hand, was "the first—he will not be the last—of the millionaire monarchs of the modern world".[18]

Rhodes's death was noted throughout the world. The authors of obituaries were at pains to find good things on which to lay stress: *de mortuis nil nisi bonum*. Rhodes was severely castigated for the Boer War, but his most criminal deeds—leading to the enslavement of millions of Africans—did not at that time, the age of the "partition of the world", meet with the widespread condemnation they merited.

It was Rhodes's wish that a pantheon of Rhodesians be created beside his own tomb. 130 metres from his grave a memorial was erected to Major Wilson and his detachment, who had perished during their pursuit of Lobengula. The monument is built in the Greek style—in accordance with Rhodes's instructions. It is massive: each of its innumerable granite slabs weighs ten tons. At the foot of the memorial are engraved the soldiers' names and a line from Kipling: "None was left alive". In 1920 the remains of "Dr Jim"—Leander Starr Jameson—were brought from Britain and interred near those of Rhodes.

Thus it was that even after death these men remained together in ground so far from their native soil. Perhaps each of them

id indeed die in the belief that he had done good for this
istant land. But to the end they remained strangers in this
and: to the people who live there their remains and their me-
morials are as foreign as the deeds done in their lifetime had
een.

The sixth and last testament left by Cecil Rhodes, opened after
is death, did not only contain instructions about the place and
manner of his burial. Rhodes had pondered long over this will,
discussing it with Rothschild, Beit, Stead, Milner and others. He
out his hand to it on July 1, 1899, the day of his final departure
rom London to South Africa on the eve of the Boer War. But
he added the appendix only on March 12, 1902, a mere two
weeks before his death.

The sixth will, like those before it, was political. His goal
emained the same: the expansion of the British Empire and of
ts influence through the world. But his approach to the prob-
em was different: he had learnt his lesson from the Jameson
Raid. In fact, even before the raid people close to Rhodes had
ried to dissuade him from his pet idea of creating a secret order
or the expansion of the British Empire. With good reason they
believed that the adverse publicity surrounding a project of that
kind could not fail to compromise both Rhodes himself and his
project in the eyes of the whole world. It would, of course, be
quite impossible to avoid the publicity.

Such arguments gradually started to sway Rhodes. In addition, his experience as a student in Oxford had graphically demonstrated to him that there are other, perhaps less obvious,
but by no means less effective methods. The influence of these
arguments can already be felt in the wills of 1892 and 1893,
but it was the shock of the Jameson Raid that finally persuaded
Rhodes radically to rethink the entire question of how to achieve
his ultimate goal.

In his final will there is not even any mention of the secret
society. Its place has been taken by scholarships to Oxford, an
idea which Rhodes nurtured during the final years of his life.
The idea of rearing the future propagators of his ideas through
the medium of Oxford University not only gained the upper
hand in his final will: it completely displaced his plan to organize a secret order.

At the same time Rhodes unequivocally declared in this final will that he had set himself the aim not of disseminating erudition and academic knowledge, but of creating men dedicated to the "union of the English-speaking people throughout the world." He instructed his executors to select candidates not merely by their application to academic study—the scholarship holders "shall not be merely bookworms", they must also be sportsmen, excelling in football, cricket or similar activities, and exhibiting manhood, truth, courage and moral force of character.[19]

In July 1899 Rhodes directed one of the executors as follows: "You should also select the best of the students and send them to different parts of the world to maintain Imperial thought in the colonies, they would be better unmarried as the consideration of babies and other domestic agenda generally destroys higher thought."[20]

In essence Rhodes sets out here the same requirements as for the members of the now abandoned secret society. This is only to be expected. After all, the goals faced by his Oxford scholars are exactly the same. Even the human catchment area is the same: the younger sons, for it was primarily these who need scholarships to study.

Rhodes created a great number of scholarships. In the process he was careful not to forget the idea of bringing together the "Anglo-Teutonic race". The German Kaiser was granted the right to award five scholarships annually to German school-leavers.

In his will Rhodes carefully explains that his bequest of five scholarships per year for a three-year degree course means that in the first year there will be five scholars, in the second ten, and from the third year onwards fifteen scholars per year.

He earmarked the majority of places for English-speaking beneficiaries: in the British Empire and the United States. British possessions were given sixty-six scholarships, the United States two scholarships for each state. The British possessions were enumerated: South Africa, Canada, Australia, New Zealand, Bermuda and Jamaica.

In other words, these were almost exclusively "white" dominions and colonies. And when Rhodes wrote that no candidate was to be rejected on the grounds of race or religion, by the word "racial" he meant, of course, "national". Rhodes intended the scholarships for whites only: a clause was included to protect the Afrikaners and the French-speaking Canadians.

With the passing of time, however, Rhodes's executors—or, to be more precise, the successors of his executors—have been forced by changing world circumstances to interpret his will in the literal sense, and Rhodes scholarships at Oxford have been taken up by students of all skin colours.

A considerable number of Rhodes scholars have subsequently attained prominence. Rhodes would certainly have been most gratified to see how many of their names figured—and still figure —in the administrative machinery of the countries of the British Empire and Commonwealth. One of his "alumni" was Dean Rusk, Secretary of State in the Kennedy administration.

But what would Rhodes have said had he learnt that one of his future scholars, by the name of Bram Fischer, an Afrikaner patrician, grandson of the Prime Minister of the former Orange Republic—a man whom destiny itself seemed to have singled out to fulfil Rhodes's behests, the "federation" of all white South Africans under the British flag—should have become the leader of the underground resistance. For which he was sentenced by the authorities in South Africa to life imprisonment.

But Rhodes was not to know this.

Rhodes did not live to celebrate his 49th birthday, and it is hard to imagine him having survived to the First World War, or to the 1920s or 1930s. Yet many of his contemporaries and people of his generation not only lived, through these years and later events, they even made their mark on them. Bernard Shaw, born three years after Rhodes, survived until 1950, Sydney and Beatrice Webb until the mid-1940s, John Hobson—one of Rhodes's most outspoken opponents—until 1940.

The armies of the First World War were commanded by Hindenburg, Joffre, Kitchener, all older than Rhodes, and by his co-eval the Russian general Brusilov. Petain, hero of the First World War and disgrace in the Second, was only three years younger than Rhodes and lived until 1951.

Rhodes's generation retained its position in world politics for a long time after his death. Balfour, Asquith, Clemenceau "the Tiger", Tomaš Masaryk were all older than Rhodes, and the newspapers of the twenties were filled with their names.

It seems as though virtually everyone with whom Rhodes's name is connected was destined to enjoy a much longer life than was allotted to him. Jameson and Hofmeyr lived for a decade and a half longer; Salisbury, Kipling and Conan Doyle —two and a half decades; Chamberlain and Kruger—three decades; Queen Victoria and Lord Rosebery—three and a half. Even Lobengula lived ten years longer than Rhodes.

Longest-live of all, Rhodes's secretary Philipp Jourdan, only died in May 1961.

In a sense Rhodes was lucky. He never experienced old age, never underwent the tragic loss of faculties and humiliation of senility and dotage. Undoubtedly, old age would have been a terrible cross for him to bear. His time was soon over: this was only too evident. New faces had entered British politics That is not to say that these men were better or worse, younger or older: they were simply new.

In the year of Rhodes's death the British premiership was assumed by Balfour. He was Rhodes's senior by five years. On the occasion of his eightieth birthday, in 1928, *The Times* published a congratulatory sonnet, whose concluding sestet was

> *Ruler, by hand of steel in silken glove;*
> *Doubtful, at times, if mending be worth while*
> *Where naught persists but ordered, smooth decay;*
> *Careless of hate, nor greatly liking love;*
> *Content, if high affairs some hours beguile*
> *With work become a finer form of play.*[21]

No one could have written these words of Rhodes. One thing which Rhodes could never have been accused of was aloofness. Whatever he did, he did with ardour, devoting himself to it body and soul and taking his work extremely seriously. The English poets extolled Rhodes in quite different terms. In his "Graveside Oration" on Cecil Rhodes Kipling writes:

> *Dreamer devout, by vision led*
> *Beyond our guess or reach,*
> *The travail of his spirit bred*
> *Cities in place of speech.*[22]

At that time, in the most frenzied stage of the scramble for the partition of the world, the rulers of Britain were in particular need of men about whom such verses could be composed. They needed men who could be presented to the public as ardent, impassioned and utterly dedicated.

This age lasted some twenty-five or thirty years: from the 1870s to the first years of this century. Rhodes's active life coincided exactly with this period. He was the very embodiment of the forces which carved up and fragmented entire continents.

But this age soon came to an end. By the beginning of the twentieth century the world was already parcelled out. The Anglo-Boer War was the culminating point of this process.

As often happens in history, when the curtain came down on this age it took with it from the stage of the world the man who had been its personification.

The zenith of the might of the British Empire, the greatest empire in the history of mankind, is marked with the name of Cecil John Rhodes, yet the empire itself did not outlive him by very long. As we now look back and review its development we cannot but marvel at the speed with which it collapsed...

In 1921 H. G. Wells foretold that in a hundred years the British Empire would no longer exist. Rider Haggard harshly criticized him for such pessimism. Yet history unfolded with far greater speed than Wells had predicted.

A mere forty years after Rhodes's death his young contemporary Winston Churchill dramatically exclaimed: "I have not become the King's First Minister in order to preside over the liquidation of the British Empire."[23]

Yet this was precisely the role Churchill was obliged to play. During his own life Dean Achison, State Secretary of the USA—a country Rhodes had so recently dreamt of bringing back to the fold of the British Empire—remarked melancholically:

"Great Britain has lost an Empire and has not yet found a role."

The last of the major British colonies to gain independence was the country conquered by Rhodes: Southern Rhodesia. In 1980, as he gave his final order as governor—to lower the British flag, Lord Soames declared that this act marked not only the end of a chapter—it completed the many-volumed history of his country: the Book of the Empire.[24]

The great poet Shelley, another compatriot of Rhodes, unwittingly wrote Cecil's epitaph with his sonnet "Ozymandias":

> *"My name is Ozymandias, king of kings:*
> *Look on my works, ye Mighty, and despair!"*
> *Nothing beside remains, Round the decay*
> *Of that colossal wreck, boundless and bare*
> *The lone and level sands stretch far away.*

How many grand monuments have met such a fate. . . Most of the statues of Rhodes proved to be very short-lived: those which were erected in Northern Rhodesia were removed from their pedestals in the mid-1960s. In Southern Rhodesia, in the early 1980s. They had stood a few decades, no more.

Conclusion

One hundred years have elapsed since, in the second half of the 1880s, the image of Cecil Rhodes as a figure of legend, the myth of Rhodes, started to take shape.

This myth continued to acquire new features even after Rhodes's death.

Almost thirty years after Rhodes's death Conan Doyle wrote these words about him, which we have already had occasion to quote: "That strange but very great man, Cecil Rhodes, a mighty leader, a man of broad vision, too big to be selfish but too determined not to be unscrupulous—a difficult man to appraise with our little human yard-sticks."[1]

For years on end newspapers and journals in Britain quoted the words of such acolytes of Rhodes as Major Leonard, a participant in his wars of conquest: "There was a magic in the name of Cecil Rhodes, as well as in the intense magnetism of his personality."[2]

The growing condemnation of racism by world public opinion has forced Rhodes's followers ever more insistently to ascribe to him the motto: "Equal rights for all civilized people". They sought to link Rhodes's name ever more closely with the names of travellers and explorers who have earned the respect of mankind, and primarily with the name of David Livingstone. In Northern Rhodesia there was even a Rhodes-Livingstone Institute.

In his acclaimed book *Der Untergang des Abendlandes* (The Decline of the West) the German philosopher Oswald Spengler prophetically sees in Rhodes a portent of the future, of a none too joyous future: in his scheme of world history Rhodes is situated mid-way between Napoléon and the men of violence of the present century.

The legend of Cecil Rhodes became so widely propagated

that even André Maurois fell under its spell, and published in 1953 his rapturous biography *Cecil Rhodes.*

We could extend almost indefinitely the list of such laudatory appraisals of the great imperialist.

Why, we might ask, should the name of Rhodes in particular have acquired such a romantic aura?

One answer suggests itself immediately: the simplest, and, in the most general terms, an undeniably correct answer.

Colonialism desperately needed to mask its ugliness and present itself to people as something magnificent and noble. After all, to conquer distant lands Europe required not only military might, to break the opposition of the peoples of Africa and Asia. It was also necessary for the general public in Europe to come to terms with colonialism, to support it or at any rate not to oppose it. This in turn engendered the urgent need for colonialism to create its own heroes: magnificent and romantic figures. These had to be heroes capable of giving a poetic embodiment to the deeds and achievements of colonialism.

Yet for all its accuracy, this answer is too sweeping and general. All it says, in essence, is that colonialism needed its own idols and that the propaganda machines of the mother countries were obliged to search them out, to create them and extol them.

Again we might ask: why should Rhodes be singled out as the most important, the foremost of these idols?

No effort was spared to create such an aura around the names of such men as the French generals Lyautey and Gallieni, the German Karl Peters, the Englishmen Harry Johnston, Lord Lugard and General Gordon... But none of them were to become legends of the order of Cecil Rhodes. Even in Britain itself no other man was placed on a pedestal with him. A great many politicians have been hailed as architects and builders of the British Empire, but Rhodes alone is described as its father.

How, then, can we account for the phenomenon of Cecil Rhodes? This same question was repeatedly asked by Mark Twain.

To a certain extent the answer can be found in the way Rhodes embodied a combination of diverse images: the industrialist; the financier; the conqueror; the ideologist; the politician and statesman—prime minister and member of the Queen's

Privy Council: even the diplomat. Rhodes acted in each of these capacities, and in every one he succeeded.

He had a fanatical belief in the cause he served—however repulsive it may seem to us today—and he devoted himself to it body and soul, applying to it all his outstanding talents.

He was able to infect others with his ideas and to inspire with his example. He could also—when it proved really necessary—display great personal courage.

He was able to provoke amazement even in people who condemned him. Such a one was the fearless Olive Schreiner: few people have exposed Rhodes so unmercifully.

But even she did not see him as an adventurer or a *nouveau riche,* rather as a modern Mephistopheles. Even in his malefactions she saw him as a man of greatness. She explained her attitude to Rhodes in the following parable. "It came to pass that Cecil Rhodes died. The Devil claimed him. However, the gates, doors and windows of Hell proved all too small to take Rhodes in. The *Bon Dieu,* hearing the commotion, asked for the reason. The Devil explained that he had tried every way but could not get Cecil Rhodes into Hell: 'He is too big!' 'Ah,' said the *Bon Dieu,* 'then, I suppose Cecil must come here after all.'"[3]

Both in Great Britain and in other European countries Cecil Rhodes's name came to stand as a symbol of success and achievement. His successes were seen not as the luck of a gambler who in a run of good fortune breaks the bank, but as the end result of actions carried out by a man inspired by the very idea of creation. His construction of railways, telegraph lines, and cities was compared favourably not only with the actions, for instance, of the Spanish conquistadors, who plundered America and constructed nothing, but also to the conduct of many other colonizers, contemporary to Rhodes, who had done nothing but plunder and pillage. It was only natural that Cecil Rhodes, even with his most deplorable actions, did not occasion such feelings of disgust and loathing as did the German Karl Peters, who had violated African women. Yet Peters also aspired to the glory of the founder of a colonial empire.

It was also easier to surround Rhodes's name with a romantic aura because he was a member of neither the aristocracy nor the monied classes. He had made his way thanks to his own talents, his energy and sense of purpose. He had not made his career thanks to the fact that he had studied at Oxford, but the reverse: he got into Oxford thanks to the career he had already made. Consequently he could almost be presented as a man of the people.

It was also with good reason that the more chauvinistic section of the British press depicted Rhodes as a man who seemingly acted in defiance of authority, of the official circles of Britain with their bureaucratic inertia and indifference to enthusiastic new ideas.

After all, some conquests are made by governments, with endless debates in parliament and the discussion of budget appropriations. To the rank-and-file tax-payer this talking shop only too often seemed a bureaucratic waste of time and public money which produced nothing but tedium and occasionally protest, particularly in Great Britain, where the attitude of the public to the authorities has always been marked by scepticism and mistrust.

But it is quite another matter when the call to go forth and conquer is sounded by a dreamer and romantic. Rhodes had discovered a new Eldorado and prophetically called on his countrymen, in the name of the greatness of their own nation, for the good of backward peoples and for the advance of civilization, to "develop" these new lands. He placed at the feet of these countrymen the countless riches of each new country: its gold and diamonds.

Rhodes himself was portrayed as an altruistic zealot working for the good of Great Britain: it was for her glory that he toiled and gave battle in the jungle and wilderness of distant Africa, beneath the blazing sun, facing innumerable dangers, at considerable risk both to his health and even his life. Those others, however, the officials back home, grew fat in their splendid, well-appointed London offices and dreamt more of their own advancement and other selfish matters.

The picture may not always have been painted in such garish colours, but the gist of newspaper and magazine articles was often on precisely these lines. Nor did it occasion any protest from the ruling circles of Britain. On the contrary: such a representation was only to be encouraged, because the aura it created around Rhodes's name only served to ennoble their colonial policies in the eyes of the ordinary man.

We might recall here that at the end of the 1840s the French government dispatched Dumas père to North Africa. It was intended that through his travel notes Dumas would excite in the breasts of the French an irresistible desire to gain new colonies. Thus even then the European ruling circles understood what an immense service a popular figure could do in asserting the ideas of colonialism.

Perhaps more than anyone before him, Rhodes embodied the spirit of colonialism such as it was during the age of the division of the world. His conscious life—from his arrival in Africa in 1870 until his death in early 1902, coincided exactly with the period of this carve-up. Everything Rhodes did and thought in life is congruent with the spirit of that colonialist and imperialist age.

The ideas of colonialism as it then existed gave purpose to his existence, and even his crimes were justified as having been committed in the name of these ideas. It was all this together that made Rhodes the most significant of the empire-builders of the end of the last century.

The colonial division of the world was effected a mere one hundred years ago. From a historical point of view this is comparatively recent—in the time of our own grandfathers and great-grandfathers. At that time, on the threshold of the twentieth century, the countries of the world were divided into the colonized and the colonizing. This distinction at the same time united their destinies: it tied them in a single knot, albeit one woven by cruel hands.

Many of the problems of the modern age are rooted in these same historical events. Not only we, but our children and grandchildren after us will seek in them answers to the issues that concern us. They will peer anxiously into the past, eager to comprehend those events, to feel the atmosphere in which the division of the world could have taken place, and in its turn have led to such far-reaching consequences.

This realization came to me with particular forcefulness during a recent study tour of Zimbabwe, Zambia, Lesotho and Mozambique, where I conducted research in the archives and libraries of these countries, and held discussions with their historians. Regrettably, the greater part of the extensive material I found there I have been unable to include in this book: it came to me too late and work had already begun on this translation. For this reason the English translation is published in approximately the same form as the original Russian edition of the book in 1984. But the historians of these countries earned my profound gratitude by drawing my attention to various debates that have arisen in recent years about the role and position of Cecil Rhodes in the history of the region.

Let me cite one example. An article was published in the *Heritage,* a yearly Zimbabwean historical bulletin in the early '80s, in which the author argued against practically everything written about Rhodes before—against Michell, Williams and the other early biographers, right up to Flint, Galbraith, Robinson and Gallagher, who published their accounts in more recent years.

The idea of the article is conveyed by its title, which suggests that Rhodes was more of an agent than an initiator. The author, Stephanie Stevenson, rebukes her predecessors for having, to a man, greatly exaggerated the role played by Rhodes in determining British policies in Southern Africa and underestimating the role of the Imperial government. The image has gradually been created and maintained of Rhodes as an all-powerful figure, extraordinarily influential and autonomous in his political activities—and this image, argues Stevenson, entirely suited the leaders of the Imperial government.[4]

The ideas expressed by this Zimbabwean article fully coincide with the conclusions to which I came myself. Yet can one justifiably consider Rhodes as a mere "agent"? I still feel that such an extreme opposition between Rhodes and the ruling circles of Great Britain is hardly supportable. It would be closer to the truth to see both him and the forces he controlled as a component part of that ruling hierarchy.

This example demonstrates that the debates around Rhodes are by no means resolved. Neither do these debates only concern historians. Politicians and industrialists are also involved, and, naturally enough, ordinary people—those whose views rarely appear in print, but whose opinions are the ones that really matter.

Disputes over Cecil Rhodes's historical role were carried on not only in the press. The documents kept at Rhodes House in Oxford under the heading "Confidential" include, for example, four short assessments of Cecil Rhodes, all of the same type. One of these is dated June 1956; the others are undated, but they, too, are most likely from the 1950s or '60s. Each of them ends with a short conclusion.

These conclusions are contradictory. One of the documents concludes thus: "Could his way of life be emulated today? It is our opinion that his political, business and administrative ability would have led him to great heights today." Another, on the contrary: "Today we see no place for him in the British of South African political scene." The third: "Moral judgement of the inner powers which drove him on could not be agreed upon even in his own day." In yet another document, the answer is evasive.[5]

Unfortunately, it was difficult for me as a foreigner, to understand by whom and for whom these documents were written, especially since they are not signed. Perhaps they were prepared in order to decide how to interpret Rhodes's image in today's world, where the countries he once conquered have become independent states.

The leading South African financier and industrialist Harry Oppenheimer has often embroiled himself in this controversy. He delivered a memorial lecture on the centenary of Rhodes's arrival in South Africa. "Let us admit it frankly," he said, "Rhodes's reputation probably now stands lower than at any time since his death."[6] Yet even with the title of his lecture—"The vision of Cecil Rhodes"—Oppenheimer was hoping to restore some of that lost reputation.

Of course Oppenheimer is not alone in his campaign to preserve the myth of Cecil Rhodes. For further evidence we may cite the Johannesburg magazine *Stag* of March 1985: "It's good to see the spirit of Cecil Rhodes and Barney Barnato did not die with the pioneers of South Africa".[7]

All this only goes to show that scholars will continue to return to the figure of Cecil Rhodes, and hope to evaluate his role with increasing objectivity. These will include not only European scholars, as has tended to be the case hitherto, but also those working in the young historical schools of Zimbabwe, Zambia and other African countries. Their research and their labours will bring forth new materials and new approaches, and in turn new assessments.

Among them will also be many of Rhodes's countrymen, of course. Much toil and talent has already been expended by them in studying the historical tendencies and events connected with Rhodes, yet it is highly unlikely that they have said their final word on the subject.

Appendix

THESE EVENTS THROUGH
THE EYES OF CONTEMPORARY
RUSSIAN OBSERVERS

Since this book was written in Moscow and Leningrad, the author was anxious to ascertain how his own countrymen had viewed Cecil Rhodes and the events connected with his name.

I believe this curiosity was quite justified. It is comparatively well-known how people regarded Rhodes in his own country and in such European states as Germany or France. But little attention has been given to his reputation in Russia.

Despite its geographical remoteness from the countries in which Rhodes was born and where he spent his life, Russia was well-informed about his activities: being one of the great powers it keenly followed everything of importance going on in the world.

First let us examine how Rhodes was regarded by official circles in Russia, and what importance he had for the Russian public. Were the Russian people, for example, at all interested in this man, and if so how did they view his activities? To what can we attribute the different attitudes to him?

By shedding light on all this we are able to gain a better understanding of Russia's attitude to Great Britain, to British colonialism and to Africa—in other words, to everything connected with Rhodes's life-work.

Naturally in Russia this man was not the focus of attention that he was in England. Nevertheless, a great deal was written about him. Articles appeared in the most prestigious journals of St Petersburg, and also in publications intended for the less educated reader. Naturally, there was also frequent mention of his name in the newspapers, and he even cropped up in adventure novels and other forms of pulp literature. Photographs and caricatures of Rhodes were no rarity in the Russian press of the time.

He received almost universal condemnation, although for different reasons. The social democrats reviled him as an imperialist. The Black Hundreds, enemies of the "rotten liberalism" of Britain, damned him as a representative of loathsome Great Britain. Many others, who were not directly concerned with politics, deprecated his cruelty towards the weak.

Often, however, this condemnation was laced with a reluctant amazement, such as we have already seen with Mark Twain and Olive Schreiner.

This is found, for example, with the well-known Russian journalist Emilia Pimenova. She wrote a long essay entitled: "Cecil Rhodes, Napoléon of the Cape", which first appeared in June 1900 in *Mir Bozhiy* (God's World), one of the most respected political and literary journals of St Petersburg. Later the same essay, slightly reworked, appeared in her book *The Political Leaders of Contemporary England and Ireland*, which was published in St Petersburg in 1904.

It is clear from Pimenova's essay that she was well acquainted with the English literature on Cecil Rhodes, and in general with political and public life in Britain at that time.

Her biographical information about Rhodes is given in detail and is basically accurate. What is of more interest, however, is Pimenova's attitude to the "Napoléon of the Cape".

At the beginning of her essay she asks: "Was Cecil Rhodes in actual fact the great Englishman that the English newspapers make him out to be?"

And gives as her answer:

"That he was a major figure, perhaps the most significant in England at that time, of that there can be no doubt. Never before has any individual brought upon himself so many curses and earned such universal hatred from all nations as Cecil Rhodes, but at the same time no one, neither before, nor today, after his death, can accuse him of having pursued narrow self-interested goals. Even his enemies acknowledge that he was not a seeker after wealth, and that he always regarded money as a means rather than an end...

"He dreamt of creating a mighty bond, which would unite

the white population of South Africa, scattered over an immense area, and would set in motion a South African political life. He realized how daunting this undertaking was and endeavoured to fulfil it using all the means at his disposal, working to the Jesuit rule that the end justifies the means; he freely practised bribery on a wide scale; he willingly spent his own millions on the equipping of troops and the organization of the notorious Jameson Raid; but when his plans failed and all Europe gloatingly derided him he showed no pusilanimity, no cowardice, even his enemies admit that at this most difficult time for him he displayed courage and generosity of heart and proved that he was a man of outstanding qualities. After suffering defeat he did not hide behind anyone's back or resort to subterfuge to exonerate himself; he did not try to shift the blame and responsibility onto the shoulders of others..."

At the end of her essay Pimenova reaches the following conclusion: "He was indeed a gigantic figure in the true sense of the word. He could be made into a hero and a brigand, depending on one's viewpoint".[1]

This was a fairly widely held view in Russia. It can be seen with particular clarity in the articles published on the occasion of Rhodes's death, both in the capital and the provincial press.

"The 'South African Napoléon', Cecil Rhodes, ended his days in terrible torment, after a grave sickness," the St Petersburg journal *Niva* informed its readers. "Rhodes's enemies, who were many in number, could see in him nothing but vice, self-interest and egotism, but they were wrong... Consider the position of a British imperialist, utterly dedicated to the idea of his country dominating the world... He was an ardent patriot, and patriotism is a two-bladed weapon. In bringing benefit to one's own country, one cannot but cause harm to the people of another."[2]

The newspaper *Odesskiye Novosti* wrote: "England has lost one of its most outstanding political figures, a man of great intelligence and extraordinary energy, who dedicated the whole of his rich and eventful life to the glorification of his own country, although he had a most original interpretation of its greatness and he sought to increase this greatness by still more original means."[3]

This dual attitude to Rhodes was an attribute not only of journalists. The Russian Consul General in London, reporting back to St Petersburg in 1899 about the situation in Rhodesia, noted, on the one hand "the undoubtedly brilliant results" (which he enumerates: the construction of 300 miles of railway and telegraph lines, the building of seven towns, etc.) and, on the other, "the bankruptcy of Rhodes's methods of government."[4]

The embassy of the Russian Empire in London reported to St Petersburg: "The death of Cecil Rhodes, which occurred on March 13, new style 26, has brought to his grave one of the most outstanding figures of modern Great Britain. This event ... has left an immense impression in England and its colonies, and the columns of all the newspapers, whatever their political tendency, were filled with details of the last minutes of the life of this great adventurer, who embodied the ideals and the aspirations of British imperialism. . ."[5]

Of the Russian writers of the turn of the century it was probably "Dioneo", Isaak Shklovsky, who had the most to say about Rhodes. Shklovsky was a leading political commentator of pre-revolutionary Russia and the London correspondent of Russian liberal journals. He was interested in events not only in Britain itself, but throughout the British Empire, and he also followed the newspapers published in Africa.

The figure of Rhodes exercised such a fascination over Shklovsky that, having read a large number of books about him, he even travelled to Oxford to observe Rhodes "receiving his doctor's mantle". Shklovsky describes this ceremony, attended by large numbers of people, in close, although perhaps not very accurate, detail for the readers of the influential St Petersburg journal *Russkoye bogatstvo* (The Wealth of Russia).

"I, together with many Londoners, repaired to Oxford to witness Cecil Rhodes receiving his doctor's mantle, which was to be conferred upon him despite the protest of the professors. The situation was as follows: in 1891 a legate of Oxford University informed Cecil Rhodes that the degree of doctor *honoris causae* had been conferred upon him. At that time Rhodes had not yet become another Napoléon; his image had not yet been formed; his name had not yet become so strangely associated with the story of the villainous raid. At that time Rhodes was in fact unpopular among the jingoists for having contributed £10,000 for agitation for Home Rule. For many years Cecil Rhodes did not come to receive his mantle, and only arrived when his 'fame' was firmly established. The Oxford professors protested, but the decisions of the Senate do not expire with time. The jingoists decided to make use of Rhodes's arrival to stage a demonstration against the 'anarchists', as they so colourfully dubbed all the professors who had signed the protest. People in the crowd shouted 'Hooray!' and sang 'For he's a jolly good fellow!' On the stage there appeared a tall, heavily-built man, who had started to grow quite stout, with fat jowls, glistening and fleshy. Most memorable of all were his brown eyes, quick and slightly impudent, and his sensuous, deep red lips.

" 'Don't look like a Boer!' shouted one voice from the gallery.

" 'How is Kruger?' shouted another. 'Haven't you sent him to his ancestors yet?'

" 'Veni, vidi, vici!'

" 'How do you say Rhodes in Latin?' asked one group, and another answered: 'The Colossus of Rhodes'. Once again the hall erupted in cheers."[6]

Shklovsky wrote about Rhodes in numerous articles. He also discusses him in the best of his books: the undeservedly neglected *Sketches of Contemporary England,* which was published in St Petersburg in 1903. In the section "Imperialism" Cecil Rhodes figures at the head of his list of "high priests" of the Stock Exchange, which he calls the "Temple of Mammon".[7]

Shklovsky was interested to see how the ruling circles in England viewed Rhodes. He quotes Prime Minister Lord Salisbury as saying:

"We still live in an age in which heroes are possible. One of the most glorious heroes is alive in our midst. Our grandsons will say of us with envy: 'How lucky they were! They were contemporaries of the great Cecil Rhodes!' "[8]

Shklovsky was also the author of an account of Barnato's life-work, albeit slightly apocryphal. It was published in 1897 in the journal *Russkoye bogatstvo.*

"Barney Barnato could have been the central figure in a novel about the gold rush. Twenty years ago a clown plied his trade on the pavements of Whitechapel, performing his acrobatics on a shabby horsecloth before an equally shabby public. But the Whitechapel poor offered an insufficient reward for his 'art', and the clown was young and ambitious. He decided to emigrate to South Africa and try his fortune there. At that time the first rumours had started to circulate about ... the diamond fields. When the clown disembarked in Cape Town he had in his pocket no more than five shillings; but Barney Barnato, for such was the acrobat's name, did not lose heart. He at once joined a party of prospectors. They were lucky and within ten years Barney Barnato was worth one million."

In actual fact, of course, things were not quite so simple and straightforward as Shklovsky would have us believe. Was it merely a matter of "luck"? After all, apart from Rhodes, Barnato was the only one among thousands of prospectors to enjoy such good fortune. He must surely have been endowed by nature with the sort of talents that made him the envy of all his rivals. Shklovsky admits this too:

"Notwithstanding his rich harvest of diamonds the young man thirsted for even quicker profits. Thus he became head of a shareholders' company. Now he was truly in his element. Just as a general dispatches battalions of soldiers into battle, so did Barney send hosts of shares into the market. In his hands these shares wrought miracles.

"...To this day the jobbers on the London Stock Exchange vividly recall Barney Barnato's reappearance after his original departure from London. This was the return of a prince—no, the word 'prince' is too bland: it was like the appearance to his people of an Indian godhead. The ecstatic worshippers were eager to fling themselves beneath the wheels of his juggernaut. Nor was the Stock Exchange the only place where Barnato was accorded such a welcome. His palatial house near Green Park was the scene of lavish balls, invitations to which were eagerly sought by duchesses endowed with lineages even longer than the aunt of Mlle Cunégonde in Voltaire's *Candide*".[9]

Of course, ten years previously, during his tussle with Rhodes, Barnato had not achieved all this, but even then, in 1887, he was regarded as one of South Africa's richest men.

With regard to the bitter struggle between Rhodes and Barnato, Shklovsky wrote that this was remembered afterwards by the London stock-brokers with the sort of "rapture with which, no doubt, Napoléon's own guardsmen recounted to their grandsons the story of Jena, Austerlitz and Wagram".[10]

Vlas Doroshevich, an even better known Russian journalist

of that time, devoted an entire essay to Cecil Rhodes under the title "A Napoléon of Our Time". It is Doroshevich's view that in Rhodes "the entire patriotic feeling of capitalism" found its embodiment.

In April 1899 the St Petersburg liberal journal *Mir Bozhiy* published an article on Rhodes under the heading: " 'The Great Adventurer' and His Idea of a Trans-African Railway". This article presented the Russian reader with a relatively objective account of Rhodes's life. It also quoted some of Rhodes's own pronouncements, and other people's opinions of him. According to one of these, Rhodes was a man with the face of Caesar, the ambition of Ignatius Loyola and the wealth of Croesus.

Turning to Rhodes's idea of a trans-African railway the journal commented: "Bearing in mind the energy and persistence of Cecil Rhodes, we may be quite certain that the coming century will witness the completion of the giant engineering project of which Rhodes dreams."

The essence of this plan, however, is seen by the journal in the following form: "...many people harbour the suspicion that Cecil Rhodes is not only thinking of travelling the entire length of Africa in one and the same train: he is aiming much higher. By laying railway and telegraph lines he will make possible the transport of materials and troops when required to any part of Africa and will assert the might of Britain, placing under its influence an immense portion of the black continent. Some people even believe that he dreams of seizing Abyssinya. In support of all these surmises and hypotheses about the true intentions behind Rhodes's grand design, it is adduced that this trans-African railway will offer no financial benefits, since there are unlikely to be many travellers who will use it; as far as freight is concerned, to this day any trade distant from the coastal strip is so negligible that the conveyance of commodities into Central Africa cannot be considered as a profitable venture for the railway."[11]

Rhodes's activities were described by the liberal Narodnik S. Yuzhakov, a sociologist and journalist,[12] and they were also commented on by the prominent historian Yevgeny Tarle in his writings.

Cecil Rhodes has also entered the pages of Russian literature. For example, he figures in M. Zlatkovsky's play "John Bull of the End of the Century", which was published in St Petersburg in 1898.[13]

Rhodes was a fruitful source of material for the pulp literature of the time, too. One example is a cheap novelette of the type published in the early twentieth century in serial form, three or four times a week, in gaudy covers, costing five copecks an issue. It was called *Rosa Burgher, Heroine of the Boers, or the Gold Prospectors in the Transvaal*.[14] In this composition Rhodes is portrayed as the evil genius of South Africa. A handsome lord at the centre of high society. The king of Cape Town.

In early 1900 a pamphlet was published in St Petersburg under the title *The New Napoléon of the South African War between the Transvaal and Britain*.[15] Its author Sergei Glebov (Gnedich) published a considerable number of pamphlets, all of a sensational nature, with titles like: *Bald-headed St Petersburg and the Hygiene of Headwear. A Helpful Book for Everyone, The Hygiene of Living or How to Live for Hundreds of Years.*

We can imagine the hullaballoo raised around Rhodes's name if even the author of *Bald-headed St Petersburg* decided to climb aboard his bandwagon! He heaps abuse upon Rhodes, "this deplorable character", as well as upon the whole of Britain. As for the Afrikaners: "they are all orthodox believers and a nation of the utmost piety."

But even in this meretricious pamphlet Rhodes is the new Napoléon.

It was during the years of the Anglo-Boer War that interest in Rhodes among the Russian public reached its highest point.

"The Boers and everything to do with the Boers are now of interest to every single level of society: in the high society salon, the newspaper's editorial office, the footman's pantry, and even the coachman's inn one hears on all sides conversations about the Boers and the African war." This was affirmed in 1900 in a pamphlet published in St Petersburg, many thousands of versts from the Transvaal front.[16]

Nor were these conversations confined to inns, pantries and salons. Nicholas II wrote to his favourite sister Xeniya: "I am utterly absorbed by the war between England and the Transvaal; I daily read and re-read all the details in the English newspapers, from the first to the very last line..."[17]

All sympathies were for the Afrikaners. Regrettably, at that time in Russia, as in most countries in the world, people had not yet gained a true picture of the life and struggle of the black population of South Africa: this only came much later. Nonetheless, this upsurge of interest in the first major war of the twentieth century did not pass without a trace. These were the first steps towards gaining a better understanding of the what life was really like in Southern Africa.

One of the most popular songs in Russia of that time, the early twentieth century, was about the Anglo-Boer War, about the courage and suffering of the Afrikaners, with the refrain "Transvaal, Transvaal, my own true land". Composed in St Petersburg by a relatively obscure poetess, it soon became a Russian folk song.

Throughout Russia collections were held for the wounded Afrikaners. Many young men came forward, eager to volunteer for service, but they were impeded by the great expense of the journey halfway across the world. Nevertheless, Russians constituted a prominent contingent in the foreign volunteer force fighting on the side of the Afrikaners. According to information gathered by the French general staff, no less than 225 Russian volunteers took part in the Anglo-Boer War.[18]

They included representatives of the various nationalities in the Rusian Empire, of different social strata, and of different political convictions. They were all inflamed by a shared aspiration: to assist the weak in his fight against the strong.

A retired Russian army officer, Lieutenant Colonel Yevgeni Maximov, took over the command of the multi-national European volunteer detachment, after the death of the French count Vilbois de Mareuil.

Several of these Russian volunteers were later to acquire considerable fame. Fighting on the side of the Afrikaners was one Alexander Essen, a social-democrat, and later a Bolshevik, who from 1925 to 1929 was deputy head of the State Planning Committee of the Russian Federation (Gosplan RSFSR). A young engineer Vladimir Semyonov was to go on and become the chief architect of Moscow in the 1930s. Alexander Guchkov, who was wounded by the British during the war, went on to become Chairman of the State Duma, and War and Navy Minister in the Provisional Government of 1917; it was he who received

Nicholas II's abdication from the throne. Fighting with the volunteer force was also the Georgian prince Nikolai Bagrationi –the British took him prisoner and dispatched him to St Helena. After Bagrationi's return from the Anglo-Boer War his countrymen in Georgia continued to call him "the Boer" to the very end of his life. "Boer" also became Party nickname of the Bolshevik Essen during the years of his underground revolutionary activity.

Vassily Gurko, Russian military attaché with the armies of the Boer republics, was later, as a general in the First World War, to perform the duties of chief of staff for the supreme commander, Czar Nicholas II.

Russians also worked in two medical detachments in the Boer War: one Russian, and the other a combination of Russian and Dutch. The sisters of mercy from St Petersburg treated the wounded at the battle of Pietermaritzburg.

On their return home these volunteers frequently wrote memoirs of what they had seen in South Africa. Such memoirs were published by the journalist Yevgeny Avgustus[19], the engineer V. Rubanov[20], the doctor M. Chistovich[21], the sisters of mercy Sophia Izedinova[22] and Olga Baumgarten.[23]

Books and pamphlets about the Anglo-Boer War and about the situation in Southern Africa in general were being published not only in St Petersburg and Moscow, but in many other cities of the Russian Empire: Kiev, Warsaw, Odessa, Smolensk, Tiflis (now Tbilisi), Borisoglebsk, Tashkent, Yuryev (now Tartu) and Yekaterinoslav (now Dnepropetrovsk).

Of major interest are the publications of the body then known as the Military Scholars' Committee of the General Staff. Between 1900 and 1905 this committee published a series of "Collected Materials on the Anglo-Boer War in South Africa". For the most part these were translations of the more interesting foreign articles, reviews, pamphlets and even entire books, devoted not only to specifically military matters, but also to the historical preconditions for this military conflict. All in all twenty one such collections were published.[24]

The Military Scholars' Committee also published the hefty (335 pages long) report by Colonel V. Gurko[25], as well as the reports of other military attachés.[26]

Numerous collections of documents pertaining to the Anglo-

Boer War and the situation in South Africa were also publish
ed.[27]

The memoirs of President Kruger were translated and publish
ed in Russian, together with books and articles by General
Joubert and General De Wet as well as other Afrikaner politi
cians and army commanders.

The impression made by this war on the Russian public
attested to by the memoirs of well-known Soviet novelists an
poets whose childhood coincided with the turn of the twentiet
century.

Cecil Rhodes's reputation, however, was not only sprea
through Russia by his detractors. His supporters, albeit far fewe
in number, also made their views known in the press and i
other publications. Arthur Conan Doyle's book *The War i
South Africa: Its Causes and Conduct*, was published in Russia
translation in 1902 in Odessa.[28] A pamphlet was published i
St Petersburg in 1900 entitled *The Anglo-Boer War and th
Russian Press*. Its author was "The Briton".[29]

Among the many Englishmen who visited Russia there wer
a considerable number who supported and admired Rhodes. I
addition the highest governmental and industrial circles of th
Russian Empire were able to glean information on Rhodes fror
a man who was very close to him: the American John Hammond
Yes, this was the very same Hammond who had helped organiz
the ill-starred anti-Boer conspiracy in Johannesburg at the en
of 1895.

Hammond visited Russia on three occasions. The first tim
he travelled at the invitation of Sergey Yulievich Vitte, th
minister of finance, and subsequently chairman of the Counci
of Ministers of the Russian Empire. This was in the winter o
1897-1898, two years after the Jameson Raid.

Of course it was not in his capacity as Rhodes's confeder
ate that Hammond was invited to Russia, but as a mining engi
neer, regarded at the time as one of the world's leading ex
perts on the gold-mining industry (it was with good reaso
that Rhodes had paid him such a fabulously high salary). Ham
mond was invited to Russia as a consultant to explore the pros
pects of the Russian gold-mining industry. He inspected the gol
and platinum deposits in Siberia and in the Urals; he even vis
ited the Yenisey River and the Altai mountain range.

In 1910 and 1912 Hammond travelled to Russia again, this time not as a mining expert, but on behalf of the financial circles of Great Britain and the United States.

He stayed at the *Yevropeiskaya,* one of the most fashionable hotels of St Petersburg. He was received by Czar Nicholas II. He held talks with the Chairman of the Council of Ministers, Pyotr Stolypin, with the minister of foreign affairs, Sergey Sazonov, with the minister of finance Vladimir Kokovtsov, with Alexander Krivosheyin, who was both minister of agriculture and head of the Bank of the Gentry and Peasantry.

Hammond described Rhodes as undoubtedly the greatest Englishman of this century.[30] These words were actually pronounced in 1895, but Hammond never lost his deep admiration for Rhodes. This can clearly be seen in the assessment of Rhodes he gave minister Vitte, whom he regarded as the most dynamic, energetic and in general most capable of the statesmen of Russia. As the highest compliment he could pay him Hammond constantly compared him to Rhodes.[31]

A considerable mass of information about the attitude of the Russian public to the events in Southern Africa of that time is assembled in the book *Russia and the Anglo-Boer War 1899-1902,* written and published in Pretoria in 1981 by the daughter of a Russian emigré family, Elizaveta Kandyba-Foxcroft.[32] Several years before this an English translation had been published in Johannesburg of the memoirs of the Russian sister of mercy, Sophia Izedinova, *A Few Months with the Boers. The War Reminiscences of a Russian Nursing Sister.* This book was published in St Petersburg in 1903, and it informed its Russian readers of Rhodes's policies. It also contained a description of Dr Jameson.

The Anglo-Boer War was one important reason, but not the only reason, behind the interest shown by Russia in events connected in one way or another with the activities of Cecil Rhodes. There are several other reasons, which, while not as important, cannot be ignored.

Significant among these—and a factor regarded as fundamental by many historians—is the relationship which existed then between Britain and the Russian Empire. After the Crimean War this remained tense for the entire duration of the second

half of the nineteenth century. This tension was further exacer
bated by the Russo-Turkish War of 1877-1878, and then by th
intensifying rivalry in the Middle East. Nicholas II's govern
ment followed with deep suspicion the expansion and consolida
tion of British influence in the gold- and diamond-rich territor
of South Africa. This meant that they also followed the activi
ties of Cecil Rhodes.

There were other important reasons besides this. At the end
of the nineteenth century the people of Russia, in common with
those of Western Europe, took a growing interest in the life
of distant parts of the world. South Africa, with its rapid growth,
was of particular interest. Russian engineers were dispatched
there to study the methods of gold-mining used, with a view to
applying this knowledge in the gold-mining regions of Siberia
and the Urals. There was a considerable flow of emigration from
the western regions of the Russian Empire to Southern Africa
from the end of the nineteenth century onwards.

But even long before this Southern Africa had occasioned
great interest in Russia, more than any other part of the continent with the possible exception of Egypt and Ethiopia.

This interest first arose in the early eighteenth century, during
the reign of Peter the Great, when Russian publications first
started giving information about the countries of Southern Africa
and the idea was conceived of sending ships from St Petersburg
into the Indian Ocean, by way of the Cape of Good Hope.

By the early nineteenth century Russian vessels were frequent
visitors in Cape Town and Simonstown. The recollections of
Russian travellers about the Cape Colony appeared in many
St Petersburg and Moscow journals, and were even published in
book form. Some of these attracted such interest in South Africa
itself that they were translated into English and published in
Cape Town. Examples of these are the travel notes of Vassily
Golovnin, a well-known seafarer[34], and the writings of Ivan
Goncharov, one of the major Russian authors of the nineteenth
century[35].

A significant contribution to the process of informing the
Russian people about life in Southern Africa was also made
by translations of the works of Olive Schreiner. Literally everything written by this great South African authoress was translated
and published in Russia. A full translation of her novel *The*

tory of an African Farm appeared in the St Petersburg journal
Vestnik inostrannoy literatury (Bulletin of Foreign Literature),
in four issues between September and December 1893. The story
"Trooper Peter Halket of Mashonaland" was published on several
occasions, in journals and as a separate edition.

Olive Schreiner proved to be so popular in Russia that her
short allegorical stories were printed not only in the capital
cities, but also in a provincial newspaper, the *Nizhegorodsky
Listok* in which, furthermore, they were presented to the reader
with a foreword by Maxim Gorky.

The present author has made a study of the voluminous material chronicling Russia's gradual acquaintance with the countries and peoples of Southern Africa in the eighteenth and nineteenth centuries, and he has summarized his findings in two
books[36], and a number of articles, one of which has been published in Cape Town[37]. It seems to me that the material contained
in these publications furnishes ample evidence of the noticeable
interest displayed in Russia towards Southern Africa and the
events taking place in that part of the world even before the
appearance of Cecil Rhodes on the historical stage.

In other words, there are a great number of reasons behind
the attention paid in Russia to Cecil Rhodes and his activities.

Lenin wrote about Rhodes on a number of occasions. He
included Cecil Rhodes's conquests in his lists of the most important colonial conquests and in general most significant events in
world history after the year 1870.[38]

In his conspectuses of the writings of western scholars on imperialism, Lenin annotated a mass of information pertaining to
Rhodes. In his book *Imperialism, the Highest Stage of Capitalism* he observes: "...At the end of the nineteenth century the
British heroes of the hour were Cecil Rhodes and Joseph Chamberlain, who openly advocated imperialism and applied the imperialist policy in the most cynical manner." He gives the following description of Rhodes: "Millionaire, a king of finance, the
man who was mainly responsible for the Anglo-Boer War".[39]

Elsewhere Lenin quotes one of Cecil Rhodes's most important pronouncements:

"I was in the East End of London [a working-class quarter]
yesterday and attended a meeting of the unemployed. I listened

413

to the wild speeches, which were just a cry for 'bread! bread!' and on my way home I pondered over the scene and I became more than ever convinced of the importance of imperialism. .
My cherished idea is a solution for the social problem, i.e., in order to save the 40,000,000 inhabitants of the United Kingdom from a bloody civil war, we colonial statesmen must acquire new lands to settle the surplus population, to provide new markets for the goods produced in the factories and mines. The Empire, as I have always said, is a bread and butter question. If you want to avoid civil war, you must become imperialists".

These words, uttered by Rhodes in 1895, are quoted by Lenin as an example to make the point "that even these leading British bourgeois politicians saw the connection between what might be called the purely economic and the socio-political roots of modern imperialism"[40].

On social issues, as, for that matter, on all others, Rhodes's pronouncements were not outstandingly original, but merely an expression of ideas that were already in the air. Lenin quotes the remark of a French author, who, as Lenin puts it, while "developing and supplementing, as it were, the ideas of Cecil Rhodes quoted above," also wrote that the social causes of colonial policies must be borne in mind alongside the economic causes. This author felt, and he was not alone in this, that the growing complexity of life and the hardships which weighed both on the working masses and on the middle strata, were generating impatience, irritation and hatred in all European countries and threatening their social calm. In consequence, the author concludes, the energy which has been dislodged from certain proper class bearings requires a new application, it needs to be deployed outside the country lest it lead to an explosion within.[41]

At the dawn of the age of imperialism Cecil Rhodes was one of the first to personify that union which Lenin was later to describe as a characteristic of that age: the personal union of banks with industry, and then of both of these with the state apparatus.

Other prominent figures in the Bolshevik party displayed a keen interest in Rhodes, too. Anatoly Lunacharsky, People's Commissar for Education in the first Soviet government, made the following observation about the European bourgeoisie of the

414

eginning of the twentieth century in a report delivered in
overmber 1921:

"The bourgeoisie needed strong men who would save it as it
ursues its colonial policies and its policy to partition the world
y the use of arms. By this time the bourgeoisie had been
oined, mainly thanks to the colonial market, by a fairly large
umber of adventurers like Rhodes, and a serious rift began
vithin the ranks of the bourgeoisie. They declared: down with
lecadence. Instead let us promote aviation, sport, automobiles,
wift propulsion, machinery, the poetry of machinery, the poetry
of capitalism, everything inherent in imperialism. It was at this
ime that imperialism started to grow within the bourgeoisie and
o change its previous sentiments. This is manifested concurren-
ly in art, in the cultivation of heartiness, vigour, strength and
bellicosity. The spirit of war can be smelt in the air. While the
elder brother in the bourgeois home whined and played the
cello, the younger signed up for military service, set off for
Turkestan or Africa, returning with a bronzed complexion and
bronzed heart and telling everyone that the proletarian scum
had to be cleaned up with machine-guns."[42]

This is a most interesting statement. To Rhodes and the
forces which he personified decadence was alien. This is not
to say, however, that the age of Rhodes ushered out that of
decadence: decadence was born during Rhodes's time and, as we
know, it outlived him.

More than half a century ago Maxim Gorky rebuked some
world-renouned writers for failing to show the capitalist in all
the "strength and beauty" of his cynicism, and, most important, for not displaying him in the element where he was most
"colourful": colonial politics. Even Rudyard Kipling and Jack
London, who so loved to portray strong men, projected in their
writings strong-willed characters of only medium calibre, rather than major historical figures. To make his point, Gorky
cited as an example of such a prominent historical personality
none other than Cecil Rhodes and expressed his regret that to
date no really talented novel had been written about Rhodes.[43]

Thus we have seen that a long tradition of interest in the
figure of Cecil Rhodes and in the events surrounding his activities exists in Russia. It is this tradition that inspired the
writing of the present book.

References

TESTAMENT OF A YOUNG MAN

1 Konstantin Balmont, *Stikhotvoreniya* (Poems), Moscow, 1980, p. 66 (in Russian).

2 Y. Charles Shee (Bulawayo), *The Heart of Cecil Rhodes*, Abbotempo (Chicago), 1968, p. 35; see also: Lewis Michell, *The Life of the Rt. Hon. Cecil John Rhodes 1853-1902*, Vol. 1, Edward Arnold, London, 1910, p. 54.

3 Basil Williams, *Cecil Rhodes*, Constable and Company Ltd., London, 1938, p. 51.

4 Cecil Rhodes, "Confession of Faith" of 1877. In: John Flint, *Cecil Rhodes*, Hutchinson of London, London, 1976, pp. 248-252.

5 Vassily Shulgin, *Tri Stolitsy. Puteshestvie v Krasnuyu Rossiyu*, (Three Capitals. Travels in Red Russia), Medny vsadnik, Berlin, 1927, pp. 194-195.

6 J. Flint, *Op. cit.*, pp. 30-32.

7 Basil Williams, *Op. cit.*, p. 51.

8 Osip Mandelstam, "Shum vremeni" (Roar of the Time), *Time*, Leningrad, 1925, p. 31 (in Russian).

9 J. Flint, *Op. cit.*, p. 33.

10 L. Michell, *Op. cit.*, Vol. 1, p. 86.

11 *The Labour Leader*, Vol. VIII, No. 112, New Series, May 23, 1896, p. 177.

12 *The Letters of Queen Victoria*, Third Series, Vol. II (1891-1895), John Murray, London, 1931, p. 13.

13 Erich Eyck, *Das persönliche Regiment Wilhelms II*, Eugen Rentsch Verlag, Erlenbach-Zürich, 1948, p. 236.

14 Mark Twain, *Following the Equator*, Vol. II, The American Publishing Company, Hartford, Conn., 1899, pp. 402-405.

15 *Illustrated London News*, May 1980, p. 28.

16 *Ibid.*, August 1980, p. 87.

17 Lord Soames, "From Rhodesia to Zimbabwe", *International Affairs*, Vol. 56, Summer 1980, No. 3, p. 417.

18 *The Journal of African History*, London, Vol. X, 1969, No. 4, p. 684.

19 George Shepperson, "Cecil Rhodes: Some Biographical Problems", *South African Historical Journal*, Johannesburg, November 1983, No. 15, pp. 54, 67.

20 Thomas Carlyle, *Critical and Miscellaneous Essays*, A New Edition,

complete in one volume, Phillips, Sampson and Company, Boston, 1857, p. 7.

[21] Ye. Yevtushenko, "To S. Preobrazhensky", *Selected Works* in two volumes, Vol. I, Moscow, 1975, p. 221 (in Russian).

[22]
> *Listen, my friend: the ages that are past*
> *Are now a book with seven seals protected*
> *What you the Spirit of the Ages will call:*
> *Is nothing but the spirit of you all,*
> *Wherein the Ages are reflected.*

Johann Wolfgang von Goethe, *Faust,* translated into English by Bayard Taylor, Grosset and Dunlap, New York, w.d., p. 49.

[23] Charles E. Finlason, *A Nobody in Mashonaland or the Trials and Adventures of a Tenderfoot,* George Vickers, London, 1894, p. V.

[24] *The Works of Lord Byron,* complete in one volume, John Murray, London, 1837, p. 29.

"HOW CECIL RHODES MADE HIS FORTUNE"

[1] Mark Twain, *Following the Equator. A Journey Around the World,* Vol. 1, *Op. cit.,* pp. 139-148.

[2] Bernard Shaw, *Collected Plays,* Vol. VI, Max Reinhardt, London, 1973, pp. 769-770.

[3] *"Rimbaud,* Introduced and edited by Oliver Bernard", Penguin Books, Harmondsworth, 1966, p. 99.

[4] "Flowers of Evil", From the French of Charles Baudelaire. By George Dillon. Harper and Brothers Publishers, N.Y., 1936, p. 231.

[5] *Ibidem.*

[6] Arthur Rimbaud, "A Season in Hell", in a new English translation by Louise Varèse. The New Classics Series, Norfolk, Conn., w.d., p. 13.

[7] L. Michell. *Op. cit.,* Vol. 1, p. 17.

[8] André Maurois, *Cecil Rhodes,* Collins, London, 1968, p. 23.

[9] Osip Mandelstam, *Op. cit.,*

[10] André Maurois, *Op. cit.,* p. 26.

[11] Alexandre Dumas, *Le Vicomte de Bragelonne ou Dix Ans plus tard,* Vol. 5, Calmann-Lévy, Paris, s.d., p. 222.

[12] Sam Kemp, *Black Frontiers, Pioneer Adventures with Cecil Rhodes' Mounted Police in Africa,* George G. Harrap & Co. Ltd., London, 1932, pp. 9-10.

[13] J. Flint, *Op. cit.,* p. 14.

[14] B. Williams, *Op. cit.,* p. 42.

[15] N. Bates, *Cecil Rhodes,* Hove, East Essex, 1976, p. 15.

[16] Georges Ohnet, *L'inutile richesse,* Paul Ollendorf, Paris, 1896, pp. 5, 12.

[17] Dioneo, "Ocherki sovremennoi Anglii" (Essays on Contemporary England), *Russkoye bogatstvo* (Wealth of Russia) magazine, St Petersburg, 1903, p. 254.

[18] Fyodor Tyutchev, *Complete Works*, Moscow, 1935, p. 55 (in Russian).

[19] Sarah Gertrude Millin, *The People of South Africa*, Constable and Co. Ltd., London, 1951, p. 17.

[20] Ivan Goncharov, *Fregat "Pallada"* (Frigate "Pallada"), Moscow, 1950, p. 227.

[21] Rudyard Kipling, "South Africa", in *Rudyard Kipling's Verse*, Definitive Edition, Hodder and Stoughton, London, 1948, pp. 207-209.

[22] B. Williams, *Cecil Rhodes*, p. 15.

[23] Charles A. Beard, Mary R. Beard, *The Rise of American Civilization*, Vol. I, The Macmillan Company, New York, 1928, pp. 609-610.

[24] Kipling, "The Song of the Dead".

[25] Mark Twain, *The Stolen White Elephant*, Chatto & Windus, London, 1902, p. 1.

[26] B. Williams, *Op. cit.*, pp. 27-28.

[27] B. Williams, *Ibid.*, p. 29.

[28] J. Flint, *Op. cit.*, p. 16.

[29] Kipling, "The Song of Diego Valdes".

[30] B. Williams, *Op. cit.*, p. 29.

[31] Gwayi Tyamzashe, "Life at the Diamond Fields". In: *Outlook on a Century. South Africa 1870-1970*, Ed. by F. Wilson and D. Perrot, Lovedale Press, Lovedale, 1973, pp. 18-20.

[32] Kipling, "The Mary Gloster".

[33] S. G. Millin, *Rhodes*, Chatto and Windus, London, 1933, p. 1.

[34] L. Michell, *Op. cit.*, Vol. 1, p. 67.

[35] S. G. Millin, *Rhodes, Op. cit.*, pp. 19-20.

[36] *Ibid.*, p. 4.

[37] Yevgeny Tarle, *Napoleon*, Moscow, 1957, p. 33 (in Russian).

[38] Richard Lewinsohn, *Barnato roi de l'or*, Payot, Paris, 1937, pp. 72-74.

[39] S. G. Millin, *Op.cit.*, p. 19.

[40] Felix Gross, *Rhodes of Africa*, Cassell and Co., London, 1956, p. 386.

[41] Charles Kingsley, *Poems to Enjoy*.

[42] Hedley A. Chilvers, *The Story of De Beers*, Cassell and Co., London, 1939, p. 48.

HIS ROAD TO POLITICS

[1] L. Michell, *Op cit.*, Vol. 1, p. 86.

[2] *Ibid.*, p. 81. See also : James Halliday "Oriel Men Do Well", *Blackwood's Magazine*, Edinburgh, Vol. 321, No. 1937, March 1977, pp. 229-235.

[3] F. Gross, *Op. cit.*, p. 39.

[4] B. Williams, *Op. cit.*, p. 41.

[5] William Stead, Ed., *The Last Will and Testament of Cecil John Rhodes*, "Review of Reviews" Office, London, 1902, p. 88.

[6] Peter Gibbs, *The True Book about Cecil Rhodes*, London, 1956, p. 7.

Louis A. C. Raphael, *The Cape-to-Cairo Dream. A Study in British Imperialism*, Columbia University Press, New York, 1936, p. 7.

S. G. Millin, *Op. cit.*, p. 45.

B. Williams, *Op. cit.*, p. 59.

J. Flint, *Op. cit.*, p. 53.

Kipling "Pagett, M. P."

Kipling, "Tomlinson".

J. G. Lockhart, C. M. Woodhouse, *Rhodes*, Richard Clay and Co., London, 1963, p. 91.

Hansard's Parliamentary Debates, Third Series, Vol. 277, London, 1883, col. 413.

B. Williams, *Op. cit.*, p. 75.

On the Passage of Corvette *Skobelev* from Pacific Ocean to Kronstand, USSR Central State Navy Archives, File 283, Leaf 3, Item 6257, p. 38 (in Russian).

[7] *Southern African Dictionary of National Biography*, Frederick Warne and Co., London, 1966, pp. 349-350.

Robert Louis Stevenson, *Treasure Island*, The Spencer Press, (Reading, Pa.,), p. 48.

[9] Watkin W. Williams, *The Life of General Sir Charles Warren*, Basil Blackwell, Oxford, 1941, p. 154.

[20] William Johannes Leyds, *The Transvaal Surrounded*, T. Fisher Unwin Ltd., London, 1919, pp. 217-218.

[21] Charles L. Norris Newman, *Matabeleland and How We Got It*, T. Fisher Unwin, London, 1895, pp. 6-7.

BATTLE OF THE MAGNATES

[1] B. Williams, *Cecil Rhodes*, p. 98.

[2] J. Flint, *Cecil Rhodes*, p. 49.

[3] Ian Colvin, *The Life of Jameson*, Vol. 1, Edward Arnold and Co., London, 1922, p. 69.

[4] W. T .Stead, Ed., *Op. cit.*, p. 62.

[5] Friedrich Engels, "Under den Verfall des Feudalismus und das Aufkommen der Bourgeoisie", in: Karl Marx, Friedrich Engels, *Werke*, Vol. 21, Dietz Verlag, Berlin, 1962, p. 392.

[6] Sam Kemp, *Black Frontiers, Pioneer Adventures with Cecil Rhodes' Mounted Police in Africa*, pp. 9, 15-17, 20-28.

[7] William Plomer, "Conquistadors", *Collected Poems*, Jonathan Cape, London, 1973, p. 18.

[8] Eric Rosenthal, *Gold! Gold! Gold! The Johannesburg Gold Rush*, The Macmillan Company, London, 1970, pp. 150-151.

[9] *Ibid.*, pp. 137-138.

[10] William L. Langer, *The Diplomacy of Imperialism. 1890-1902*, Vol. 1, Alfred A. Knopf, New York, 1935, p. 227.

[11] Dioneo, "Iz Anglii" (From Britain), *Russkoye Bogatstvo*, 1897, No. 8, p. 61.

THE LAND OF OPHIR BETWEEN THE ZAMBEZI
AND THE LIMPOPO

1 Edward C. Tabler, Ed., *Zambezia and Matabeleland in the Seventies*, Chatto and Windus, London, 1960, p. 76.
2 Walter Montagu Kerr, *The Far Interior: a Narrative of Travel and Adventure from Cape of Good Hope Across the Zambezi to the Lake Regions of Central Africa*, Vol. 1, Sampson Low, Martson, Searle and Rivingston, London, 1986, p. 67.
3 Ernest A. Ritter, *Shaka Zulu. The Rise of the Zulu Empire*, G. P. Putnam's Sons, N. Y., 1957, p. 273.
4 W. M. Kerr, *Op. cit.*, Vol. 1, p. 67.
5 Eduard Mohr, *Nach den Victoriafällen des Zambesi*, Verlag von Ferdinand Hirt & Sohn, Leipzig, 1875, pp. 195-196.
6 *Ibid.*, p. 215.
7 *Ibid.*, p. 220.
8 *Ibid.*, p. 221.
9 *Ibidem.*
10 *Ibid.*, pp. 250, 306.
11 J.P.R. Wallis, Ed., *The Northern Goldfields Diaries of Thomas Baines*, Vol. 3, Chatto and Windus, London, 1946, p. 805.
12 Robert Patterson, Capt. "Notes on Matabeleland". *Proceedings of the Royal Geographical Society*, New Monthly Series, Vol. 1, No. 8, August 1879, London, p. 511.
13 W. M. Kerr, *Op. cit.*, Vol. 1, pp. 65-66.
14 R. Patterson, *Op. cit.*, p. 511.
15 H. Rider Haggard, *Maiwa's Revenge; or, the War of the Little Hand*, Longmans, Green and Co., London, 1891, p. 10.
16 *Ibid.*, p. 26.
17 Kipling, *The Lost Legion*.
18 R. Patterson, *Op. cit.*, p. 509.
19 W. M. Kerr, *Op. cit.*, Vol. 1, p. 72.
20 *Further Correspondence Respecting the Affairs of Bechuanaland and Adjacent Territories*, [C-5237] London, 1887, pp. 18-19.
21 *Ibid.*, p. 18.
22 Edward P. Mathers, *Zambesia, England's El Dorado in Africa*, King, Sell and Railton, London, 1891, p. 88.
23 Karl Marx and Frederick Engels, *Selected Works* in three volumes, Progress Publishers, Moscow, 1976, Vol. 3, p. 267.
24 *Ibid.*, p. 266.
25 Élisée Reclus, *Nouvelle Géographie universelle. La terre et les hommes*, Vol. 13 "L'Afrique Méridionale", Hachette et Cie, Paris, 1888, p. 580.
26 André Maurois, *La vie de Disraeli*, Librairie Gallimard, Paris, 1927, p. 312.
27 H. Blauvelt, "Vast Reservoir of Warriors for Allies in Africa", *New York Herald Tribune*, January 25, 1942.
28 Matabele Thompson, *An Autobiography*, Faber and Faber, London, 1936, p. 207.

[9] W. M. Kerr, *Op. cit.*, p. 67.

[10] E. A. Ritter, *Op. cit.*, p. 232.

[11] *Ibid.*, p. 339.

[12] John Mackenzie, "Native Races of South Africa and Their Policy", In: *The British Empire Series*. Vol. II, *British Africa*. Kegan Paul, Trench, Trübner and Co., London, 1899, p. 192.

[13] E. Mohr, *Op. cit.*, p. 176.

[14] James Theodore Bent, "The Ruins of Mashonaland, and Explorations in the Country", *Proceedings of the Royal Geographical Society*, New Monthly Series, Vol. XIV, No. 6, May 1892. pp. 288, 289.

[15] Pierre Lerov-Leaulieu, *Les nouvelles sociétés anglo-saxonnes,* Armand Colin et Cie, Paris, 1897, pp. 271-272.

[16] Charles New, *Life, Wanderings, and Labours in Eastern Africa,* Frank Cass and Co., Ltd., 1971, p. 162.

[17] John Stuart Mill, *System of Logic, Ratiocinative and Inductive, Being a Connected View of the Principles of Evidence, and the Methods of Scientific Investigation*, Vol. II, Longmans, Green, and Co., London, 1865, pp. 344-345.

FROM THE "WHITE QUEEN" TO INKOSI LOBENGULA

[1] L. Raphael, *Op. cit.*, p. 151.

[2] C. E. Nowell, *The Rose-Coloured Map. Portugal's Attempt to Build an African Empire from the Atlantic to the Indian Ocean*. Junta de investigoçoes cientifica do ultramor, Lisboa, 1982; M. Newitt, *Portugal in Africa. The Last Hundred Years*, C. Hurst and Co., London, 1981.

[3] James Percy Fitzpatrick, *The Transvaal from Within*, Frederick A. Stokes Company Publishers, N. Y., 1900, p. 54.

[4] *Further Correspondence...*, p. 23.

[5] *Ibid.*, p. 19.

[6] Karl Marx and Frederick Engels, *Selected Works*, Vol. 3, p. 216.

[7] Arno Karlen, *Sexuality and Homosexuality. A New View*, W. W. Norton & Co., N.Y., 1971, p. 463.

[8] E. P. Mathers, *Op. cit.*, p. 271.

[9] Harry H. Johnston, *The Story of My Life*, Garden City Publishing Company, Inc., N. Y., 1923, p. 221.

[10] "The Concession Journey of Charles Dunell Rudd", *Gold and the Gospel in Mashonaland 1888*, Chatto and Windus, London, 1949, p. 222.

[11] Matabele Thompson, *Op. cit.*, pp. 114-115.

[12] *Ibid.*, pp. 38-39, 116.

[13] *Gold and the Gospel...*, p. 194.

[14] *Ibid.*, p. 225.

[15] W. Plomer, *Cecil Rhodes*, Edinburgh, 1933, p. 58.

[16] Matabele Thompson, *Op. cit.*, pp. 131, 128.

[17] *Gold and the Gospel...*, p. 201.

[18]   M. Thompson, *Op. cit.*, p. 130.

[19]   *Gold and the Gospel . . .*, p. 227.

[20]   *Ibid.*, pp. 219, 220.

[21]   J. A. Hobson, *Imperialism*, The University of Michigan Press, Anr Arbour, 1965, p. 259.

[22]   M. Thompson, Op. cit., p. 178.

[23]   N. M. B. Bhebe, "Ndebele Politics during the Scramble", *Mohlomi Journal of Southern African Historical Studies*, 1978, Vol. II, pp. 31-32.

[24]   M. Thompson, *Op. cit.*, pp. 141, 156-158, 170, 172, 181-183.

[25]   John S. Galbraith, *Crown and Charter. The Early Years of the British South Africa Company*, University of California Press, Berkely, Los Angeles, London, 1974, p. 76.

[26]   E. A. Maund, "On Matabele and Mashona Lands", *Proceedings of the Royal Geographical Society*, New Monthly Series, Vol. XIII, No. 1, January 1891, p. 7.

[27]   E. Mathers, *Op. cit.*, p. 145.

[28]   *Ibid.*, p. 146.

[29]   David Livingstone, *Missionary Travels and Researches in South Africa*, John Murray, London, 1857, pp. 682-683.

[30]   J. Galbraith, *Op. cit.*, p. 77.

[31]   E. Mathers, *Op. cit.*, p. 148-151.

[32]   J. Galbraith, *Op. cit.*, pp. 112-113.

[33]   E. Mathers, *Op. cit.*, p. 157.

[34]   *Ibid.*, p. 159.

[35]   *Der Papalagi. Die Reden des Südseehäuplings Tuiavii aus Tiavea*, Herausgegeben von Erich Scheurmann, Felsen-Verlag Buchenbach, Baden, 1922, pp. 14, 15, 24, 35, 45, 45, 46, 51, 52, 55, 58 59.

[36]   An, *Naivnost ili mudrost* (Naïvety or Wisdom), *Zori*, No. 10, 1924, p. 14.

[37]   Anatole France, *Pierre Nozière*, Calmann-Lévy, Paris, w.d., pp. 156-157.

[38]   "Engels to Margaret Harkness in London [Draft]" (London, beginning of April 1888), in Karl Marx, Frederick Engels, *Selected Correspondence*, Progress Publishers, Moscow, 1982, p. 380.

[39]   M. Tikhomirov, "Letopis nashei epokhi" (A Chronicle of Our Age), *Izvestiya*, October 30, 1962 (in Russian).

[40]   *The Life of Olaudah Equiano, or Gustavus Vassa The African*, Ed. by Paul Edwards, Vol. I, Dawsons of Pall Mall, London, 1969, p. 104.

[41]   A. C. Jordan, "Towards an African Literature (VI): Literary Stabilization", *Africa South*, Vol. 3, No. 1, Oct-Dec. 1958, pp. 115-116.

[42]   J. A. Chalmers, *Tiyo Soga*, Glasgow, 1978, p. 430.

[43]   *Swahili Prose Texts. A Selection from the Material Collected by Carl Velten from 1893 to 1896*, London-Nairobi, 1965.

[44]   Stanlake Samkange, *Origins of Rhodesia*, Heineman etc., London, 1968, pp. 87-110.

[45]   E. Mathers, *Zambesia. . .*, p. 279.

[46]   B. Williams, *Cecil Rhodes*, p. 128.

[47] *The Times,* Aug. 5, 1890, p. 6.
[48] B. Williams, *Op. cit.,* p. 173.

SETTING UP HIS OWN STATE

[1] Arthur Silva White, "Chartered Government in Africa", *The Nineteenth Century,* London, Vol. XXXV, 1894, p. 131.
[2] *The Times,* May 21, 1891, p. 10.
[3] *East Africa and Rhodesia,* London, Vol. 26 (New Series), No. 1309, November 3, 1949, p. 268.
[4] *Arkhiv vneshney politiki Rossii* (Russian Foreign Policy Archives), F. kantselyarii, 1894, d. 56, Ye. Ye. Staal to N. K. Girs, January 26 (new style February 7), 1894, p. 27.
[5] L. S. Vulf, *Ekonomicheski imperialism v Azii i Afrike* (Economic Imperialism in Asia and Africa), Petrograd, 1923, p. 57.
[6] Karl Marx, *Capital,* Vol. III, Progress Publishers, Moscow, 1971, p. 910.
[7] John S. Galbraith, *Op. cit.,* p. X.
[8] *The Economist,* Vol. 47, No. 2, 414, Nov. 30, 1889, pp. 1530-1531.
[9] J. S. Galbraith, *Op. cit.,* p. 116.
[10] Kipling, "The Press".
[11] Bernard Shaw, "The Simpleton, the Six and the Millionairess", Constable and Company Ltd., London, 1936, p. 62.
[12] "Engels an Karl Kautsky in Stuttgart. London, 25, Okt. 91", in Karl Marx, Friedrich Engels, *Werke,* Vol. 38, Dietz Verlag, Berlin, 1968, p. 191.
[13] *Parliamentary Debates,* Third Series, Vol. 333, London, The Hansard Publishing Union, Ltd., 1889, col. 255.
[14] *Ibid.,* Vol. 334, col. 337-339.
[15] Kipling, "A Smuggler's Song".
[16] "British South Africa Company. Charter of Incorporation". In : *Copy of Correspondence between the British South Africa Company and the Colonial Office about the Administration of Matabeleland and Mashonaland,* [C-7383], London, 1894, No. 1.
[17] B. Williams, *Op. cit.,* p. 164.
[18] "Power of Attorney of the British South Africa Company to C. J. Rhodes", London, 1896.
[19] B. Williams, *Op. cit.,* p. 164.
[20] J. A. Hobson, *Imperialism,* The University of Michigan Press, Ann Arbor, 1965, p. 231.
[21] John Mackenzie, "The Chartered Company in South Africa: A Review and Criticism", *The Contemporary Review,* London, Vol. 71, March 1897, p. 309.
[22] John Marlowe, *Cecil Rhodes. The Anatomy of Empire,* Paul Elek, London, 1972, p. 123.
[23] *Hansard's Parliamentary Debates,* Third Series, Vol. 349, 1891, col. 1142.
[24] V. I. Lenin, "Notebooks on Imperialism", *Collected Works,* Vol. 39, Progress Publishers, Moscow, 1976, p. 694.

[1] *Southern African Dictionary of National Biography*, p. 184.

[2] I. Colvin, *The Life of Jameson*, Vol. 1, p. 116.

[3] *Ibid.*, p. 132.

[4] S. Kemp, *Op. cit.*, pp. 52-53.

[5] I. Colvin, *Op. cit.*, Vol. 1, p. 139.

[6] Charles L. Norris Newman, *Matabeleland and How We Got It*, T. Fisher Unwin, London, 1895, p. 99.

[7] S. Kemp, *Op. cit.*, pp. 54-55, 130-131.

[8] Kipling, "The Galley-Slave".

[9] S. Kemp, *Op. cit.*, p. 181.

[10] Raymond Roberts, "The Settlers", *Rhodesiana*, September 1978, No. 39, p. 55.

[11] J. Flint, *Op. cit.*, p. 181.

[12] *Ibid.*

[13] Kipling, "The Lost Legion".

[14] S. Kemp. *Op. cit.*, pp. 54-55.

[15] *Ibid.*, pp. 57-58.

[16] *Ibid.*, p. 70.

[17] E. Mathers, *Op. cit.*, p. 344.

[18] *The Times*, August 5, 1890, p. 6.

[19] J. Galbraith, *Op. cit.*, pp. 150-151.

[20] The quotations have been submitted by Dr Solomon M. Mtswairo, Senior Lecturer, University of Zimbabwe and are reproduced by his kind permission.

[21] *The Times,* September 17, 1890.

[22] E. P. Mathers, *Op. cit*, p. 461.

[23] *The Times,* September 23, 1890.

[24] C. Finlason, *Op. cit.*, pp. 63-64.

[25] *Ibid.*, p. 119.

[26] *Ibid.*, p. 162.

[27] *Ibid.*, p. 175.

[28] *Ibid.*, p. 111.

[29] *Ibid.*, p. 114.

[30] *Ibid.*, p. 123.

[31] *Ibid.*, p. 43.

[132] *Ibid.*, p. 177.

[33] S. Kemp, *Op. cit.*, pp. 136, 206.

[34] C. Finlason, *Op. cit.*, p. 211.

[35] S. Kemp, *Op. cit.*, p. 159.

[36] *The Times*, February 28, 1891.

[37] Brian Roberts, *Churchills in Africa,* Hamish Hamilton, London, 1970, pp. 3, 11-13, 17-18, 19.

[38] C. Finlason, *Op. cit.*, p. 74.

[39] B. Roberts, *Op. cit.*, pp. 34-35.

[40] C. Finlason, *Op. cit.*, pp. 77-78.

[41] B. Roberts, *Op. cit.*, p. 59.

[42] *Ibid.*, p. 58.

[43] Winston Spencer Churchill, *Lord Randolph Churchill*, Vol. II, Macmillan and Co., Ltd., London, 1906, p. 451.

[44] Randolph Churchill, *Men, Mines and Animals in South Africa*, Sampson Low, Marston and Co., London, 1893.

[45] J. Galbraith, *Op. cit.*, pp. 277, 278.

[46] *The Times*, August 5, 1890.

AND THE FIRST WAR

[1] S. Kemp, *Op. cit.*, p. 175.

[2] J. Flint, *Op. cit.*, p. 150.

[3] B. Williams, *Op. cit.*, p. 174.

[4] *Report by Mr. F. J. Newton upon the Circumstances Connected with the Collision between the Matabele and the Forces of the British South Africa Company at Fort Victoria in July 1893 and Correspondence Connected Therewith*, [C-7555], London, 1894, p. 47.

[5] J. Flint, *Op. cit.*, p. 151.

[6] *Report by Mr. F. J. Newton. . .*, p. 49.

[7] "Personal Reminiscences of Mr. Rhodes", by Dr Jameson. In *Cecil Rhodes. A Biography and Appreciation*. By Imperialist. Chapman and Hall, London, 1897, pp. 399-401.

[8] *Parliamentary Debates*, Fourth Series, Vol. 17, 1893, col. 1789.

[9] *Ibid.*, Vol. 16, col. 1215-1216.

[10] *The Times*, August 16, 1893, p. 3.

[11] *South Africa. The British South Africa Company in Mashonaland and Matabeleland*, [C-7196] London, 1893, p. 28.

[12] *Ibid.*, p. 16.

[13] *Ibid.*, pp. 50-51.

[14] *Ibid.*, pp. 76-77.

[15] *Ibid.*, p. 93.

[16] *Ibid.*, p. 39.

[17] *Ibid.*, p. 80.

[18] *Ibid.*, p. 47.

[19] *The Edinburgh Review*, Vol. 149, No. 36, April 1879, p. 564.

[20] *South Africa. The British South Africa Company in Mashonaland and Matabeleland*, p. 75.

[21] *Ibid.*, p. 73.

[22] Mayford Sibanda, "Song of the Warrior from Gadade Battlefield", *Mambo Book of Zimbabwean Verse in English*, Gweru, Mambo Press, 1986, p. 322. Ndebele original: "Ingoma Yebutho Livela Egadadi", in *Inkundla Yezimbongi*, Gweru, Mambo Press, 1979, p. 139.

[23] J. A. Pitout, "Lobengula's Flight and Shangani Battle as Told me by Siyatsha—an Eye Witness of the Battle", *NADA* (The Southern Rhodesia Native Affairs Annual), Salisbury, 1963, Vol. 40, p. 73.

[24]

> Nobody knows what happened to you Lobengula,
> Son of our King,
> We know that you, son of Ndaba,
> Disappeared—
> But you are not dead.

From the personal collection of Mr Caleb Dube, of the University of Zimbabwe Department of African Languages and Literature. Reproduced by kind permission of Mr Dube.

[25] Ben Shephard, "Showbiz Imperialism. The Case of Peter Lobengula" in *Imperialism and Popular Culture*, Ed. by J. M. Mackenzie, Manchester University Press, 1986, pp. 94-109.

[26] V. I. Lenin, "War and Revolution", *Collected Works*, Vol. 24 Progress Publishers, Moscow, 1974, p. 406.

[27] C. L. N. Newman, *Op. cit.*, p. 144.

[28] *Ibid.*, p. 99.

[29] *The Pall-Mall Gazette*, October 23, 1893.

[30] *The Times*, March 24, 1894, p. 6.

[31] *The Times*, January 4, 1899, p. 5.

[32] *The Economist*, January 19, 1895, No. 2682, pp. 76-77.

[33] P. Leroy-Beaulieu, *Op. cit.*, p. 271.

[34] Parker Thomas Moon, *Imperialism and World Politics*, The Macmillan Company, N. Y., 1927, pp. 394-395.

[35] V. I. Lenin, "War and Revolution", *Collected Works*, Vol. 24 p. 401.

[36] *The Matabele—Scandal and Its Consequences* by One Who (1) Remembers the Punishment which fell upon Cain for Killing His Brother, and (2) is Jealous of the Honour of Great Britain, Cambridge, February 1894, pp. 5-7, 25, 44, 46.

[37] *Justice*, London, No. 509, Vol. X, October 14, 1893.

[38] *Justice*, No. 511, Vol. X, October 28, 1893.

[39] F. Gross, *Op. cit.*, p. 241.

[40] *The Parliamentary Debates*, Forth Series, Vol. 18, 1893, col. 1-2 111.

[41] *Justice*, No. 516, Vol. X, December 2, 1893.

[42] *The Pall-Mall Gazette*, November 14, 1893, p. 11.

[43] *Report by Mr. F. J. Newton. . .*, p. 38.

[44] *Ibid.*, p. 1.

THE IDOL OF HIS DAY

[1] L. Raphael, *Op. cit.*, p. 70.

[2] J. L. Garvin, *The Life of Joseph Chamberlain*, Vol. 3, Macmillan and Co., London, 1934, p. 34.

[3] P. Th. Moon, *Imperialism and World Politics*, The Macmillan Company, N. Y., 1927, p. 66.

[4] Dioneo, "Ocherki sovremennoi Anglii" (Essays on Contemporary England), *Russkoye bogatstvo*, St Petersburg, 1903, p. 38.

[5] *Reports from the Consuls of the United States*, Vol. 36, Washington, D. C., 1891, pp. 593-594.

[6] P. Th. Moon, *Op. cit.*, p. 216.

[7] William E. Gladstone. "Aggression on Egypt and Freedom in the East", *The Nineteenth Century*, London, Vol. 2, No. 6, August 1877 pp. 158-159.

[8] L. Raphael, *Op. cit.*, p. 135.

[9] Kipling, "The Native-Born".

[10] *Ibidem.*

[11] L. A. C. Raphael, *Op. cit.,* p. 80.

[12] W. T. Stead, Ed., *Op. cit.,* p. 190.

[13] A. G. Kenwood, A. L. Lougheed, *The Growth of the International Economy, 1820-1960,* George Allen and Unwin Ltd., London, 1971, p. 60.

[14] Vindex, *Cecil Rhodes. His Political Life and Speeches, 1881-1900,* Chapman and Hall, London, 1900, pp. 701-702.

[15] V. I. Lenin, "The Valuable Admissions of Pitirim Sorokin", *Collected Works,* Vol. 28, 1977, p. 187.

[16] Kipling, "The Widow at Windsor".

[17] B. Williams, *Op. cit.,* p. 234.

[18] M. Twain, *Following the Equator,* Vol. II, p. 403.

[19] *The Letters of Queen Victoria,* Third Series, Vol. II, 1930, p. 12.

[20] *The Times,* May 21, 1891.

[21] Afrikaner. "Cecil Rhodes—Colonist and Imperialist." *Contemporary Review,* March 1896, Vol. 69, pp. 374-390.

[22] V. O. Klyuchevsky, *Pisma. Dnevniki. Aforizmy i mysli ob istorii* (Letters. Diaries. Aphorisms and Meditations on History), Moscow, Nauka Publishers, 1968, pp. 260-261 (in Russian).

[23] M. E. Saltykov-Shchedrin, *Collected Works,* Moscow, Vol. 5, 1937, p. 335 (in Russian).

[24] Jerome K. Jerome, *Idle Ideas in 1905,* Bernhard Tauchnitz, Leipzig, 1905, pp. 143-144.

[25] J. Flint, *Op. cit.,* p. 168.

[26] *Ibid.,* pp. 168-169.

[27] George Honour, "What Cecil John Rhodes thought about the 'Native question' ", *The New Rhodesia,* Vol. 18, May 4, 1951, p. 6.

[28] B. Williams, *Op. cit.,* p. 212.

[29] Vindex, *Op. cit.,* p. 296.

[30] *Ibid.,* p. 297.

[31] *Ibid.,* p. 376.

[32] *Ibid.,* p. 383.

[33] W. Plomer, *Op. cit.,* pp. 119-120.

[34] O. Schreiner, *Trooper Peter Halket of Mashonaland,* Roberts Brothers, Boston, 1897, p. 37.

[35] Catalogue of Library of late Rt. Hon. C. J. Rhodes at Groote Schuur [S.d., s.l.].

[36] Gordon Le Sueur, *Cecil Rhodes, The Man and His Work,* John Murray, London, 1913, p. 47.

[37] M. Twain, *Following the Equator,* Vol. II, pp. 379, 402-403.

THE CONSPIRACY AGAINST THE AFRIKANERS

[1] Margot Asquith, *Autobiography,* Vol. II, Thornton Butterworth Ltd., London, 1922, pp. 17-19.

[2] E. Rosenthal, *Gold!...,* p. 267.

[3] O. Schreiner, *Op. cit.,* pp. 4, 6, 9.

⁴ Kipling, "Screw-guns".

⁵ E. Rosenthal, *Op. cit.*, p. 275.

⁶ *Ibid.*, p. 276.

⁷ *Ibid.*, p. 278.

⁸ *Ibid.*, pp. 282-283.

⁹ Kipling, "Soldier, Soldier".

¹⁰ Die Grosse Politik der Europäischen Kabinette 1871-1914. Sammlung des Diplomatischen Akten des Auswärtigen Amtees", Vol. 11, Deutsche Verlagsgesellschaft für Politik und Geschichte, Berlin, No. 2597, pp. 24-25.

¹¹ W. Langer, *The Diplomacy of Imperialism*, Vol. 1, p. 237.

¹² *Ibid.*, p. 248.

¹³ *Die Grosse Politik. . . ,* Vol. 11, No. 2636, p. 53.

¹⁴ M. Twain, *Following the Equator*, Vol. II, pp. 381-382.

¹⁵ Paul Darmstädter, *Geschichte der Aufteilung und Kolonisation Afrikas seit dem Zeitalter der Entdeckungen,* Vol. II, Vereiningung wissenschaftlicher Verleger, Leipzig, 1920, p. 123.

¹⁶ E. Rosenthal, *Gold!. . . ,* pp. 258-259.

¹⁷ J. Flint, *Op. cit.*, p. 194.

¹⁸ B. Williams, *Op. cit.,* p. 271.

RHODESIA AGAINST RHODES

¹ *The Times,* March 31, 1893.

² *The Times,* August 14, 1894.

³ Philip Jourdan, *Cecil Rhodes. His Private Life by His Private Secretary,* John Lane the Bodley Head, London, 1911, pp. 46-48, 50-53.

⁴ *Report of the Land Commission of 1894 and Correspondence Relating Thereto,* [C-8130], London, 1896, p. 3.

⁵ H. C. Thomson, *Rhodesia and Its Government,* Smith, Elder and Co., London, 1898, p. 82.

⁶ *The Parliamentary Debates,* Fourth Series, Vol. 57, 1898, col. 597-598.

⁷ *The Times,* December 4, 1894.

⁸ *British South Africa Territories. Report by Sir R. E. Martin on the Native Administration of the British South Africa Company. Together with a Letter from the Company Commenting Upon that Report,* London, 1897, p. 32.

⁹ *The Times,* April 8, 1896, p. 3.

¹⁰ Frederick Courteney Selous, *Sunshine and Storm in Rhodesia,* Rowland Ward and Co., London, 1896, pp. 58-59.

¹¹ *The Times,* May 6, 1896.

¹² *The Parliamentary Debates,* Fourth Series, Vol. 39, London, 1896, col. 1175.

¹³ *Ibid.,* Vol. 41, col 418.

¹⁴ Kipling, "Fuzzy-Wuzzy".

¹⁵ F. Gross, *Op. cit.,* p. 327.

¹⁶ *Ibidem.*

[17] J. Flint, *Op. cit.*, p. 204.
[18] S. G. Millin, *Op. cit.*, p. 303.
[19] *The Times,* June 25, 1896.
[20] S. G. Millin, *Op. cit.*, p. 301.
[21] *Ibid.*, p. 305.
[22] Terence O. Ranger, *Revolt in Southern Rhodesia. 1896-7,* Heinemann, London, 1967, pp. 241-242.
[23] J. G. Lockhart, *Op. cit.*, p. 353.
[24] T. O. Ranger. *Op. cit.*, p. 246.
[25] *Ibid.*, pp. 247-248.
[26] *Ibid.*, pp. 241-258.
[27] H. C. Thomson, *Op. cit.*, pp. 142-143.
[28] Matabele Thompson, *Op. cit.*, pp. 192-193.
[29] Apollon B. Davidson, *Matabele i Mashona v borbe protiv angliiskoi kolonizatsii, 1888-1897,* (The Matabele and the Shona in the Struggle against British Colonization, 1888-1897), Vostochnaya Literatura Publishers, Moscow, 1958.
[30] David N. Beach, *War and Politics in Zimbabwe 1840-1900,* Gweru, Mambo Press, 1986; Ngwabi M. B. Bhebe, *Lobengula of Zimbabwe,* London, Heinemann, s.d.; H. H. K. Bhila, *Trade and Politics in Shona Kingdom,* Essex, Longman, 1982; David Chanaiwa, "African Initiatives and Resistance in Southern Africa", in: *General History of Africa,* Vol. VII, UNESCO, 1985; Raymond S. Roberts, "Rhodes, Rhodesia and the Jameson Raid", *Zambezia,* Vol. I, No. 2, Jan. 1970; Stanlake Samkange, *Origins of Rhodesia,* London, Heinemann, 1968.

MERE SETBACK OR UTTER DEBACLE?

[1] See also: E. Aveling, "Filibuster Cecil Rhodes and His Chartered Company", *Social-Democrat,* Vol. 1, 1897.
[2] S. G. Millin, *Op. cit.*, p. 317.
[3] Margot Asquith, *Autobiography,* Vol. II, p. 25.
[4] Dioneo, "Iz Anglii" (From Britain), *Russkoye Bogatstvo,* August 1897, No. 8, pp. 61-62.
[5] R. Lewinsohn, *Barnato...*, pp. 207-211.
[6] L. Michell, *Op. cit.*, Vol. 2, p. 180.
[7] M. Twain, *Following the Equator,* Vol. II, p. 403.
[8] J. van der Poel, *The Jameson Raid,* Cape Town, 1951, pp. 203-207.
[9] L. Michell, *Op. cit.*, Vol. 2, p. 201.
[10] Kingsley Amis, *Rudyard Kipling and His World,* Thames and Hudson, London, 1975, p. 85.
[11] Kipling, "The White Man's Burden".
[12] Frederick L. Knowles, *A Kipling Primer,* Chatto and Windus, London, 1900, p. 60.
[13] "Great Man on a Great Man", *The African Review,* October 22, 1898, p. 135.
[14] M. N. George, "Recollections of Rhodes", *The Hampshire Countryside,* Vol. 1, No. 10, October-December 1948, p. 270.

[15] See also: Rhodes House (Oxford), *Misc. Papers concerning C. J. Rhodes* (MSS Afr, S 8), *Letters from R. Kipling to Sir Herbert Baker Relating to the Rhodes Memorial etc.*, 1900-1934.

[16] Arthur G. Barlow, *Almost in Confidence*, Juta & Co., Ltd., Cape Town—Johannesburg, 1952, p. 83.

[17] Kipling, "If—".

[18] Peter Schirmer, *The Concise Illustrated South African Encyclopaedia*, Central News Agency, Johannesburg, 1981, p. 43.

[19] A. Wilmot, *Monomotapa (Rhodesia). Its Monuments, and Its History from the Most Ancient Times to the Present Century*, T. Fisher Unwin, London, 1896, p. VIII.

[20] Arthur Conan Doyle, *The Great Boer War*, Smith, Elder and Co., London, 1902.

[21] Arthur Conan Doyle, *The War in South Africa. Its Causes and Conduct*, Smith, Elder and Co., London, 1902.

[22] Arthur Conan Doyle, *Our African Winter*, John Murray, London, 1929, p. 148.

[23] Arthur Conan Doyle, *Our African Winter*, pp. 148-149.

[24] "Men You Know. Mr. 'Matabele' Wilson", *South Africa*, March 18, 1899, p. 554.

[25] Frederick R. Burnham, *Scouting on Two Continents*, Books of Rhodesia, Bulawayo, 1975, p. VII.

[26] Margot Asquith, *Autobiography*, Vol. II, p. 26.

[27] *Ibid.*, Vol. II, pp. 23-24.

[28] *The Parliamentary Debates*, Fourth Series, Vol. 75, 1899, col. 715-716.

"TERUG NA DIE OU TRANSVAAL"
("BACK TO THE OLD TRANSVAAL")

[1] A. A. Ignatiev, *Pyatdesyat let v stroyu* (Fifty Years in the Ranks), Vol. 2, Moscow, 1959, p. 24.

[2] L. Michell, *Op. cit.*, Vol. 2, p. 246.

[3] *Ibid.*, p. 247.

[4] *Ibidem.*

[5] *Die Grosse Politik. . .*, vol. 15, 1924 No. 4320, p. 306.

[6] George W. F. Hallgarten, *Imperialismus vor 1914*, Vol. I, C. H. Beck'she Verlagsbuchhandlung, Munich, 1951, p. 408.

[7] *Die Grosse Politik. . .*, Vol. 14, Part Two, 1924, No. 4022, pp. 550-551, 554.

[8] F. A. Rotshtein, *Mezhdunarodnye otnosheniya v kontse XIX veka* (International Relations in the Late 19th Century), Moscow-Leningrad, 1960, pp. 558, 565.

[9] Bernhard von Bülow, *Denkwürdigkeiten*, Bd. I, Im Verlag Ullstein, Berlin, 1930, S. 289.

[10] L. Michell, *Op. cit.*, Vol. 2, p. 250.

[11] W. Plomer, *Op. cit.*, p. 101.

[12] S. G. Millin, *Rhodes*, p. 345.

[13] E. Eyck, *Op. cit.*, S. 236.

[14] J. L. Garvin, *Op. cit.*, Vol. 3, p. 508.

[15] W. Langer, *Op. cit.*, Vol. II, p. 448.

[16] *Die Grosse Politik...*, Vol. 13, No. 3530, p. 199.

[17] Bernhard von Bülow, *Op. cit.*, Bd. I, S. 258.

[18] *Die Grosse Politik...*, Vol. 15, No. 4384, p. 395.

[19] B. von Bülow, *Op. cit.*, Bd. I, S. 289.

[20] John Galsworthy, *The Forsyte Saga*, Book 2, Progress Publishers, Moscow, 1975, pp. 84, 88, 89, 91, 98, 99, 131.

[21] *The Complete Poems of Thomas Hardy*, Macmillan, London, 1976, pp. 90-91.

[22] Kipling, "The Song of the Dead".

[23] J. Galsworthy, *Op. cit.*, pp. 185-186.

[24] Kipling, "Two Kopjes".

[25] W. T. Stead, "Shall I Slay My Brother Boer? An Appeal to the Conscience of Britain", *Review of Reviews* Office, London, 1899; W. T. Stead, "Are We in the Right? An Appeal to the Honest Men", *Review of Reviews Office*, London, 1899; "Manifesto of the Knights of Labour of South Africa. The First Report..." /s.d., s.l./; see also *Rhodes Triumphant! England's Future Premier*, by Exile and others, [s.d., s.l.].

[26] James Milne, "The Epistles of Atkins, Being Some of the Lights on Human Nature in the Ordeal of War, which Illumine the Letters of the Common Soldier, Written from South Africa to His People at Home; and So an Answer to Question 'How Does It Feel to Be In Battle?' " Bernhard Tauchnitz, Leipzig, 1902.

[27] Kipling, "Wilful-Missing".

[28] *Arkhiv vneshnei politiki Rossii. Fond posolstva v Londone.* (Russian Foreign Policy Archives.), Catalogue 520, File 1029, Message by Chargé d'affaires Lessary, January 17 (new style January 30), 1901, p. 4 (in Russian).

[29] Kipling, "The Widow's Party".

[30] "Mark Twain's Letter", Vol. II, Harper and Brothers Publishers, N. Y., 1917, p. 695.

[31] André Maurois, *Édouard VII et son temps*, Editions Bernard Grasset, Paris, 1937, pp. 126-127.

[32] S. G. Millin, *Op. cit.*, p. 348.

[33] L. Michell, *Op. cit.*, Vol. 2, p. 267.

[34] *A. P. O.* (Cape Town), December 18, 1909.

[35] W. Plomer, *Op. cit.*, p. 132-133.

[36] L. Michell, *Op. cit.*, Vol. 2, p. 289.

[37] *Ibid.*, p. 290.

[38] Paul Morand, *1900*, Les Éditions de France, Paris, 1931, pp. 198-200.

[39] Kipling, "Bobs".

[40] *The Parliamentary Debates*, Fourth Series, Vol. XCVIII, 1901, col. 48. See also: Dioneo, "Ocherki sovremennoi Anglii" (Essays on Contemporary England), pp. 137-138.

431

FADING AWAY

1. ·Kipling, "The Merchantmen".
2. Kipling, "If—".
3. Kipling, "The Vampire".
4. S. Yu. Vitte, *Vospominaniya* (Reminiscences), Vol. 3, Leningrad, 1924, p. 270.
5. *Ibid*, p. 274.
6. Comte Paul Vasili, "La Société de Berlin", *La Nouvelle Revue*, Vol. 24, September-October 1883, pp. 223-238, 667-691.
7. H. Rogge, *Holstein und Hohenlohe*, Stuttgart, 1957, pp. 208-209.
8. J. Flint, *Op. cit.*, p. 225.
9. *South African Dictionary of National Biography*, p. 110.
10. A. Maurois, *Prométhée ou la vie de Balzac*, Paris, 1965, p. 615.
11. *Spectator*, London, January 6, 1979, p. 19.
12. A. C. Addington, *The Royal House of Stuart. The Descendants of King James of Scotland James I of England*, Vol. II, London, 1971, p. 316.
13. Brian Roberts, *Cecil Rhodes and the Princess*, Hamish Hamilton, London, 1969.
14. J. Flint, *Op. cit.*, p. 219.
15. Rhodes House Library Oxford, *Report on supplementary collections relating to Cecil J. Rhodes, 1980. Papers relating to the Princess Radziwill*, 1899-1902.
16. Jomes Rose Innes, *Selected Correspondence (1884-1902)*, Cape Town, 1972, pp. 338-339.
17. L. Michell, *Op. cit.*, Vol. 2, pp. 297, 310, 313.
18. W. T. Stead, Ed., *Op. cit.*, pp. 51, 55.
19. "Copy of the Will of the Rt. Hon. C. J. Rhodes", in L. Michell, *Op. cit.*, Vol., 2, pp. 318, 321.
20. J. Flint, *Op. cit.* p. 218.
21. Cited from *Problems of Contemporary History* by R. Palme Dutt, International Publishers, New York, 1963, pp. 123-124.
22. Kipling, "The Burial".
23. *The End of the Beginning. War Speeches by the Right Hon. Winston S. Churchill*, Little, Brown and Company, Boston, 1943, p. 268.
24. Lord Soames, "From Rhodesia to Zimbabwe", *International Affairs*, Summer 1980, Vol. 56, No. 3, p. 416.

CONCLUSION

1. A. Conan Doyle, "Our African Winter", p. 148.
2. Arthur Glyn Leonard, *How We Made Rhodesia*, Kegan Paul, Trench Trübner and Co., Ltd., London, 1896, p. 355.
3. F. Gross, *Op. cit.*, p. 395.
4. S. B. Stevenson, "Rhodes 'More an Agent Than an Initiator' ", *Heritage*, No. 1, 1981.
5. Rhodes House, Oxford, *Misc. Papers concerning C. J. Rhodes (MSS*

Afr. S.8), pp. 35, 104, 102, 125.

6 Harry Oppenheimer, "The Vision of Cecil Rhodes", *The Pioneer*, Journal of the Rhodesia Pioneer' and Eartly Settlers' Society, August 1972, Vol. 2, p. 65.

7 *Stag* (Johannesburg), March 1985, Vol. IV, No. 4, p. 4.

THESE EVENTS THROUGH THE EYES
OF CONTEMPORARY RUSSIAN OBSERVERS

1 Emilia Pimenova, *Politicheskiye vozhdi sovremennoy Anglii i Irlandii* (The Political Leaders of Contemporary England and Ireland), St Petersburg, 1904, pp. 59-60, 94.

2 *Niva*, March 30, 1902, p. 258.

3 *Odesskiye novosti*, March 15, 1902.

4 Baron R. Ungern-Shternberg, *Zametka o Rodezii [Doneseniye Generalnogo konsula v Londone]* (A Note on Rhodesia [Report of the Consul General in London]), Collection of Consular Reports, Issue I, St Petersburg, 1899, pp. 12, 13.

5 *Arkhiv vneshnei politiki Rossii. Fond posolstva v Londone* (Foreign Policy Archives of Russia. Reports from the Embassy in London), Catalogue 520, File 1073, Message from March 21/April 9, 1902 p. 18.

6 Dioneo, "Iz Anglii" (From Britain), *Russkoye bogatstvo*, 1899, No. 7(10), Part II, pp. 75-76.

7 Dioneo, "Ocherki sovremennoi Anglii (Essays of Contemporary England), St Petersburg, 1903, p. 114.

8 Dioneo, "Iz Anglii" (From Britain), *Russkoye bogatstvo*, 1899, No. 7(10), Part II, p. 74.

9 *Ibid.*, p. 61.

10 *Ibid.*, p. 78.

11 " 'Velikii avantyurist' i ego ideya transafrikanskoi zheleznoi dorogi" ('The Great Adventurer' and His Idea of a Trans-African Railway), in *Mir bozhiy*, April 1899, No. 4, pp. 48-49.

12 S. Yuzhakov, "Dnevnik zhurnalista" (Diary of a Journalist), in *Russkoye bogatstvo*, 1897, No. I, Part II, pp. 137-141.

13 M. Zlatkovsky, *Dzhon Bul kontsa veka* (John Bull of the End of the Century), St Petersburg, 1898.

14 *Roza Burger, burskaya geroinya, ili zolotoiskateli v Transvaale. Roman iz anglo-burskoi voiny* (Rosa Burgher, Heroine of the Boers, or the Gold Prospectors in the Transvaal. A Novel of the Anglo-Boer War), St Petersburg, 1902.

15 S. Glebov, *Novyi Napoleon iz yuzhnoafrikanskoi voiny Transvaalya s Angliei* (The New Napoléon of the South African War Between the Transvaal and Britain), St Petersburg, 1899.

16 Burofil *V pomoshch buram! Prichiny voiny i eyo techeniye. Vozmozhnye posledstviya anglo-burskogo stolknoveniya* (Boerophile. Aid the Boers! The Causes and Course of the War. Possible Consequences of the Anglo-Boer Conflict), St Petersburg, 1900, p. 25.

[17] "Nikolai Romanov ob anglo-burskoi voine" (Nikolai Romanov on the Anglo-Boer War), in *Krasny arkhiv*, 1934, Vol. 2(63), p. 125.

[18] *Voina anglichan s burami. Redaktirovano 2-m byuro frantsuzskogo generalnogo shtaba* (The British at War with the Boers. Ed. by the Second Bureau of the French General Staff), translated from the French, St Petersburg, 1905.

[19] Ye. Avgustus, *Vospominaniya uchastnika anglo-burskoi voiny 1899-1900* (Recollections of a Participant in the Anglo-Boer War 1899-1900), Warsaw, Bristol Printing House, 1902.

[20] V. Rubanov, *Ot Peterburga do Pretorii* (From St Petersburg to Pretoria), St Petersburg, Printing House of the Journal *Stroitel*, 1900.

[21] M. Chistovich, *Meditsinskaya pomoshch v Transvaale* (Medical Aid in the Transvaal), St Petersburg, Publishing House of M. Stasyulevich, 1901.

[22] S. Izedinova, *Neskolko mesyatsev u burov. Vospominaniya sestry miloserdiya* (A Few Months with the Boers. War Reminiscences of a Nursing Sister), Printing House of A. S. Suvorin, St Petersburg, 1903.

[23] O. Baumgarten, *Vospominaniya o Transvaale sestry miloserdiya obshchiny Sv. Georgiya, 1899-1900* (Recollections about the Transvaal by a Sister of Mercy of the St George Community, 1899-1900), Government Press, St Petersburg, 1901.

[24] *Sbornik materialov po anglo-burskoi voine v Yuzhnoi Afrike* (Collection of Materials on the Anglo-Boer War in South Africa), Issues 1-21, Military Scholars' Committee of the General Staff, St Petersburg, 1900-1905.

[25] V. [Romeiko]-Gurko, *Voina Anglii s yuzhnoafrikanskimi respublikami 1899-1901. Otchet komandirovannogo ... k voiskam yuzhnoafrikanskikh respublik Generalnogo shtaba polkovnika Romeiko-Gurko* (Britain at War with the South African Republics 1899-1901. Report by the General Staff Colonel Romeiko-Gurko, Attaché to the Armies of the South African Republics), Military Scholars' Committee of the General Staff, St Petersburg, 1901.

[26] *Doneseniye Generalnogo shtaba podpolkovnika Gurko, komandirovannogo na teatr voennykh deistvii v Yuzhnoi Afrike* (Report by the Lt Colonel Gurko of the General Staff on His Mission to the Theatre of Operations in South Africa), 1900; *Doneseniya voennogo agenta v Londone Generalnogo shtaba polkovnika Yermolova* (Reports of the Military Agent in London Colonel Yermolov of the General Staff), 1900; *Doneseniya voennogo agenta v Bryussele i Gaage Generalnogo shtaba podpolkovnika Myullera* (Reports of the Military Agent in Brussels and the Hague Lt Colonel Müller of the General Staff), 1900.

[27] A. Vinogradsky, *Anglo-burskaya voina v Yuzhnoi Afrike* (The Anglo-Boer War in South Africa), Issues 1-3, St Petersburg, 1901-1903; *Anglo-Transvaalskaya voina. Protest Burov i ikh istoriya. Perevedeno s broshyur, sostavlennykh na osnovanii dokumentalnykh dannykh, opublikovannykh Transvaalskim komitetom v Amsterdame i generalnym konsulom Oranzhevoi Respubliki Myullerom v Gaage* (The Anglo-

Transvaal War. The Boers' Protest and Their History, Translated from the Brochures Compiled on the Basis of Documents Published by the Transvaal Committee in Amsterdam and by Müller, Consul General of the Orange Republic in the Hague), Khudozhestvennaya Pechat Press, 1900; V. Markov, *Voina v Yuzhnoi Afrike. Ocherk takticheskikh deistvii anglichan i burov* (The War in South Africa. An Essay on the Tactics of the British and the Boers).

[28] Arthur Conan Doyle, *Voina v Yuzhnoi Afrike, eyo prichiny i sposob eyo vedeniya* (The War in South Africa: Its Causes and Conduct, translated from the English, Odessa, 1902.

[29] Britanets, *Anglo-burskaya voina i russkaya pressa* (The Anglo-Boer War and the Russian Press), St Petersburg, 1900.

[30] H. Wright, "Cecil John Rhodes Through American Eyes", *The American Oxonian*, July 1946, p. 150.

[31] J. H. Hammond, *Autobiography*, Vol. II, N. Y., 1935, pp. 455, 469-470.

[32] E. Kandyba-Foxcroft, *Russia and the Anglo-Boer War 1899-1902*, Pretoria, 1981.

[33] S. Izedinova, *A Few Months with the Boers*, Johannesburg, 1977.

[34] V. M. Golovnin, *Detained in Simon's Bay. The Story of the Detention of the Imperial Russian Sloop "Diana" from April 1808 to May 1809*, Cape Town, 1964.

[35] "A Russian View of the Cape in 1853 (Translated by N. W. Wilson from I. A. Goncharov's *Frigate Pallada*, with Additional Notes by D. H. Varley)", in *Quarterly Bulletin of the South African Library*, Cape Town, Vol. 15, Nos. 2-4. Vol. 16. 1 December 1960-September 1961.

[36] A. Davidson, V. Makrushin, *Oblik dalyokoi strany* (The Image of a Remote Land), Nauka Publishers, Moscow, 1975; A. Davidson, V. Makrushin, *Zov dalyokikh morei* (Draw of Far-Away Seas), Nauka Publishers, Moscow, 1979.

[37] Apollon Davidson, "The Russian Experience", in *The New African*, Cape Town, March 28, p. 1964.

[38] V. I. Lenin, "Notebooks on Imperialism", *Collected Works*, Vol. 39, Progress Publishers, Moscow, 1976, pp. 511-515.

[39] V. I. Lenin, "Imperialism, the Highest Stage of Capitalism", *Collected Works*, Vol. 22, Progress Publishers, Moscow, 1977, p. 257.

[40] *Ibidem.*

[41] *Ibid.*, p. 262.

[42] Anatoly Lunacharsky, "Doklad na vtorom Vserossiiskom s'ezde Proletkulta [Noyabr 1921]" (Report to the Second All-Russia Congress of the Proletkult), *Voprosy literatury*, 1976 No. 10, p. 199.

[43] Maxim Gorky, "Eshche raz ob 'Istorii molodogo cheloveka XIX stoletiya' " (Once Again About 'The Story of a 19th Century Young Man'), *Collected Works in 30 volumes*, Vol. 26, Moscow, 1953, p. 311.

Name Index

441

Progress Publishers

Will soon publish

of *The Russian Orthodox Church 10th to 20th
Centuries A.D.* Ed. by A. Preobrazhensky

Written by prominent Soviet historians and
students of religion, this is an exhaustive piece
of research into the past and present of the
Russian Orthodox Church.

The authors review the evolution of Russian
Orthodoxy and the Church over the one thous-
and years of their existence. There are charters
on the appearance of Christianity in ancient
Rus and the initial financing of the Church by
the Prince, its transformation into a landowner
and a major force in the country's economic and
political life, the Church's role in the formation of the Russian centralised state, the struggle between secular and ecclesiastical authorities over land and peasants, attempts by the
cleargy in the 17th century to subordinate the
tsar's power, the reforms of Peter the Great
which placed the Church under state control,
and other major landmarks.

The authors also make a detailed study of
the present   state of the   Russian   Orthodox
Church.

The volume is richly illustrated, has a bibliography and name and subject indexes.

Progress Publishers

Will soon publisin

Ancient Civilisations of East and West. Ed. by
Grigory Bongard-Levin

In this book, leading Soviet scientists analyse
the history and culture of ancient civilisations
and their social development. They describe
and assess the contribution made by various
countries and peoples to world civilisation,
stressing the unity of the world-historical
process. The book embraces the period from the
origin of man on Earth through the early Middle Ages: from Spain in the West to China and
Japan in the East.

The book is based on the latest findings in
archaeology and history, and is supplied with
bibliography and maps.

The book is intended for wide readership.

Progress Publishers

Will soon publish

Feudal Society and Its Culture. Ed. by V. I. Ruthenburg, Associate Member of the USSR Academy of Sciences

This is an exhaustive study by prominent Soviet mediaevalists of the history of feudal society and its culture in Western Europe, the East and America from the 5th to the 18th century. The authors devote much space to European feudal expansion during the discovery of America, penetration into India, and formation of the first colonial systems.

The book examines the relations between Africa and Europe in the years of the great geographical discoveries and the forcible transportation of Africans overseas. The section on Africa also concentrates on the formation and development of feudal states peculiar to northern Africa and Ethiopia.

A major part of the book is devoted to the feudal societies of the East and their unique culture.

The history of feudalism in Russia is reviewed from the 9th century to the formation of the Russian Empire.

The edition is lavishly illustrated and intended for broad readership.

REQUEST TO READERS

Progress Publishers would be glad to have your opinion of this book, its translation and design and any suggestions you may have for future publications.

Please send all your comments to 17, Zubovsky Boulevard, Moscow, USSR.